psychosomatic medicine

psychosomatic medicine
Its Clinical Applications

edited by
Eric D. Wittkower

M.D., L.R.C.P., L.R.C.S., L.R.F.P.S., F.R.C.P.S., F.R.C.P.(c). Professor Emeritus, Department of Psychiatry, McGill University; Consulting Psychiatrist, Royal Victoria Hospital, Montreal General Hospital and Queen Elizabeth Hospital, Montreal, Quebec, Canada

Hector Warnes

B.Sc., M.D., F.R.C.P. (C)., F.A.P.A. Professor and Chairman, Department of Psychiatry, University of Dublin, Trinity College; Clinical Director, Department of Psychiatry, St. James's Hospital; Consultant Psychiatrist, St. Patrick's Hospital and Sir Patrick Dun's Hospital, Dublin, Ireland

With 49 contributors

Medical Department
Harper & Row, Publishers
Hagerstown, Maryland
New York, San Francisco, London

DRUG DOSAGE

The authors and publisher have exerted every effort to ensure that drug selection and dosage set forth in this text are in accord with current recommendations and practice at the time of publication. However, in view of ongoing research, changes in government regulations, and the constant flow of information relating to drug therapy and drug reactions, the reader is urged to check the package insert for each drug for any change in indications and dosage and for added warnings and precautions. This is particularly important when the recommended agent is a new and/or infrequently employed drug.

77–78–79–80–81–82—10–9–8–7–6–5–4–3–2

Cover and text designed by Alice J. Sellers

Psychosomatic Medicine: Its Clinical Applications. Copyright © 1977 by Harper & Row, Publishers, Inc. All rights reserved. No part of this book may be used or reproduced in any manner whatsoever without written permission except in the case of brief quotations embodied in critical articles and reviews. Printed in the United States of America. For information address Medical Department, Harper & Row, Publishers, Inc., 2350 Virginia Avenue, Hagerstown, Maryland 21740.

Library of Congress Cataloging in Publication Data

Main entry under title:
Psychosomatic medicine.

    Includes bibliographies and index.
    1. Medicine, Psychosomatic. I. Wittkower,
Eric David, 1899–   II. Warnes, Hector.
[DNLM:
1. Psychosomatic   medicine.   WM90
P975]
RC49.P82   616.08   76–44472
ISBN 0–06–142768–3

To Claire and Phyllis

Contents

Part I: General Considerations

Part II: Models of Intervention

Part III: Psychotherapies

Part IV: Specific Disorders

List of Contributors

HARRY S. ABRAM, M.D.
CHAPTER 4
Professor of Psychiatry, Department of Psychiatry, Vanderbilt University School of Medicine, Nashville, Tennessee

LESTER BAKER, M.D.
CHAPTER 12
Director of the Clinical Research Center, Children's Hospital of Philadelphia; Professor of Pediatrics, Department of Pediatrics, The University of Pennsylvania School of Medicine, Philadelphia, Pennsylvania

JAN BASTIAANS, M.D., F.I.C.P.M.
CHAPTER 9
Professor of Psychiatry and Chairman, Department of Psychiatry, State University of Leiden, Oegstgeest, Holland

S. R. BLUMBERGER, M.D., C.M.
CHAPTER 15
North Hero, Vermont

WALTER BRÄUTIGAM, M.D.
CHAPTER 10
Professor of Psychosomatic Medicine, University of Heidelberg, Heidelberg, West Germany

HILDE BRUCH, M.D.
CHAPTER 23
Professor of Psychiatry, Department of Psychiatry, Baylor College of Medicine, Houston, Texas

EWALD W. BUSSE, M.D.
CHAPTER 32
Associate Provost and Director, Department of Medical and Allied Health Education, Duke University School of Medicine, Durham, North Carolina

PIETRO CASTELNUOVO-TEDESCO, M.D.
CHAPTER 8
James G. Blakemore Professor of Psychiatry, Department of Psychiatry, Vanderbilt University School of Medicine, Nashville, Tennessee

MAURICE DONGIER, M.D.
FOREWORD
Professor of Psychiatry and Chairman, Department of Psychiatry, McGill University, Montreal, Quebec, Canada

DINSHAW R. DOONGAJI, M.D., M.S., M.A.M.S., M.R.C. PSYCH, D.P.M.
CHAPTER 19
Hon. Professor, Department of Psychiatry, King Edward VIII Memorial Hospital, Seth G.S. Medical College, Bombay, India

CALVIN EZRIN, M.D.
CHAPTER 28
Professor, Department of Medicine, Associate Professor, Department of Pathology, University of Toronto; Director, Medical Endocrine Clinic, Toronto General Hospital, Toronto, Ontario, Canada

GEORGE G. FISHMAN, M.D.
CHAPTER 2
Instructor in Psychiatry, Harvard Medical School; Assistant Psychiatrist, Department of Psychiatry, Beth Israel Hospital, Boston, Massachusetts

CHARLES V. FORD, M.D.
CHAPTER 8
Adjunct Associate Professor, Department of Psychiatry, University of California School of Medicine, Los Angeles; Director, Residency Training Program, Department of Psychiatry, Harbor General Hospital; Head Physician, Psychiatric Liaison Service, Harbor General Hospital, Torrance, California

RENATA DE BENEDETTI GADDINI, M.D., A.A.C.P., I.P.A., A.C.P.
CHAPTER 31
Associate Professor of Pediatrics, Department Head, Mental Hygiene Unit, Department of Pediatrics, University of Rome Medical School, Rome, Italy

DAN G. HERTZ, M.D.
CHAPTER 25
Director, Psychiatric Clinic and Psychosomatic Research, Department of Psychiatry, Hadassah University Hospital; Senior Lecturer in Psychiatry, Hebrew University-Hadassah Medical School, Jerusalem, Israel

HENRY A. JORDAN, M.D.
CHAPTER 24
Assistant Professor of Psychiatry, Department of Psychiatry, University of Pennsylvania School of Medicine, Philadelphia, Pennsylvania

GORDON M. KIMBRELL, Ph.D.
CHAPTER 24
Associate Professor and Chairman, Department of Psychology, Denison University, Granville, Ohio; Visiting Associate Professor of Psychology in Psychiatry, Department of Psychiatry, University of Pennsylvania School of Medicine, Philadelphia, Pennsylvania

PETER H. KNAPP, M.D.
CHAPTER 21
Professor, Department of Psychiatry, Boston University School of
Medicine, Boston, Massachusetts

ADAM J. KRAKOWSKI, M.D.
CHAPTER 3
Senior Attending Neuropsychiatrist and Director, Psychosomatic
Service and Research, Champlain Valley-Physicians Hospital Medical
Center, Plattsburgh, New York

LEONARD S. LEVITZ, Ph.D.
CHAPTER 24
Assistant Professor of Psychology, Department of Psychiatry,
University of Pennsylvania School of Medicine; Co-Director, Behavioral
Weight Control Program, Hospital of the University of Pennsylvania,
Philadelphia, Pennsylvania

CHOH-LUH LI, M.D., Ph.D.
CHAPTER 5
Associate Neurosurgeon, National Institute of Neurology and
Communicative Disorders and Stroke, National Institutes of Health,
Bethesda, Maryland; Clinical Professor, Department of Neurological
Surgery, George Washington University School of Medicine,
Washington, D.C.

RONALD LIEBMAN, M.D.
CHAPTER 12
Psychiatrist-in-Chief, Children's Hospital of Philadelphia; Medical
Director, Philadelphia Child Guidance Clinic; Associate Professor of
Psychiatry and Pediatrics, The University of Pennsylvania School of
Medicine, Philadelphia, Pennsylvania

LOUIS LINN, M.D.
CHAPTER 1
Clinical Professor, Department of Psychiatry, Mt. Sinai School of
Medicine and City University of New York; Attending Psychiatrist,
Department of Psychiatry, Mt. Sinai Hospital, New York, New
York

W. LUTHE, M.D.
CHAPTER 15
Scientific Director, Oskar Vogt Institute, Kyushu University School of
Medicine; Professor of Psychophysiologic Therapy, Visiting Faculty of
Medicine, Kyushu University, Fukuoka, Japan

ARNOLD J. MANDELL, M.D.
CHAPTER 17
Professor and Co-Chairman, Department of Psychiatry, University of
California at San Diego School of Medicine, La Jolla, California

GEORGE J. MATHEWS, M.D., F.R.C.S. (C)
CHAPTER 5
Chief of Neurosurgery, Department of Neurosurgery, Veterans
Administration Hospital; Associate Professor, Department of
Neurological Surgery, George Washington Medical Center; Clinical
Associate Professor, Division of Neurological Surgery, Georgetown
University Hospital, Washington, D.C.; Consultant in Neurological
Surgery, Department of Neurological Surgery, National Institutes of
Health, Bethesda, Maryland

LEROY MILMAN, M.D.
CHAPTER 12
Private Practice, Cherry Hill, New Jersey

SALVADOR MINUCHIN, M.D.
CHAPTER 12
Professor of Child Psychiatry and Director, Division of Child Psychiatry,
University of Pennsylvania; Director, Family Therapy Training Center
and Philadelphia Child Guidance Clinic, Philadelphia, Pennsylvania

HANS MOLINSKI, M.D.
CHAPTER 27
Professor of Psychosomatic Medicine, Department of Obstetrics and
Gynecology, Duesseldorf University, Federal Republic of Germany

RUDOLF H. MOOS, Ph.D.
CHAPTER 20
Professor, Department of Psychiatry and the Behavioral Sciences,
Stanford University, Stanford; Director, Social Ecology Laboratory,
Veterans Administration Hospital, Palo Alto, California

HERMAN MUSAPH, M.D. F.R.C. Psych.
CHAPTER 30
Head, Department of Psychodermatology, University of Amsterdam,
Binnengasthuis, Amsterdam, Holland

THEODORE NADELSON, M.D.
CHAPTER 2
Associate Psychiatrist, Department of Psychiatry, Beth Israel Hospital;
Assistant Professor of Psychiatry, Department of Psychiatry, Harvard
Medical School, Boston, Massachusetts

JOHN B. NOWLIN, M.D.
CHAPTER 32
Senior Research Associate, Duke Center for the Study of Aging and
Human Development, Durham, North Carolina

GEORGE PETERFY, M.D., F.R.C.P.(C)
CHAPTER 13
Senior Psychiatrist, Department of Psychiatry, Allan Memorial Institute;
Assistant Professor, Department of Psychiatry, McGill University,
Montreal, Quebec

R. ALEC RAMSAY, M.D.
CHAPTER 6
Associate Psychiatrist and Chief, Psychiatric Consultation Service,
Royal Victoria Hospital; Psychiatric Consultant, Pain Unit, Montreal
Neurological Hospital; Assistant Professor of Psychiatry Faculty of
Medicine, McGill University, Montreal, Quebec

BERNICE ROSMAN, Ph.D.
CHAPTER 12
Director of Research and Evaluation, Philadelphia Child Guidance
Clinic; Assistant Clinical Professor, Department of Psychiatry, The
University of Pennsylvania School of Medicine, Philadelphia,
Pennsylvania

W. DONALD ROSS, M.D., F.R.C.P.(C)
CHAPTER 29
Professor of Psychiatry and Associate Professor of Environmental
Health, College of Medicine, University of Cincinnati; Attending
Psychiatrist and Director, Psychiatric Consultation-Liaison Service,
Cincinnati General Hospital, Cincinnati, Ohio

MILTON ROSENBAUM, M.D.
CHAPTER 25
Professor of Psychiatry, Department of Psychiatry, Hebrew University
and Hebrew University-Hadassah Medical School; Medical Director,
Jerusalem Mental Health Center-Esrath Nashim, Jerusalem, Israel;
Visiting Professor of Psychiatry, Department of Psychiatry, Albert
Einstein College of Medicine, Bronx, New York; Clinical Professor of
Psychiatry, Department of Psychiatry, Georgetown University Medical
School, Georgetown, D.C.

ALMUTH RÜPPELL
CHAPTER 10
Dr. phil., Dipl-Psych., University of Heidelberg, Heidelberg, West
Germany

JOSEPH D. SARGENT, M.D.
CHAPTER 16
Chief of Internal Medicine, Department of Neurology, Neurosurgery
and Internal Medicine, Menninger Foundation; Project Director,
Headache Research and Treatment Project, Menninger Foundation,
Topeka, Kansas

BERNARD SCHOENBERG, M.D.
CHAPTER 7
Professor of Clinical Psychiatry, Department of Psychiatry; Associate Dean for Academic Programs; Director, Office of Educational Planning in the Health Sciences, Columbia University; Attending Psychiatrist in Psychiatry Service, Department of Psychiatry, Presbyterian Hospital, New York, New York

A. B. SCLARE, M.B., Ch. B., F.R.C.P., M.R.C.P., F.R.C.PSYCH., D.P.M.
CHAPTER 11
Consultant Psychiatrist, Department of Psychiatry, Duke Street Hospital and Royal Infirmary; Honorary Clinical Lecturer in Psychological Medicine, University of Glasgow, Glasgow, Scotland

TOMONORI SUZUKI, M.D.
CHAPTER 18
Director, Suzuki Clinic, Tokyo, Japan

RYU SUZUKI, M.D.
CHAPTER 18
Psychiatrist, Department of Psychiatry, Yowa Hospital, Tokyo, Japan

HARRY A. TEITELBAUM, M.D., Ph.D.
CHAPTER 26
Assistant Professor of Psychiatry, Emeritus, The Johns Hopkins University School of Medicine; Assistant Professor Neurology, Department of Neurology, University of Maryland Medical School, Baltimore, Maryland

THOMAS C. TODD, Ph.D.
CHAPTER 12
Chief Psychologist, Harlem Valley Psychiatric Center, Wingdale, New York

N.S. VAHIA, M.D., F.R.C.Psych.
CHAPTER 19
Professor Emeritus, Department of Psychological Medicine, Seth G.S. Medical College; Professor Emeritus, Department of Psychological Medicine, King Edward VIII Memorial Hospital; Head of the Department, Department of Psychological Medicine, Dr. Balabhai Nanavati Hospital, Vile Parle, Bombay, India

G. TERENCE WILSON, PH.D.
CHAPTER 14
Associate Professor, Graduate School of Applied and Professional Psychology, Rutgers University, New Brunswick, New Jersey

STEWART WOLF, M.D.
CHAPTER 22
Professor and Director, The Marine Biomedical Institute, University of Texas Medical Branch, Galveston, Texas

Foreword

The psychosomatic approach to medicine has been promoted essentially by psychiatrists and psychoanalysts. Eric Wittkower has been one of the pioneers of this movement and one of its most energetic proponents over the past fifty years. Despite extensive developments in the field of psychosomatic medicine, internists, surgeons, gynecologists, pediatricians, and general practitioners who attend psychosomatic meetings and who take part in colloquia or demonstrations of interviews and psychotherapy have been *rarae aves*. Witness the list of contributors to this book, among whom psychiatrists are in overwhelming majority. As Wittkower and Warnes point out in their Preface, psychiatrists are now more readily accepted by nonpsychiatrists, particularly by colleagues in hospitals. Unfortunately, however, the job of psychosomatic evaluation and treatment of patients is still left largely in the hands of psychiatrists by their nonpsychiatric colleagues.

The psychosomatic movement has been conceived, hatched, and nurtured at universities. Scientific societies, congresses, journals, and books devoted to psychosomatic medicine have proliferated all over the world. Yet, because research in this area has been carried out mainly at universities, the psychosomatic approach has predominantly been practised at teaching hospitals.

This state of affairs exists equally in North America and in Europe; its deplorable existence makes this book very timely. Is it true that despite innumerable clinical, laboratory, and epidemiologic studies during the past four decades, the relevance of psychological factors to the understanding and treatment of disease has failed to gain substantial ground? Why have not psychiatrists "sold" the psychological approach to their nonpsychiatric colleagues?

Although it is true that there is more evidence of the efficiency of various psychotherapeutic methods in psychosomatic disorders than in psychoneuroses (3), a very small minority of physicians are using them for psychosomatic patients. This lack of impact constitutes an interesting parallel to the failure of psychotherapy research to influence psychotherapeutic practice, a leitmotiv of Bergin and Strupp's excellent book (1). Conversely, research in biological psychiatry has evinced no problems in achieving rapid translation of findings into daily practice, e.g. insulin coma was generally given up soon after its outcome proved inferior to other forms of treatment in schizophrenia; selection of psychopharmacologic drugs is becoming more and more accurate; and electroconvulsive therapy has retained its legitimate place in certain diagnostic categories.

Explanations for these discrepancies between research and practice in the field are probably both internal resistance by physicians to unfamiliar insights into the role of the doctor's personality and the doctor-patient relationship) and external (the time-consuming nature of the psychotherapeutic process). They may also have some scientific basis, i.e., the "softer" nature of much research data in this field.

Just as psychiatry has to face an antipsychiatric movement, medicine at large now has to face antimedical attacks from various professionals, politicians and governments. A prominent example is Ivan Illich who, after his radical and impassioned criticism of the schooling system of transportation and of the hypertrophy of the industrial civilization in general, turns in Medical Nemesis (2) a bitter attack on the modern medical enterprise; he views it as a paradigm of the industrial society with all its alienating powers. Iatrogenic effects take place, according to him, at the clinical, social, and psychological levels, and they outgrow the largely mythical beneficial effects of medicine. While many of these antimedical claims are excessive, some present valid viewpoints which may indicate the right direction for medicine in the future.

The dehumanization of health care has probably increased rather than decreased since 1954 when Wittkower and R.A. Cleghorn (4) edited a more theoretical book (Recent Developments in Psychosomatic Medicine) where they clearly describe this danger of dehumanization. One of the best answers to Illich and his supporters is to demonstrate how efficient a humanistic approach to medicine may be. Without doubt the present book is an excellent and timely contribution which will aid the diffusion of the psychosomatic approach from teaching hospital services to the daily practice of all categories of physicians.

REFERENCES:

1. Bergin AE, Strupp H: Changing Frontiers in the Science of Psychotherapy. Chicago, Aldine, 1972

2. Illich I: Medical Nemesis: The Exploration of Health. McClelland and Stewart, in association with Marion Boyars Publishers, Ltd., London, 1975

3. Malan DH: The outcome problem in psychotherapy research. A historical review. Arch Gen Psychiatry, 1973, pp. 719–729

4. Wittkower ED, Cleghorn RA (eds): Recent Developments in Psychosomatic Medicine. Philadelphia, Lippincott, 1954

Maurice Dongier, M.D.
Chairman, Department of Psychiatry,
McGill University
Montreal, Quebec, Canada

Preface

"It is more important to know what sort of person has a disease than to know what sort of disease a person has."

Hippocrates

Psychosomatic medicine has been emerging in the past decade from dichotomous fallacies based on Cartesian dualism into a fertile area of clinical and physiologic research. Individuals tend to show highly characteristic and consistent patterns of physiologic reaction under various well-studied conditions and settings. Individual susceptibility and the perpetuation of the disease process are two ends of a circular multifactorial spectrum of etiologically interrelated elements. In this chain of pathogenic events, characteristic vulnerabilities to stress, conflict avoidance and affect, disturbed patterns of coping under physiologic and psychological stress, immune response deficiencies, neuroendocrine and autonomic shifts and ecologic and psychosocial impingements have been implicated as playing a major or minor role in various disease processes.

The psychosomatic or holistic approach to medical practice has developed as a result of clinical observations and humane concern for the sick individual. It probably reached its peak after World War II when hopes were raised that diseases previously regarded to be of unknown origin had found a psychological explanation and were likely to be amenable to psychotherapy. Subsequently, proponents of psychosomatic medicine moved in two directions: toward basic research in psychophysiology and toward application of its principles to clinical practice.

As regards the latter, the concept of psychosomatic specificity, i.e., the relevance of specific personality factors to the etiology of certain disorders, has increasingly given way to the psychosomatic approach, i.e., to the psychological and psychosocial approach to anyone suffering from any disorder. Centers have sprung up in various parts of the world—mostly at universities—at which enthusiastic researchers and clinicians have pursued their orientation, and the psychosomatic approach has to some degree permeated the practice of medicine.

The purpose of this book is 1) to take stock of the present situation, i.e., to assess to what extent the psychosomatic approach has become part and parcel of the practice of medicine, 2) to reinforce cooperation between psychiatrists and nonpsychiatrists with the ultimate aim of absorption of psychological, psychiatric and psychophysiologic techniques by physicians, 3) to illustrate the multitude of situations ranging from the dying patient to the asthmatic in which psychological help may be needed, and 4) to present a multitude of techniques ranging from psychoanalysis to relaxation therapies with which such help can be offered. This last goal constitutes the largest portion of this book.

A great deal of interesting psychophysiologic research has been carried out within recent years, and a large body of psychosomatic theory has been accumulated. To deal with these issues is *not* the purpose of this book which is meant to be of practical value with a predominant clinical orientation.

Twenty years ago in the preface to *Recent Developments In Psychosomatic Medicine,* edited by one of us (E.D.W.) and R. A. Cleghorn, the hope was expressed that the psychosomatic approach be absorbed by medicine. Has this hope materialized? Certainly not. There are still any number of physicians who practice—and pride themselves on practicing—an impersonal approach to their patients, who aim at repairing damaged organs rather than at treating diseased and dis-eased persons. A good deal has been done to bridge the gap between psychiatry and medicine, but much more remains to be done. This book has been designed and is primarily destined for general practitioners; we hope that it will also be of interest and benefit to many others, including psychiatrists.

PSYCHOSOMATIC MEDICINE is divided into five parts, beginning with a discussion of basic principles in patient management and a review of particular problems in consultation. Models of intervention for particular conditions, such as hemodialysis, are dealt with in the next few chapters. A variety of treatment procedures ranging from psychoanalysis to yoga are presented in the next twelve chapters, and an account of special therapeutic considerations in relation to disorders of various organ systems concludes the book.

With the stated objectives in mind we invited practitioners to report on the field of their expertise. In choosing them, we have been guided solely by their high scientific standing. Most of them are psychiatrists; some are internists. A majority of the contributors are North Americans; a few are Europeans and Asiatics.

Deliberately we disregarded their theoretical orientation. The result of this has been that, analogous to the familiar blind-man-elephant simile, numerous approaches to the same overall problem have been used. Just as there are many medical approaches to treatment, there are more than one psychosomatic approach. The authors have been encouraged to express their views freely, and some have taken an extreme position. When this happened we asked a proponent of a different viewpoint to express his views. We do not necessarily share the views of all the contributors to this book, but we believe that presentation of a multitude of approaches is an asset rather than a liability.

Our contributors interpreted their assignments in different ways, some confining themselves to reporting their own experiences, others augmenting these by observations culled from the literature, and still others giving an overview of the field of their expertise. However, as regards the topics included here, we are dealing with illustrative examples rather than with comprehensive overviews.

What can be learned from this book? On comparison with *Recent Developments In Psychosomatic Medicine,* the following changes have taken place during the last twenty years:

The growth of consultation and liason psychiatry indicates that psychiatrists are now more readily accepted by nonpsychiatrists than in the past. New fields for cooperation between psychiatrists and surgeons have developed, e.g., in cardiac surgery and hemodialysis. Interest has been focused on pain and grief over loss of a beloved person, and team cooperation in dealing with these issues has been established.

Initial enthusiasm for the application of psychoanalysis for the so-called psychosomatic disorders has cooled, though it is still regarded as the treatment of choice for highly selected patients. New forms of group therapy adapted to patients with psychosomatic complaints have been developed. The efficacy of family therapy and of behavior therapy for the treatment of these patients has been demonstrated. The introduction of pharmacotherapy has had a tremendous impact on medical treatment, especially in the area of affective disorders and reactive psychophysiologic derangements, though it has been less notable in patients with chronic emotional conflicts and severe personality disturbances. Autogenic training employed for a long time in Europe has of late been enthusiastically received in some quarters in North America. Biofeedback is still very much on trial. Interest has been shown in the application of Asiatic methods of treatment to Western patients.

Good therapeutic results have been reported by all procedures adopted depending rather on the doctor who uses them than on the patient to whom they are administered. Criteria for choice of procedure are sorely lacking.

Even in the early phases of the psychosomatic movement it was recognized that the term *psychosomatic* was not equivalent to *psychogenic.* As time went on, the multifactorial etiology of disorders once labeled psychosomatic has increasingly been acknowledged. Consequently, a pluralistic therapeutic approach to these disorders has gained ground. As stated before, cooperation between psychiatrists and nonpsychiatrists has been somewhat strengthened. Not infrequently, as some chapters here illustrate, application of psychotherapy to patients suffering from psychosomatic complaints has been taken over by nonpsychiatrists.

As one turns the pages of the section entitled "Specific Disorders" it becomes obvious that the necessity for the employment of psychotherapy in the treatment of these patients is unanimously stressed. However, the authors who report on specific disorders are a good deal more guarded in the results obtained than the authors of the section "Psychotherapies," who report on the psychotherapies which they apply and obviously favor. An approach to disturbed life-situations predominates over a personality approach.

Our thanks are due to the authors for willingly accepting our invitation to contribute to this book; to those of them who goodnaturedly complied with our request for editorial revisions; to Mrs. Joan McGilvary for her valuable help in script editing; and to Miss Katherine P. Vidmér for carrying out the arduous task of typing the manuscript.

E.D.W.
H.W.

psychosomatic medicine

Part I
General Considerations

1 Basic Principles of Management in Psychosomatic Medicine

LOUIS LINN

MEDICINE IS BIOPSYCHOSOCIAL

Emotion is present in every stage of illness: during the premonitory stage, in the acute, the subacute, and the convalescent stages, and throughout chronicity. However, during each period of illness, the importance of the emotional factor varies: it may be minimal or even absent at one time but of primary importance at another (12).

The symptoms of all illness arise from three separate sources (16). The *biological factor* is the body's attempt to cope with the nonhuman environment; it is represented, for example, by a cough to expel a foreign body from the respiratory tract, vomiting or diarrhea to expel noxious agents from the gastrointestinal tract, or an inflammation with pain, swelling, and fever to contain a bacterial invasion. The *psychological factor* relates to specific attitudes and feelings that are inculcated within the family circle as a result, largely, of interactions with parents and siblings in early childhood. An excessively strong maternal attachment based on the frustration of the dependency needs of early childhood may, for instance, contribute to peptic ulcer formation or bronchial asthma later in life. The *social factor* refers to personal interactions outside the home after the early childhood developmental period, *i.e.,* to the impact of school, work, recreation, and the community. Failure in school or a period of unemployment may be cited as examples of social pressures that may initiate physical changes leading to disabling disease.

We will not consider the biological factor in this chapter, except as one of the given data in referring to a clinical picture such as that of diabetes, hypertension, or myocardial infarction. On the other hand, we will consider the psychological and social factors in detail.

THE SICK ROLE

To comprehend symptom formation in psychosocial terms, a few words about the so-called sick role are in order (20, 22). The sick role implies a contractual arrangement between the patient and the physician that involves the rights, privileges, and duties of the sick person as well as of those who are to perform certain services for him. Sociologists refer to the patient's part in this arrangement as the "sick role." If the physician is to perform his role effectively, the patient must comply with at least some of the social prescriptions for the role of patient. The latter involves a constellation of thoughts, feelings, and actions expressed by the patient for the purpose of engaging the attention and active assistance of other persons whose help he is seeking. The patient may believe his very survival is in danger as a result of abnormal changes within his own body. These changes may be variously experienced as pain, nausea, bowel and urinary urgency, fatigue, anxiety, depression, and so forth. He may express these subjective states with varying degrees of intensity and overt drama. In response to pain, for example, he may scream in agony at one extreme or give no outward evidence of discomfort at the other; more frequently, he will display the various intermediate stages of weeping, vocalizing, or stoically controlled verbalizations of suffering. Again, in relation to fatigue, he may display lassitude and total collapse at one extreme, or he may continue to drive himself at his accustomed rate of productivity in spite of an accompanying inner sense of uneasiness. Similar variations can occur in the expressions of anxiety and depression.

What determines the qualitative and quantitative aspects of these overt expressions of discomfort and the effectiveness with which they engage the attentions and ministrations of helping agencies? First, there is the degree of actual physical disorder, or at any rate the degree to which the patient is affected by his discomfort. Second, there is the degree to which the helper is actually responsive to the patient's plight, or the extent to which the patient has been programmed to expect a response from helpers in general.

It is clear that the way the patient perceives and unconsciously symbolizes his sickness is important; indeed, these highly subjective impressions are of primary importance. To understand how a patient arrives at his particular version of the sick role, it is necessary to review certain psychological developmental facts. The infant learns the sick role in the earliest interactions with his mother, and what he learns at this time sets the stage for his subsequent sick-role behavior. For example, if she is sensitive to his needs, if she does not withdraw her love even though he has soiled himself through vomiting or loss of sphincter control or has suffered disfigurement, and if she responds swiftly and effectively to relieve his discomfort, he learns one sick-role pattern. In this instance, the child will be less likely to panic when he becomes ill. He will express his discomfort in an appropriate, self-disciplined manner. He will enter into cooperative and reasonably trusting relationships with helping individuals. On the other hand, when the mother-child relationship is disturbed, the sick role will tend to reflect this disturbance. A chronically unresponsive mother, for example, will tend to encourage panic reactions and excessive displays of discomfort.

To some degree, every mother views her child as an extension of her own body (26). In this spirit, she may, for example, scold him if he injures himself in a fall. In every instance of illness, she acts as if the child had been careless with her property and warns, in effect, that he will lose her love if he gets sick. From extreme forms of this interactional pattern, a child may come to believe that illness is somehow sinful or morally wrong. In time, he will tend to react to illness with guilt, shame, and fear of loss of love. As a result, he becomes inclined to conceal or deny illness and not to signal his distress when in pain. In short, he does all in his power to avoid the sick role as a way to avoid the loss of love and the loss of self-esteem.

The sick role in adult life is regularly associated with the phenomenon of *regression*. The latter is a point of view adopted by an adult in response to emotional distress in which he regards himself as very small and helpless, in short, as a child again. In this state of regression, he not only underestimates his own powers but tends to overestimate the powers of those who are supposed to help him. The same mental state that evokes in the patient the feeling that he is a little child causes him to cast his helpers, symbolically, into the exaggeratedly powerful role of parent surrogates. This latter aspect of regression is known as *transference*. As a consequence of regression, a patient tends to repeat his childhood patterns of coping with sickness. For example, a lifelong tendency to ambivalence—*i.e.,* to feel hostile to those very people whose love and help one needs—may create a tendency to excessive guilt in settings of helpless dependency due to illness.

Cultural factors are also involved in the manifestations of the sick role. In a study of the patients in a clinic for example, Zola (33) found that Irish patients tended to limit and understate their complaints, whereas Italian patients in the same clinic tended to dramatize their complaints and to generalize them to involve other body parts.

ADHERENCE AND NONADHERENCE TO MEDICAL ADVICE

Implicit in the foregoing discussion of the sick role is the proposition that there is an appropriate pattern of adherence to medical advice, which is characterized by the lack of panic, appropriate self-disciplined expressions of discomfort, and a reasonably trusting relationship with helping individuals (21).

Some patients may be described as overly adherent. Paradoxically, these patients are usually not seriously ill from a physical point of view. In spite of this, they will brave the most inclement weather to keep a clinic appointment. Typically, these are aged patients for whom the medical clinic provides the most significant human contact. When some such individuals are provided with supportive social programs in nonmedical settings, they quickly surrender the sick role and the associated pattern of overcompliance.

For patients with hypochondriasis, a doctor, a nurse, or some other parent-surrogate caretaker may often be the only person with whom anxiety-free social interaction is possible. The "sick role" for such patients provides an escape from more complex relationships involving family, employers, and friends—relationships that generate intolerable levels of anxiety. Emotionally disturbed children in institutional settings often tend to adopt the hypochondriacal sick role as a way of evading intolerable social interactions.

In each of these instances, all attempts by the physician to discourage the sick role are doomed to failure unless the underlying social needs of the patient are understood and solved. The social needs of many aged patients are more easily met. They tend to respond well to "golden age" programs in geriatric day-care centers (13). For many hypochondriacal patients, however, the social issues are more complex. Commonly, the outlets that are available to these patients are studiously avoided because of intolerable anxiety on social contact. On the other hand, social isolation can generate a feeling of loneliness that is no less painful. In short, the patient finds himself between the horns of a "need-fear" dilemma—his need for human contact *versus* his fear of human contact (4). The sick role with its highly circumscribed repertoire of social interactions can provide an extraordinarily effective way of solving this dilemma. This explains why the typical hypochondriacal patient wards off all attempts on the part of others to discourage the sick role.

Behavior which is nonadherent to medical advice may be manifested by a failure to take prescribed medications or to follow treatment procedures, by missed clinic appointments, or by the decision to sign out of a hospital against medical advice. Some instances of nonadherence to medical advice result from faulty communication between the patient and his physician. In the doctor's office, the patient may be too panic-stricken to ask all his questions. The patient should therefore be encouraged to formulate his questions in writing in the calm of his own home and with the assistance of his family. The physician should take enough time to review these questions in detail. Similarly, a panic-stricken patient may not be in the best mental state to understand what the physician is saying. As a result, he may leave the clinic grossly misinformed and, perhaps inappropriately, expecting "the worst." The physician should therefore make free use of printed forms which explain clearly to the patient the nature of his illness and the treatment regimen he is expected to follow.

By and large, people are motivated by a desire to be well. This gives rise almost universally to an ongoing, mild *attitude of denial.* Physical deviations from normal tend to be disregarded. A lesion on a concealed part of the body may be ignored longer than a highly visible facial lesion. A potentially serious lesion may be neglected due to a lack of education. Lesions that do not interfere with customary family, work, or play relationships tend to be ignored, as are symptoms which are present only intermittently (19). The patient's denial may be reinforced by a spouse who cannot tolerate the idea of a physically disabled marital partner.

These attitudes of denial and the rejection of the sick role figure significantly in the emergence of nonadherent behavior. A patient who complies religiously with the doctor's orders may run the risk of alienating an illness-intolerant spouse. In the ensuing conflict, the doctor's wishes may get lost. Similarly, conflict between a doctor's orders and an adolescent's need for independence may lead to noncompliance. An authoritarian approach to diet with an adolescent diabetic, for example, may lead to self-destructive, rebellious acting out. That this rebellion takes place, nevertheless, in a setting of basic respect for the physician is shown when the adolescent diets carefully on the day preceding a clinic visit so as not to displease his doctor with a urine test which is positive for sugar. By the same token, addicts will commonly bring someone else's "clean" urine for laboratory examination so as not to provoke disappointment in the clinic physician.

In brief, the problem of noncompliance is a complex one, involving not only the patient's own basic attitude toward the sick role, but also the attitude of certain other persons of significance, such as a spouse, a parent, or an employer. The physician has to decipher the puzzle and recruit adherence by providing appropriate explanations to the patient and his family (3).

We cannot omit the physician's role in this discussion of the patient-doctor contract (9). Some physicians function best with the totally compliant patient. The surgeon operating on the anesthetized patient is the best example of this. Some other physicians manage satisfactorily with the patient who is conscious but only as long as he is helpless as a result of acute illness. The problem of treating the patient with a chronic illness is an altogether different matter. Here, the aim of the doctor is to help the patient to help himself. This requires respect for individual differences. The physician must be able to respond flexibly to the rigidities and eccentricities of specific patients, and he must possess sufficient self-esteem so that he is not threatened if the patient does not comply.

Many physicians are brilliant technicians and even contribute mightily to human welfare, but yet they cannot relate with warmth to a fully conscious patient. We must learn not to harass such colleagues with ill-advised entreaties to join the psychosomatic medicine fold. It is well to recall at this point that people choose medicine as a career for unconscious and even irrational reasons as well as from motivations that are conscious and rational (30). Neurotic fears based on the death of an ambivalently loved parent or sibling, for example, may lead to exaggerated fears of death, which lead in turn to the choice of a medical career as a counterphobic defense (7). Some such physicians may maintain their equilibrium only by keeping an emotionally safe distance from their patients. Others may turn to alcoholism, drugs, or other forms of pathological behavior to relieve anxiety, depression, and guilt (8, 28). Such physicians, naturally, require intensive psychiatric treatment, and some may prove unfit to remain in practice.

ANTECEDENTS OF ILLNESS

The final decision to visit a doctor is an expression not so much of abnormality within the patient as of a life change to which the patient cannot adapt (23). Losses of one kind or another are predominant factors: loss of a spouse, a child, or a parent, loss of one's accustomed work role through unemployment, retirement, or promotion, loss of health or a body part which leads to a loss of accustomed social roles, or loss of self-esteem. Often the loss involves unconscious mechanisms. Physical symptoms may erupt, for example, at the time of an anniversary of a loss. Even though the fact of the anniversary is not consciously perceived, it may nevertheless activate memories of previous periods of "giving up." A work promotion with new responsibilities may elicit complex anxiety, guilt, and depressive reactions because of unconscious childhood competitive strivings with a parent. The experience of being mugged, robbed, or burglarized is not uncommonly followed by a loss of self-esteem and by physical symptoms necessitating medical care. A sense of helplessness and hopelessness, a loss of satisfaction with one's customary relationships, and a loss of the sense of continuity with one's past, present, and future are feeling states which commonly precede the eruption of incapacitating physical illness (5).

Holmes and Rahe (10) have compiled a list of commonly encountered life changes and have attempted to quantitate the traumatic impact of each event as measured by what they call *life-change units* (LCU) (see Table 1–1). According to their findings, the accumulation of over 200 LCUs in a year is associated with a very high incidence of reported illness. The latter may, in some instances, be an old illness which the patient previously denied or neglected but which is now used as a ticket of entry into the health-care system. A patient may decide, for example, to enter a hospital for the repair of a long-neglected hernia as an escape from a life situation that has become intolerable. The continuation of his acute life problems postoperatively may lead to a protracted convalescence and even to unexpected chronic invalidism.

In other instances, the reported illness may consist of various symptoms without a discernible organic basis. This reaction is commonly misinterpreted or misunderstood. A patient may exasperate an emergency-room physician because of the seeming triviality of the complaint, and the physician may cite this as an example of the misuse of the emergency room. This is not a misuse of the emergency room so much as it is an inaccurate diagnosis of the nature of the clinical situation. For example, a mother who is about to lose control of her self-destructive impulses may bring her physically normal child to the emergency room. Too often, the true meaning of her clinic visit is not recognized; she is sent home without help, only to return a few hours later with a seriously injured, battered child.

The following case history illustrates the danger of misinterpreting the clinical significance of seemingly minor physical complaints.

A 43-year-old married man with two teenage daughters and a newborn son presented himself on sick call at the factory one day with a complaint of headache without apparent physical cause. He was dismissed with two aspirins. During the ensuing months, he was on sick call repeatedly, each time for minor physical complaints. It was noted that he was becoming irritable and argumentative with fellow workers. After 20 years with an unblemished work record, he took to drinking on the job. He also incurred a number of minor injuries while at work.

These striking personality changes went unheeded until he sustained a relatively mild concussion which became the nidus of a protracted neurotic disorder. After years of physical examinations, treatments, compensation payments, and litigation, he was officially retired and given a lump-sum financial settlement by his employers.

A retrospective study of this case suggested quite strongly that his wife's unplanned pregnancy and the birth of a son in his middle years gave rise to life changes to which this man could not adapt. A scientific medical response during the premonitory stage of his "accident" neurosis would have included a proper evaluation of the emotional impact of this event. It would also have included

Table 1-1. THE STRESS OF ADJUSTING TO CHANGE*

EVENTS	SCALE OF IMPACT
Death of spouse	100
Divorce	73
Marital separation	65
Jail term	63
Death of close family member	63
Personal injury or illness	53
Marriage	50
Fired at work	47
Marital reconciliation	45
Retirement	45
Change in health of family member	44
Pregnancy	40
Sex difficulties	39
Gain of new family member	39
Business readjustment	39
Change in financial state	38
Death of close friend	37
Change to different line of work	36
Change in number or arguments with spouse	35
Mortgage over $10,000	31
Foreclosure of mortgage or loan	30
Change in responsibilities at work	29
Son or daughter leaving home	29
Trouble with in-laws	29
Outstanding personal achievement	28
Wife begins or stops work	26
Begin or end school	26
Change in living conditions	25
Revision of personal habits	24
Trouble with boss	23
Change in work hours or conditions	20
Change in residence	20
Change in schools	20
Change in recreation	19
Change in church activities	19
Change in social activities	18
Mortgage or loan less than $10,000	17
Change in sleeping habits	16
Change in number of family get-togethers	15
Change in eating habits	15
Vacation	13
Christmas	12
Minor violations of the law	11

*Holmes TJ: The New York Times, June 10, 1973

appropriate assistance in the psychological and social spheres and thereby might have averted years of invalidism (15).

The experience of a traumatic life change may set the stage for the onset of disease involving any organ system of the body and with any degree of severity. The cardiovascular system may be involved with acute myocardial infarction, hypertension, and cerebrovascular accidents; the respiratory system, with asthma, hyperventilation, increased cigarette smoking, and so on; the gastrointestinal system, with peptic ulcer and ulcerative colitis. Immune mechanisms may be altered, rendering an individual more prone to infectious diseases and perhaps to certain malignancies (25). Associated endocrine upheavals may mark the onset of thyroid disease or diabetes. Changes in the levels of cholesterol, uric acid, or various amines accompany these emotional upheavals and are probably causative in a variety of organic diseases (27).

In summary, a major life change may result in symptoms without organic disease, or it may lead to complaints arising from old but previously tolerated diseases, to new organic diseases, or to a combination of any of the foregoing.

PERSONALITY FACTORS IN ILLNESS

In any large population, a small percentage of the people accounts for a disproportionately large percentage of illness. As a result, we have come to speak of people who are "illness prone," "pain prone," or "accident prone" (11). Many years ago, it was hypothesized that certain personality types were specifically prone to certain organic diseases. Alexander, in particular, elaborated this point of view (2). He felt, for example, that peptic ulcer patients were basically passive and dependent but had been thrust by life circumstances into unwanted positions of leadership and responsibility. Chronic hypersecretion of gastric juices as an expression of ongoing, unfulfilled, infantile longings was especially emphasized. Arterial hypertension seemed to be related to conflicts concerning poorly controlled aggression. The asthmatic attack seemed to be the outcome of an underlying depression and to represent a cry for help from a mother whose love was not forthcoming. Dermatological disorders seemed to relate to conflicts concerning exhibitionism, and colitis to unresolved conflicts concerning bowel control.

Although the issues are perhaps not as neatly compartmentalized as Alexander suggests, there remains some residual validity to these formulations. In any event, Alexander's basic principle is valid, namely, there is an obligation to elucidate the specific life conflict which characterizes a specific patient and his physical disorder. Such an individualized approach in psychotherapy is more likely to lead to both insight and symptom relief.

In recent years, attention has been called to the so-called type-A personality, which is characteristic of individuals who are work addicts, who are rigid and overconscientious, and who tend to become prisoners of time schedules. These inflexible, type-A people are said to be more apt to break down physically in the face of life changes that call for new patterns of adaptation.

The traditional psychiatric concept concerning personality is to view it as a rather inflexible life-style which is rooted deeply in the experiences of early childhood and which is relatively unresponsive to psychotherapy. Contemporary learning theory, on the other hand, tends to see a chronic life pattern as a consequence of current and relatively superficial human interactions which act as positive reinforcers or reward-givers and which have the effect of perpetuating these old patterns on a day-to-day basis. In relation to certain chronic disabilities, for example, the patient may be rewarded in various ways by his family, friends, and physicians for maintaining the sick role. By separating the patient from his customary environment (by hospitalization, for example) and by rewarding him for the success with which he controls his pathological somatic manifestations, it is sometimes possible to improve a chronic sick pattern in a relatively short period of time (24). Unfortunately, however, improvements achieved within the sheltered setting of a hospital often do not persist when the patient is returned to his customary environment. It is exactly at this point—after discharge from the hospital—that the real test of any treatment plan begins (17).

In any case, the long-term life pattern which we call personality is only one element in the disease process. The vicissitudes of living which generate the antecedents of acute illness constitute a second element. The psychological developmental history, which contributes to daily experience the dimension of symbolism and unconscious mentation, is a third, and finally the organic factor, the biological vulnerability to specific disease entities, is a fourth element. The last is often an inherited factor and may be the ultimate determinant in specific instances. Some patients, for example, are born gastric hypersecretors. However well-equipped a given patient may be psychologically to cope from within, we cannot protect him from the external pressures of everyday life. As a result, the best-adjusted hypersecretor may, under sufficient provocation, acquire a peptic ulcer (6).

GENERAL PRINCIPLES OF TREATMENT

PHYSICAL EXAMINATION

Never underestimate the psychotherapeutic value of a careful physical examination. Often a patient who is brooding needlessly over the possibilities of a malignancy will develop insomnia, anorexia, and weight loss—symptoms which seem to confirm his worst fears. A careful physical examination with negative results, followed by suitable reassurances, may suffice in themselves to produce a full remission of symptoms. On the other hand, the morbid somatic preoccupation may be part of a deeper psychiatric disorder, requiring referral for special care. In some instances, the patient rejects positive reassurances and so distorts what he hears that he goes home more frightened than ever. It is well to recall the propensity of frightened patients to distort and misunderstand medical communications before judging too harshly a colleague who may have seen the patient previously and who, according to the patient's report at least, apparently misguided him.

THE PATIENT'S HISTORY

A careful history is probably the single most important item in the physician's diagnostic and therapeutic armamentarium. Such a history necessarily includes a detailed account of psychological and social factors. The erstwhile family doctor knew about family problems and difficulties at work; he investigated the psychosocial antecedents of a complaint as a matter of course. Due to the technical refinements of modern medicine, however, with its fragmentation into organ specialities, it is not so easy anymore to see the patient in his entirety, *i.e.,* as a human being who is enveloped in a social net which can, in turn, support him or strangle him. The influence of the past as well as the impact of the current plight must be taken into account. To omit them is to reduce medical care to a series of sometimes spectacular technological successes which do not really affect the health of the individual or of the community in any long-lasting way.

FAMILY INVOLVEMENT IN TREATMENT

A corollary of the preceding section is the fact that medical practice must be family centered.

One of the most significant contributions by Masters and Johnson (18) is their insistence that a sexual impairment seemingly within an individual is really the outcome of a general communication breakdown within a marriage. They have emphasized repeatedly that they cannot treat a specific potency disturbance in a husband or frigidity in a wife, but that the target of their treatment plan is the marital unit as a whole. This profound observation has implications that go far beyond the confines of so-called sex therapy. According to one hypothesis, for example, schizophrenia is caused by faulty communication patterns within the family and cannot be treated without treating this intrafamilial communication disturbance (14). In one study of myocardial infarction, it was found that in 30% of the cases, severe family disturbances were reported and that in this group, in particular, the poorest clinical outcome could be expected (32).

When one marital partner becomes ill, the other may become ill, too, on the basis of identification associated with guilt and anxiety. A resentful spouse in an attitude of reaction formation may become destructively overprotective. A pathologically dependent spouse may be intolerant of illness in the partner and, as a result, participate in patterns of denial or nonadherence which interfere with proper medical care. A spouse may encourage addictive states in the partner, thereby effectively eliminating any possibility of cure in the home setting. A child may repeatedly ingest poisonous substances in the home as part of a pathological mother-child interaction. A husband's highly successful career may be the cause of emotional deprivation and symptom formation in an overly dependent wife (31).

On the other hand, family interactions may be maximally supportive—so much so that the individual cannot survive apart from the family. Studies of morbidity and mortality rates in marital partners who lose a spouse regularly show an abnormally high illness rate in the survivor. In one study, for example, widowers age 54 or older had 67% more deaths due to coronary heart disease than did their nonbereaved controls.

A wife's report about a husband's symptoms may be crucial for diagnosis or treatment. The importance of the mother's presence at a hospitalized child's bedside is now widely recognized. Parents are permitted to spend the night in the child's hospital room as a matter of routine and to be present at mealtimes in order to feed the child.

Many procedures which were once regarded as necessarily requiring an inpatient setting are now carried out safely at home. In addition, many procedures are now carried out in day-hospital settings to reduce the trauma of uninterrupted separation from the family. By the use of such relatively new patterns of health-care delivery, it has become possible to provide the patient with the maximum benefits of hospital technique while preserving, at the same time, the nurturing effects of loving family relationships and familiar home surroundings.

PSYCHOPHARMACOLOGICAL ADJUNCTS

The availability of potent psychotropic medications has made it possible for the physician to treat successfully many somatic equivalents of emotional disorders. Depression, for example, may play an etiologic role in a broad range of addictive states (including alcoholism, obesity, and excess smoking), in some types of headache, in certain intractable pruritic states, in insomnia, as well as in phobic panic states that may present symptoms of cardiac neurosis. Indeed, in any somatic condition in which a depressive component is suspected, a trial of antidepressant medication is warranted. Major tranquilizers may be indicated in certain somatic complaints associated with schizophrenia.

THE FAMILY PHYSICIAN AND THE PSYCHIATRIC CONSULTANT

Many psychiatric problems can be treated effectively by the family physician with some guidance from a psychiatric consultant. The consultant, for example, may effectively pinpoint target symptoms and advise the physician concerning the proper choice of medications and dosage. He may identify crucial psychodynamic factors concerning key people in the patient's environment who reinforce the sick role. He may then guide the family doctor concerning appropriate family interventions in the patient's behalf. A consultant may be able to point out unconscious factors in the clinical picture. The anniversary of a bereavement may arrive unawares, for example, and effective treatment may depend on the physician's recognition of this fact and his ability to encourage the patient to complete the work of mourning. The consultant may recognize instances of emotional overinvolvement with the patient's problems on the part of the family doctor and thus help him to play a more objective role.

The consultant can help the family doctor to decide which cases require referral for specialized psychiatric treatment. These may include cases of psychosis that require the use of neuroleptic medications, shock therapy, and in-patient treatment, or there may be cases with indications for long-term "insight" psychotherapy that only the specially trained psychiatrist can provide. The consultant may also be privy to personal secrets that the patient does not wish to share with his family physician, who may be, among other things, an old family friend.

IATROGENIC FACTORS IN PSYCHOSOMATIC DISORDERS

Some current problems in psychosomatic medicine are a consequence of specialization, technology, and overemphasis on hospital care. We are familiar, for example, with the plight of the patient who is doomed to die among strangers in a gadget-filled intensive care unit (ICU). The main insights of thanatology seem to lead back to simpler, kindlier times when dying occurred more often at home in the company of loved ones. ICU patients suffering from attacks of panic and delirium remind us that these patients need a few words of explanation concerning the physical arrangements of such units. They need contact with a window, a clock, and a calendar, and, most of all, they need contact with the human face, particularly with those people on whom their very lives depend. In addition, young nurses and technicians may have fears and frustrations with which they need help and which can lead to poor morale. In the long run, a sense of dedication and an *esprit de corps* are as important as technical skill in determining mortality outcome in an ICU* (1, 29).

Many medications in current use are associated with psychiatric complications.

Reserpine, which is used in the treatment of hypertension, causes depression in about 20% of the cases. This is particularly likely to occur in patients with a previous history of depression. Once it has started, the depression will often continue after the reserpine is stopped and may require a course of shock treatment to bring it to an end.

Oral contraceptives may exacerbate migraine or precipitate migraine in a previ-

---

*One elderly, postcoronary Miss Malaprop told me recently how relieved she was to leave the "intensive scare unit."

ously headache-free individual. The continued use of oral contraceptives in a patient with vascular headaches increases the risk of cerebral infarction.

In cases of hypothyroidism, overly rapid replacement therapy may precipitate a psychotic reaction or temporarily aggravate an existing psychosis.

When barbiturates are used to produce sleep, there is a rapid-eye-movement (REM) sleep rebound when the medication is discontinued. Patients recovering from myocardial infarction are particularly prone to further myocardial damage during this time.

Digitalis, quinidine, and propranolol can produce reactions of delirium in some sensitive patients.

Diuretics may produce delirium due to an excessive lowering of blood pressure or blood sodium level.

Many psychotropic agents can complicate the medical management of nonpsychiatric problems. The phenothiazines, for example, may increase the tachycardia of hyperthyroidism. They may also produce amenorrhea and lactation in nonpregnant females, and may induce hyperglycemia in previously well-regulated diabetic patients. Benzodiazepines may produce false normal values for iodine-131 uptake in hyperthyroid patients. Lithium therapy may cause the growth of thyroid nodules and produce thyroid dysfunction.

The use of tricyclic antidepressants may increase intraocular tension in patients with glaucoma. They may also reduce blood sugar levels in diabetics and produce dangerous reductions in blood pressure. They also have a direct cardiotoxic effect which can be dangerous in patients with myocardial infarction. Moreover, they can neutralize the hypotensive action of guanethidine, which is used in the treatment of severe hypertension.

To conclude this discussion of iatrogenic factors in psychosomatic disorders, it must be clear that a physician can no longer ignore the fallacies and pseudosimplicities of a medical approach which is not solidly based on a biopsychosocial point of view.

REFERENCES

1. Abram HS: Psychologic aspects of intensive care units. Med Ann DC 43:59–62, 1974
2. Alexander F: Psychosomatic Medicine: Its Principles and Application. New York, WW Norton, 1950
3. Balint M: The Doctor, The Patient and the Illness. London, Pitman, 1964
4. Burnham DL, Gladstone SI, Gibson RW: Schizophrenia and the Need–Fear Dilemma. New York, International Universities Press, 1969
5. Engel GL: A life setting conducive to illness. Intern Med 69:293–299, Aug 1968
6. Engel GL: Psychophysiological gastrointestinal disorders: peptic ulcer. In Freedman AM, Kaplan HI, Sadock BJ (eds): Comprehensive Textbook of Psychiatry. Baltimore, Williams & Wilkins, 1975
7. Feifel H: Death and dying: attitudes of patient and doctor vs the function of attitudes toward death. Group Adv Psychiatry 5:633–641, 1965
8. Garb J: Drug addiction in physicians. Anesth Analg 48:129–133, 1969
9. Hollender MH, Knopf WF, Szasz TS: The doctor–patient relationship and its historical context. Am J Psychiatry 115:522, 1958
10. Holmes TH, Rahe RH: The social readjustment rating scale. J Psychosom Res 11:213, 1967
11. Joseph ED, Schwartz AH: Accident proneness. In Freedman AM, Kaplan HI, Sadock BJ (eds): Comprehensive Textbook of Psychiatry. Baltimore, Williams & Wilkins, 1975
12. Kaufman MR, Margolin SG: What is psychosomatic medicine? In Medical Clinics of North America, New York Issue. Philadelphia, WB Saunders, 1948, pp 609–611
13. Kubie S: Group Work with the Aged. New York, International Universities Press, 1953
14. Lidz T, Fleck S, Cornelison AR: Schizophrenia in the Family. New York, International Universities Press, 1965
15. Linn L: Neurosis following head injury. In Feiring EH (ed): Injuries of the Brain and Spinal Cord. New York, Springer, 1974, pp 614–637
16. Linn L: Clinical manifestations of psychiatric disorders. In Freedman AM, Kaplan HI, Sadock BJ (eds.): Comprehensive Textbook of Psychiatry. Baltimore, Williams & Wilkins, 1975
17. Linn L, Weinroth LA, Schamah R: Occupational Therapy in Dynamic Psychiatry: An Introduction to the Four–Phase Concept in Hospital Psychiatry. Washington DC, American Psychiatric Association, 1962
18. Masters WH, Johnson VE: Human Sexual Inadequacy. Boston, Little, Brown & Co, 1970
19. Mechanic D: Medical Sociology. New York, Free Press of Glencoe, 1968
20. Mumford E: The patient's role: what is it? Why? What can the doctor do about it? In Kaufman MR (ed): The Medical Clinics of North America: Psychiatry for the Non-Psychiatrist. Philadelphia, WB Saunders, 1967, pp 1507–1514
21. Mumford E: Response of patients to medical advice. In Pardes H, Simon R (eds): Human Behavior in Health and Illness (in press)
22. Parsons T: Definition of health and illness in the light of American values and social structure. In Jaco G (ed): Patients, Physicians and Illness. New York Free Press of Glencoe, 1968, pp 165–187
23. Rahe RH, Gunderson E, Arthur RJ: Demographic and psychosocial factors in acute illness reporting. J Chronic Dis 23:245–255, 1970
24. Sargent JD, Green EE, Walters ED: Preliminary report on use of autogenic feedback training in treatment of migraine and tension headaches. Psychosom Med 35:129–135, 1973
25. Schmale AH: Relationship of separation, depression to diseases. I. A report on a hospitalized medical population. Psychosom Med 20:259, 1958
26. Seidenberg R: Who owns the body? Exist Psychiatry (Summer–Fall): 93–105, 1969
27. Theorell T, Lind E, Froberg J, Karlsson CG, Levi L: Longitudinal study of 21 subjects with coronary heart disease: life changes, catecholamine excretion and related biochemical reactions. Psychosom Med 34:505–516, 1972
28. Vaillant GE, Sobowale NC, McArthur C: Some psychological vulnerabilities of physicians. N Engl J Med 287:372–375, 1972

29. Wilson LM: Intensive care delirium: effect of outside deprivation in windowless unit. Arch Intern Med 130:225–226, 1972

30. Wittkower ED, Stauble W: Psychiatry and the role of the general practitioner. Psychiatry Med 3(4):287–301, 1972

31. Wittkower ED, White KL: Bedside manner. Br Med J 50:1432–1434, 1954

32. Zohman BL: Emotional factors in coronary disease. Geriatrics 28:110–119, 1973

33. Zola IK: Culture and symptoms: an analysis of patients presenting complaints. Am Sociol Rev 31:615–630, 1966

2

Crisis Intervention in Psychosomatic Medicine

GEORGE FISHMAN, THEODORE NADELSON

Many patients enter the psychiatrist's office or clinic with a definitive "emotional crisis" (2, 23). In every such instance, the patient has become unable to bear a variable admixture of anxiety and depression. In turn, these affects have been provoked in intolerable degree by a psychological issue, such as a loss or major life change. The patient may present with a bodily symptom but intuitively senses that the real province of his difficulty is his emotions.

When the nonpsychiatric physician is presented with a patient in a true "psychosomatic crisis," the underlying emotional ingredients are often the same as those encountered by the psychiatrist. What muddies the waters, however, is the fact that the patient complains mainly or exclusively of bodily symptoms. He sees his emotional distress as an accompaniment and not a cause of his sickness. The doctor's problem, as he usually presents it to himself, is to sort out the "real" from the "nonreal," the "objective" from the "subjective," the "organic" from the "functional." Often the physician has an impossible task in pursuing these diagnostic dichotomies.

To illustrate this further, let us consider the following:

Case 1. Mr. H., an obese, 39-year-old man, was well known by his internist. The doctor recognized that he was a nervous and dependent person who had never fully met his adult responsibilities. The patient characteristically blamed his difficulties on a vaguely defined state of ill health. He frequently absented himself from work or social obligations because of complaints of abdominal or chest pain, diarrhea, or joint stiffness. With each symptom, he called or visited his physician for empathy and reassurance. Within a short time, the doctor recognized that the patient was dependent on his attentions. His constant availability was demanded by the patient. When the doctor's time off or busy schedule blocked telephone access, the patient felt "very sick." A day prior to the doctor's summer vacation, the patient presented with crushing substernal chest pain, nausea, and sweating. An ECG demonstrated inverted T waves in the lateral precordial leads. The man was hospitalized. The ECG immediately reverted to normal, and enzymatic changes consistent with myocardial injury were not found.

In this case, there are factors consistent with psychiatric crisis. Mr. H. could not bear the anxiety attendant upon separation from strong and giving persons. The additional element, however, that makes this a *psychosomatic crisis* is the diffusion of the issues between the body and the mind into which the doctor is pulled (4). Despite his psychiatric common sense, any physician is at first compelled by his medical responsibility to attempt to reduce the confusion of such a situation by asking: "Is this sick man suffering a coronary?" When the results of the examination prove negative, the doctor then usually asks: "Is this sickness due to nerves?" Each form of the question is an attempt to understand the whole problem in terms of either its somatic or psychic aspects.

We would like to present an alternative focus for this very common dilemma. Our general approach is one that emphasizes the inseparability of mind and body. The doctor may ask himself, "To what extent and in what ways are the psychological factors manifested?" instead of asking, "Is this a psychosomatic disease?" (24). More specifically, the focus of this approach is on the varying degrees and kinds of emotional investment in one's body. In the example just presented, Mr. H. brings his symptoms to his doctor as a way of saying, "Do not leave me alone to face the world as an adult." He also invested the symptoms of "real" disease—his coronary insufficiency—with the same emotional message.

We suggest that the patient's distress and his communication of it merge to define a pattern or scheme that can be recognized whether or not one is certain "real" disease is present. Moreover, the physician's human response differs for each such pattern. In the case above, for example, the doctor is reflexively torn between a sense of responsibility and a feeling of being imposed upon. The patient's mode of complaint and the doctor's reactions are characteristic of the scheme that we call the "body as communicator of emotions." Several discrete schemes have been observed, and two others will be described in detail: the body as depot of the emotions and the body as separated from mind. It is our premise that most psychosomatic crises can be understood in terms of these three patterns. Each requires nothing more than the doctor's awareness of the patient, his investment in his "sickness," and the doctor's responses. Most importantly, each pattern suggests specific, practical operations to solve the crisis.

THE BODY AS DEPOT OF THE EMOTIONS

This crisis scheme is involved in all problematic instances when a patient dissociates his feelings from the significant persons and events in his life and displaces them into or onto his body.* It is most likely to impose itself when the doctor and patient are not well known to each other. Two major elements define this pattern. The patient persistently focuses all his attention on his body, and although the physician is perplexed by the symptoms and often zealous in the attempt to make a diagnosis, his findings never put his question at rest. He still remains somewhat doubtful about his understanding of the "sickness," and he may then feel challenged to renew his efforts. A psychosomatic crisis may ensue in his interaction with the patient, however, when he yields to his own annoyance with the state of affairs between them. At such a point, he may throw up his hands in exasperation and tell the patient, "There is nothing wrong," or, "I can do nothing more for you."

This pattern often arises when the physician accepts a patient with an acute disease, *e.g.,* trauma, heart attack, cancer, or infection. The onset of the illness may have occurred in the midst of stress (19), family crisis (13, 15), or despair (6, 21). Nevertheless, the physician may come to feel that the disease is invested, or has been reinvested, with energies derived from the ongoing emotional conflict.

Case 2. While trying to board a trolley, Ms. G., a 67-year-old woman, was trapped outside the door and dragged along the tracks. Amputation of her right leg and part of her left foot became necessary. She bore the initial shock, acute surgery,

---

*This has been termed the "mysterious leap from the mind to the body" (7).

and months of painful stump revision with appropriate grieving admixed with humor and spunk.

The moment her rehabilitation was begun, she underwent a marked shift in her attitude. She became very attentive to her limb pains and complained of unsteadiness and vertigo while using the parallel bars to walk. Repeated physical examinations were unremarkable. The surgical staff were puzzled and concerned by these symptoms, and a psychiatric consultation was requested. The consultant learned that the symptoms had their onset when the patient began to fear that she would fall and incur amputation of her left leg. Nightmares relating to this fear began to occur regularly. It was also learned that the patient lived with an older brother and sister throughout her life. It was seen that she had worked to mitigate and to deny the fact of her childlike entrenchment in the family home. She accomplished this in part by spending her evenings alone in her room with travel books. She frequently entertained fantasies of a ballet career stunted by circumstance. This continent of adventure that she defensively established in her mind relied heavily on the idea of mobility. In reality, she traveled only to work and back. Three months prior to admission, she was forced to retire. The day of the accident, she was en route to the airport with her sister who was going on an extended tour of Europe.

Thus, the nightmare and the symptoms could be understood as part of this patient's central life theme and emotional conflict: whether or not to give up the ability to stand on her own feet in order to be held more closely by family. Her problem with posttraumatic rehabilitation was then also caught up in the core conflict.

Another example of this concept is revealed in a commonplace dilemma seen by cardiologists: the patient's emotional overlay of concern about anginal attacks often retards his leaving the hospital. Here, lifelong conflicts concerned with the consequences of aggressivity and choice often are bound up with a real threat, *i.e.,* that a wrong choice can mean sudden death (11). Classic psychosomatic illness—such as peptic ulcer, ulcerative colitis, asthma, and so on (8, 17, 18)—as well as conversion, hypochondriasis, and factitious disease, very frequently result in a crisis formulated by this scheme (22).

Case 3. Ms. T., a 25-year-old woman, was admitted to the hospital with a recurrent bout of ulcerative proctitis. She experienced tenesmus that was severe enough to result in several episodes of soiling. She had noted a crescendo of tension tied to her job and relationship with her boyfriend just prior to the eruption of symptoms. Her work involved coordinating all aspects of construction projects for a group of hard-driving, often difficult, male bosses. Her boyfriend was employed by the same firm. She had been attracted to him when she noticed that he often seemed troubled and drank. She fantasized being able to help him. The relationship ended just before the relapse of symptoms, when she learned that he was a homosexual.

A medical regimen of rest, diet, and salicylazosulfapyridine (Azulfidine) was instituted. The patient left her job and apartment, returned to her parents' home, but experienced no relief from the tenesmus and soiling. It became clear that the symptoms had become locked in a new and tenacious psychological feedback system: going out of the home engendered fear that the symptom would occur. There was a consequent sense of panic followed by autonomic discharge and the onset of more symptoms. In summary, the initial symptom had become invested with all the elements of a typical phobia.

Depression may often be concealed in the body (16). This displacement of this particular affect must be distinguished for two reasons: first, depression can often be recognized by the patient and treated promptly and second, covert depression frequently governs covert suicidal intent.

Case 4. Ms. I, a 52-year-old married woman, developed severe anorexia shortly after the death of her niece from carcinoma of the stomach. The patient's symptoms were similar to those of her niece. Her depression was encapsulated in bodily symptoms that mimicked those of her lost relative and simultaneously kept at least a part of the dead person within her.

THERAPEUTIC INTERVENTIONS

The "mysterious leap" from the mind to body serves a function. Although maladaptive, it is the best that can be done for the psychic economy at the time (20, 26); the patient does not have the emotional means to do otherwise. The patient relegates the otherwise unbearable affects to his body and, in turn, gives his body to the physician for cure. In that sense, the doctor is asked to contain the problems within the body (20), and for most patients with this problem, it may be best to do just that.

Use of the Relationship

The physician may feel impelled to herd the trespassing issues back from the body to the mind. He gains his best chance of doing so *if he does not try*. Instead, he may direct his efforts toward understanding and validating the patient's view of the situation (1). For example, the doctor worked at understanding Ms. T.'s panic when she left the house (Case 3). His words conveyed nothing more than that he was empathetic. He would say, simply, "I can see how leaving the house must terrify you." At the same time, the doctor may scan what the patient brings into their discussion to try to find a possible access route to the core issue. For instance, Ms. G. usually confined the discussion to her fears of losing her other leg or her reading (Case 2). On one particular day, she scowled as her sister left the room. The doctor merely responded with "Difficult visit?" and the patient began to detail her lifelong difficulties in maintaining her mature sense of self in the midst of her family. The point here is that if the door readily opens, walk in; if it does not, do not force entry. Thus, confrontations, directives, or "deep interpretations" invariably fail to prod the issues out into the open; it is best to hold empathetically still.

Use of Regimen

Good psychosomatic treatment regards all aspects of medical process, diagnosis, and treatment as potentially creative vehicles for psychotherapy. For Ms. G. (Case 2), a series of exercises did more to rest her fears of further calamity than to strengthen her limbs. The strategy is to direct and mold all efforts toward *mitigating* the symptoms, regardless of their cause. The doctor caring for Ms. T. (Case 3) prescribed a meditation program to help her allay the panic.

Basic Corrective Maneuvers

Kellner (10) and Minuchin (15) as well as other contributors to this volume take up the use of psychotherapy for psychosomatic disorders. Psychiatric consultation is often advisable to help answer the question of the feasibility of therapy in helping to establish more adaptive ways of accommodating feelings.

THE BODY AS THE COMMUNICATOR OF THE EMOTIONS

Crisis within this scheme is defined by the particular action-directed mode that often arises between the doctor and patient once their relationship has become well-established. The physician first usually notices that he is going out of his way to respond to the patient's distress. He feels that he is urgently being called on to intervene actively, rather than merely to attend to a medical situation, but he is often unable to perceive the specific nature of the request. The patient's body becomes the medium for an elusive message. Awareness of this pattern usually develops slowly. The physician initially feels that the patient's behavior either is justified by the illness or reflects an insoluble emotional problem. He may try to muster maximum empathy, solicitation, and involvement in the hope that whatever the difficulty may be, good intentions will solve it.

The crisis point occurs when the physician despairs of either understanding or adequately answering the implicit request. It is then that he grasps the notion that he has been "manipulated" or "controlled" by the patient. Responsibility to the medical tasks at hand often clashes with antipathy to the patient's "monkey business," and this conflict sometimes produces in the doctor a varying sense of hopelessness and guilt. The patient is then often confronted with an ultimatum: either he yields in his behavior or else the doctor will give him up as a patient. The former action seldom brings about enduring success; the latter only insures that the same crisis will occur with another physician.

The major goal of this section is to present some definitions of "message" and "manipulation" so that more successful crisis interventions may be employed. We shall expand the discussion through consideration of two case examples.

Case 5. Mr. B., a 73-year-old man, was diagnosed as having chronic glomerulonephritis. He underwent bilateral nephrectomy at a university-based hospital and began hemodialysis in the same institution, three times a week. Initially he beguiled the nursing staff with stories from his early life. He had grown up in Asia Minor and maneuvered his way through World War I with cunning and strength. From an early time in his life, he complained of vague symptoms that could never be definitely traced to somatic causes. He praised manhood, authority, and the rearing of sons, and he demeaned women. He equated all that was feminine with passivity. This man's devastating illness was becoming invested with lifelong conflicts concerning his masculine self-esteem and with related, more contemporary ones concerning the worth of an old man. During the present hospitalization, a dilemma of the second pattern developed. Mr. B. began to complain of continual cough and to request that tissues be brought one at a time, even if a whole box was left at his bedside. He never obeyed his food and fluid restrictions, especially if these were imposed by women. He also employed many remedies borrowed from the folklore, and extensive dialysis was required to remove the excesses due to indiscretion. However, whenever he sensed the dialysis had considerably reduced his weight, he complained of agonizing leg cramps. He attributed this symptom to ineptitude on the part of his attending nurse and reported this typically feminine blunder to the head nurse or physician in charge. On several occasions, the staff overtly lied about the extent of the dialysis weight loss, and the cramps instantly disappeared.

At one point, a woman suffered a cardiac arrest and died in the unit. The staff was absorbed for hours by the resuscitation effort. The patient responded at first by apparent indifference. Then he chastised the staff for ignoring him during the arrest and for devoting so much effort to a mere woman. This became "the last straw"; the staff felt they had suffered enough of this increasing manipulation and confronted the patient. The objectionable behavior redoubled in intensity. The staff finally spoke about transferring the patient to a local dialysis unit.

The staff often experiences a vague sense of *manipulation* and *message* coming from patients with a chronic, life-threatening disease. A frequent explanation is that the stress of illness intensifies preexisting manipulative or incorrigible character traits. We suggest, rather, that the diathesis for this crisis is universally present in patients undergoing sustained medical care, and the crisis is explained by the inherently *transitional* nature of the helper-patient relationship.

The idea here is that the patient and the doctor share a common, real fabric of their relationship. In the above example, Mr. B. initially accepted a bare outline of facts, prescription, and limitation. This common fabric, however, becomes additionally imbued with a hierarchy of meanings rooted in emotional need. Such emotional needs are directed at reestablishing the elements of selfhood that the illness has destroyed. These needs are of three kinds (3): first, the chronically ill patient needs to recreate dignity and worthiness. To accomplish this, he must interpret the quality of specialness into his care. For example, he could perceive himself as having a special case of disease X, and especially liked by Dr. Y. Mr. B's arrogant reaction (Case 5) can be understood as an attempt to reclaim his worth from the degrading insult of death. Second, the chronically ill patient must reinstate the universal sense of timelessness that is annihilated by severe illness but without which there can be no sense of being alive (5, 12). In healthful existence, the constancy of daily inconstancy continually guards the sense of timelessness. In illness, other rhythmic, consistent processes are used instead; for example, test schedules, serial ECGs, weekly 5-fluorouracil (5-FU) injections, and, most importantly, the tempo of contacts with the helpers provide the illusion of timelessness. In the example above, Mr. B's demands for one Kleenex tissue at a time is a disguised request for a frequency of nursing visits that is adequate to "neutralize" the deadening experience of the dialysis treatment. Third, the patient must recreate his sense of potential action and consequence: the force of "being" instead of the sense of being forced. Mr. B's demeaning control of the women who attended him was an attempt to counter the emasculation consequent on age and illness.

Let us consider another factor operating within this particular mind-body pattern: that of the perceived omnipotence of the physician. The case of Mr. H. (Case 1) is illustrative of this point. He continued to deteriorate until his absenteeism from work was extremely frequent. He became paralyzed with the fear that sickness would strike him precisely when his physician was unavailable. He began to carry a walkie-talkie in his car in order to relay the merest nuance of symptoms to an amateur radio operator who in turn could seek out his doctor. He continually petitioned his physician for more frequent office visits.

The background of his decompensation became clear with time. His father had died in a motorcycle accident when he was seven. His mother died six years later of a misdiagnosed ruptured appendix. These losses permanently damaged his belief in the constancy of others. For this reason, he had difficulty in tolerating his own anger because it, too, threatened to destroy those people he needed. His family, well aware of his vulnerability to loss, was extremely protective. The psychosomatic crisis arose when the sons were preparing for college and his wife also began school to start a career she had long deferred. The patient resented the loosening of the protective family ties. His strongly repressed anger engendered anxiety, and symptoms he had always harbored were acutely exacerbated.

Into the fabric of the relationship between Mr. H. and his doctor, which was predicated on the patient's medical problems, was woven an important private message rooted in emotional need. The approximate translation into words was: "Be always accepting and able to bear and repair whatever I cannot." This is the feeling of the child that is expressed to an all-good, powerful parent at the beginning of the life cycle. At the end of a long growth process, the child can usually accept the image of himself and his parents as good or powerful "enough" (25). When the "all-powerful" parent is not given up, however, it is transferred on to other figures (doctors, for example) and becomes fixed as a psychosomatic dialog.

THERAPEUTIC INTERVENTIONS

The major step in responding in a covert psychosomatic dialog is the realization that the symptom may represent disease, but it also stands for an unmet emotional need. Since the symptom is a message, the removal of the symptom—even if possible—is not sufficient. In the long run, the patient's requirement includes a reading of the meaning of the message.

Use of the Relationship

The doctor must allow himself to be used *according* to the patient's needs, but he must also pay attention to his own human limitations. For all physicians, including psychiatrists, this is a most difficult skill to master. The doctor may accept the impossibility of ever totally satisfying the patient's needs, yet he does not give up in frustration. In the case of Mr. B. (Case 5), resentment of his demeaning attitude by the female staff decreased as understanding of his needs increased. As they were able to understand one or another aspect of his behavior—*e.g.*, his intense need for restituting self-esteem—they were able to allow themselves to be compliantly in charge, *e.g.*, they conformed to the patient's illusion of control, except where they realistically had to be in charge on medical grounds. Similarly, the physician who cared for Mr. H. (Case 1) was consistently available within a firmly limited frequency, *e.g.*, three telephone calls per week for not longer than five minutes.

Use of Regimen

The specific regimen is best geared to the implicit needs of the patient as perceived in the hidden bodily communication. Mr. H. was asked to keep a careful list of his vital signs, which provided him an extension of the physician's "omnipotent" presence. In another example, Mr. B.'s area of control—*e.g.*, his use of folk remedies—was a necessary allowance even if it required more dialysis. With Mr. H., the regular administration of small doses of minor analgesics and tranquilizers helped to extend his sense of the doctor's consistent presence, while making the patient comfortable (9).

Basic Corrective Maneuvers

In cases of chronic or life-threatening illness, the doctor-patient relationship is continually punctuated by the patient's explicit and implicit messages of crisis. These signals are always directed toward the primary physician, and it is his role to understand, respond, and accommodate to shifts in the patient's needs. This task cannot be delegated, because the physician usually has the heavily invested position of caretaker of the body.

A significant crisis mode may arise when the patient achieves a remission and wants the doctor to turn off excess supports. For example, an 80-year-old woman had diabetes and coronary vascular disease; she became blind secondary to retinopathy and adapted remarkably to her home life. Several years later, she required two below-knee amputations in close succession. The hospital course was complicated and stormy, but the entire staff responded with devotion and respect. As the last wounds began to heal, the staff decided to extend the hospitalization in order to make the best plans for discharge. The patient abruptly developed throat tightness and began to regurgitate all of her meals. A brief psychiatric interview revealed that she could no longer "swallow" the kindness of her medical hosts, because she feared becoming too attached to them. The message in her seeming anorexia was finally properly understood: the patient both desired and feared the physician's ministrations. She needed their care because she felt weak; she also felt that their attention was sapping her strength and reducing her "will." The staff's kindness was then similar to an addiction she wished to shake off in order to get back to her usual functioning at home.

Family interviews are almost always helpful. They often reveal confused or implicit communications as a style of interaction among the members, just as the body is used implicitly as a communicative mode (14). Furthermore, the intensity of the message to "do something different" that is addressed to the physician may be contributed by the family rather than arising solely from the patient.

Case 6. Mr. K., a 63-year-old man, immobilized himself in the hospital after he had suffered a myocardial infarction. The hospital staff was frustrated and confounded by his adamant refusal to participate in any activity. He ate little unless fed by his wife. His complaint was of bowel discomfort, diffuse aches, and fatigue. His physician enjoined and exhorted him to activity, as a way of relieving his symptoms, but he refused. In this he seemed supported by his wife, who encouraged his "lifelessness" by literally spoon-feeding him every meal. His physician turned some of his frustration on her, and at one point barred her presence in her husband's room. Psychiatric consultation was requested. The psychiatrist, after hearing about the case from the doctors and nurses, met with both the patient and his family and confirmed the extent of the devitalizing interaction between the wife and husband. In a separate meeting, the wife revealed to the consultant and her husband's intern that her mother had suddenly died in her home during a visit. We inferred that this catastrophic event had increased a tendency toward carefulness to one of excruciating, universal concern. This concern was particularly evident when her husband's sudden heart attack occurred; it revived all her guilt with regard to her own aggressiveness. She thus controlled all his movements and insisted that he not make any excess effort. She "successfully" conveyed her fears to him. Confirmation of the correctness of our guess occurred when the wife was given specific instructions. The physician insisted on defining the limits of the patient's activities. At the same time, the wife was kept nominally "in charge" (her usual position with her husband) by helping to carry out the doctor's orders. She aided her husband in walking and dressing, and she stopped feeding him. The doctor's stronger position also allowed her, we again assumed, not to feel totally responsible for her husband's life.

THE BODY AS SEPARATED FROM THE EMOTIONS

A formidable crisis often arises when a patient can no longer accept either his sickness or its attendant meaning. The body is more or less relinquished by the mind. A sense of urgency may be precipitated in the patient's physician by a parallel feeling that he must responsibly attend to that which the patient denies. The doctor may first increase his vigilance. The concerned doctor may variously encourage, exhort, or scare. He may be reluctant to proceed with more complex therapy, because that would require even more direct cooperation from the patient. Alternatively, he may feel pressed to do something that will take the responsibility for treatment completely out of the patient's hands. Several case examples are presented to illustrate the various shadings of this pattern.

Case 7. Mr. R., a 55-year-old man, was admitted to the medical intensive-care unit with an acute inferior myocardial infarction. He had previously cherished the heartiness and vitality with which he conducted his hectic life. He was the hard-working editor-in-chief of several technical journals, and his weekends were devoted to hunting, sailing, or similarly vigorous pursuits. From the moment of admission, he became a beguiling "nonpatient." His warmth and charm made it difficult for the staff to address him on his infractions of recuperative law: he stole smokes, bounced out of bed, and made calls to business associates. The staff's watchfulness and concern matched the intensity of his apparent calm. A psychiatric consultation was requested. The psychiatrist opened every potential avenue for discussion of the issue—heart attack—but the patient detoured the talks back to sailing and business.

Case 8. Ms. M., a 56-year-old woman who looked older than her age, lived alone in unfamiliar cities for the 15 years following the loss of her husband and children through divorce and custody proceedings. Her shame about the circumstances of these events led her to regard her solitude as a gratifying source of punishment. Her rapid aging was accompanied by an inner, increasing despondency. Nevertheless, she maintained an outward dignity and supported herself.

A few weeks prior to her hospital admission, she faced the loss of her living quarters from circumstances that, for the first time since the divorce, remained beyond her control. She abruptly suffered a severe myocardial infarction. Continuing cardiac decompensation neccessitated the use of aortic-balloon assistance. Throughout the prelude to this procedure, she remained conspicuously indifferent to what the staff saw as her tenuous physical status. She said she was confident that if left alone she would recover. At the time of the procedure, she became paranoid. She railed at the medical staff and accused them of capricious tortures. Attempts at explanation only increased her accusations. The procedure was stopped and the psychosis disappeared.

Case 9. Ms. P., a 20-year-old married woman, had spent two years in a dialysis program in preparation for a homograft kidney transplantation. As the time approached for surgery, the staff became wary of her extreme optimism. She expressed convictions that the procedure would bring an end to her disease. After the transplantation, she continued to act as though she had shed all her medical burdens. The staff remained concerned about whether or not she would maintain her steroid and immunotherapy after discharge. A psychiatric consultation was requested, and the patient spoke mainly of plans for decorating her apartment. In the middle of her description, she made a passing allusion to the fact that she had rented space in her grandmother's house and felt that was best in case she should have further troubles, such as graft rejection. After that reference, she quickly changed the subject.

All three examples reflect a human need to turn from a realization of catastrophic fact. These patients took emotional leave of their bodies. Such denial is often neccessary for maintaining psychological integrity in the face of massive stress. Temporary "disembodiment" allows the mind a respite from the preoccupation with disease, so that it may muster additional coping energy.

THERAPEUTIC INTERVENTIONS

The overall goal of good psychosomatic therapy in this sort of crisis is to support the patient's use of the defense of "disembodiment."

Use of the Relationship

The physician must attempt to engage the patient without insisting on "reality." (In Case 7, the doctor and Mr. R. confined much of their talks to sailing.)

Medical instructions may be given, but detailed explanations are rarely helpful for those patients who fall within this pattern. Confrontations about facing reality are not indicated. Paradoxically, the patient is more likely to make a compromise with grim necessity if he senses that his need to remove himself from the facts is respected.

Use of Regimen

Frequently, such patients ignore or reject the doctor's advice. The physician's task in such cases is to accept the idea that judgment cannot be forced onto the patient. For example, Mr. R. (Case 7) was duly cautioned about his activity. His persistence must be regarded *not* as a rejection or devaluation of the doctor's concerns, but rather as a yielding to higher priority, *i.e.*, the neccessity for preserving emotional balance. If the doctor can *allow* imperfect compliance in some less essential matters, he can often achieve complete compliance with that which is most important. When the aortic-balloon assist was stopped, for example, Ms. M. (Case 8) became more accepting of digitalis, diuretics, and central-venous-pressure monitoring.

Basic Corrective Maneuvers

When a crisis fails to resolve, psychiatric consultation is often helpful. The psychiatrist may be able to clarify the reasons why the patient is unable to face his sickness. In addition, the very process of consultation may mobilize the patient's attention to psychological issues.

REFERENCES

1. Balint M, Balint E: Psychotherapeutic Techniques in Medicine. London, Tavistock, 1961
2. Balint M, Ornstein PH, Balint E: Focal Psychotherapy. London, Tavistock, 1972
3. Bibring E: The mechanism of depression. In Greenacre P (ed): Affective Disorders. New York, International Universities Press, 1968
4. Crisp AH: Therapeutic aspects of the doctor–patient relationship. In Pierloot RA (ed): Recent Research In Psychosomatics. Basel, S Karger, 1970, pp 12–33
5. Eissler K: The Psychiatrist and the Dying Patient. New York, International Universities Press, 1955, pp 87–94
6. Engel GL, Schmale AH: Psychoanalytic theory of somatic disorder: conversion, specificity and the disease onset situation. J Am Psychoanal 15:344–365, 1967
7. Freud S: A General Introduction to Psychoanalysis. New York, Boni & Liveright, 1920
8. Freyberger H: The doctor/patient relationship in ulcerative colitis. In Pierloot RA (ed): Recent Research In Psychosomatics. Basel, S Karger, 1970, pp 80–89
9. Kahana RJ, Bibring GL: Personality types in medical management. In Zinberg NE (ed): Psychiatry and Medical Practice in a General Hospital. New York, International Universities Press, 1964, pp 108–123
10. Kellner R: Psychotherapy in psychosomatic disorders. Arch Gen Psychiatry 32: 1021–1028, 1975
11. Kits Van Heijningen H, Treurniet N: Psychodynamic factors in acute myocardial infarction. Int J Psychoanal 47: 370–374, 1966
12. Mann J: Time Limited Therapy. Cambridge, Harvard University Press, 1973
13. Meissner WW: Family process and psychosomatic disease. Int J Psych Med 5: 411–430, 1974
14. Minuchin S: Families and Family Therapy. Cambridge, Harvard University Press, 1974
15. Minuchin S et al.: A conceptual model of psychosomatic illness in children. Arch Gen Psychiatry 32: 1031–1038, 1975
16. Nadelson T: Engagement Before Alliance: Treatment Of Ego Depleted States.
17. Nemiah JC, Sifneos PE: Psychosomatic illness: a problem in communication. In Pierloot RA (ed): Recent Research in Psychosomatics. Basel, S Karger, 1970, pp 154–160
18. Nemiah JC, Sifneos PE: Affect and fantasy in patients with psychosomatic disorders. In Hillow (ed): Modern Trends in Psychosomatic Medicine. New York, Appleton–Century–Crofts, 1970, pp 1–25
19. Rahe RH: Subjects' recent life changes and their near-future illness susceptibility. In Lipowski ZJ (ed): Advances in Psychosomatic Medicine, Vol 8. Basel, S Karger, 1972, pp 2–19
20. Russell P: The Theory of the Crunch (unpublished manuscript)
21. Schmale AH: Giving up as a final common pathway to changes in health. In Lipowski ZJ (ed): Advances in Psychosomatic Medicine, Vol 8. Basel, S Karger, 1972, pp 20–40
22. Schmale AH, Meyerowitz S, Tinling DC: Current concepts of psychosomatic medicine. In Hill OW (ed): Modern Trends in Psychosomatic Medicine. New York, Appleton–Century–Crofts, 1970, pp 1–25
23. Sifneos PE: Short-Term Psychotherapy and Emotional Crisis. Cambridge, Harvard University Press, 1972
24. Weiss JH: The current state of the concept of a psychosomatic disorder. Int J Psych Med 5: 473–482, 1974
25. Winnicott DW: The Maturational Processes and the Facilitating Environment. New York, International Universities Press, 1965
26. Zetzel ER: The Capacity for Emotional Growth. New York, International Universities Press, 1970

3   The Process of Consultation

ADAM J. KRAKOWSKI

Consultation-liaison psychiatry constitutes the most essential service rendered by general hospital psychiatrists in the practical application of the tenets of psychosomatic medicine (39). Its growth followed other related developments: 1) the popularization of psychiatric units in general hospitals as a result of the departure from state-hospital to community psychiatry; 2) the introduction of modern psychopharmaceutical agents; and 3) biological research into the roots of mental illness. Bringing psychiatric treatment into the community created an increased awareness of somatic-psychic indivisibility and involved clinicians of various specialties in the care of mental patients (43, 44). These developments in turn produced a need for assisting nonpsychiatric physicians through consultation psychiatry.

Although technological advances have been unquestionably beneficial, the doctor's prestige and the truly humane doctor-patient relationship have, nonetheless, gradually eroded. Without a doubt, both will further decline, but consultation psychiatry may serve to counteract this dehumanization of medical practice.

The review that follows will be addressed to the present status of consultation-liaison work and will elucidate its practical aspects, its role, its functions, and its practice patterns.

THE SCOPE

Consultation psychiatry may be defined as the services rendered by psychiatrists outside of the psychiatric department of the general hospital 1) to assist the nonpsychiatric physician both in his diagnoses of patients on whose behalf psychiatric intervention is required and in rendering appropriate treatment to these patients; and 2) to provide appropriate training for such physicians. A separate though related activity consists in gathering data for research (55).

The diagnostic and therapeutic work aims at facilitating the care of those patients whose problems may be primarily psychiatric, although they may have been admitted to the hospital for somatic illness. In other instances, the psychiatric illness may stem from or complicate somatic illness, or psychosocial problems may interfere with the process of recovery.

The instructional task may be achieved through consultation or by more formal procedures (50). Its object is to train medical and nursing students in the comprehensive approach to patient care and to instruct residents, both in psychiatry and in other specialties, in the nuances of the psychosomatic approach and of consultation-liaison psychiatry.

The research, mostly clinical, that is performed by consultation psychiatrists, is in the field or psychosomatic medicine. Recently, a strong trend has emerged in the direction of physiological research and interdisciplinary collaboration (61).

26

Numerous publications have dealt with the conceptual aspects and methodology of consultation techniques as well as with the psychiatric precursors of illness and the psychopathology of organic illness. The current literature focuses on the behavioral characteristics and the management problems of patients treated in intensive care and coronary care units and of those who undergo hemodialysis, cardiac and vascular surgery, and organ transplantation. The "older" services—such as geriatrics and work with terminal patients and the dying—still remain topics of interest.

THE PSYCHOSOMATIC SIGNIFICANCE OF CONSULTATION PSYCHIATRY

The consultation psychiatrist performs bona fide psychosomatic work and should maintain the psychosomatic approach in relations with his medical or surgical counterparts. To achieve this, he must reorient the consultees from their purely medical model to the psychosomatic view that stresses the coexistence of the psychosocial phenomena of health and disease. Such reorientation may be difficult, especially for those physicians whose position is based on the long-standing tradition of the medical model of diagnosis-by-exclusion and on the use of an orthodox, dominant role in the doctor-patient relationship (6). It is not easy to renounce a disease-oriented approach and substitute a patient-oriented, comprehensive approach (7).

The importance of the close link between the psychosomatic approach and consultation psychiatry cannot be overemphasized. Without it, the usefulness of this service becomes doubtful (59). In some hospitals in various parts of the world, the absence of such a close link has rendered the consultation service inadequate and barely useful (51). A psychosomatic orientation requires the consultant to be well-versed in both the biological and the psychogenic components of pain and physical illness, in the effects of somatic illness on psychic disability, and in the possible psychosocial adjustment problems of the patient and his family. The consultant must also be expert in understanding the quality of patients' adaptation to illness and to the hospital environment with all its potential untoward effects, and he must know how to mitigate or ward off all negative influences arising from these sources.

The consultant must consider the influence of factors related to personality and their effect upon the progress and outcome of the illness, and, in this regard, he must pay particular attention to chronic and disabling illness (74). He must have a thorough knowledge of the psychodynamics of illness (86) as well as a clear understanding of the doctor-patient relationship, of its nuances, and of its changes following serious medical complications (80). He must also have an understanding of the effects of consultation upon the patient and of the inner workings of the consultation process in terms of the consultee-consultant relationship (48, 49).

Consultation psychiatry, like psychosomatic medicine, is not, of course, a specialty, yet those engaged in it either have been trained in more than one specialty, psychiatry being an essential one, or have undergone special training (59).

THE FUNCTION

The four functions of consultation psychiatry—diagnosis, therapies, instruction, and research—have already been listed. The organization and the size of the service are usually determined by the size of the institution served as well as by the size and degree of sophistication of its parent service, the psychiatric unit of the general hospital. In small hospitals the service may be run by a sole psychiatrist.

In the larger teaching institutions, the service may employ several senior members and an appropriate number of trainees including residents, and one or more psychologists, social workers, and specially trained nurses (14). On the whole the departments of consultation psychiatry are understaffed. The exact number of such departments is not known (51). In the United States, where they originated, they are still expanding (5). In some countries, *e.g.*, West Germany, psychosomatic medicine is found predominantly in the area of internal medicine, and in many others it is entirely in the domain of the internists. In the underdeveloped and Communist countries (40, 82) consultation services resemble our psychiatric emergency services. They are usually obtained by referral to mental hospitals or to outpatient departments, and follow-up treatment is rarely offered.

The usual structure of a well-organized service requires that the consultants serve as members of the appropriate departments and, in addition to their specialized work, participate in ward rounds and conferences. An active interest in the business of the specialty to which the consultant is assigned assures him of acceptance, although his assimilation into the therapeutic team may be only gradual (9) and may require patience, tact, availability, and understanding of the specific approaches, needs, wishes, biases, and even idiosyncrasies of other members of the professional team. His diagnostic and therapeutic work must also facilitate the consultee's work (39).

THE CLINICAL ASPECTS

Psychiatric consultation consists of aiding in the diagnosis and management of the referred cases in a way that does not interfere with the primary treatment of the patient. Three basic approaches are at the consultant's disposal. Probably the most useful of these is the *situation-oriented approach* (30), which aims at resolving the difficulty for the patient, his family, and the consultee, as well as those due to the total environment of the patient including the hospital. Necessity may dictate, however, the use of the *patient-oriented approach*, in which primary attention is focused on the need of the patient. This is the method closest to the medical model of therapy and has its usual shortcomings. The *consultee-oriented approach* aims at helping the consultee. This, under certain circumstances, may improve the doctor-patient relationship and simultaneously enhance the quality of care of the patient.

In choosing a method, an eclectic approach is demanded that is guided by the particular need of the patient and the overall situation (75).

THE TACTICS

The tactics of the consultant require some elaboration. Some authors advise the psychiatrist to avoid the use of the expertise of the medical specialty to which he happens to be attached (39); others, however, recommend that the consultant become an expert in both fields (22). Whichever position is taken, he must be flexible and tactful, and he must avoid professional one-sidedness, condescension, and the use of psychiatric jargon and excessive theorizing. In this sense the psychiatrist should not identify too strongly with the specialist whom he intends to help, nor should he expect the consultee to identify with the role of the psychiatrist (48). Otherwise, resistance to or rejection of the consultant and the service will be created.

The diagnostic part of the consultation consists of several phases: the consultation request, a review of the patient's history and of the care already rendered, the examination proper, and the report (56).

Whether the request is made in writing or verbally, it should be carefully evaluated because it contains clues regarding the patient and the doctors and nurses caring for him. The approach to referral usually seems to reflect the consultee's feelings regarding his own usefulness to the patient as well as his attitude toward mental illness in general and toward psychiatry and psychiatrists in particular, with all its hidden meanings that may indicate a pattern of resistance. Furthermore, the consultant must be sure that the patient and his family have been properly informed of and prepared for the consultation.

Various conditions motivate physicians to seek psychiatric consultation, since each doctor shows a different sensitivity to his patients' problems. Some are alarmed by what is—or what they consider to be—abnormal behavior of the patient; others are interested in the confirmation of their diagnostic impression. Still others are motivated by a need for assistance in management, in the control of disrupting behavior, in amelioration of a strained doctor-patient relationship, in hastening a delayed convalescence, in treating untoward drug reactions, in preparation for surgery, or in the care of the dying. A suspicion of suicidal behavior and the threat of suicide are perhaps the most frequent causes of emergency consultation.

A well-scrutinized request may necessitate a shift in emphasis from the apparent problem to the real disturbance. In preparing for the examination of the patient, one must review his record, procure information from another hospital if necessary, and possibly interview the family. Such a process may, however, have to be postponed beyond the first contact with the patient in cases of urgency (67).

The consultation proper, *i.e.,* the examination of the patient, is performed on the ward under conditions of satisfactory privacy. Its first task is to make at least an approximate diagnosis to determine the presence or absence of a psychosis, especially delirium. In cases involving organic illness, the psychiatrist *must not aim at determining whether the disease is organic or not,* but rather at discerning the influences of both intrinsic and extrinsic psychopathological factors. Similarly, when pain is involved in the patient's complaint, he must endeavor to detect the coexistence of depression, schizophrenia, hypochondriasis, hysteria, "compensation neurosis," or malingering. Except for the last, the above-mentioned diagnostic impressions do not negate the coexistence of organic illness.

The search for diagnosis must involve the survey of the patient's personality and his ability to adapt to illness, his assets and liabilities as a member of his family, and his position with regard to his work situation and all its stresses (24). Personality evaluation may have to be postponed if urgency is indicated, in which case the interview must be directed toward the specific problem responsible for the consultation (72). The preliminary report must be promptly rendered.

Additional factors linked with the patient's personality include those related to his educational and cultural level (73), his past medical history in terms of its psychological experience (8), and his acceptance of his role as a patient (62). The quality of his interpersonal relationships—including the doctor-patient relationship and the socioeconomic problems involved in his temporary or permanent invalidism and the anticipated loss of earning capacity—are not any less important.

The psychological adaptation is intimately interrelated with the organ affected: disfiguring injuries or diseases affecting the eyes or genitals create more severe untoward effects than do those involving other organs (86). Physical illness creates or increases self-centeredness and heightens the demand for gratification of dependency needs; it also lowers self-esteem, since the state of illness is not equal in value to the state of health. The sense of burden, which may result in depression, may also be caused by guilt when the illness possesses an aggressive meaning or when rejection (real or imagined) increases the feeling of uselessness. What needs to be emphasized is the fact that illness with all its stresses usually exacerbates the so-called ordinary, premorbid traits

(37). Such considerations are useful, since even abnormal adaptation to illness, such as denial, if well recognized, may be of value (12, 22, 31). The mechanism of denial, however, may have a negative effect if it is improperly handled or allowed to lead to reckless behavior.

The whole phenomenon of denial is so important to the consultation psychiatrist that it should be seriously considered; information on it abounds (25, 28, 83, 84). Because it is not a permanent defense, appropriate psychiatric treatment is imperative to help the patient accept the "sick role" through such mechanisms as desensitization, rationalization, and dependence on the environment and the supernatural. In all these changes, reassurances from the physician play an important role.

Denial on the part of the physicians and nurses must be recognized (4), since it not only leads to resistance against psychiatric consultations, but it may also result in instances of suicidal depression among the patients (2).

Denial may be linked with alexithymia, a phenomenon which appears in patients with psychosomatic disorders and which is said to be manifested by a difficulty in describing one's feelings (68, 78).

DOCTOR-PATIENT RELATIONSHIP

The doctor-patient relationship has a profound influence upon the reaction of the patient to illness. This relationship may be viewed in terms of the following three operational models (80). In the *activity-passivity model,* the physician performs for or on the patient, who remains inactive, as in anesthesia. Dynamically, this represents the parent-infant relationship, though the doctor acts with necessary "scientific detachment." Empathy is of no particular importance, but the doctor's skill and fame are invaluable. In the *guidance-cooperation model,* the doctor directs and performs a dominant role while the patient obeys, as in the treatment of an acute infection. Such treatment represents a dynamic model of parent-child relationship. In addition to competence and skill, the doctor offers sympathetic advice and assistance, while the patient responds with gratitude. In the *model of mutual-participation,* an alliance exists between the empathetic doctor and the patient, who is helped to help himself. This situation is present in psychotherapy, where the dynamic meaning is the adult-adult relationship.

Physical illness creates in the patient some regression and dependence, which may become excessive and even crippling unless there is a satisfactory doctor-patient relationship. Failure to produce a prompt cure may jeopardize it and may have untoward effects upon both the patient and the doctor. The consultant must readily perceive such disturbances, since he is in a position to restore the satisfactory balance.

Physical illness is at times manifested by psychological symptoms, especially anxiety and depression, during its early prodromal phases (6). Denial is utilized at this stage, but when it ceases, illness is accepted. If denial ceases too abruptly, however, the anxiety may become severe and lead to a projection mechanism against the physician. The doctor must endeavor to restore the positive nature of the doctor-patient relationship in such cases by encouraging overdependence upon himself, the nursing personnel, and the family.

PSYCHOLOGICAL ADAPTATION IN ILLNESS

Psychological symptoms accompanying physical illness represent an exaggeration of the usual personality adaptations. These and other symptoms may be present as a result of organic involvement of the central nervous system, such as an intracranial lesion (13), or may be secondary to an organic disease process located remotely from the central nervous system.

Of special importance are those depressions in the aged which, because they are often accompanied by confusional states, imitate the clinical picture of senile dementia (53). The nonorganic causality of the latter condition emphasizes that senile individuals should not be hospitalized unless absolutely necessary, because they may become depressed and exacerbate a mild chronic brain syndrome that heretofore had not interfered with an independent or semidependent existence.

The truly organic brain syndromes are usually of multiple causes; the organic condition, the psychogenic influences, and the basic personality makeup are equally contributory (18, 20). The incidence of such syndromes is sufficiently high to warrant the watchfulness of the consultant, particularly because the milder forms or those in the initial stages are rarely diagnosed early by the primary physician. Furthermore, their incidence is rising (1, 3, 10, 17, 27, 32, 42, 55).

PSYCHOLOGICAL SYNDROMES MANIFESTED BY SOMATIC SYMPTOMS

On the opposite end of the spectrum are those psychological syndromes that are manifested by somatic symptoms. Hysteria is frequently seen in medical-surgical wards, though conversion symptoms are not always present (29). Many chronic hysterics manifest a superimposed depression and "psychogenic regional pain" (20, 64, 81). The diagnosis is not always simple, and it may require involved workup, including psychological testing.

The consultation psychiatrist should be well versed in the problems of pain, since he is often consulted regarding patients with chronic pain, especially when medical and surgical methods have failed for them. Besides psychogenic regional pain, other forms may be present: 1) psychogenic manifestations of physical pain, 2) psychogenic muscular pain (tension), 3) vascular pain, 4) miscellaneous conditions (low back pain, cranial neuralgias, causalgias, or phantom limb pain), and 5) hypochondriacal and delusional pain (81). It should be noted that the *pain threshold* as a biological factor cannot be readily altered, but *pain tolerance* may be influenced from without (65). For a detailed discussion of the psychosomatic aspect of pain the reader is referred to Chapters 5 and 6.

DEPRESSION

Depression has been called the greatest imitator of organic illness, and its vegetative symptoms are mostly responsible for it (19, 36). Denial in psychotically depressed patients is particularly strong if there is some concurrent physical illness. When the symptoms become exacerbated, psychiatric consultation is finally sought for the chronically depressed patient, who may have been unsuccessfully treated for a perennial "run down" condition and subjected to all sorts of laboratory tests.

Depressed patients are frequently referred to the psychiatrist because of coexistent frigidity or impotence, especially after unsuccessful hormone therapy. In other instances, referral follows the family's alarm over the patient's excessive alcohol intake, especially if he is a middle-aged "social" drinker.

NEUROTIC ILLNESS

Cases of anxiety neurosis and hypochondriacal neurosis are frequently referred for psychiatric consultation. In the former, pain, tension, and hyperventilation with its numerous sequelae frequently lead to an erroneous somatic diagnosis, such as organic heart disease, convulsive disorder, cerebrovascular insufficiency, and the like, all of which are physical symptoms related to the autonomic nervous system (59). Hypochondriacal neurotics are chronic complainers who lack the blissful indifference of hysterics (20).

PSYCHOPHYSIOLOGICAL ILLNESS

The *Diagnostic and Statistical Manual of Mental Disorders* (16) offers a very vague definition of this category.

In my experience, physicians of all specialties claim that these disorders belong to their own respective domains. The psychiatric consultant, however, is called in and is given some role in their management, though he is rarely considered the primary physician in these cases. Ironically enough, the exception sometimes occurs in cases of gross severity when the medical-surgical approach has failed (44, 49).

SCHIZOPHRENIA

Until a schizophrenic patient displays a blatant form of behavior, his illness may go unrecognized and be treated by nonpsychiatric physicians, since among these patients, somatic symptoms are frequent and often misdiagnosed (69). Such patients resist being referred for psychiatric examination (35), but their cases may be identified earlier if they can be induced to elaborate on their interpretation of pain and other symptoms (20).

On the other hand, the patient with a known psychiatric illness may arouse prejudicial feelings in the hospital personnel, and many of his symptoms may be ascribed to mental illness, even to the point where the physical illness is overlooked.

REPORTING THE CONSULTATION FINDINGS

The customary written report, supplemented by a conference with the consultee, should be promptly rendered, especially in cases of emergency. It should be concise, and easily understood (15), and should contain relevant, practical recommendations for immediate or long-term management of the patient. A patient's request for further psychiatric care should be considered, even though the consultee may have reservations regarding such care.

The conference that follows may serve several purposes: 1) to explain why the patient may need immediate psychiatric care or why such care should be postponed, 2) to make clear that the interview with the patient's family was undertaken solely for prediagnostic purposes, 3) to correct diplomatically any erroneous diagnosis made by the consultee, and 4) to perform the didactic role for which the consultation conference is so well suited (50).

THE THERAPEUTIC SERVICE

Therapeutic activities, which are usually adapted to a relatively short hospitalization, must include psychotherapy, and this may be combined with chemotherapy. Crisis intervention therapy (32, 34, 84) includes the psychodynamic formulation of the conflict that is caused or complicated by the illness and hospitalization, as well as establishing the plan for therapeutic action correlated with the conflict. The therapist, who is an active participant in the treatment process, serves as a source of identification for the patient. The therapy aims at strengthening the patient's existing defenses primarily to overcome the current difficulties.

Moreover, the therapist may have to carry out counseling regarding sick leaves, employment in general, vocational rehabilitation, and retirement. Knowledge of the appropriate state laws and of local resources, as well as conferences with the proper personnel, may be extremely valuable.

SPECIAL ASPECTS OF MANAGEMENT AND LIAISON WORK

Special aspects of management include selection of patients for elective surgery or hemodialysis; assistance with patients who disrupt the primary therapeutic management, whose convalescence is unusually prolonged, or who threaten or attempt suicide; and assistance with terminal and dying patients.

In connection with most of these situations, we should mention the phase of consultation work referred to as *liaison*. Although the terms "consultation" and "liaison" are often used interchangeably, liaison is a somewhat different aspect of the consultant's work. It involves the interpretation of the psychosocial aspects of illness and their correlation with the biological aspects. Liaison mediates between the patient and his physician and the entire medical team, and it interprets the meaning of the team's work to the patient or the meaning of the patient's illness and behavior to the team.

DISRUPTIVE BEHAVIOR

Disruptive behavior may be due to an initial attack of mental illness that occurs only after admission, to panic states created by diagnostic procedures or the physicians' stressful statements, or to a failure to understand that some personalities are prone to anxiety unless given reassurance and satisfactory explanations. The patient may react by refusing completely to cooperate with diagnostic and therapeutic procedures, including surgery, or he may sign out against medical advice. Although the latter occurs more often among patients with personality disorders, the former often represents situations in which adequate explanations are found wanting. The antagonistic behavior of the patient toward the nonmedical members of the staff may represent a conflict with the doctor, or the patient's initial denial of his illness.

THE SUICIDAL PATIENT

The suicidal patient is the subject of consultation when a history of suicide attempts is discovered or when the patient threatens or attempts suicide while in the hospital. The rate of suicide attempts given in one study is 1.55 per 10,000 admissions (26), the attempts being made mostly by jumping from windows. Suicide-prone patients are usually those who are severely ill and who have a great deal of pain and dyspnea (11); especially suicide-prone are older males suffering from severe physical illness who have few relatives (79).

UNTOWARD EFFECTS OF DRUGS

Such effects occur quite frequently and may be caused by a host of new agents, either because of direct toxic effects or because of drug interactions. The list of such drugs is extensive, and space limitations prevent a detailed elaboration here (42).

THE DELAYED CONVALESCENCE

In my experience, patients showing late convalescence have passive-dependent personalities with hypochondriacal characteristics. Their voluminous hospital records usually show longer than average hospital stays and frequent changes from one doctor to another, usually in the direction of the physicians who have newly settled in the community. For these patients, the hospital appears to be a safe place, and mention of discharge may create separation anxiety (58) and newly developed symptoms.

SELECTION OF PATIENTS FOR SURGICAL PROCEDURES

The factors that may lead to psychiatric complications among surgical patients include a previous history of psychiatric illness, old age, the coexistence of chronic pulmonary and cardiac disease, and alcoholism (42). In patients admitted for cardiac or cataract surgery, sensory deprivation may be responsible for delirium (66); its cause is probably both psychological and organic in nature.

THE DYING PATIENT

An important contribution made by the psychiatrist is the consultation and liaison work with terminal patients and the dying. Such situations always call for therapy, and the liaison work involves the patient's family and sometimes the clergy and others. The fear of death and dying is as severe in the minds of lay people (54, 83) as it is among physicians. The reasons given for this fear have been elaborated in detail in a hypothesis offered as an explanation of the motivation for the choice of medicine as a vocation (39). This became the subject of further theoretical elaborations and of a study that will subsequently be described (45–49).

The assistance given by the consulting psychiatrist in caring for terminal patients may also have to become a consultee-oriented task, since the death of a patient creates a strain on the doctor's self-esteem, regardless of the degree of "scientific detachment" he employs in resolving his own fear of death (49).

TEACHING AND TRAINING

In larger hospitals, notably in those with psychiatric departments of medical schools, the departments of psychosomatic medicine and the divisions of consultation psychiatry perform teaching and training activities. The nature of these activities varies from school to school (7, 21, 50, 60, 62, 70, 85), and it may also involve the training of undergraduate medical students in the various aspects of the comprehensive interview and the comprehensive approach to patients. The interview techniques may be so construed as to lead to a holistic approach, a comprehensive diagnosis, a humanistic tendency, and the lessening of orthodox one-sidedness (71).

The consultation itself may be utilized as a tool for the continuing education of physicians. The well-constructed written report can become the basis of a conference with the consultee. In my experience, this procedure seems superior to formal, didactic techniques, since it takes place at the request of the consultee and therefore diminishes the usual "student-teacher" type of resistance. Moreover, the written report is usually accessible, and it utilizes the actual patient material supplied by the consultee. It is, therefore, dictated by the patient's realistic needs (50).

RESISTANCE TO REFERRAL

Although the exact psychiatric morbidity in the nonpsychiatric departments of general hospitals is not known, the consensus is that the actual need for psychiatric consultation greatly exceeds the rate of referral (57). Analysis of the causes of this situation awaits a more thorough investigation. Meanwhile, it seems unlikely that the under utilization of psychiatric resources is due solely to the resistance of the patient causing the doctor to fear that the referral might drastically change the doctor-patient relationship (74); but such fear undoubtedly does exist (49).

A worldwide survey of consultation psychiatry showed that among our nonpsychiatric colleagues, the acceptance of psychiatry and psychiatrists is generally unsatisfactory, though our image is improving (51). Generally, such acceptance seems to be hampered by misconceptions regarding mental illness, its supposed incurability, and its stigma. Even when psychiatric intervention is requested, the consultee often expects an instant resolution of all difficulties and a precise recommendation for management. Such an attitude usually indicates the consultee's resistance to consultation.

Resistance may arise in a patient who is opposed to consultation because of his denial of illness, his fear of the stigma of mental illness and psychiatry, and a general ignorance of what psychiatry is all about. Moreover, the patient may be insufficiently prepared for the consultation.

When it comes to the resistance shown by physicians, the problem may be complicated by more intricate factors. In approaching this problem, I have postulated theoretically in another work (45) that the whole process of consultation —including the triadic relationship between the consultee, the consultant, and the patient—is but a part of the doctor's practice of medicine, which in turn stems from his motivations for choosing medicine as his vocation. There is little doubt that the entire triad—two doctors and one patient—is dominated by transference-countertransference phenomena that influence the consultation above and beyond the usual elements of medical practice.

In studying this triadic relationship, I conjectured that therapeutic success or failure affects the physician's self-esteem in a positive or a negative way. The lowering of self-esteem that occurs when the patient does not improve or when he shows complications causes the physician to feel professionally threatened by his inability to intervene satisfactorily. His self-esteem is then further endangered by the necessity to seek help. At this point, the doctor's self-esteem may be at a dangerously low level, and the request for consultation may be perceived as a defeat.

The consultant's attitude toward the consultee may be very helpful if it is ego-supporting; it may, however, become ego-deflating, if not truly traumatic, when the consultant is unaware of the consultee's idiosyncrasies and the state of his current lowered self-esteem. Inappropriate handling of the consultation may, for these reasons, cause further self-devaluation.

These theoretical assumptions were tested systematically and confirmed in an attitudinal research study among 50 physicians practicing in four rural general hospitals (46–48). The attitudes of nonpsychiatric physicians toward medical or surgical consultations were grossly influenced by a strong concern, and in some instances, an apprehension, lest consultants accuse them of inadequate patient management. They also feared a negative influence upon the previously satisfactory relationship with the patient and his family. Psychiatric consultation, however, did not create such apprehension, but the surveyed physicians expressed fears regarding their own ability to care for psychiatric patients, because of their claimed lack of experience. There was also strong sympathy felt toward psychiatric patients which was magnified by an exaggerated, and often hopeless, prognostic attitude about such patients. Here, too, a very direct relationship was observed: those who considered themselves more "scientific" in the performance of their specialty were more resistant than those who felt that medicine is only partially a science.

Specific resistances to psychiatric consultations must be caused, however, by other factors, since they have not diminished even in the light of the increased role played by the primary physicians in community psychiatry. These factors may be due to a yet unsatisfactory level of training or to the personality of some doctors being not well suited for such a specific role. In connection with the specifics of resistance, the purely personal problems must be considered (54). The doctor's feelings regarding his own usefulness to the patient are important. We all realize that the confrontation with the patient may awaken in the physician his own fear of illness; the confrontation with psychiatric patients probably causes similar feelings, except that mental illness is feared more severely.

The same causes must be responsible for the psychiatrists' own unpopularity among nonpsychiatric physicians, which is magnified perhaps by their own isolation from other specialties and the condescending, patronizing attitude shown by some of them who may feel that they do have the answers to all questions.

The consultation psychiatrist must strive to improve his relationship with other professionals. To achieve this, his own prescription should be: respond promptly to a consultation request, prepare reports in understandable language, and give recommendations that are practical and readily achieved. His follow-up assistance must be offered, but so construed that the consultee will not perceive it as an attempt at a total takeover of the patient (76).

CONCLUSION

The great proliferation of scientific knowledge in the past fifty years has brought in its wake the subtle evil of fragmentation within specialized fields. As a result, the medical approach to the patient and his illness has been more mechanistic than psychosomatic. Hence, the medical or surgical specialist may minimize the psychosocial factors of health and illness or ignore them completely in the management of the patient. If the quality of medical practice is to keep pace with the quality of medical knowledge, however, a total approach to diagnosis and management must be made. The consultation psychiatrist is in a unique position to assist the primary physician in the psychosomatic approach to health and illness. Above all, however, he must strive to make the consultee aware that the soma and the psyche are indivisible and that a prerequisite of any positive treatment is a holistic approach.

REFERENCES

1. Abram HS: Adaptation to open heart surgery: a psychiatric study of response to the threat of death. Am J Psychiatry 122:659, 1965

2. Abram HS: Suicidal behavior in chronic dialysis patients. Am J Psychiatry 127:1199, 1971

3. Abram HS: The psychiatrist, the treatment of chronic renal failure and the prolongation of life. Am J Psychiatry 128:1534, 1972

4. Abram HS: Frontiers in psychiatry: a challenge in psychosomatic medicine. Psychosomatics 14:131, 1973

5. American Hospital Association: Personal communication, 1974

6. Balint M: The Doctor, His Patient and the Illness. London, Pitman, 1964

7. Balint M, Ball DH, Hale ML: Training medical students in patient centered medicine. Compr Psychiatry 10:249, 1969

8. Bard M, Dyk KB: Psychodynamic significance of beliefs regarding the cause of serious illness. Psychoanal Rev 43:146, 1956

9. Beigler JS, Robbins FP, Lane EW, Miller AA, Samuelson C: Report on liaison psychiatry at Michael Reese Hospital 1950–1958. Arch Neurol Psychiatry 81:733, 1959

10. Blachly PH, Star A: Postcardiotomy delirium. Am J Psychiatry 121:371, 1964

11. Brown W, Pisetsky JE: Suicidal behavior in a general hospital. Am J Med 29:307, 1960

12. Cassem MH, Hackett TP: Psychiatric consultation in a coronary care unit. Am Int Med 75:9, 1971

13. Chapman LF, Wolff HC: Disease of the neopallium. Med Clin North Am 42:677, 1958

14. Cleghorn JM: Organization of psychosocial care in a teaching hospital. Psychother Psychosom 23:55, 1974

15. Dean E: Writing psychiatric reports. Am J Psychiatry 119:759, 1963

16. Diagnostic and Statistical Manual of Mental Disorders, 2nd ed. Washington DC, American Psychiatry Association, 1968

17. Dlin BA, Stern A, Poliakoff SJ: Survivors of cardiac arrest. Psychosomatics 15:61, 1974

18. Doran JC, Spaulding WB: The Organic Psychoses. Toronto, University Press, 1958

19. Dorfman W: The recognition and management of masked depression. In de la Fuente R, Weisman MU (eds): Int Congr Series No. 274. Amsterdam, Excerpta Medica Foundation, 1973

20. Engel GL: "Psychogenic" pain and the pain prone patient. Am J Med 26:899, 1959

21. Engel GL: Medical education and the psychosomatic approach. A report of Rochester experience 1944–1966. J Psychosom Res 2:27, 1967

22. Engel GL, Green WL Jr, Reichsman F, Schmale A, Ashenburg N: A graduate and undergraduate teaching program on the psychological aspects of medicine. J Med Educ 32:859, 1957

23. Engel GL, Romano J: Delirium, a syndrome of cerebral insufficiency. J Chronic Dis 9:260, 1959

24. Faucet RL: Psychiatric interview as a tool of medical diagnosis. JAMA 12:537, 1956

25. Fenichel O: The Psychoanalytic Theory of Neurosis. New York, WW Norton, 1945

26. Fleminger JJ, Mallett BL: Psychiatric referrals from medical and surgical wards. J Med Sci 108:182, 1962

27. Fox HM, Rizzo ND, Gifford S: Psychological observations of patients undergoing mitral surgery. Psychosom Med 16:186, 1954

28. Freud A: The Ego and the Mechanisms of Defense. London, Hogarth Press, 1948

29. Gatfield PD, Guze SB: Prognosis and differential diagnosis of conversion reaction. Dis Nerv Syst 23:623, 1962

30. Greenberg IM: Approaches to psychiatric consultation in a research hospital setting. Arch Gen Psychiatry 3:691, 1960

31. Hackett TP, Cassem NH: Psychological reactions to life threatened-illness-acute myocardial infarction. In Abram HS (ed): Psychological Aspect of Strain. Springfield Ill, CC Thomas, 1970

32. Hackett TP, Cassem NH, Wishnie HA: The coronary–care unit, an appraisal of its psychological hazards. N Engl J Med 279:1365, 1968

33. Hackett TP, Weisman AD: Psychiatric management of operative syndromes. I. The therapeutic consultation and the effect of noninterpretive intervention. Psychosom Med 22:267, 1960

34. Hackett TP, Weisman AD: Psychiatric management of operative syndromes. II. Psychodynamic factors in formulation and management. Psychosom Med 22:356, 1960

35. Hollender M: Ambulatory schizophrenia. J Chronic Dis 9:249, 1959

36. Jones D, Hall SB: Significance of somatic complaints in the patients suffering from psychotic depression. Acta Psychother (Basel) 11:193, 1963

37. Kahana RJ, Bibring GL: Personality types in the medical management. In Zinberg EN (ed.): Psychiatry and Medical Practice in a General Hospital. New York, International Universities Press, 1964

38. Kasper AM: The doctor and death. In Feifel H (ed): The Meaning of Death. New York, McGraw–Hill, 1959

39. Kaufman RM: The role of the psychiatrist in a general hospital. Psychiatr Q 27:367, 1953

40. Kiev A (ed): Psychiatry in the Communist World. New York, Science House, 1968

41. Kleghorn JM: Organization of psychosocial care in a teaching hospital. Psychother Psychosom 23:55, 1974

42. Krakowski AJ: Common acute psychiatric complications in medical and surgical patients in the general hospital. Med Times 78:180, 1969

43. Krakowski AJ: The role of medicine in community psychiatry. Psychosomatics 11:13, 1970

44. Krakowski AJ: Psychosomatic or comprehensive? The role of the physician in the total management of the patient. Psychosomatics 11:587, 1970

45. Krakowski AJ: Doctor–doctor relationship. I. Psychosomatics 12:11, 1971

46. Krakowski AJ: Doctor–doctor relationship. II. Conscious factors influencing the consultation process. Psychosomatics 13:158, 1972

47. Krakowski AJ: Doctor–doctor relationship. III. A study of feelings influencing vocation and its tasks. Psychosomatics 14:156, 1973

48. Krakowski AJ: The practical implications of psychosomatic principles in patient management. In de la Fuente R, Weisman MN (eds): Int Congr Series No. 274. Amsterdam, Excerpta Medica Foundation, 1973

49. Krakowski AJ: Liaison psychiatry: factors influencing the consultation process. Psychiatry Med 4:439, 1973

50. Krakowski AJ: Role of consultation psychiatry in teaching psychopharmacology in the general hospital. NY State J Med 73:1987, 1973

51. Krakowski AJ: Consultation psychiatry, present global status—a survey. Psychother Psychosom 23:78, 1974

52. Krakowski AJ: Psychiatric consultation in the general hospital. Exploration of resistances. Dis Nerv Syst 36:242, 1975

53. Krakowski AJ, Langlais LM: Acute psychiatric emergencies in a geriatric hospital. Psychosomatics 15:72, 1974

54. Kubler–Ross E: On Death and Dying. Riverside, MacMillan, 1970

55. Lenzner A: Psychiatry in the coronary care unit. Psychosomatics 14:70, 1974

56. Lipowski ZJ: Review of consultation psychiatry and psychosomatic medicine. I. General principles. Psychosom Med 29:153, 1967

57. Lipowski ZJ: Review of consultation psychiatry and psychosomatic medicine. II. Clinical aspects. Psychosom Med 29:201, 1967

58. Lipowski ZJ: Review of consultation psychiatry and psychosomatic medicine. III. Theoretical issues. Psychosom Med 30:395, 1968

59. Lipowski ZJ: Consultation psychiatry in the general hospital. Compr Psychiatry 12:461, 1971

60. Lipowski ZJ: Psychiatric liaison with neurology and neurosurgery. Am J Psychiatry 129:21, 1972

61. Lipowski ZJ: Consultation liaison psychiatry: an overview. Am J Psychiatry 131:623, 1974

62. McKegney JP: Consultation liaison teaching of psychosomatic medicine. Opportunities and obstacles. J Nerv Ment Dis 154:198, 1972

63. Mechanic D: The concept of illness behavior. J Chronic Dis 15:189, 1962

64. Merskey H: The characteristics of persistent pain in psychological illness. J Psychosom Res 9:291, 1965

65. Merskey H, Spear FG: Pain: Psychological and Psychiatric Aspects. London, Bailliere, Tindall, Cassell, 1967

66. Meyer BS, Blacher RS, Brown P: A clinical study of psychiatric and psychological aspects of mitral surgery. Psychosom Med 23:194, 1961

67. Meyer E, Mendelson M: The psychiatric consultations with patients on medical and surgical wards: patterns and processes. Psychiatry 24:197, 1961

68. Nemiah JC: Denial revisited, reflections on psychosomatic theory. Presented at the 10th European Conference on Psychosomatic Research, Edinburgh, Scotland, 1974

69. Offenkrantz W: Multiple complaints as a precursor of schizophrenia. Am J Psychiatry 119:258, 1962

70. Pierce CM: Psychiatric teaching in a general hospital. Compr Psychiatry 9:258, 1968

71. Reichsman F: The role of psychosomatic medicine in medical education. The current state and future trends of psychosomatic medicine. Hanover, 1972

72. Reush J: Psychiatric Care. Psychiatry Simplified for Therapeutic Action. New York, Grune & Stratton, 1964

73. Saunders L: Cultural Differences and Medical Care. New York, Russell Sage Foundation, 1954

74. Schwab JJ: Medical patient's reactions to referring physicians after psychiatric consultation. JAMA 195:1120, 1966

75. Schwab JJ: Handbook of Psychiatric Consultation. New York, Appleton–Century–Crofts, 1968

76. Schwab JJ, Brown J: Uses and abuses of psychiatric consultation. JAMA 205:55, 1968

77. Schwab JJ, Clemmons RS, Marder L: The self–concept: psychosomatic applications. Psychosomatics 7:1, 1966

78. Sifneos PE: Short-Term Psychotherapy and Emotional Crisis. Cambridge, Harvard University Press, 1972

79. Stoller RJ, Estes FM: Suicides in medical and surgical wards of general hospitals. J Chronic Dis 12:592, 1960

80. Szasz TS, Knoff WF, Hollender MH: The doctor–patient relationship in its historical context. Am J Psychiatry 115:522, 1958

81. Walters A: Psychogenic regional pain alias hysterical pain. Brain 84:1, 1961

82. Wardaszko–Lyskowska H: Konsultacje psychiatryczne na oddzialach wielospecialistycznego szpitala klinicznego (Psychiatric consultations in the department of a multidisciplinary hospital of a university medical center). Psychiatria Polska 5:525, 1971

83. Weisman AD: On Dying and Denying. New York, Behavioral Publications, 1972

84. Weisman AD, Hackett TP: Denial as a social act. In Levin D, Kahane R (eds): Psychodynamic Studies on Aging, Creativity and Dying. New York, International Universities Press, 1967

85. Williams RL: The educational potential of the psychiatric consultation. Psychosomatics 9:63, 1968

86. Wittkower ED, Stauble WJ: Psychiatry and the role of the general practitioner. Psychiatry Med 3:287, 1972

Part II
Models of Intervention

4 Therapeutic Consultation with the Surgical Patient

HARRY S. ABRAM

Two questions are usually foremost in the minds of physicians and surgeons when problems arise concerning a patient's psychological response to an operation: Are there preoperative psychiatric contraindications to the proposed operation? How should I treat the patient who has developed a postoperative psychosis? This chapter concentrates upon these two questions, particularly regarding the roles of psychological preoperative intervention and postoperative care.

PREOPERATIVE CONSULTATION

In preparing the patient for an operation, it is obviously important to inform him regarding the procedure and to allow time for him to discuss his doubts, worries, and fears about it. Likewise, if the physician or surgeon requests a psychiatric opinion, he should prepare the patient for the consultation. The preparation need not be complex but merely a straightforward statement about the necessity of the consultation; *e.g.,* "I am asking a psychiatrist to talk with you before your operation, as often as a patient's psychological state can affect how he adjusts postoperatively. It is not uncommon for me to make such a referral."

Preoperative intervention—whether by the physician, the surgeon, or the psychiatrist—has a twofold purpose: 1) to assess the patient's mental functioning, affective state, and attitudes toward the proposed surgical procedure and 2) to establish a therapeutic relationship that will carry over into the postoperative phase. The initial assessment should be nonthreatening and informal, though with specific goals in mind. In general, the discussion with the patient should proceed along the following lines and include the following topics:

1. The proposed surgical procedure
   A. Physical difficulties giving rise for the need of an operation
   B. Patient's factual information and psychological conception concerning procedure ("What will be done to you during the operation?")
   C. Patient's attitudes and expectations ("What do you expect the operation to do for you?" "How will your life be different after the operation?")
   D. Symbolic significance and psychological meaning of the operation ("How do you feel about having your uterus removed, or having your heart operated upon, etc.?")
   E. Reactions to past surgical procedures (including delirious episodes, periods of amnesia surrounding past operations, evidence of polysurgical addiction, etc.)

F. Attitude toward present and past surgeons (trusting, paranoid, idolatrous, etc.)
2. Mental functioning and affective state
   A. Use of defense mechanisms (denial, repression, displacement, etc.)
   B. Evidence of psychosis or brain damage
   C. Presence and intensity of anxiety
   D. Presence and intensity of depression
3. Family and psychosocial background
   A. Family's attitude toward operation (supportive, indifferent, anxious, etc.)
   B. Evidence of family or psychosocial stress leading up to or surrounding operation
   C. Response of family or acquaintances to operations similar to that proposed for patient

In the above outline, the patient's expectations, his use of denial as a major defense mechanism, and the presence and intensity of overt anxiety are probably the most important prognosticators of postoperative psychiatric complications (2) following general surgical procedures. With open-heart operations, some investigators (8, 9) believe that the presence of severe depression and neurotic, ambivalent attitudes related to the operation are harbingers not only of postoperative psychiatric morbidity but of an increased mortality as well. In evaluating expectations, one considers what the patient anticipates from the proposed procedure, in particular, whether his anticipations are *realistic* or *unrealistic*. If they are realistic in that the patient expects the operation to produce results that are surgically possible (*i.e.,* that the extirpation of a gallbladder will remove the epigastric distress associated with cholecystitis), as opposed to unrealistic or surgically impossible results (*i.e.,* that the cholecystectomy will bring back a spouse who recently deserted the patient), then the likelihood of an adverse emotional reaction is less.

Anxiety in the preoperative period plays a major role in determining the postoperative psychological adjustment. Deutsch (4) emphasized this role many years ago, based upon her clinical experience. Janis (7) some years later demonstrated that moderate anticipatory anxiety portended satisfactory psychological adaptation, whereas excessive anxiety or a lack of anxiety led to postoperative panic or depression, respectively. In brief, the patient who "worries" before an operation has a better psychological prognosis than the patient who blandly accepts the procedure or becomes irrationally terrified preoperatively. Likewise, the patient who uses denial as a major defense mechanism and is unable consciously to look at the threatening aspects of an impending operation is apt to have postoperative difficulties.

In answering the first question posed at the beginning of this presentation—Are there preoperative psychiatric contraindications to the proposed operation?—one should be reluctant to prohibit a procedure solely on grounds of the patient's emotional state if it is surgically indicated. For years, psychiatrists have stated that "neurotic" or "unstable" individuals react adversely to operations, but they have not presented sufficient information to defend such a stand. In fact, the only specific contraindication is when the operation is to be performed for psychological rather than for surgical reasons, *e.g.,* when the surgeon knows the patient does not have a surgically treatable illness but operates to "prove" to the patient that there is "nothing wrong" physically. If one detects potential conflicts (*e.g.,* the use of excessive denial, overwhelming anxiety, unrealistic expectations, depression, ambivalence, and so forth), then he may recommend *postponement* of the procedure until he is able to work through the problem areas related to the operation with the patient. One should also be alert for the "polysurgical addict" (14), so that unnecessary surgery in the patient who receives neurotic gratification from having an operation may be avoided, as well as for the rare patient with a predilection to death (19), who may well die postoperatively. On the other hand, there are occasions when a surgical procedure may have a positive psychological effect, such as rhinoplasties performed on patients with nasal deformities (13).

Of equal or greater importance than the preoperative assessment and carried out concomitantly with it is the establishment of a therapeutic relationship that continues into the postoperative period. Ample evidence exists that such a relationship prevents postoperative psychoses, especially following cataract and open-heart operations. With the former, Weisman and Hackett (18) observed that establishing a specific preoperative doctor-patient relationship, which provides other sensory modalities and cues for the temporarily blinded patient after cataract removal, decreased the occurrence of "black-patch delirium." Thus, for example, if the psychiatrist in his preoperative interviews were to detect that a patient took particular pleasure from gustatory or olfactory sensations, he could prevent delirium by providing and sharing with the patient food or flowers in the preoperative and postoperative periods.

Although the causes of postcardiotomy delirium remain obscure and are undoubtedly multifaceted (1), with physiological, psychological, and environmental factors being involved, Lazarus and Hagens (12) demonstrated that psychosis after open-heart surgery is less likely when preoperative intervention has been employed. Such intervention includes discussion and preparation for the operation, and it provides a familiar, constant person who continues contact with the patient in the postoperative phase. This type of relationship not only allows the patient to ventilate fears and concerns about the operation, but it also allows one to prepare the patient by describing what he can expect postoperatively, especially in the intensive care unit with its concomitant physiological stresses.

In sum, preoperative intervention which then develops into an ongoing relationship is a potent therapeutic measure for the psychiatrist, the patient's physician, and his surgeon. Establishing the relationship is not a complicated procedure, and mainly it requires of the interviewer a straightforward, honest approach through which he shows interest and instills the patient with hope and trust. The preoperative interview not only permits the assessment of the patient's attitude toward the approaching operation but also opens up areas of misconception, fears, and doubts that require clarification and discussion. In addition to giving a baseline from which to evaluate the patient's postoperative behavior, it forms the foundation for continued contact with a familiar person known to the patient and someone with whom he can communicate postoperatively.

POSTOPERATIVE CONSULTATION

The necessity for postoperative consultation increases in proportion to the lack of preoperative intervention. Adequate preparation, establishing an early relationship, and the assessment of operative attitudes diminish the need of postoperative psychological measures, which are more difficult to establish, because there is insufficient prior knowledge of the patient. The major psychiatric disturbance in the postoperative period is that of psychosis or delirium, although other complications, such as depression, overdependency, and delayed recovery (6), can be just as or more troublesome.

POSTOPERATIVE PSYCHOSIS

As noted earlier, there is evidence that the establishment of a preoperative relationship diminishes the likelihood of postoperative psychosis, especially after open-heart operations. Most studies report postcardiotomy delirium developing in 30–60% of patients undergoing cardiac surgery; the incidence after general surgery is more difficult to determine, since it depends upon the manner in which the investigator collects his data. The main variable seems to depend upon whether the investigator includes only those patients referred for psychiatric consultation or if he bases his data upon patients randomly selected from surgical wards. As after open-heart surgery (3), it is often difficult to detect patients with subtle signs of psychiatric syndromes (*e.g.,* the so-called "quiet" deliria), especially if they are not verbal in their complaints. Thus, Knox (10), who included only patients referred for psychiatric consultation following general surgical procedures, reported the occurrence of postoperative psychoses as one case per 1600 patients, whereas Titchener *et al.* (17), in a study of randomly selected surgical patients, found major disturbances in 44 of 200 patients.

It is important to note that just as there is no distinct entity as a "postpartum psychosis," neither is there a specific postoperative psychosis. In both situations, one encounters a variety of psychiatric syndromes, ranging from deliria and schizophreniclike states to depression and attacks of panic. However, when the surgeon asks the second question posed at the beginning of this chapter—How should I treat the patient who has developed a postoperative psychosis?—he is usually speaking of a delirium or a schizophreniclike state that becomes manifest on the third to the fifth postoperative day. As Morse and Litin (15) have observed, these states are causally multidetermined and are related to the physical and psychological stress of the procedure, the postoperative environment, and the underlying psychological conflicts brought to the fore by the operation. Clinically, one usually observes clouding of the sensorium, confusion, and a labile affect. Illusions, hallucinations, and paranoid delusions are common (*e.g.,* the patient may mistake nurses or physicians for spies, have visions, hear voices, and believe that he is being harmed or is in danger). Experiences of being taken surreptitiously out of the hospital at night frequently occur. The patient often has a dazed, frightened, or inappropriate facial expression, and he may even deny that he has had an operation.

Therapeutic measures for these psychotic states include the following.

Correction of Physical Disturbances

The correction of electrolyte imbalances and other physical insults (*e.g.,* infection or drug intoxication) that potentially could attribute to the patient's altered mental state demands initial attention. Here one should also consider the possibility of alcohol withdrawal as a contributing factor in the so-called "hidden" alcoholic or the presence of a subdural hematoma if conditions of confusion and diminished sensorium persist.

Use of the Preoperative Relationship and Human Contact

It is in this area that the preoperative relationship comes into play through providing a continuum with someone known to the patient, who then becomes a source of support and a person whom the patient uses as a reality base. If a preoperative relationship has not been established, intervention at this point can still be effective even though more difficult. The intervenor directs the relationship toward orienting the patient to reality and establishes human contact by means of becoming a constant, familiar object in his environment. If the patient is disoriented, hallucinating, or delusional, then one makes every effort to orient him and to cut through the psychotic state. Thus, one does not "humor" the patient and go along with his misperceptions and thinking. Helpful are such statements as, "You are very confused, as people can become after an operation. Today is Friday, two days after your surgery. You are in the intensive care unit and doing fine. The doctors and nurses who are dressed in green are not the police but are here to help you.

You may think they are out to harm you because of the pain you are in or because this place seems so scary to you." Contacts with the patient at this point need not be lengthy, and indeed should not be, but rather they are carried out two to three times daily for short intervals. It is important to encourage nurses, family members, and other persons important to the patient to make similar visits. Restraining the patient physically or with mechanical restraints should be avoided if at all possible; having a sitter with the patient is always preferable to tying him down to the bed.

Use of Familiar Environmental Stimuli

The intensive care unit (ICU) most vividly illustrates the effects of an estranged, forbidding milieu on patient behavior, although the principles that have evolved in this setting (11) are valid in treating any patient with a postoperative psychosis or delirium. In general, they consist of providing sensory stimuli that help to orient the patient and to keep him in touch with reality; *e.g.*, a clock and a calendar may be provided to relieve the confusion of the temporally disoriented patient. It is of interest that in a controlled study (16), postoperative delirium occurred three times as frequently in a windowless ICU room as it did in one with windows. One should also consider the effects of sleep deprivation in the psychotic ICU patient, particularly when there are bright overhead lights that are left on 24 hours a day. When postoperative psychoses occur outside the ICU and when the patient is less critically ill, the use of a radio or a television and a small night-light may also improve orientation (20).

Psychopharmacological Medication

As in any patient with a clouded sensorium, it is wise to keep sedatives to a minimum in the patient with a postoperative delirium. Barbiturates should be avoided, particularly in elderly patients. If the patient is agitated, overtly psychotic, and difficult to manage, however, there is indication for psychopharmacological medication. If the possibility of alcohol or drug withdrawal exists or if the patient's physical condition is perilous, diazepam (Valium) in a dosage range from 5 mg, three times daily, to 10 mg, four times daily, is in order. Otherwise, an antipsychotic agent, such as haloperidol (Haldol) or chlorpromazine (Thorazine), is indicated. The former is preferable, particularly in patients with cardiovascular disease and when excessive sedation is undesirable, and it may be administered in a dosage range of 0.5 mg twice daily up to 2 mg four times daily. If sedation is necessary and hypotension is not a problem, then chlorpromazine (ranging from 25 mg three times daily up to 50 mg four times daily) is helpful.

POSTOPERATIVE DEPRESSION

Postoperative depression is usually less acute than the psychotic states described above, and it is more likely to occur later in the patient's hospital course or even after discharge. It is encountered more frequently after the loss of an organ that has special symbolic meaning, such as the uterus (5) or a breast (16). Preoperative intervention is especially important in this group of patients to assist them in working out the conflicts related to their anticipated losses. Postoperatively, a continued relationship—or the establishment of one if it was not present preoperatively—with the goal of allowing the patient to express whatever underlying feelings of loss, resentment, or hopelessness he may have, will aid the patient in resolving any conflicts that are associated with the operation. Gaining the support of the family may also be of therapeutic value in these situations. If the patient's depression persists or begins to reach severe levels, then the use of an antidepressant is indicated, such as amitriptyline (Elavil), starting at 75 mg and building up to 200 mg per day, if necessary, in divided doses or at bedtime.

POSTOPERATIVE OVERDEPENDENCY AND DELAYED RECOVERY

Finally, cases of postoperative complications include those patients with over-dependency and delayed recovery. These patients gain excessive gratification from their illness and the attention associated with the operation. Although such reactions occur normally in any patient who is physically ill and incapacitated, an individual with excessive and unresolved independency-dependency conflicts may find himself unable to give up the comforts of hospital care after an operation. In distinction to the rebellious patient who fights his dependency needs by means of refusing treatment, he reacts by giving in to his dependent feelings and is unable to assume the responsibilities associated with the stresses of everyday life. As Hackett and Weisman (6) note in their discussion of therapeutic consultation, this form of postoperative syndrome is most effectively managed through tipping the balance toward the patient's independency strivings by giving him as much responsibility as possible for his own care. By demonstrating to him that he can be "master of his own ship," he regains his psychological strength and finds that he does not have to rely so heavily upon others.

SUMMARY

This presentation emphasizes the preoperative and postoperative measures that aid in the overall adaptation of the surgical patient. These measures may be employed not only by the psychiatric consultant but by the patient's physician and surgeon as well. If at all possible, psychological intervention should begin preoperatively and continue into the postoperative phase. The purpose of preoperative intervention is twofold: 1) to determine a baseline assessment of the patient's behavior, mental functioning, and attitudes toward the approaching operation and 2) to establish an ongoing therapeutic relationship that continues postoperatively. The latter purpose is as important as or perhaps more important than the former. There are no specific psychiatric contraindications to an operation as long as it is *surgically* indicated. The surgeon should be wary of the "polysurgical addict" and be aware of surgical patients with a predilection to death. Postponing an operation, especially an open-heart procedure, may be indicated in the presence of severe depression and ambivalence. Unrealistic expectations, extreme anxiety, and denial are often prognosticators of postoperative psychiatric complications.

Postoperative psychiatric complications consist mainly of psychoses, deliria, depressions, as well as those of patients with delayed recovery and overdependency. In treating psychosis or delirium, therapeutic principles are directed toward 1) treating and correcting the underlying physiological disturbances, 2) maintaining a relationship with the patient that provides a base for reality testing and support, 3) providing a nonthreatening and familiar postoperative environment, and 4) using appropriate and adequate psychopharmacological medications when indicated. Postoperative depression occurs most frequently after the loss of an important symbolic organ (*e.g.,* the uterus or the breast), may require psychological support to work through feelings of grief and resentment, and may require the use of antidepressant medication. In patients with delayed recovery and over-dependency, a conflict often exists between dependency and independency, which requires a shift of the responsibility of care onto the patient to insure proper recovery.

REFERENCES

1. Abram HS: Psychotic reactions after cardiac surgery: a critical review. Semin Psychiatry 3:70–78, 1971
2. Abram HS, Gill BF: Predictions of postoperative psychiatric complications. N Engl J Med 265:1123–1128, 1961
3. Blacher RS: The hidden psychosis of open-heart surgery. JAMA 222:305–308, 1972
4. Deutsch H: Some psychoanalytic observations in surgery. Psychosom Med 4:105–115, 1942
5. Drellich MG, Bieber I: The psychological importance of the uterus and its functions. J Nerv Ment Dis 126:322–336, 1958
6. Hackett TP, Weisman AD: Psychiatric management of operative syndromes. I. The therapeutic consultation and the effect of noninterpretive intervention. Psychosom Med 22:267–282, 1960
7. Janis IL: Psychological Stress: Psychoanalytic and Behavioral Studies of Surgical Patients. New York, John Wiley & Sons, 1959
8. Kennedy JA, Bakst H: The influence of emotion on the outcome of cardiac surgery: a predictive study. Bull NY Acad 42:811–845, 1966
9. Kimball CP: Psychological responses to the experience of open-heart surgery. I. Am J Psychiatry 126:348–359, 1969
10. Knox SJ: Severe psychiatric disturbances in the postoperative period—a five-year survey of Belfast hospitals. J Ment Sci 107:1078–1096, 1961
11. Kornfeld DS, Zimberg S, Malm JR: Psychiatric complications of open-heart surgery. N Engl J Med 273:288–292, 1965
12. Lazarus HR, Hagens JH: Prevention of psychosis following open-heart surgery. Am J Psychiatry 124:1190–1195, 1968
13. Linn L, Goldman IB: Psychiatric observations concerning rhinoplasty. Psychosom Med 11:307–314, 1949
14. Menninger KA: Polysurgery and polysurgical addiction. Psychoanal Q 3:173–199, 1934
15. Morse RM, Litin EM: Postoperative delirium: a study of etiologic factors. Am J Psychiatry 126:388–395, 1969
16. Renneker R, Cutler M: Psychological problems of adjustment to cancer of the breast. JAMA 148:833–838, 1952
17. Titchener JL, Zwerling I, Gottschalk L, Levine M: Psychosis in surgical patients. Surg Gynecol Obstet 102:59–65, 1956
18. Weisman AD, Hackett TP: Psychosis after eye surgery: establishment of specific doctor–patient relationship in prevention and treatment of "black-patch" delirium. N Engl J Med 258:1284–1289, 1958
19. Weisman AD, Hackett TP: Predilection to death: death and dying as a psychiatric problem. Psychosom Med 23:232–256, 1961
20. Wilson LM: Intensive care delirium. Arch Intern Med 130:225–226, 1972

5 Evaluation and Management of Intractable Pain

GEORGE MATHEWS, CHOH-LUH LI

Many forms of pain are self-limiting and amenable to standard medical or surgical measures. In cases of chronic or intractable pain, however, treatment often becomes a difficult undertaking with meager rewards. Errors in either diagnosis or management may add immeasurably to the medical and emotional complexities of the treatment transaction.

In this chapter, the subject of pain is discussed under three aspects: 1) possible errors in diagnosis and treatment, 2) recent advances in pain evaluation, and 3) recent advances in pain management.

POSSIBLE ERRORS IN DIAGNOSIS AND TREATMENT

WRONG DIAGNOSIS, WRONG TREATMENT

Wrong diagnosis leads to incorrect treatment. Less often, the correct diagnosis is made, but the wrong treatment is instituted. In both cases, the results are the same, *i.e.*, the pain persists. A major source of error is to insist on the label "pain syndrome" even if it has to be squeezed into a diagnostic straitjacket. Thereafter, the wrongly labeled entity is treated with earnest perseverance; failure prompts greater therapeutic vigor, rather than a revision of the diagnosis.

In the diagnosis and management of causalgiform syndromes, for example, many pitfalls are encountered that thwart successful treatment. In causalgia, more than in any other pain syndrome, chronicity leads to intractability, and, in some instances, the diagnosis is made only after well-entrenched symptoms and signs have appeared. These symptoms consist of burning, hyperpathia, trophic changes, and responsiveness to emotional tone. Although a sympathetic nerve block may abort the condition in its early stages, in intermediate stages a surgical sympathectomy becomes necessary, and in the late stages even frontal lobotomy may be futile. Sometimes causalgia in its early stages is correctly diagnosed but the sympathetic pathways are left alone. Instead of treating the nerves directly, a regimen of analgesics is begun and may be expanded to include opiates. Valuable time is lost, and intractability and narcotic dependence are ushered in *pari passu*.

On the other hand, there are a number of painful conditions that share some features with causalgia without meeting all the criteria; these conditions are sometimes designated *minor causalgia* or *sympathetic dystrophies*. These variations, as it were, extend the perimeter of the diagnostic domain until unrelated entities are included because they bear some resemblance to a sympathetic disturbance.

49

These unrelated disorders may be treated as cases of causalgia, with an understandable lack of success.

Another example where imprecise diagnosis and improper treatment may be encountered in our daily practice is provided by low back pain. To regard as radiculopathy all pain that radiates from the axial spine into the extremities is a common but avoidable error. When rigid criteria are used in determining the localization of a patient's pain, (not merely down the leg, but strictly down the back of the leg), when the straight leg-raising test is properly performed and interpreted, and when segmental reflex, myotomal, and dermatomal deficits are verified and correlated, then a diagnosis of sciatica may be made that will rest on a firm clinical basis. Roentgenographic information provides further confirmation, and surgery, if it is performed after an appropriate conservative trial, seldom fails. Laxity—either in diagnostic concept or in clinical examination—can easily mislead the physician into suspecting sciatica where none exists. If minor changes in the myelogram and other roentgenograms are overinterpreted, surgery is bound to be followed by dismal results. Thereafter, the saga of myelograms redone, disc spaces reexplored, fusions, cordotomies, psychiatric referrals, and abandonment is a familiar one. Why does this continue to occur in the face of so many bad results? First, the surgical correction of the true sciatica of disc disease is gratifying, second, the basis of nonradicular pain radiating into the leg is poorly understood, and third, the optimism that results from the first reason contaminates proper evaluation regarding the second.

A parallel exists in cases involving the cervical spine. Arm pain that is clearly radicular and related to a disc disorder responds dramatically to surgery. Nonradicular arm pains—whether following whiplash injuries, in spondylosis, from psychosomatic causes, or from other unknown factors—respond less well to treatment of any sort, and, in particular, they respond poorly to surgical interference. As in the treatment of causalgia, the converse situation—*i.e.*, the failure to operate when surgery is indicated—is less prevalent but is nevertheless encountered in practice. Herniated discs with unmistakable radiculopathy are treated with dogged conservatism until serious weakness or sphincter disturbances supervene, and permanent alterations in the affected nerves preclude any successful outcome of surgical treatment.

Trigeminal neuralgia and other facial pains constitute another large group where accurate diagnosis and treatment can be as rewarding as the opposite can be catastrophic. Those physicians experienced in the treatment of tic douloureux repeatedly stress the importance of a rigorous approach to the problem. The age of onset, the predilection for the two lower divisions of the trigeminal nerve, the paroxysms of pain, the trigger points, and the absence of sensory or motor deficits must be carefully evaluated. The possibility of multiple sclerosis and of the involvement of the trigeminal nerve in tumors or vascular abnormalities to cause pain in the face must also be explored. Appropriate medical or surgical treatment of trigeminal neuralgia meets with reasonable success. This, however, is not always found to be the sequence. Not uncommonly, dental extractions and orthodontic work have been performed en route. Other patients have been treated with narcotic painkillers, either because the ineffectiveness of such agents in this condition was not appreciated, or because there was the notion that in so doing, surgery could be fended off until spontaneous remission occurred.

Many facial pains masquerade as tic douloureux. The unwary surgeon who operates on these patients may soon be disappointed. Chemical, thermal, or surgical destruction of the trigeminal system in atypical trigeminal neuralgia carries a high risk of precipitating anesthesia dolorosa, a severe and intractable form of pain that is considerably worse than the original condition.

Complacency and error are difficult to avoid in treating something as commonplace as headaches; besides they are mostly situational, insipid, and self-limiting.

Frequently, when they are found to occur on a psychogenic or psychosomatic basis, headaches are the hallmark of hypochondriasis. Even the more clearly identified entities such as migraine incorporate a wide spectrum of vascular headaches, often termed *migraine like* or *migraine variants.* Here again, a limited understanding of the basic mechanisms is the reason for diagnostic and therapeutic ambiguity. It has long been fashionable to contrive psychodynamic explanations for headaches; Inevitably, headaches due to brain tumor, aneurysm, or arteriovenous malformation have been called "psychogenic" until the true cause surfaced. This danger has been the subject of much reiteration.

Somewhat less well known is the role of disorders of the cervical spine in the genesis of headache; cervical disc disease, degenerative changes, and acute flexion-extension injuries (whiplash) can cause occipital, temporal, frontal, or retroocular pain. The almost invariable trapezius muscle spasm that is found in conjunction with such disorders, is sometimes mistaken for the cause, and "muscle tension headache," a psychosomatic disturbance, is then the diagnosis. Nothing less than treatment of the primary cervical spine problem, however, affords relief.

INADEQUATE TREATMENT

Whenever a precise diagnosis is followed by appropriate medication but in less-than-effective doses, over protracted intervals, or for insufficient periods of time, or when a less potent drug is used where the stronger is called for, then the therapy is inadequate and so is relief. Failure to take advantage of the adjunctive use of psychotropic drugs or physical therapy slows progress; failure to explain the pain problem, the treatment schedule, and the expectations for relief to the patient and his family is a tactical error, and failure to enlist the specialists' assistance when necessary may prove a costly omission.

The personal biases of the attending physician as to how much pain is involved and how much medication is needed provide the usual reason for inadequate treatment. A suspicion of exaggeration or dissimulation of pain, the conclusion that the pain is psychogenic in origin, or the suggestion that "secondary" pain is involved (whether in the psychoanalytic or social sense) may cause many doctors to assume an unsympathetic or even punitive posture, which often is reflected in a curtailment of analgesic medication.

Physicians are generally apprehensive that narcotic dependence may develop in the course of treatment and hence dispense these drugs parsimoniously. Thus, neither adequate pain control nor absolute prevention of drug addiction is insured. Agitation, which may be felt with the pain but even more acutely with partial relief, is briefly allayed by the narcotic, and the patient begins to identify these agents more with relief from anxiety than with relief from pain. Supplying narcotic analgesics, when required, in a dosage and frequency that permits uniform comfort during the phase of acute pain is the best provision for a smooth transition into the use of milder analgesics as the pain subsides.

Inadequate control of pain is most often seen in the treatment of patients during the postoperative period. In large measure, this is because some surgeons have no talent for pain management. The unprepared patient is distressed by the intensity and uncertain about the duration of his suffering. Whether to request pain medication sooner or to endure it stoically for hours is a dilemma that may easily be avoided by providing a few moments of instruction. The surgeon may restrict analgesics, fearing drowsiness and improper clearing of tracheobronchial secretions, but in doing so, he fails to consider that postoperative pain effectively discourages coughing and imposes immobility. Good pain control engenders the patient's trust and cooperation, two valuable assets in any therapeutic situation.

Pain in the late stages of cancer is treated ungrudgingly, but the pain that is manifested early in the course of the disease is often considered an annoying diversion in the battle against cancer. Since in most cases, the pain subsides as the lesions regress as a result of chemotherapy or radiation therapy, it is not often considered necessary to expend any particular effort to control the pain. Oncologists and radiation therapists, like surgeons, may be dilatory in their approach to pain and often seek assistance only when nothing else avails.

MISMANAGEMENT OF INTRACTABLE PAIN

The tragedy of intractable pain is that there always seems to be one more treatment that might help and must, in all good faith, be tried. No pain is called "intractable" until a number of surgical and nonsurgical failures clutter its wake. This often results because in a number of patients, what might be considered "intractable" pain has responded to medical or surgical therapy of one form or another, which thus provides the impetus for many subsequent and unsuccessful ventures along the same lines. The history of surgery for pain lists many techniques that were initially reported in glowing terms, quickly embraced, widely applied, and then relegated into an uneasy oblivion. The elusive quality of intractable pain is typified by its prompt response to surgery, a brief respite lasting weeks or months, and the inevitable return of the pain with renewed intensity. Nonetheless, the surgeon can always be found who is willing to try his particular surgical variation in an attempt at a cure.

Some forms of intractable pain are recognized as such from the outset. Phantom-limb pain, thalamic syndrome, post-herpetic neuralgia, and arachnoiditis are known to be refractory to therapy. As noted before, an occasional cure may be obtained, but that is accomplished by destruction of the pain pathways. Although a sacrifice of function may well be accepted in lieu of the pain, a return of the pain despite continuing functional loss is a serious burden.

Intractable pain should be recognized as early as possible and the patient made privy to that conclusion. Its treatment should be mainly supportive in a holistic sense. The danger of drug addiction, emotional disturbances, and a deterioration of the doctor-patient relationship may continually be present. Any noninvasive modality, no matter how novel or mystifying, is worth trying in these cases. Yoga, meditation, faith-healing, acupuncture, or the pain-clinic approach may all be useful to a degree and may be tried in these desperate cases.

RECENT ADVANCES IN PAIN EVALUATION

The purpose of this section is to mention certain newer investigative techniques that might be used to elucidate pain problems. It is not often that a method is used exclusively in the diagnosis of pain; more frequently, tests developed for other purposes are found to be useful in the investigation of pain syndromes. A familiarity with the existence of such tests and the information that can be gained from them may expand the physician's demesne and provide implements for his specific needs.

ROENTGENOGRAPHY

Standard methods such as carotid and vertebral angiography have long ago established their usefulness. Magnification and subtraction techniques have been added to improve the resolution of the more subtle findings. The ability to study selectively small vascular territories has been of assistance in specific problems. Pain within the orbit traversing the orbital fissures or the cavernous sinus due to involvement of the nerves in the orbit can now be investigated with orbital venography. Spinal angiography has become a valuable tool, and on occasion it helps to elucidate the genesis of pain of spinal origin (3). The complicated anatomy of the cerebellopontine angle is well depicted by the cisternal myelogram when a small quantity of contrast medium is run into the posterior fossa and the area of the internal auditory meatus, and the gutters on either side of the brain stem are visualized.

The most significant advance in roentgenographic technique has been the development of computerized axial tomography. A very accurate cross-sectional view of the brain and its ventricular system can be obtained with this system, and lesions within the head that cause pain—such as infarctions, hematomas, tumors of the thalamus, or tumors along the paths of cranial sensory nerves—are visualized with startling clarity (6, 7).

NERVE BLOCKS

Somatic and sympathetic nerve blocks have remained important methods in pain evaluation. Although no major modifications have appeared recently, improvements such as the use of fluoroscopy to enable accurate needle placement and electrical stimulation to localize the tip of the needle have been gaining more refinement with usage.

The use of more dilute local anesthetic solutions to block the autonomic nerves while sparing the somatic nerves is being investigated, and this technique may enhance the value of nerve blocks (17). Epidural catheterization of the lumbar, thoracic, and lower cervical regions enables the blocking of wide areas for prolonged periods. Placebo trials or repeated injections using varying concentrations or volumes of the anesthetic agent can be effected by this means (2).

PSYCHOLOGICAL TESTING

Psychological testing has become an integral part of pain evaluation. Personality inventories, pain threshold, anxiety and depression scales, and placebo reactivity can be measured, and the information gained from these tests is generally felt to be of assistance in the management of chronic and difficult pain problems. The Minnesota Multiphasic Personality Inventory (MMPI) is probably the most commonly used test for such purposes in pain cases (5).

RECENT ADVANCES IN PAIN MANAGEMENT

PHARMACOLOGICAL AGENTS

Pentazocine (Talwin), a weakly narcotic antagonist of the benzomorphan series, is gaining wide use as an effective injectable and oral analgesic, and it has a lower capacity for abuse than the more potent narcotic analgesics. The precipitation of acute withdrawal symptoms, addiction, as well as fibrosis of the muscles in sites of frequent and repeated injections have, however, been noted with the use of pentazocine (14).

Propoxyphene napsylate (Darvon-N) has been introduced as an agent with advantages over the older propoxyphene hydrochloride (Darvon). Greater effectiveness, longer action, a larger margin of safety, and greater stability in the presence of aspirin are some of the improvements over the original preparation (14).

Perhaps the most important advance in this field is the combined use of pharmacological agents in the treatment of denervation dysesthesia. In conditions like post-herpetic neuralgia, anesthesia dolorosa, and peripheral neuropathy, pain amelioration has been reported with the administration of fluphenazine (Prolixin), 1 mg three times a day, and amitriptyline (Elavil), 75 mg at bedtime. The use of psychotropic drugs as adjuncts in pain therapy is by no means recent, but this combination of a tricyclic antidepressant with a substituted phenothiazine is both new and of proved effectiveness (16).

PHYSICAL METHODS

An old method that has been rejuvenated and enhanced by modern technology is the use of electrical surface stimulation for pain control. Percutaneous electroanalgesia consists of applying electrodes to sites that are found most effective by trial anderror. An electrical current is passed through the electrode and adjusted with regard to frequency, amplitude, and duration so as to procure maximum relief. When used in a variety of benign chronic pain situations and for pain due to cancer, significant relief seems to occur in about 60% of cases (10).

Acupuncture, which has recently been imported from the East (8), is a modality in the throes of a scientific "jet lag." Wildly enthusiastic reports of success, especially those generated by practitioners in acupuncture clinics, have been countered with extreme scepticism by the scientific community. At the present time, it would appear that acupuncture does not suppress, to any great extent, experimentally produced pain (9). Many institutions are currently addressing the question of its value as a medical technique, and useful data should be forthcoming in the near future.

PSYCHOLOGICAL METHODS

Many psychological techniques of pain control are being explored. Apart from a few preliminary reports, however, no substantive data are available. Behavioral and environmental modification, biofeedback, transcendental meditation (TM), or a combination of these modes are being used both in and out of pain clinics. The best enunciated of these seems to be operant conditioning or contingency management, in which pain behavior is analyzed, reinforcers are identified, and the environment is programmed so that "the occurrence of positive reinforcement becomes contingent upon the occurrence of the behavior to be decreased and, conversely, positive reinforcers are withdrawn from behavior to be decreased" (4).

SURGICAL TECHNIQUES

In recent years, an increase has occurred in the use of radio-frequency irradiation to destroy pain-conducting pathways in a graded and controllable manner. Thermocoagulation of the trigeminal ganglion for neuralgia and percutaneous chordotomy are examples of such applications (11, 15). Stereotaxic pain-relief operations have maintained a status quo; the technical complexities of the procedure have not been matched by results that are sufficiently good to encourage its wider use (12). Dorsal column stimulation, which was considered an exciting new method for a period of time, is described in somewhat more guarded terms in recent reports. Here again, the initial enthusiasm has given way to a more circumspect approach, particularly because it has been found that with time, the pain returns, despite a well-functioning stimulation (13).

THE MULTIDISCIPLINARY CLINIC

No discussion of modern pain management is complete without mentioning the pain clinic. A proliferation of such clinics throughout the country has been the result of the pioneering efforts of Dr. John Bonica. The team approach and the organizational structure of the clinic involve personnel from various disciplines, such as anesthesiology, neurosurgery, radiology, physiology, psychiatry, psychology, sociology, and nursing. The director, the patient manager, the executive committee, the clinic coordinator, and the conference constitute the functional roles that have been described for the clinic, and this organization has, by and large, been followed by the various existing clinics (1). Since only one or two patients, however, can be considered at a conference that includes a sizable number of participants over a one- to two-hour period, the time and cost factors are not inconsiderable. Further data as to how many patients may benefit and for what length of time will have to become available before the practical worth of pain clinics in pain management can be evaluated.

REFERENCES

1. Bonica JJ: Organization and function of a pain clinic. In Bonica JJ (ed.): Advances In Neurology, Vol 4. New York, Raven Press, 1974, pp 513–515

2. Bonica JJ: Current role of nerve blocks in diagnosis and therapy of pain. In Bonica JJ (ed): Advances In Neurology, Vol 4. New York, Raven Press, 1974, pp 445–453

3. Di Chiro G, Wener L: Angiography of the spinal cord. J Neurosurg 39: 1–29, 1973

4. Fordyce WE: Treating chronic pain by contingency management. In Bonica JJ (ed): Advances In Neurology, Vol 4. New York, Raven Press, 1974, pp 665–672

5. Hathaway SR, McKinley JC: Minnesota Multiphasic Personality Inventory. Minneapolis, University of Minnesota Press, 1942

6. Hounsfield GN: Computerized transverse axial scanning (tomography). Part 1. Description of system. Br J Radiol 46:1016–1022, 1973

7. Ledley RS, Di Chiro G, Luessenhop AJ, Twigg HL: Computerized transaxial x-ray tomography of the human body. Science 186:207–212, 1974

8. Li CL: A brief outline of Chinese medical history with particular reference to acupuncture. Perspect Biol Med 18:132–143, 1974

9. Li CL, Ahlberg D, Lansdell H, Gravitz MA, Chen TC, Ting CY, Bak AF, Blessing D: Acupuncture and hypnosis: effect on induced pain. Exp Neurol, 1975 (in press)

10. Long DM, Carolan MT: Cutaneous afferent stimulation in the treatment of chronic pain. In Bonica JJ (ed): Advances in Neurology, Vol 4. New York, Raven Press, 1974, pp 755–759

11. Mullan S: Percutaneous cordotomy (RF). In Bonica JJ (ed): Advances in Neurology, Vol 4. New York, Raven Press, 1974, pp 677–682

12. Pagni CA: Place of stereotactic technique in surgery for pain. In Bonica JJ (ed): Advances in Neurology, Vol 4. New York, Raven Press, 1974, pp 699–706

13. Shealy CN: Six years' experience with electrical stimulation for control of pain. In Bonica JJ (ed): Advances in Neurology, Vol 4. New York, Raven Press, 1974, pp 775–782

14. Sunshine A: Recent advances in non-narcotic analgesics. In Bonica JJ (ed):Advances in Neurology, Vol 4. New York, Raven Press, 1974, pp 513–515

15. Sweet WH, Wepsic JG: Controlled thermocoagulation of trigeminal ganglion and rootlets for differential destruction of pain fibers. 1. Trigeminal neuralgia. In Bonica JJ (ed): Advances in Neurology, Vol 4. New York, Raven Press, 1974, pp 665–672

16. Taub A, Collins WF: Observations on the treatment of denervation dysesthesia with psychotropic drugs: postherapetic neuralgia, anesthesia dolorosa, peripheral neuropathy. In Bonica JJ (ed): Advances in Neurology, Vol 4. New York, Raven Press, 1974, 309–315

17. Winnie AP, Ramamurthy S, Durrani Z: Diagnostic and therapeutic nerve blocks: recent advances in techniques. In Bonica JJ (ed): Advances in Neurology, Vol 4. New York, Raven Press, 1974, 455–460

6 Psychiatric Considerations in Chronic Pain States

R. ALEC RAMSAY

Before the early part of the nineteenth century, the phenomenon of pain was viewed as an essentially emotional event. This concept had for many centuries changed little from that expressed in the early dissertations of Aristotle, who placed pain in the same category as pleasure and assigned its study more to the realm of the philosopher than of the physician. Szasz (23), in a volume appropriately titled *Pain and Pleasure,* outlines the fascinating historical and psychodynamic relationships between these two concepts.

With the rise of the scientific method and the explosion of knowledge concerning the structure and function of the body, neurophysiology and neurology increasingly challenged these philosophical ideas and succeeded in establishing the importance of considering pain as a sensory phenomenon. Much interest has subsequently been generated in clarifying the nature of pain phenomena in neurophysiological terms and in employing the resultant knowledge to understand clinical pain phenomena in neurolopathic and other disease states. Despite significant advances in the study of what is undoubtedly the commonest of reasons for seeking medical help, pain still remains uncommonly difficult to define and characterize in a comprehensive sense. No theoretical model has as yet been devised that can account for all the experimental and clinical observations concerning it, but there is widespread agreement among workers in the field that pain, especially chronic pain, is much more complex than the traditional neurophysiological explanations would suggest. An excellent account of the classical specificity and pattern theories of pain is provided by Melzack in *The Puzzle of Pain* (14), as well as a modified version of the gate-control theory first proposed a decade ago by himself and Wall (15). As recently reviewed by Kroger (11), the gate-control theory is able to account for a variety of previously unexplained phenomena in chronic pain states, including the possibility of spinal mechanisms being modified by descending impulses that originate in either the cortical or the limbic structures, or both. Although these latter phenomena are difficult to investigate in their complexity, they are of great importance in the attempt to understand how cognitive and affective factors interact with the better understood peripheral mechanisms.

The reasons for the relatively primitive understanding of the psychological factors in pain are several, in my opinion, and include the following:

1. As part of the reaction of the early and later scientific community against the somewhat nebulous philosophical characterizations of the ancients, emphasis in the study of pain has been placed, until recently, almost exclusively on its neurophysiological aspects as a sensory modality.
2. Psychological phenomena are enormously complex, often difficult to characterize in the form of testable hypotheses, and subject to varying interpretation

depending upon the other variables in the situation, including the theoretical orientation of the observer. Although most clinicians can identify readily enough those patients for whom the emotional factor, or so-called psychological overlay, is influencing the clinical picture of pain, the precise nature, proportion, and cause-or-effect relationship of this component in relation to the more concrete sensory phenomena are often difficult to ascertain. It thus stands to reason that the peripheral components of the pain experience should have received first attention.

3. Psychology and psychiatry have only very recently turned significant attention to the study of pain. This is somewhat surprising, since the studies by Merskey (17, 18) have shown that the incidence of pain in identified psychiatric patients is very high and is often intimately intertwined with their emotional problems. Despite these observations (which were probably no less true 100 years ago), standard textbooks of psychiatry, even those by authors with a basic organic orientation, have paid little attention to the subject.

4. Despite gradual progress in many medical schools, there remain formidable problems in the teaching of the psychosocial aspects of medicine and the understanding of psychosomatic and somatopsychic relationships. As a result, the soma-psyche dichotomy persists in much of clinical practice, making it more difficult to develop integrated conceptual models that might prove very useful in the understanding and treatment of many complex cases commonly encountered in medical practice, including those of patients who make a career of their pain and attempts to obtain relief from it.

The recent establishment of interdisciplinary pain clinics, such as those described by Bonica (1) and Maline and Crue (12), has been very beneficial in pooling the resources of clinicians and investigators from varying backgrounds. As an extension of this trend, the International Association for the Study of Pain was created this year, and this should, through its congresses and the journal *Pain*, do much to foster necessary dialog among the many basic scientists and clinical practitioners interested in the subject. The development of a comprehensive theory of pain will require the establishment of a common ground in language, and each specialized discipline must depart far enough from its own traditional position to encompass the concepts of others.

PROBLEMS OF CONCEPT AND DEFINITION

Many attempts have been made to define what pain is, and Sternbach (22) has noted that, whatever else might be said about it, pain is an abstraction used to refer to a great variety of different feelings that have little in common except the quality of physical hurt. He points out that the word is also sometimes used to describe the stimuli for the experience, and in behavioral terms, it has more recently been applied to a class of behaviors, whether verbal, reflex, voluntary, or physiological. These behaviors are referred to as "pain responses," and their concept has been found useful as an operational definition of pain for the purposes of experimentation and objective clinical evaluation.

Merskey and Spear (20), in a volume that summarizes well the writings on the psychological and psychiatric aspects of pain prior to 1967, discuss in detail the semantic problems and propose, after Merskey (16), the following operational definition of pain: "an unpleasant experience which we primarily associate with tissue damage or describe in terms of tissue damage or both" (20). This definition emphasizes the essentially experimental nature of pain, and it can be used to refer to pain whether of organic, psychogenic, or mixed origin. In many patients with chronic pain, particularly of the so-called intractable variety, the establishment of any distinction between its organic and psychogenic origins can be extremely difficult if not impossible, but it is usually unnecessary, though, since management in the light of current knowledge is similar in either case.

Among others, Sternbach (22) and Szasz (23) have discussed the conceptual and practical pitfalls of insisting on classifying a pain as psychogenic or somatogenic, and Sternbach outlines the usefulness of Graham's (8) concept of "linguistic parallelism" in which psychosomatic disorders, including chronic pain states, can be described in the language of psychology or physiology or both, according to which provides the greater value in understanding patients and planning management. With regard to management, a treatment plan that combines organically aimed and psychologically based modalities in parallel offers the best chance of success in many patients with chronic pain.

It follows from this theory of parallelism that it is important for the physician to be aware that psychogenic pain should never be labeled as "imaginary." From the viewpoint of the experience of the person affected, there is no reason to suspect that psychogenic pain is any different in either quality or intensity from so-called true pain, a term which is also misleading and should be discarded.

CLINICAL PRESENTATION AND DYNAMIC PROFILE

Although patients with chronic pain states constitute numerically a small proportion of those seen in a typical medical practice, they characteristically make inordinate demands on the time and patience of the physician. Most readers involved in clinical practice will recognize familiar elements in the following account:

The patient is likely to approach Dr. X with an impassioned plea, often at a time when he might anticipate a less than sympathetic ear, such as late Friday afternoon. He is most likely to have a complaint referable to the musculoskeletal system, the lumbosacral and cervical regions of the spine being favorite targets. Dr. X is never the first doctor to be consulted but is more likely to be the 15th or the 20th, none of whom, according to the patient, could diagnose or cure his painful back or shoulder or face. Dr. X is told of his good reputation as a diagnostician and that he represents the patient's last hope for a cure. There is usually a background of multiple investigations for a bewildering variety of symptoms, and often a history is given of several surgical procedures, at least one of them at one of the famous clinics. All these procedures produced dramatic relief for one to several weeks, followed by the appearance of identical or new symptoms. The patient expresses confidence that Dr. X will make the correct diagnosis. He may insist on extensive reinvestigations or surgery. He will express his conviction that although the previous six operations were useful or harmful, the one that Dr. X can arrange will solve his misery at last. Dr. X may decide to reinvestigate or operate, perhaps against his better judgment and partly as a response to the patient's insistence. There is an initial improvement, and Dr. X becomes the world's best doctor. Soon, however, the honeymoon is over and the pain returns, the phone calls come more frequently and insistently, disillusionment sets in on both sides, a rupture of the doctor-patient relationship may occur, and the process starts off again with a new doctor or in another hospital's outpatient department.

For most doctors, an important part of our professional gratification depends on our patients getting better. Chronic disease of any kind is an increasingly common source of frustration because of the elusiveness of "cure" in these conditions, and this is especially true in the case of chronic pain patients who may complain bitterly about their symptom but often cannot give it up. Needless to say, injudicious or repeated surgical interventions often complicate, rather than alleviate, the clinical picture. Experienced clinicians, such as Crue (3), are wary of surgical procedures in those patients whose suffering is due either to unknown causes and mechanisms or alternatively, to trauma or a disease that is considered too minor or to have taken place too long ago to constitute a likely explanation for their symptoms.

These patients are often discovered to be "pain prone," a term that has been used by Engel (5) and more recently by McCranie (13). As Engel points out, these patients, throughout their life history, are repeatedly or chronically suffering from one or another painful complaint, and the understanding of certain of the psycho-dynamic mechanisms involved may be crucial in the consideration of treatment. In some of these patients, the pain may be adaptive in the sense of serving as a kind of symbolic, self-inflicted punishment for misdeeds, whether real or imagined. Usually, pain is only one of several mechanisms used in the service of the same unconscious need. Such patients often manifest a generally masochistic life-style, subjecting themselves unnecessarily to humiliation by others or provoking sadisti-cally inclined partners to attack or exploit them.

Another type of common situation involves the patient who develops pain which is identical to that suffered by a loved one who is dying or who has died. This often represents a psychological defense against the reality of the loss or impending loss; by becoming like the person, the reality of the loss is denied. Characteris-tically, such a patient is not aware of these connections, no matter how obvious they may be to the observer. This pattern is commonly associated with an absent or incomplete mourning capacity, and unfinished grief reactions may persist for years in a large number of patients with chronic pain.

PSYCHIATRIC DIAGNOSTIC CATEGORIES

The dynamic mechanisms in pain states cut across diagnostic lines. The establish-ment of a psychiatric diagnosis in such patients involves the consideration of other features that the patient presents. Although mixtures commonly occur, there are, as noted by Pinsky (21), four primary diagnoses in which pain may be a prominent feature:

Hysterical Neurosis

This disorder is also known as conversion hysteria. The patient's history may provide evidence of other conversion symptoms, such as globus hystericus, faint-ing, aphonia, hyperventilation, and various sensory and motor disturbances. Lack of concern *(la belle indifférence)* about the symptoms *may* be seen. Female pa-tients may be exhibitionistic, overdramatizing, and seductive. Such patients may develop intense emotional involvement with the physician, and this is often as-sociated with dramatic remissions and relapses of symptoms. In men, there may be findings of relative passivity and feminine identification.

Frequently, there is a history of an actual physical illness in the past that had the same symptoms, perhaps in childhood. The return of the symptoms at the present time is often unaccompanied by sufficient organic evidence to explain their pres-ence or intensity.

It should be remembered that conversion, as a mechanism, can occur in any diagnostic category. The term "hysterical pain" is probably too well established to be easily replaced, although it has been justifiably criticized by Walters (24), who suggested the alternative designation of "psychogenic regional pain."

Depression

Depression, whether neurotic or psychotic, is often associated with pain. There is a generally depressed appearance, and behavior may be retarded or agitated. The affects expressed are those of sadness, guilt, and shame, although in some patients these may be denied, and the depression is referred to as "masked." There may be previous episodes of depression with or without pain. In some cases, the occurrence of the pain protects these patients against more intense depression and even suicide.

Hypochondriacal and Obsessional States

These patients are obsessed with the idea of pain and the meaning thereof. They are little or not at all reassured by the doctors' negative findings. Such patients shower a great deal of attention on the painful part, ruminating endlessly and often driving their families to distraction by insistent trips to the emergency room for still another roentgenogram or electrocardiogram. Some patients in this category are essentially psychoneurotic and may be excellent candidates for insight psychotherapy; others have a deeper level of personality disorganization and should be considered prepsychotic.

Schizophrenia

Schizophrenic patients with pain are usually paranoid. The pain may represent a true hallucination, or there may be a delusional interpretation of a painful physical process. Often the patient feels persecuted by the pain, and bizarre descriptions of the pain and explanations of the cause are commonly given; for example, in explaining an abdominal pain, one patient said, "There is a tapeworm chewing at my spleen." Generally, one can find other paranoid qualities, including withdrawal and suspicious attitude, accompanied at times by accusations against other physicians, relatives, or neighbors as being responsible for the pain.

THE LEARNING THEORY EXPLANATION OF PAIN BEHAVIOR

The learning theory model has proved very useful in understanding certain aspects of pain behavior, and it employs the concepts of operant conditioning to explain the persistence of pain despite apparent "organic recovery." A good account of the principles involved can be found in Fordyce *et al.* (7) or in Sternbach (22), and very useful applications of these techniques in treating the patients with chronic pain who are seen in an office practice are provided in a more recent work by Fordyce (6). The usefulness of the biofeedback model in handling these patients has yet to be proved, but Coger and Werbach (2) feel that further investigation is justified.

MANAGEMENT CONSIDERATIONS

An understanding of some of the psychiatric aspects of pain can be important to the clinician who is faced in daily practice with the management of patients having chronic pain, and the following points may prove useful in this regard.

Much pain can be alleviated or completely removed, at least temporarily, by the psychological device of strong suggestion, whether in "pure" form, within the context of a more specific technique such as hypnosis (9) or acupuncture (10), or as part of the placebo effect of any treatment or agent which is "given" to the patient, such as analgesic, psychotropic or other drugs. This applies whether the origin of the pain is psychogenic or organic or both. As an example of the clinical application of this principle, a study by Egbert *et al.* (4) reported on the effectiveness of suggestion, reassurance, and cognitive rehearsal in decreasing postoperative pain, which was measured by the amount of analgesic required.

The reaction to severe pain in any illness involves anxiety. Such anxiety can be treated with psychotropic drugs, which may reduce the dose of the analgesic required. Phenothiazines in particular are useful in reducing the pain and attendant anxiety in many chronic, organically based conditions, and Merskey (19) has written of his broad experience in this regard.

Pain that is related to or associated with depression may be significantly improved by primary treatment of the depression using the antidepressant drugs. In retarded depression, imipramine is still the drug of choice, and for those patients in whom anxiety is a prominent component, an agent such as amitriptyline or doxepin is indicated. It is important to stress that these medications should be increased stepwise to full therapeutic doses of up to 100–200 mg/day and continued for several months if effective. The disappointing response to these agents is often due to the prescription of inadequate doses.

With regard to the pain-prone patients described previously, many of them are unlikely to be able to give up their symptoms, because of the entailed secondary gain that they derive. Recognition of the dynamics involved can relieve the physician of considerable feelings of frustration and possible guilt in dealing with these patients. In addition, gentle but firm limit-setting concerning the physician's availability and frequency of contact is essential in the long-term management of such patients.

Early rather than late psychiatric consultation is of crucial importance in cases of suspected psychogenic pain. With multiple investigations and surgery, the symptoms become fixed and exceedingly difficult to modify with any kind of treatment. Such referrals may require the greatest of skill and tact on the part of the primary physician, since these patients are often actively hostile to the idea of any emotional element in their clinical picture.

Many situations are not "either/or" in the sense of being either organic or psychogenic, and this is especially true of the conversion reactions. It is pointless and counterproductive to dispute with the patient whether the pain is "real" or not. The absence of detectable organic pathology should alert the physician to the possibility that the patient is employing pain as a communicative device.

As a final note on management, it is worth reiterating the importance of what the clinical psychiatrist calls "secondary gain" and the behaviorist calls "operant reinforcement" in the maintenance of pain symptoms in patients with susceptible personality structures. Common reinforcers for these patients consist of increased attention from relatives, friends, or doctors (which may not be attainable in any other way), excessive or repeated diagnostic investigation, removal from undesired positions of responsibility, and, most importantly, the availability of monetary compensation for their injury or painful disability. In particular, careful thought should be given to obtaining a psychiatric assessment before one approves compensation or disability pensions for patients whose pain is without an apparent or significant organic basis.

In conclusion, pain is the commonest symptom in medical practice yet one of the least understood. The problem of chronic pain states is particularly baffling and frustrating for the patient, his family, and his physician. Increasingly, pain clinics of various sorts are being established to provide consultative help and advice to the medical practitioner who is faced with the management of these patients in the community. Referral to such a facility may be useful in that it may throw new light on the problem and revive the physician's enthusiasm for the long-term management required.

REFERENCES

1. Bonica JJ: Organization and function of a pain clinic. Adv Neurol 4:433–443, 1974
2. Coger R, Werbach M: Attention, anxiety, and the effects of learned enhancement of EEG and in chronic pain: a pilot study in biofeedback. In Crue BL Jr (ed): Pain, Research and Treatment. New York, Academic Press, 1975
3. Crue BL Jr: The present status of therapy for clinical pain states. In Crue BL Jr (ed): Pain, Research and Treatment. New York, Academic Press, 1975
4. Egbert LD, Battit GE, Welch CE, Bartlett MK: Reduction of postoperative pain by encouragement and instruction of patients. N Engl J Med 270:196, 1964
5. Engel GL: "Psychogenic" pain and the pain-prone patient. Am J Med 26:899–918, 1959
6. Fordyce WE: The office management of chronic pain. Learning factors. Minn Med 57:185–188, 1974
7. Fordyce WE, Fowler RS Jr, Lehmann JF, De Lateur BJ: Some implications of learning in problems of chronic pain. J Chronic Dis 21:179–190, 1968
8. Graham DT: Health, disease, and the mind–body problem: linguistic parallelism. Psychosom Med 29:52–71, 1967
9. Hilgard ER: The alleviation of pain by hypnosis. Pain 1:213–231, 1975
10. Krager WS: Hypnotism and acupuncture. JAMA 220:1012, 1972
11. Kroger WS: Behind Chinese acupuncture—hypnosis? In Crue BL Jr (ed): Pain, Research and Treatment. New York, Academic Press, 1975
12. Maline DB, Crue BL Jr: Evolution of the pain center at the City of Hope National Medical Center. In Crue BL Jr (ed): Pain, Research and Treatment. New York, Academic Press, 1975
13. McCranie EJ: Conversion pain. Psychiatr 47:246, 1973
14. Melzack R: The Puzzle of Pain. London, Penguin, 1973
15. Melzack R, Wall PD: Pain mechanisms: a new theory. Science 150:971–979, 1965
16. Merskey H: An Investigation of pain in psychological illness. Oxford, DM Thesis, 1964
17. Merskey H: Psychiatric patients with persistent pain. J Psychosom Res 9:299–309, 1965
18. Merskey H: The characteristics of persistent pain in psychological illness. J Psychosom Res 9:291–298, 1965
19. Merskey H: Psychological aspects of pain relief; hypnotherapy; psychotropic drugs. In Swerdlow M (ed): Monographs in Anesthesiology. I. Relief of Intractable Pain. London, Excerpta Medica, 1974
20. Merskey H, Spear FG: Pain. Psychological and Psychiatric Aspects. London, Ballière, Tridall & Cassell, 1967
21. Pinsky JJ: Psychodynamics and psychotherapy in the treatment of patients with chronic intractable pain. In Crue BL Jr (ed): Pain, Research and Treatment. New York, Academic Press, 1975
22. Sternbach RA: Pain Patients. Traits and Treatment. New York, Academic Press, 1974
23. Szasz T: Pain and Pleasure. A Study of Bodily Feelings. London, Tavistock, 1957
24. Walters A: Psychogenic regional pain alias hysterical pain. Brain 84:1–18, 1961

7 Grief in General Practice

BERNARD SCHOENBERG

Most physicians are not aware of the degree to which human beings are repeatedly confronted with separation and loss, since frequently these events are not readily acknowledged by the individual and therefore are not easily recognized by an observer. In fact, however, at some time during his life, every individual is confronted with the loss of a valued possession. The valued possession may be a loved person, a body part or function, an opportunity, a hope, an aspiration, or the like. The extent of the reaction to such a loss is directly related to the strength of the attachment to the lost object; the stronger the bond, the more intense the sense of loss and the feeling of grief.

Some losses may be anticipated and prepared for, but others may be sudden and unpredictable. The most intense loss is that of a loved person—a parent, spouse, child, or sibling—through death, estrangement, or separation. Another type of profound loss involves the person's mental or physical function and may include the loss of youth, beauty, strength, or sexual ability. The loss of external objects—such as valued possessions, wealth, position, property, or reputation—may also result in profound grief.

The reaction to meaningful loss varies with each individual and is related to early life experiences regarding loss, the relationship that existed with the lost object, the nature of the event, the opportunity to prepare for it, and the environment in which the bereaved individual continues to function, particularly the extent to which it offers social and emotional support and new life opportunities (12).

The usual underlying process observed in the reaction to meaningful loss is mourning, and the subjective experience or feeling of the bereaved person is grief. The term *mourning* is used to describe the normal, adaptive, psychological healing processes that are initiated by the loss, and *grief,* to describe the subjective state that accompanies mourning. Freud stated that the function of mourning ". . . is to detach the survivors' memories and hopes from the dead. When this has been achieved the pain grows less and with it the remorse and self reproach" (6). One of the primary functions of mourning is to permit the withdrawal of emotional attachment from the lost object and allow for attachments to new objects.

THE MOURNING PROCESS

The mourning process is complex, since a variety of contrasting responses coincide and the phases of grief cannot easily be separated from each other. The loss of a loved person, for example, can stimulate only conflicting feelings: the yearning desire to regain the loved individual, intense hatred toward the individual for abandoning the survivor, and feelings of helplessness, despair, and dependency toward others in the environment but still anger toward them for not recovering the lost person, fulfilling dependency needs, or relieving the painful anguish. The balance struck among these conflicting responses varies from individual to individual and is patterned to a large extent by the manner in which experiences of loss were responded to in earlier life. Very likely, the happier the relationship with the lost object, the less conflict experienced. The anger is not as intense, and it is easier for the individual to experience sadness without conflicting feelings of hostility.

Bowlby graphically described the process:

". . . mourning is best regarded as the whole complex sequence of psychological processes and their overt manifestations, beginning with craving, angry efforts at recovery, and appeals for help, proceeding through apathy and disorganization of behavior, and ending when some form of more or less stable reorganization is beginning to develop. Like all biological processes, however, mourning may take one of several different courses. Those which enable the individual ultimately to relate to new objects and to find satisfaction in them are commonly judged healthy, those which fail in this outcome pathological" (2).

Lindemann (1 0), Bowlby, and Klein (7) have described an orderly sequence in the normal mourning process. In the first phase, the bereaved individual is still attached to the original object and strives for reunion. He therefore repeatedly experiences disappointment, severe separation anxiety, and grief. The painful affect associated with the attempts to retain the lost object persists, but despite the individual's conscious awareness of the uselessness of the effort, he is compulsively obliged to continue it. At this time, comfort, reassurance, and sympathy are not appreciated and are, in many instances, resented, since they confront the bereaved with the reality of the loss. The feelings of weakness and helplessness are manifested by lamentation and an appeal to others for assistance in regaining the lost object. Anger may be directed toward the lost person as well as toward those who are held responsible for the loss or who do not help to achieve reunion. In uncomplicated mourning, the futile efforts to maintain or recover the lost object gradually diminishes, and it is eventually relinquished.

In the second phase of mourning, the realization of loss ushers in anguish and despair. Patterns of behavior become disorganized, with restless, aimless, apathetic, searching activity occurring. The individual appears lost and depressed, and his accustomed behavior patterns no longer yield their previous satisfactions.

During the third phase, a reorganization takes place. Emotional investment in the lost object continues, but there is also an orientation toward new individuals and activities. With the resolution of mourning, an equilibrium is gradually reestablished in an environment where the lost person no longer exists and where hope of new relationships is gradually regained.

Recovery may proceed in an uncomplicated way, or mourning may be accompanied by sequelae that interfere with function or cause crippling disability. The rate of recovery may be fast, or in some cases it may be prolonged and last for the remainder of the individual's life.

Difficulties in mourning arise when the anger toward the lost loved person is repressed and displaced to other situations. Abnormal mourning appears to be related largely to an inability to relinquish the love object, that is, to pass through the first phase. Instead, there is a persistent striving to recover the lost person.

TYPES OF GRIEF

Grief has been described as inhibited, delayed, prolonged, absent, or anticipatory; it may be normal or unresolved.

In order to protect oneself against the overwhelming stress of death, psychological defense mechanisms such as denial are usually employed. When the death is expected because of chronic illness, debilitating disease, or old age, the mourning process may have been initiated previously and the degree of shock reduced. Exhaustion, fatigue, anorexia, irritability, and brief episodes of rage are not unusual. Before long, the initial shock diminishes and the reality of the loss gradually penetrates consciousness. The acute phase may last for a short time, or it may continue for a period of months. Most patients begin to improve in six to ten weeks following the loss.

In some cases, the manifestations of the mourning process may not occur for some time after the occurrence of death. The first evidence of grief may be expressed on an anniversary of the death or of marriage or on the deceased person's birthday.

Anticipatory grief is the term used to describe the occurrence of grief prior to loss. Aldrich (1) has recently identified several important differences between conventional and anticipatory grief. He indicated that the latter has a finite end point, dependent on the external circumstances of the physical occurrence of the anticipated loss. Another important difference is that unlike conventional grief, which ordinarily diminishes with the passage of time, anticipatory grief increases in degree as the loss becomes more imminent. In anticipatory grief, there is always an element of hope, and therefore the added responsibility exists of making important decisions that may save the patient from death or delay the loss.

Like grief itself, anticipatory grief may serve an adaptive function in preparing the individual for an impending loss. The common assumption is that if the interval between the time of giving the prognosis and the time that death is expected is considerable, there is opportunity for emotional preparation. Likewise, anticipatory grief can serve an adaptive function for the patient who is awaiting death by allowing him to express feelings which in turn may permit him closer communication with family members.

A number of investigators have described grief as an illness. Engel (4) has pointed out that mourning corresponds closely to other processes that we customarily regard as disease. The grieving person is often manifestly distressed and disabled to a degree that is quite evident to an observer. We can identify a constant causative factor, namely, the real, threatened, or even fantasized object loss. The symptoms and signs of mourning meet the criteria of a discrete syndrome, with a predictable symptomatology and a definite course.

GRIEF AND SOMATIC SYMPTOM FORMATION

Normal grief includes a variety of physical symptoms that frequently require medical attention. Some symptoms are similar to the complaints of depressed or anxious patients, and they may include anorexia, weight loss, insomnia, weakness, fatigue, feelings of debility, impotence, constipation, hypochondriasis, pain, dyspnea, palpitations, restlessness, and a multiplicity of other somatic complaints. Other symptoms include guilt, shame, self-reproach, anxiety attacks, lassitude, fear of death, and a sense of unreality. The prominent symptoms that the dead person had may also be seen in either a direct or modified form.

In recent years, increasing attention has been directed toward the relationship between the death of, or separation from, a loved person and the development of somatic disorders, including death (3). Numerous studies have supported the concept that the mourning process is associated with increased mortality and morbidity. In one study by Rees and Lutkins (13), relatives of a person who died were found to have a much higher mortality rate during the first year of bereavement. During this period, 12.2% of widowed people died, as compared with 1.2%

of a control group. The risk that close relatives would die during the first year was significantly greater when the death that led to bereavement occurred away from home.

In 1964, Parkes (11) compared the medical records of bereaved widows with their records during a period preceding the bereavement. The medical consultation rate for all causes during the first six months of mourning increased by 63%. The rate of utilization of physicians for treating nonpsychiatric symptoms increased by nearly a half in widows of all age groups. It became evident that aged patients, in particular, tend to express their grief through somatic symptoms. Another study by Schmale (15) focused on 42 unselected hospitalized medical patients. He noted that 41 patients experienced actual, threatened, or symbolic loss, accompanied by feelings of helplessness and hopelessness, immediately prior to the onset of disease. In 31 patients, the onset of disease followed within a week of the real or threatened loss that evoked feelings of helplessness or hopelessness. The loss of a loved person has been described as a precipitating factor in the onset or intensification of such diverse diseases as ulcerative colitis, peptic ulcer, asthma, pulmonary tuberculosis, coronary occlusion, heart failure, thyrotoxicosis, rheumatoid arthritis, diabetes, leukemia, pernicious anemia, and multiple sclerosis. Schmale emphasized that loss itself does not establish a cause but rather a setting for the disease.

In 1885, Parker, an American surgeon, singled out the emotion of grief as being especially associated with cancer of the breast. Eight years later, Snow affirmed that the number of breast and uterine cancers that immediately followed antecedent emotions of a depressing character was greatly above chance expectations. Modern studies (9) have also supported the viewpoint that severe loss precedes the development of cancer.

More recently, I and my colleagues (17) have investigated a syndrome, the burning mouth, that has been variously referred to in the scientific literature for the past 50 years as stomatodynia, glossodynia, glossopyrosis, and idiopathic orolingual pain. It has been described as a burning, painful sensation of the oral cavity without a specific, demonstrable organic cause. Of 21 patients studied, 81% were judged to be overtly depressed, and the remaining 19% showed signs of covert depression. The sources of grief included the loss of parents, parental surrogates, siblings, or children, of vision, the uterus, or teeth, and of reproductive function, as symbolized by the menopause. In agreement with others, we postulated that unresolved grief is one of the conditions that allows a number of disease processes to appear.

ABNORMAL MOURNING AND GRIEF

Less than 5% of individuals may become fixed in the first phase of the mourning process and be unable to extricate themselves from the compulsive striving to reunite with the lost person. This inability to move on and gradually invest emotionally in other relationships is the major constituent of pathological or unresolved mourning. Unresolved grief may take a number of forms, and it may include a variety of neurotic or psychotic reactions, psychophysiological reactions, and asocial or sociopathic behavior. Its protracted course and its exaggerated and excessive nature provide common warnings that the grief may be abnormal or pathological.

The bereaved may persist in the denial of death and behave as if the lost individual is still alive. The painful feelings of grief may be denied, and feelings and actions in relation to the deceased may be expressed whose inappropriateness is easily recognized. The bereaved individual will typically refer to the deceased in the present tense and report repetitive dreams wherein the survivor may struggle to rescue the dead person.

Doubt regarding the person's death will at times come to the surface unexpectedly, and illusions of seeing the dead person in a crowd on the street are not uncommon. In other situations, the death is verbally acknowledged, but the emotional impact and the significance of the loss remain unconscious. The intense emotional reaction may be displaced or projected by the bereaved onto others, onto a sibling or child, for example. At times, the survivor may turn to others in an unrealistic way to fulfill the needs previously gratified by the dead person.

The failure to resolve grief is illustrated in the following case (3):

Case 1. Ms. A. was a 46-year-old married woman who reported that following extensive dental work, she suffered a sharp, excruciating, burning pain, which she described as "if my mouth would go up in flames." Her pain became worse, and she received treatment from dentists, otolaryngologists, oral surgeons, neurologists, internists, and a psychiatrist, with no relief of symptoms. Five years before, following the death of her mother, she had had insomnia. She readily stated that she had never accepted her mother's death and has been in a state of continuous mourning. She was still unable to dispose of her mother's clothes and dreamed of her frequently. She compared her present state to the postpartum reaction after the birth of her first child, stating that she "was deathly ill for three years, depressed, and neurasthenic."

She agreed to start psychotherapy, following repeated complaints of despair, guilt, and depression. She made frequent slips in referring to her mother in the present tense, and she complained of her inability to accept the reality of previous deaths of other family members. Despite frequent interpretations indicating to her that her pain was psychogenic, she continued to seek a physical explanation for her symptoms. One day prior to the anniversary of her mother's death, she persuaded a dentist to extract another tooth, although "we both knew it was a perfectly healthy tooth." Several days later, following her husband's unexpected business failure and her inability to find the relief promised by an oral surgeon through local injections, she committed suicide by ingesting large quantities of drugs that she had collected over a period of time.

The identification of the survivor with the deceased person was evident in the case of another patient who was unable to resolve the mourning process (17):

Case 2. A 69-year-old woman complained of soreness and burning of the upper and lower lips. Other complaints included indigestion, paresthesias, vague bodily concerns, and insomnia. Her husband had died of oral carcinoma about six years earlier, and following his death, she was cautioned by her physician to suppress her grief since she had previously had a myocardial infarction. Shortly after his death, she developed mouth ulcers, and five years later, a she began to have burning sensation of the mouth. Her physicians could find no physical basis for her complaints.

Symptoms can also develop preceding a loss, when grief is precipitated by an anticipated death:

Case 3. A 53-year-old subway worker complained of having had a burning sensation and irritation of his mouth and tongue for the past two years. He attributed his symptoms to extreme nervousness over a period of five years, which had been relieved somewhat through the use of tranquilizers.

When interviewed, he dated the onset of his symptoms to his mother's colostomy following surgery for carcinoma of the colon five years before. Since that time, he had been markedly depressed and in fear of death.

Following the development of organic symptoms, the grief may at times be gradually dissipated (14):

Case 4. A 50-year-old married woman lost her adult daughter, who died of disseminated cancer. The patient responded with intense sorrow and anger, and she isolated herself from any social contact. Within the first two years following her loss, she began to suffer from Meniere's syndrome and cholecystitis, and she had a coronary occlusion. As she gradually recovered and renewed her social relationships, the somatic complaints diminished.

LOSS OF BODY PARTS

Physicians frequently treat patients who have experienced many significant kinds of loss in addition to the death of an individual. The loss of a body part or its functioning—including limb amputation, mastectomy, or bodily disfigurement—is psychologically comparable to the loss of a significant person. If the mourning process is prolonged or unusually severe, emotional complications may occur. In evaluating the effect of the loss, the special or unique significance to the individual should be considered.

Case 5. A 54-year-old unmarried man had compensated for an unhappy childhood, in which his parents contributed to his feeling weak, ineffective, and feminine. He placed undue emphasis on physical strength and athletic ability, discontinuing his graduate studies to become a high school football coach. He prided himself on his ability to surpass his students in athletics. He refused to cooperate in the control of his diabetes, and gangrene of one leg developed. Following its amputation, he showed signs of withdrawal and depression. Despite strenuous efforts at rehabilitation by his physician, he committed suicide.

The loss of reproductive function may initiate a mourning process with the manifestations of severe grief. Failure to resolve the mourning process may lead to physical symptoms and complaints.

Case 6. A 60-year-old married woman described her presenting problem as a "burning sensation in the oral cavity which travels." The sensation started nine years previously with the onset of menopause. Numerous attempts by a variety of medical specialists to treat her symptoms were unsuccessful. She had suffered from attacks of migraine headache accompanying the menses for 25 years. The migraine headaches disappeared with the onset of her current symptoms. She denied any feelings of grief, but she apparently was depressed.

The previous medical history of a patient may indicate how a patient will deal with loss.

Case 7. A 42-year-old woman with a lifelong history of somatic complaints and hypochondriacal symptoms was discovered to have a lump in her breast. Prompt treatment by mastectomy and radiotherapy resulted in a five-year cure. Despite reassurance, however, she remained a chronic invalid, dependent upon her mother and older sisters to manage her household.

GRIEF AND THE PHYSICIAN

Recent advances in biomedical science and technology have resulted in increasing numbers of patients being treated for longer periods of time. The lives of cancer patients have been significantly prolonged because of methods for earlier detection, more effective surgical methods, new chemotherapeutic agents, progress in the utilization of radiotherapy, and combinations of modalities, which have not only increased the chances of survival but have also increased the period of illness preceding death. Thus, the care of the dying has become a more significant aspect of health care.

Health personnel, nevertheless, continue to receive meager support in providing care for the dying and a minimal opportunity to deal with their emotional reactions to death. The physician's reactions to his own feelings will determine, to a considerable degree, how the patient deals with his anticipated death and the course of the patient's future relationship with his family. Health personnel place great emphasis on the preservation of life and generally view a patient's death as a personal failure. For the physician, avoiding the issues associated with death is related to prized professional values of success and to maintaining self-esteem. Studies have validated the view that physicians, in general, have a greater fear of death than others, and they may use their profession as a means of controlling this fear of death (5).

In caring for the dying patient and the bereaved family, the primary goal of the physician should be to establish a relationship based on trust and confidence, in which they feel free to express their fears, feelings, and thoughts. For the physician, the usual gratifications may be absent in the care of the dying patient or the bereaved family. In his identification with the patient, his own childhood feelings of separation, abandonment, and injury are recalled, as well as the consequent feelings of grief. In order to overcome his feelings of helplessness and grief, the physician may become emotionally and physically inaccessible, or he may engage in premature activity or needless procedures.

As a result of the trend in modern medical care toward strict division of labor in caring for patients, many traditional functions of the physician have been transferred to others, and, as a consequence, have diluted the physician's most useful therapeutic method, the traditional one-to-one relationship. This division of labor allows the physician to withdraw by delegating his responsibility to others. The result of this process is the disruption of that continuity of care which is of primary importance in establishing a feeling of security in the patient.

The emotional withdrawal of health personnel is frequently based on their need to protect themselves against their own feelings of loss and consequent feelings of grief. The unfortunate result is that the patient is dealt with as if he were already dead. It is therefore especially important that physicians become more aware of their reactions to loss. They need to understand that grief is a normal response and that providing an opportunity to express and discuss their feelings with colleagues and others will lead to better management of their patients and the bereaved family members. If physicians remain unaware of their own feelings and have no outlets for expressing them, these feelings will undoubtedly interfere with effective treatment of their patients.

MANAGEMENT

In order to develop information on which to base specific recommendations for the management of bereaved patients, a number of surveys were conducted. One recent survey was distributed to general practitioners, surgeons, internists, psychiatrists, and psychoanalysts (8). More than three-fourths of the respondents predicted in bereaved persons the appearance of common signs of grief—such as weight loss, anorexia, sleeplessness, and feelings of helplessness and despair—prior to the death of the patient. There was common agreement that the one concerned with the deceased person would have dreams of him and would experience illusions. The same number expected that angry thoughts and feelings toward the deceased would be expressed at times, and more than half predicted the development of guilt feelings. Again, more than half thought that the bereaved would sometimes have subjective symptoms similar to those of the deceased. A large percentage of physicians predicted diminished sexual desire, impotence, or an inclination to masturbation in the bereaved. More than three-fourths of the physicians expressed the opinion that guilt feelings would be less when there had been a free expression of feelings between the bereaved and the patient.

In this survey, more than 70% suggested that during the first year of bereavement, regular visits to the physician should be encouraged. Of significance is the strong agreement that the bereaved should not be hospitalized for elective surgical procedures soon after or during the course of the bereavement. Most physicians agreed that the expression of feelings and tears, rather than repression, should be encouraged, and almost half of the group felt that the repression of distressing memories should not be encouraged. Rather, they favored encouraging the bereaved to speak about the recent bereavement and, specifically, to discuss with someone their feelings concerning the deceased. Physicians were in general agreement that the bereaved, if elderly, would profit from new companionships, a pet, a new living arrangement, or a new vocation. Three-fourths of those surveyed agreed that work should be resumed within two weeks. Most physicians regarded work as being helpful to the bereaved during the mourning period.

Parkes, in his study of 44 unselected widows (11), found that 75% had consulted their general practitioner during the first six months of bereavement. More than one-third complained of symptoms that were clearly psychological and had been treated with sedatives or tranquilizers. He concluded, "In general, physical treatments of this kind were all that the G.P. gave or was expected to give. This finding seems to reflect a change in attitude towards grief which is coming to be seen as an illness to be treated . . ." (11).

Schmale (16) recently expressed the belief that normal grief cannot be delayed or changed in any major way by drugs, and no overdependent person becomes dependent on drugs when there are substitute individuals to depend upon. Physicians have traditionally offered sedation to immediate family members to be taken the first several nights after the death. He noted that "those who cannot tolerate frustration and are heavy users of alcohol, food or drugs as a means to avoid involvement may continue to do so during a period of bereavement. Those who are able to grieve will do so and nothing including drugs will prevent the process from running its course" (16).

In abnormal or unresolved grief reactions, a wide variety of emotional disturbances are observed. Those patients suffering from acute anxiety may improve if given drugs in the sedative-hypnotic group, whereas others with more neurotic manifestations would appear to benefit from the minor tranquilizers. For patients with prolonged, severe anxiety reactions, mania, or manic depression, the administration of a major tranquilizer is indicated. This group of patients would profit from psychiatric consultation and psychotherapy. The primarily depressed, neurotic patient who has minimal anxiety is effectively treated with an antidepressant. In mixed states of anxiety and depression, combinations of tranquilizers and antidepressants can be useful. The physician's prescribing of drugs may symbolize for the patient a gratification of his dependency feelings and produce in him the realization that the physician is concerned with his welfare.

Whatever the psychopharmacological agent utilized, drug therapy should be seen as only one element in the total effort to assist the patient in his attempt to resolve the mourning process successfully. Environmental manipulation and psychotherapy are usually important adjuncts to pharmacological treatments.

Most important is the willingness of the physician to listen sympathetically and to assist the patient in his attempt to restore his emotional and social equilibrium. The unique susceptibility of the bereaved to physical and emotional illness requires that the physician give serious attention to all complaints. Above all, to be effective in assisting the bereaved, the physician should be alert to his own feelings regarding loss and be accepting of his own helplessness.

REFERENCES

1. Aldrich CK: Some dynamics in anticipatory grief. In Schoenberg B, Carr AC, et al. (eds): Anticipatory Grief. New York, Columbia University Press, 1974

2. Bowlby J: Processes of mourning. Int Psychoanal 42:317–40, 1961

3. Carr AC, Schoenberg B: Object loss and somatic symptom formation. In Schoenberg B, Carr AC, et al. (eds): Loss and Grief: Psychological Management in Medical Practice. New York, Columbia University Press, 1970

4. Engel GL: Is grief a disease? A challenge for medical research. Psychosom Med 23:18, 1961

5. Feifel H: Death. In Faberow NL (ed): Taboo Topics. New York, Atherton Press, 1963

6. Freud S: Mourning and melancholia (1917). In The Complete Psychological Works of Sigmund Freud, Vol XIV. London, Hogarth Press, 1957

7. Klein M: Mourning and its relation to manic-depressive states. In Contributions to Psychoanalysis. London, Hogarth Press, 1948, pp 311–338

8. Kutscher AH: Practical aspects of bereavement in loss and grief. In Schoenberg B et al. (eds): Loss and Grief: Psychological Management in Medical Practice. New York, Columbia University Press, 1970, pp 280–297

9. LeShan LL, Worthington RE: Personality as a factor in the pathogenesis of cancer: a review of the literature. BR J Med Psych 29: 40, 1956

10. Lindemann E: Symptomatology and management of acute grief. Am J Psychiatry 101:141–148, 1944

11. Parkes CM: Effects of bereavement on physical and mental health: a study of the medical records of widows. Br Med J 2:274, 1964

12. Parkes CM: Bereavement: Studies of Grief in Adult Life. New York, IUP, 1972

13. Rees WD, Lutkins SG: Mortality of bereavement. Br Med J 4:13, 1967

14. Romm MC: Loss of sexual function in the female. In Schoenberg B, Carr AC et al. (eds): Loss and Grief: Psychological Management in Medical Practice. New York, Columbia University Press, 1970

15. Schmale AH: Relationship of separation and depression to disease. Psychosom Med 20:259, 1958

16. Schmale AH: Normal grief is not a disease. In Goldberg IK, Malitz S, Kutscher AH (eds): Psychopharmacologic Agents for the Terminally Ill and Bereaved. New York, Columbia University Press, 1973

17. Schoenberg B, Carr AC, Kutscher A, Zegarelli E: Idiopathic orolingual pain. NY State Med 71 (5):1832–1837, 1971

8

Hemodialysis and Renal Transplantation— Psychopathological Reactions and Their Management

CHARLES V. FORD, PIETRO CASTELNUOVO-TEDESCO

The development of the artificial kidney in the late 1950s and the subsequent introduction of new immunosuppressive agents have led to new and important therapeutic opportunities. Persons previously doomed by terminal uremia now may have their lives prolonged by hemodialysis or by receiving a transplanted kidney. These new clinical interventions, though clearly beneficial, have also created new major stresses for the kidney patient and significant challenges to his psychological integrity. The frequent psychiatric complications of these forms of treatment were noted early in the history of their application, and thus the relevant literature has burgeoned since 1960; over 125 publications have been reviewed in the English language alone. Although this work has originated from scattered parts of the world (*e.g.,* from the United States, England, Australia, Scandinavia, Israel, and France), the findings that have been reported show remarkable similarity, attesting to the universality of human response. Anecdotal reports in the early 1960s were followed by well-described series and prospective studies.

This survey will emphasize the clinical aspects of the field, while acknowledging that the ethical and moral issues are also of importance (4, 55). The material has been divided into sections for ease of organization, even though such arbitrary division of the clinical syndromes is admittedly artificial, since a host of factors constantly interact in these cases.

PSYCHIATRIC ASPECTS OF HEMODIALYSIS

THE DIALYSIS SITUATION: PSYCHOLOGICAL IMPLICATIONS

The patient for whom chronic hemodialysis is recommended has generally suffered from months to years of progressive renal failure. Characteristically, he has been troubled by fatigue, apathy, drowsiness, and increasing difficulty with concentration (64). Since the patient has also experienced decreased libido, poor appetite, and irritable behavior, he may be mistakenly diagnosed as depressed. If these manifestations are more marked, and particularly if they are accompanied by disturbances of thought, the patient may be prejudged to be a chronic psychotic. It is essential that these symptoms be recognized as indicative of an organic brain syndrome secondary to uremia, rather than be regarded as a psychiatric contraindication to hemodialysis. In fact, these symptoms clear up quite promptly once dialysis treatment begins (75, 78).

The patient usually approaches dialysis with considerable apprehension, because of fears of pain, injury, or death, as well as because of the realization that his life now depends upon the proper functioning of a complex and unfamiliar machine (16, 58, 65). The patient is particularly vulnerable to anxiety while he is connected to the machine and is watching his blood move in and out of his body through plastic tubing, which, in the regressive atmosphere of dialysis, becomes like an umbilical cord. This experience inevitably influences the integrity of the patient's body image (2, 4, 12, 65). Growing familiarity with dialysis procedures gradually reduces the patient's anxiety, but it returns quite predictably whenever the complications of long-term treatment occur.

The patient who is newly started on hemodialysis generally experiences a marked increase in physical well-being together with greater optimism and cheerfulness, occasionally to the point of euphoria (2). This "honeymoon" period, however, is replaced later by a mood of disenchantment and discouragement that often amounts to a true depression (58). The realization grows that hemodialysis, though lifesaving, is demanding and imposes a very specific dependency on the machine. Other problems include a highly restricted diet, financial sacrifice, and often painful physical complications (such as clotting or infections at shunt sites). Some patients continue to struggle with the feeling that life is not worth the demands of treatment, whereas others work through their feelings about the situation and accept realistically the compromises necessary for the maintenance of life. Still others manage to exist only for the hope that in time, transplantation will free them from the machine (5).

Many authors have stressed that these patients employ denial to a marked degree (1, 7, 16, 66). It may help the patient through some of the complications of treatment by offering hope for life and improvement. Denial, however, may also be detrimental in that the patient, in denying crucial aspects of his illness, may fail to follow medical advice. Moreover, it leaves him vulnerable to severe depression if the defense breaks down.

Another frequently noted characteristic of dialysis patients is the conflict of dependency versus independency (2, 4, 33, 39, 58, 71). The dialysis patient is in a highly dependent situation that predisposes toward regression (71). His life is literally in the hands of the personnel who operate the dialysis equipment. Persons who previously have dealt with dependency conflicts by assuming counterdependent behavior cannot easily relinquish control over their lives (4). On the other hand, the patient who has been disabled for some time by progressive uremia must often face the expectations of his family and the medical staff that he resume an independent and productive life. Some patients who have surrendered to their passive-dependent longings resent demands that they now care for themselves (58). Others find hemodialysis a solution to conflicts inherent in their marriage or employment, and these patients readily accept the chronic dependency it promotes (20, 33).

Children undergoing dialysis suffer many of the same problems as adults, but in addition the experience introduces important changes in the family interaction. The child is likely to be overprotected, which may have a detrimental effect on his normal maturation. These problems, however, can be at least partially overcome if the treatment team attends to them (43, 44, 57, 73).

PSYCHOPATHOLOGICAL SYNDROMES

Overt psychotic reactions, though not the rule, are not uncommon in patients undergoing hemodialysis (4, 13, 64, 65, 71). It is difficult to separate organic from functional causes, since in these cases, both factors interact. Rapid changes in serum electrolyte levels and blood osmolarity affect brain function (52, 66), and, at the same time, the emotional stress of a life-threatening illness and of the dialysis experience with its potential for regression (71) can precipitate a psychotic decompensation. The psychotic episodes, which may be characterized by hallucinations and delusions, are generally short lived and respond well to conservative, supportive management. Psychotropic medications have been successfully used in this context (13, 40, 52).

Depression is a major problem among hemodialysis patients, and it may significantly influence their medical management. The patient on dialysis is subject to multiple losses, including the loss of body parts or functions, the failure of plans, and changes in his life pattern, finances, and occupation (76). Gratification becomes more difficult as physical and sexual capabilities diminish and interpersonal problems increase. Paradoxically, it is precisely these relationships with significant persons that most influence the patient's ability to withstand the repeated assaults on his narcissism.

Lefebvre *et al.* (46) have commented that the dialysis patient can neither view himself as healthy nor really experience the mourning work of death, since it is continually being postponed. The deaths of other patients may precipitate widespread depression in the dialysis unit (65), not only because they entail major personal losses, but also because they help break through the patients' denial that allows them to believe that they can live indefinitely on the machine.

The extent of the depression that occurs is dramatically shown by the high incidence of suicide among dialysis patients. Abram *et al.* (5) calculate that if one includes intentional suicides, those who withdraw from the program, and deaths due to not following the treatment regimen, the total incidence is 400 times that of suicide in the general population. Death may be by the usual means, by exsanguination after intentionally disconnecting the shunt or cannula (59), or by a deliberate binge of proscribed foods (60). The rejection or loss of a transplanted kidney may be a significant factor in suicidal behavior (59). Patients have an immense investment in the transplanted kidney, which is regarded as a means of escaping the dreaded dependency on hemodialysis. Typically, many look to transplantation to free them from hemodialysis once and for all. Thus, kidney rejection signals the need to return to dialysis, possibly indefinitely, and for some, this is intolerable. Patients undergoing dialysis at home have a much lower incidence of suicide. This is probably due to several factors, including the facts that the healthiest and most independent patients are generally selected for home dialysis (28) and that home dialysis patients, being actively involved in their own treatment, are less likely to become regressed or fatalistic (29).

Adherence to diet is essential for the patient on dialysis. Potassium, protein, and fluids need to be limited. The patient's failure to adhere to the diet can cause multiple problems and may result in his death. Although dietary abuse has an obvious self-destructive quality, it must not be assumed to be suicidal or presuicidal behavior in all circumstances. Goldstein and Reznikoff (29) have noted that with chronic illness and hemodialysis, the patient begins to see himself as having little control over his life. If he does not perceive his behavior as related to his condition, then the likelihood of his rejecting personal responsibility for medical treatment increases. Abuse of diet may also represent an effort to deny the illness itself and the dependency upon the machine. A well-educated man told one of the authors that periodically he "cheated" on his diet in the hope of finding that the disease magically had gone away. Dietary indiscretions can also be a transference reaction to the demands of the medical staff; by such acting out, a patient can express hostility that is otherwise repressed (36). Patients with low frustration tolerance simply may not be able to discipline themselves. Others may consciously or unconsciously abuse their diet as a means of remaining sick and reaping the secondary gains of illness (20, 36).

FACTORS PREDICTING ADJUSTMENT TO HEMODIALYSIS

Efforts have been made to predict which patients will tolerate successfully the severe stresses of hemodialysis. When dialysis programs were beginning, few patients could be accepted for treatment, and the emphasis was placed on selecting those who were, if not the most deserving, at least able to show the best response. As programs have expanded, the goal of predictive studies has shifted to that of identifying those who may need additional psychological support.

Intelligence and willingness to admit to some anxiety have been shown to be associated with better adjustment (63). Patients who used somatizing defenses did more poorly. On the other hand, depression and anxiety, as measured by the Minnesota Multiphasic Personality Inventory (MMPI) and the Multiple Affect Adjective Check List (MAACL) after one week of home dialysis, presaged a poor adjustment one year later (25). There is also evidence that the way in which patients have dealt with major changes in their lives prior to the onset of kidney disease may be used to predict their adjustment to treatment. Those who previously had adjusted well did well on dialysis and were rehabilitated sufficiently to be able to work (49, 50). The patients' expectations of rehabilitation were important; those with a negative outlook did not return to work (50). The factors of high intelligence and organ damage, when found to be present before dialysis, favored a more rapid initial adjustment to treatment, but these variables lost their predictive value after 12 months (30). A habitual disposition to react with repressive defenses in a flexible way was found to promote early adaptation, whereas the tendency to isolation and withdrawal had a negative prognostic significance (30). Similarly, a habit of maintaining regular social contacts was associated with the likelihood of good adjustment (31). Patients who had a high frustration tolerance and obsessive-compulsive features but who also rejected dependency needs did better in regard to adherence to diet and in vocational rehabilitation (19). A study of the factors associated with survival on chronic hemodialysis showed that an affiliation with the Roman Catholic faith, the continued presence of one or both parents, a low mean blood urea nitrogen (BUN) level, and an apparent indifference to fellow dialysis patients were statistically correlated with the survival group (26). From the number of parameters studied, however, some of these factors may have separated out by chance.

Successful adaptation to dialysis has often been assessed in terms of vocational rehabilitation. As Sullivan (68) has noted, however, home dialysis is in itself a full-time job, and it is hardly reasonable to expect a patient to invest another 40 hours a week in paid employment to achieve "successful rehabilitation."

PSYCHOTHERAPEUTIC MANAGEMENT

Following the early recognition of the psychological difficulties of dialysis patients, a variety of therapeutic recommendations have been made. Although several authors (3, 33, 41, 69) have written about their experiences with individual psychotherapy, little has been said about specific techniques, and one is left with the impression that the involvement was primarily supportive and relationship oriented. Principally, the patient is prompted to express feelings about approaching death (3, 33, 41), to verbalize anger and aggressive feelings toward the treatment staff (3, 33), and to discuss the dependency-independency conflicts that are so common in the dialysis setting (3, 33). Partial, time-limited regression has been allowed, as appropriate for the state of the patient's physical health (33). Abram (3) has stated that direct confrontation often is not indicated, and he has suggested the use of therapeutic maneuvers, especially environmental manipulations, based on psychodynamic understanding of the patient. This requires close liaison between the psychiatrist and the other members of the health-care team. The importance of the psychiatrist as an interpreter of the patient's behavior to the staff has also been suggested by others (40, 51), and several authors have commented on the value of regular attendance by the psychiatrist at the staff meetings of the dialysis unit (24, 35, 51). A modified group-therapy situation involving the medical staff, the patients, and their families has been described as useful (32, 67). The need to support the whole family unit, not just the patient has been emphasized (16, 45).

Patients are not alone in experiencing psychological problems in the dialysis setting (27, 35, 53). Physicians, nurses, and ancillary personnel face the continual anxiety of responsibility, suffer the despair of defeat when patients die, and are the recipients of the patients' transference reactions. Understandably, the staff often withdraws emotionally or makes inappropriate responses to the patients. Thus, the psychiatric consultant may be more effective if he works with the entire therapeutic milieu than merely with individual patients (16). The psychiatrist's involvement with the individual patient using goal-limited psychotherapy remains, however, a valuable part of the treatment program (34, 66).

Psychotherapeutic work with dialysis patients is emotionally draining. The patients' massive use of denial (3, 66) and their limited interest in people reduce their ability to form new relationships (33). The fact that the patients are struggling with a life-threatening illness (9) and have a limited life span inevitably influences the therapist's ability to maintain enthusiasm for treatment.

Group therapy has been recommended for dialysis patients (77). On the other hand, the point has been made that for highly anxious patients with a brief expected life span, the examination of interpersonal issues may do more harm than good (34).

Another factor that influences the adjustment of patients to dialysis is the expectations of the treatment team. Patients are more likely to be seen as making a good adjustment when the team has realistic expectations for their success (37, 38).

PSYCHIATRIC ASPECTS OF RENAL TRANSPLANTATION

The patient who is considered for organ transplantation has generally endured a protracted period of disability and the expectation of an early death. The acquisition of a new organ typically offers hope of prolonging life and perhaps even of returning to normal activities.

As of 1975, renal transplantation, based on the experience of over 20,000 operations, has become an accepted surgical procedure, although the transplantation of other organs continues to be regarded as experimental. Renal transplantation has a unique psychological feature in that the kidney to be transplanted may be obtained either from a cadaver or from a living donor. This has resulted in complex interpersonal relations between recipients and donors. Considerable attention has been given in the literature to the motivation of kidney donors (14, 15, 22, 23, 61, 62).

TRANSPLANT RECIPIENTS: PSYCHOLOGICAL FEATURES

A remarkably high incidence of postoperative psychiatric problems is found among renal transplantation recipients. Penn *et al.* (56) found that 32% of 292 patients had emotional difficulties, mainly depressive or anxiety reactions, and over 10% had psychotic organic brain syndromes. Other authors have also described psychotic reactions following renal transplantation (48, 74). The use of steroids in massive doses as immunosuppressive agents has been well recognized as a causative factor in these postoperative psychiatric reactions.

In the immediate postoperative period, kidney transplant patients often respond with euphoria, occasionally to the point of hypomania. This is related both to feelings of being "reborn" as well as to the influence of exogenous steroids (11, 48). Fairly soon, however, these reactions give way in most cases to less disguised psychological distress. Anxiety is a constant problem, since it is unknown, in each instance, how long the allograph will remain viable (9, 17). Episodes of rejection occur unpredictably. Depression is always just under the surface, since the patients usually realize that the transplanted kidney is but a temporary solution (7, 17, 41). Many patients, however, manage to maintain some hope by reminding themselves that, should rejection become irreversible, they can always fall back upon chronic hemodialysis or perhaps receive another transplant. Another loss that must be worked through is that of fantasied restoration of health (41). Repeated minor complications, changes in appearance secondary to the administration of exogenous steroids, and rejection crises all serve to remind the patient that he is not truly well. It is understandable, therefore, that the patient may find himself wondering whether life with a transplanted organ or with hemodialysis really is worthwhile (7).

Postoperatively, psychic conflicts regarding sexual identity are prominent and are likely to be intensified when the kidney is from a donor of the opposite sex (6, 11, 14, 18, 54). Basch (6) has described the panic of a young man upon learning that his donor brother was homosexual. This type of reaction may be more pronounced in adolescents, who are concerned about their identity as part of normal maturation. The organ transplant recipient must also deal with feelings of guilty indebtedness, whether or not the donor is living (6, 7, 14, 72). Thus, several recipients of cadaver kidneys developed hand-washing compulsions (6). When the kidney was received from a living donor, the recipient's sense of indebtedness may influence significantly his relationship with the donor (42, 72). The transplant patient also may feel as if he suddenly has acquired certain personality features of the donor (11, 47). An adolescent patient of Castelnuovo-Tedesco believed himself "more mature" after receiving the kidney of an older man (11).

The psychological integration of the new organ into the body scheme of the recipient takes some time and may not occur smoothly. Castelnuovo-Tedesco (10, 11) has stressed that transplantation is a *life-extending process* and that the body image must be enlarged to include the new organ, which at first is perceived as a foreign body. Muslin (54) has described the various stages in the incorporation of the transplanted organ, ranging from the "foreign-body" stage to that of reasonably complete integration. The opportunities for regression, accompanied by a failure to integrate the transplant, are considerable. The extent to which the recipient can psychologically accept the new organ depends largely on the quality of his relationship with the donor, both real and fantasied (72). Viederman (72) has reported the case of a black man who fantasized that his transplanted cadaver kidney was from a white woman. He repeatedly said, "The kidney will reject me." He received some relief, however, when he learned that it came from a black woman.

The relationship of the patient's psychological status to the continued acceptance of the transplanted organ has received some notice. Several authors have commented that acute rejection or death followed very soon after some major disruption of a close interpersonal relationship (6, 17, 21, 54, 70). Thus, Eisendrath (21), in reporting on the deaths of 11 kidney transplant patients, found that eight who died had experienced unusual panic, pessimism, or a sense of abandonment, whereas those who survived had not.

LIVING KIDNEY DONORS: PSYCHOLOGICAL FEATURES

Giving a part of one's self to another is a noble act, especially when the gift involves pain, permanent disfigurement (scarring), and some risk of morbidity and mortality. Many persons make this offer—some eagerly in response to the patient's needs, some reluctantly because of family coercion or from a sense of guilt (15, 22, 23, 42, 62). Individual motivations are complex and may be unconsciously determined, yet the decision to donate is often impulsive (23). Mothers tend to be the most willing donors, siblings the least. The latter, not infrequently, are negatively influenced toward the decision of donorship by their spouses.

Theoretically, when a body part is lost, some depression or grief can be anticipated. Kemph (41) has commented on this as well as on the need for the kidney donor to be supported psychologically during the postoperative period. Other authors, however, have found little such depression (22, 23, 61, 62).

Whatever the motivation, postoperatively the donor often takes a proprietary interest in the recipient (14). Since the donor is generally a close family member, this may alter family interactional patterns and reactivate old conflicts (42).

PSYCHOTHERAPEUTIC MANAGEMENT

Considering the frequency of severe psychiatric symptoms following transplantation and the probability that the patient's psychological status may affect his longevity as well as the quality of his life, it is not surprising that psychotherapeutic techniques are an important aspect of the overall medical care of such cases. Kemph (41) has stressed that both kidney donors and recipients may require support and an opportunity to ventilate feelings of guilt, anger, or loss. This may prevent the occurrence of frank depressive reactions. Crombez and Lefebvre (18) have stressed that the "giving up" syndrome should be regarded as a psychiatric emergency; the syndrome may be resolved if the treatment permits the verbalization of conflict and clarifies the distinction between past and present losses.

Various preventive psychotherapeutic techniques have been offered. Eisendrath (21) suggests the use of preoperative psychotherapy to assess family relations and establish rapport. Castelnuovo-Tedesco (10) has recommended that the patient be familiarized with the hospital personnel prior to the operation to help prevent stereotyped and infantile transferences to the staff. Brock *et al.* (8) have described how familiarization with both the staff and the medical procedures involved was achieved by means of preoperative workshops for the patients, their families, and involved friends. These workshops achieved increased rapport with the medical staff and reduced anxiety and depression.

SUMMARY

Hemodialysis and transplantation are closely intertwined modalities of treatment in the experience of most patients with chronic renal failure. Both therapies, while serving to prolong life, also create a host of psychological stresses that often give rise to distinct psychopathological syndromes. The contribution of organic factors, secondary to uremia and treatment with steroids, should not be minimized and must be responded to as much as possible. It is essential, however, that the serious psychological predicament of the patient also be understood. Specifically, the patient is subject to chronic anxiety and to the realization that treatment is still quite imperfect and does not cure his basic disease. He must be able to accept diminished function. Psychological management is necessarily *supportive* and must be based on a close knowledge of the patient's current life situation. It is most effective when it becomes a part of the total medical care and when it can make allowances for the inevitable frustrations of the staff as well as for the continuing stresses borne by the patient.

REFERENCES

1. Abram HS: The psychiatrist, the treatment of chronic renal failure and the prolongation of life. I. Am J Psychiatry 124:1351–1358, 1968
2. Abram HS: The psychiatrist, the treatment of chronic renal failure and the prolongation of life. II. Am J Psychiatry 126:157–167, 1969
3. Abram HS: Psychotherapy in renal failure. Curr Psychiatr Ther 9:86–92, 1969
4. Abram HS: Survival by machine: The psychological stress of chronic hemodialysis. Psychiatry Med 1:37–51, 1970
5. Abram HS, Moore GI, Westervelt FB: Suicidal behavior in chronic dialysis patients. Am J Psychiatry 127:1204–1207, 1971
6. Basch SH: The intrapsychic integration of a new organ. Psychoanal Q 52:364–384, 1973
7. Beard BH: Fear of death and fear of life: the dilemma in chronic renal failure, hemodialysis and kidney transplantation. Arch Gen Psychiatry 21:373–380, 1969
8. Brock D, Lawson RK, Bennett WM: Preoperative workshops with patients waiting for kidney transplants. Transplant Proc 5:1059–1060, 1973
9. Calland CH: Iatrogenic problems in end-stage renal failure. N Engl J Med 287:334–336, 1972
10. Castelnuovo–Tedesco P: Psychoanalytic considerations in a case of cardiac transplantation. In Arieti S (ed): The World Biennial of Psychiatry and Psychotherapy. New York, Basic Books, 1971
11. Castelnuovo–Tedesco P: Organ transplant, body image psychosis. Psychoanal Q 42: 349–363, 1973
12. Cazzulo CL, Invernizzi G, Ventura R, Sostero M: Psychosomatic implications in chronic hemodialysis. Psychother Psychosom 22:341–346, 1973
13. Cooper AJ: Hypomanic psychosis precipitated by hemodialysis. Compr Psychiatry 8: 168–174, 1967
14. Cramond WA: Renal homotransplantation—some observations on recipients and donors. Br J Psychiatry 113:1223–1230, 1967
15. Cramond WA, Court JH, Higgins PR et al.: Psychological screening of potential donors in a renal homotransplantation programme. Br J Psychiatry 113:1213–1221, 1967
16. Cramond WA, Knight PR, Lawrence JR: The psychiatric contribution to a renal unit undertaking chronic hemodialysis and renal homotransplantation. Br J PSychiatry 113: 1201–1212, 1967
17. Christopherson LK, Gonda TA: Patterns of grief: end stage renal failure and kidney transplantation. Transplant Proc 5:1051–1057, 1973
18. Crombez JC, Lefebvre P: The behavioral responses of renal transplant patients as seen through their fantasy life. Can Psychiatr Assoc J [Suppl] 17:19–23, 1972
19. Czaczkes JW, Kaplan-DeNour A: Selection of patients for regular haemodialysis. Proc Eur Dial Transplant Assoc 9:167–172, 1972
20. Dansak DA: Secondary gain in long-term hemodialysis patients. Am J Psychiatry 129: 352–355, 1972
21. Eisendrath RM: The role of grief and fear in the death of kidney transplant patients. Am J Psychiatry 126:381–387, 1969
22. Eisendrath RM, Guttmann RD, Murray JE: Psychologic considerations in the selection of kidney transplant donors. Surg Gynecol Obstet 129:243–248, 1969
23. Fellner CH: Selection of living kidney donors and the problem of informed consent. Semin Psychiatry 3(1):79–85, 1971
24. Fielding JM, Grounds AD, Mellsop G: Psychiatrists' roles and staff stresses in a renal homotransplantation unit. Med J Aust 1:66–68, 1974
25. Fishman DB, Schneider CJ: Predicting emotional adjustment in home dialysis patients and their relatives. J Chronic Dis 25:99–109, 1972
26. Foster FG, Cohn GL, McKegney FP: Psychobiologic factors and individual survival on chronic renal hemodialysis—a two year followup. Part I. Psychosom Med 35:64–82, 1973
27. Foy AL: Dreams of patients and staff. Am J Nurs 70:80–82, 1972
28. Freyberger H: Six years' experience as a psychosomaticist in a hemodialysis unit. Psychother Psychosom 22:226–232, 1973

29. Goldstein AM, Reznikoff M: Suicide in chronic hemodialysis patients from an external locus of control framework. Am J Psychiatry 127:124–127, 1971

30. Hagberg B: A prospective study of patients in chronic hemodialysis. III. Predictive value of intelligence, cognitive deficit and ego defense structures in rehabilitation. J Psychosom Res 18:151–160, 1974

31. Hagberg B, Malmquist A: A prospective study of patients in chronic hemodialysis. IV. J Psychosom Res 18:315–319, 1974

32. Hollon TH: Modified group therapy in the treatment of patients on chronic hemodialysis. Am J Psychother 26:501–510, 1972

33. Kaplan–DeNour A: Psychotherapy with patients on chronic hemodialysis. Br J Psychiatry 116:207–215, 1970

34. Kaplan–DeNour A: Role and reactions of psychiatrists in chronic hemodialysis programs. Psychiatry Med 4:63–76, 1973

35. Kaplan–DeNour A, Czaczkes JW: Emotional problems and reactions of the medical team in a chronic hemodialysis unit. Lancet 2:987–991, 1968

36. Kaplan–DeNour A, Czaczkes JW: Personality factors in chronic hemodialysis patients causing noncompliance with medical regimine. Psychosom Med 34:333–334, 1972

37. Kaplan–DeNour A, Czaczkes JW: Team–patient interaction in chronic hemodialysis units. Psychother Psychosom 24:132–136, 1974

38. Kaplan–DeNour A, Czaczkes JW, Lilos P: A study of chronic hemodialysis teams—differences in opinions and expectations. J Chronic Dis 25:441–448, 1972

39. Kaplan–DeNour A, Shaltier J, Czaczkes JW: Emotional reactions of patients on chronic hemodialysis. Psychosom Med 30:521–533, 1968

40. Kaye R, Leigh H, Strauch B: The role of liaison psychiatrist in a hemodialysis program: a case study. Psychiatry Med 4:313–321, 1973

41. Kemph JP: Psychotherapy with patients receiving kidney transplants. Am J Psychiatry 124:623–629, 1967

42. Kemph JP, Bermann EA, Coppolillo HP: Kidney transplant and shifts in family dynamics. Am J Psychiatry 215:1485–1490, 1969

43. Khan AV, Herndon CH, Ahmadian SY: Social and emotional adaptations of children with transplanted kidneys and chronic hemodialysis. Am J Psychiatry 127:1194–1198, 1971

44. Korsch BM, Negrete VF, Gardner JE et al.: Kidney transplantation in children: psychosocial followup study on child and family. J Pediatr 83:399–408, 1973

45. Kossoris P: Family therapy: an adjunct to hemodialysis and transplantation. Am J Nurs 70:1730–1733, 1970

46. Lefebvre P, Nobert A, Crombez JC: Psychological and psychopathological reactions in relation to chronic hemodialysis. Can Psychiatr Assoc J [Suppl] 17:9–13, 1972

47. Lunde DT: Psychiatric complications of heart transplants. Am J Psychiatry 126:369–373, 1969

48. MacDonald DJ: Psychotic reactions during organ transplantation. Can Psychiatr Assoc J [Suppl] 17:15–17, 1972

49. Malmquist A: A prospective study of patients in chronic hemodialysis. I. Method and characteristics of the patient group. J Psychosom Res 17:333–337, 1973

50. Malmquist A: A prospective study of patients in chronic hemodialysis. II. Predicting factors regarding rehabilitation. J Psychosom Res 17:339–344, 1973

51. Marshall JR: Effective use of a psychiatric consultant on a dialysis unit. Postgrad Med 55:121–125, 1974

52. Menzies IC, Stewart WK: Psychiatric observations on patients receiving regular dialysis treatment. Br Med J 1:544–547, 1968

53. Moore GL: Nursing response to the long-term dialysis patient. Nephron 9:193–199, 1972

54. Muslin HL: On acquiring a kidney. Am J Psychiatry 127:1185–1188, 1971

55. Paton A: Life and death: moral and ethical aspects of transplantation. Sem in Psychiatry 3(1):161–168, 1971

56. Penn I, Bunch D, Olenik D, Abouna G: Psychiatric experience with patients receiving renal and hepatic transplants. Semin Psychiatry 3(1):133–144, 1971

57. Raimbault G: Psychological aspects of chronic renal failure and hemodialysis. Nephron 11:252–260, 1973

58. Reichsman F, Levy NB: Problems in adaptation to maintenance hemodialysis. Arch Intern Med 130:859–865, 1972

59. Retan JW, Lewis HY: Repeated dialysis of indigent patients for chronic renal failure. Ann Intern Med 64:284–292, 1966

60. Rubini MI: The conference on dialysis as a practical workshop. New York, Proceedings of the National Dialysis Committee, 1966, p 48

61. Sadler HH: The motivation of living donors. Transplant Proc 5:1121–1123, 1973

62. Sadler HH, Davison L, Carroll C, Kountz SL: The living, genetically unrelated, kidney donor. Semin Psychiatry 3(1):86–101, 1971

63. Sand P, Livingston G, Wright RG: Psychological assessment of candidates for a hemodialysis program. Ann Intern Med 64:602–610, 1966

64. Schreiner GE: Mental and personality changes in the uremic syndrome. Med Ann DC 28:316–323, 1960

65. Shea EJ, Bogdon DF, Freeman RB, Schreiner GE: Hemodialysis for chronic renal failure. IV. Psychological considerations. Ann Intern Med 62:558–563, 1965

66. Short MJ, Wilson WP: Roles of denial in chronic hemodialysis. Arch Gen Psychiatry 20:433–437, 1969

67. Sorensen ET: Group therapy in a community hospital dialysis unit. JAMA 221:899–901, 1972

68. Sullivan MF: The dialysis patient and attitudes toward work. Psychiatry Med 4:213–219, 1973

69. Tuckman AJ: Brief psychotherapy and hemodialysis. Arch Gen Psychiatry 23:65–69, 1970

70. Versieck J, Barbier F, Derom F: A case of lung transplant: clinical note. Semin Psychiatry 3(1):159–160, 1971

71. Viederman M: Adaptive and maladaptive regression in hemodialysis. Psychiatry 37:68–77, 1974

72. Viederman M: The search for meaning in renal transplantation. Psychiatry 37:283–290, 1974

73. Walters WHG, Bonekamp ALM, Donckerwolcke R: Experiences in the development of a haemodialysis centre for children. J Psychosom Res 17:271–276, 1973

74. Wilson WP, Stickel DL, Noyes CP et al.: Psychiatric considerations of renal transplantation. Arch Intern Med 122:502–506, 1968

75. Wise TN: The pitfalls of diagnosing depression in chronic renal disease. Psychosomatics 15:83–84, 1974

76. Wright RG, Sand P, Livingston G: Psychological stress during hemodialysis for chronic renal failure. Ann Intern Med 64:611–621, 1966

77. Wysenbeek H, Munitz H: Group treatment in a hemodialysis center. Psychiatr Neurol Neurochir 73:213–220, 1970

78. Yager J: (Letter to ed): Intellectual impairment in uremic patients. Am J Psychiatry 130:1159–1160, 1973

Part III
Psychotherapies

9 Psychoanalytic Psychotherapy

JAN BASTIAANS

Treatment methods in psychosomatic medicine include techniques derived from psychiatry, psychotherapy, and related disciplines as well as from pharmacotherapy. Because the psychosomatic patient usually suffers from psychoneurosis that is accompanied by a characteristic life-style and defense and coping mechanisms, therapy is generally employed to promote a minor change in the life situation, in personality, or in behavior, which, it is hoped, will lead to the disappearance of the bodily symptoms. Some forms of therapy focus on the alleviation of superego stress, whereas others focus on strengthening the ego capacities that are necessary to counteract the pressures or stresses initiated by the environment, the superego, or the id. Because patients with psychosomatic diseases tend to be tense, it is understandable that all kinds of relaxation therapies may help the patient accept his warded-off, inner, passive-receptive tendencies and wishes. Thus, hypnosis, Yoga, autogenic therapy, or psychopharmacotherapy may be used to induce relaxation.

Theoretically, a rational therapeutic approach should be based on a preliminary multidimensional approach to the patient in his life situation. If it becomes clear that it is the life situation which has precipitated the psychosomatic syndrome, a therapy that helps change this life situation may be best. Sometimes such change can be brought about by simple social measures or by financial support, but in many cases, these simple and objective measures are not sufficient. Changes in the patient's work or housing situation, though apparently rationally indicated, may fail because of the patient's inner resistance to change. Other means of reshaping his life situation may be developed through family or group therapy, especially in those cases where the psychosomatic syndrome is unmistakably related to a special attitude or a special role in a particular interactional process.

In cases where a multidimensional approach suggests that the psychosomatic syndrome or psychosomatic reactions are predominantly the result of learned patterns of behavior, then behavior therapy may be the best therapeutic method. I believe that behavior therapy is particularly indicated in those cases in which the syndrome are largely split off from the original precipitating and unresolved conflict situations. This means that in the course of time, the symptom has gained a certain autonomy.

Because sufficient information about nonanalytic psychotherapies is to be found in other chapters, this presentation will concentrate on those forms of psychoanalytic psychotherapy that have been derived from the traditional psychoanalytic treatment of psychosomatic patients. Since 1945, my main experience has been with the traditional psychoanalytic approach as well as with the abbreviated forms of such therapy. I have followed the original approach of Alexander (1) and his co-workers, who, before World War II, started with the traditional analytic treatment, but who used their knowledge and experience in the so-called brief therapies to allow the gold of psychoanalysis to alloy optimally with the silver of already existing techniques of psychotherapy.

STAGES OF TREATMENT AND TECHNIQUES OF PSYCHOANALYTIC PSYCHOTHERAPY

THE INTRODUCTORY PHASE

The first approach to the psychosomatic patient should be based on careful screening of the precipitating life situation and of the personality factors that may have contributed to the development of his symptom. Because almost all symptoms arise in situations where the patient feels increasingly insecure or threatened, the diagnostic and therapeutic climate must be warm and understanding to encourage the patient to begin to feel more secure. Only in such a climate will the patient be able to tell the therapist about the stress situations that have led to his symptoms. For many patients, the mere fact that they have become ill is a blow to their pride and self-esteem, especially if they have never fallen ill before. The friendly and understanding atmosphere of the first contact may be of utmost importance in overcoming at least some of the implications of this kind of traumatization. I have discussed elsewhere the extent to which the technique of microanalysis of the first interview may be extremely helpful in establishing the right contact with the patient (10). This is basic for the transition to the following phases.

THE EXPLORATION OF SO-CALLED PSYCHOSOMATIC RIGIDITY

Many psychosomatic patients are rather rigid in their life-style as well as in their defense and coping mechanisms. In 1952, Groen and I wrote, "Psychosomatic patients are usually neurotics who pretend to be mentally healthy and well adapted. As the result of their increased and chronic efforts to maintain this pretension they must pay a high price in the form of the bodily symptom" (12). This attitude of the patient often means that he will reject the causal relationship between his life situation and the development of the symptom. Doctors who are not trained in the exploration or appraisal of such causal relationships may also fail to see this connection. Many patients also suppress or deny their fears, their anxieties, and their unconscious, instinctive strivings or pseudo-needs. Some training in psychoanalytic exploration is therefore needed to establish contact with psychosomatic patients. The trained therapist generally requires a few sessions to explore the extent to which the patient is aware of the relationship between his symptom and his psychic makeup.

As soon as it has become clear which stress situations or which life events may have contributed to the development of the symptom, the therapist must try to identify and discuss the patient's feelings that are related to the experiences connected with these events. Usually, the stress situations have induced or activated feelings of frustration, anger, fear, inadequacy, or powerlessness. Unfortunately, most patients with psychosomatic disorders are hardly aware of these feelings, which are usually immediately suppressed or repressed.

If psychosomatic patients are able to express these aforementioned feelings during the first interviews, a rapid diminution or disappearance of the psychosomatic symptom may be expected, provided that the mode of expression is not solely intellectual or rational. Unfortunately, most psychosomatic patients are not able to express themselves emotionally in these first interviews, at least not with such intensity that a sense of relaxation ensues. For them, the careful working through of the next phase is an indispensible condition for a therapeutic result.

THE APPROACH TO SPECIFIC SUPEREGO COMPONENTS THAT PREVENT THE EXPRESSION OF EMOTIONS AND WISHES

During this phase, the therapist must try to discuss with the patient the basic aspects of his ideals and ideal formations, especially his all too narcissistic or self-centered ideals associated with feelings of omnipotence or grandeur. These ideals and related feelings may be the most nuclear defense against his expression of emotions, especially those emotions that are regarded as childish or infantile. During this phase, which may last from a few hours to several weeks, it may be helpful to make the patient aware of his constant search for admiration, since many patients are unable to live under the pressure of such ambitious steering mechanisms. It may be explained to the patient that his attitudes could be advantageous or even beneficial under many life conditions, but at the same time, it must be made clear that some ideals, norms, or rules can demand too much from people. In this way, it is possible to avoid too rapid a blow to the narcissism of the patient; his acceptance of an easier life-style can take place without such a narcissistic injury. One might say that in this phase of the therapy, the therapist acts like a teacher who recognizes the merits of the patient's present life-style while teaching him how to adopt an even better one. If the patient's narcissistic defenses are so rigid that he cannot accept the possibility that pent-up emotions may be at the root of his symptom formation, it must then be decided whether psychoanalytic psychotherapy is the best treatment method for this patient.

If a patient can permit the expression of his repressed feelings and if such a giving in does not entail a loss of face, the patient usually reports a diminution of his symptoms at the next session. Sometimes it may be possible to avoid a traumatic blow to the patient's ideals and narcissism by telling him that he should consider the therapeutic situation as a sheltered workshop in which he can exercise his emotions without fearing that such emotions will endanger him elsewhere. The change in this phase of the treatment is from an attitude of "do it yourself" to the direction of a joint effort in the sense of "we can do it together."

EVALUATION OF THE ROLE OF THE THERAPIST

The patient's first giving in to cooperation with the therapist is usually immediately associated with the revival of early experiences with parents, other family members, or key figures outside the family. In those cases in which the patient's early contact with his father or mother was deficient, a therapeutic alliance can develop only slowly, especially if the patient identifies the therapist with one of his parents. Some psychosomatically ill patients prefer a predominantly fatherly contact with the therapist; others, a motherly contact. Many patients, however, are overly sensitive to a parental approach and prefer a contact on the basis of neutral understanding or a superficial friendship that may remind them of a preferable contact with siblings, teachers, or other key figures. Another group of psychosomatic patients expects the therapist to function as a transitional object in the sense that Winnicott (15) described. Such a longing is generally more specific in cases of addiction or other extreme ego disorders than it is in psychosomatic patients, who have usually been attached to real persons in an all too rigid way. The therapist must become aware as soon as possible of which role is expected from him by the patient, and he must decide to what extent he will engage in active role-playing in the desired direction.

RELEASE OF FOCUSING ON REPRESSED FEELINGS, EMOTIONS, AND AFFECTS

As soon as the first approach to the narcissistic or self-centered attitudes of the patient is successful and at least some of the suppressed or repressed emotions of frustration and the like have come to the fore, the therapist must begin to deal with the fact that different types of psychosomatic patients unconsciously prefer to express their feelings of alarm and related affects in different ways. Patients with an active and sthenic personality structure are apt to express feelings related to aggressiveness and hostility, instead of feelings related to passivity, fear, and anxiety. The former feelings are more in line with their built-in fighting attitude. Patients who are characterized by ego weakness and passivity in contact and adaptation usually express their feelings of fear and anxiety much sooner than their aggressive or hostile feelings.

It is a rule of thumb in psychoanalytic therapy that a noticeable alleviation of bodily symptoms takes place as soon as patients can express their aggressive feelings. Until such expression is possible, the therapist must keep in mind that a surrender to regressive, passive behavior may allow the patient to relax sufficiently so that his symptoms may disappear, at least temporarily. In fact, in this phase of treatment, the therapist should be satisfied with the expression of those feelings that are activated just below the level of consciousness. Another rule of thumb is that he must continuously evaluate which expressed feelings are most closely associated with the patient's experiences of being traumatized, being rejected, or being injured, *i.e.*, with states of extreme powerlessness. A display of feelings and emotions should never be made synonymous with unwanted surrender or capitulation.

THE EXPRESSION OF FANTASIES AND DREAMS

Some authors, especially those of the French psychosomatic school (15), have observed that psychosomatic patients have no capacity for fantasy formation. Similarly, Ammon (2), called attention to the remarkable fact that many psychosomatic patients are unable to dream, or at least, they are unable to verbalize their dreams. I am of the opinion, however, that this may be true only as long as the patient feels threatened by the therapeutic situation or by the therapist. As soon as the therapeutic process takes a favorable course, it becomes clear that it is not a matter of fantasy or dream deficiency, but rather that it is a question of inhibition of related intrapsychic functions. Analysts who have reported on dreams and fantasies in psychosomatic patients have shown to what extent these dreams and fantasies manifest the basic disturbances of the body scheme or the basic preoccupation with bodily functioning.

Much attention must be paid to the unconscious fantasies or dreams related to warded-off rivalry, jealousy, and passivity. Other fantasies may reveal destructive strivings in the sense of destroying one's rivals, parents, siblings, or therapist. Because psychosomatic patients are usually hyperactive in their daily life, one may also find fantasies related to creation, especially regarding aspirations that could not be realized in childhood (*e.g.*, having a child). One has to remember that the patient's fantasies related to castration anxiety are usually far more repressed than his fantasies related to pleasurable situations, creation, or aggression. The working through of fantasies related to activity and creativity may contribute to the disappearance of the bodily symptom.

ACCEPTANCE OF OTHER IMPORTANT ALARM EMOTIONS

I have used the term "alarm emotions" to summarize the complex set of emotions that are activated under conditions of stress and are characterized as painful. "Pain" may imply bodily pain, anxiety, or feelings of shame and guilt. When the patient suffers from pain or one of its components, or when his pain is more or less equated with the experience of suffering, the therapist has to investigate what is at fault in the actual situation, especially within the body. One must determine what has happened to the patient's perception of the actual state of his body and what ideas or fantasies he may have about the ideal state of his body and his existence (8). This means that the aforementioned working through of fantasies and dreams must be related to emotions, feelings, and affects as they are progressively expressed or verbalized. Some feelings and some affects—*e.g.,* anxiety, anger, or grief—may be inseparably connected with feelings of shame, guilt, or pain. The activation of one pain component may also imply the activation of other pain components. The patient may feel guilty or may experience an intense feeling of shame, for example, because he gives vent to feelings of anxiety and anger. Again, the therapist must be reminded of the need to be as tactful as possible in his sometimes too ambitious attempts to mobilize such repressed feelings and emotions in the course of brief psychotherapy. Although this psychotherapy is in line with Freud's recommendation, *"wo Es war soll Ich werden"* (where id was, ego shall be), overly urgent pressure in the direction of mental growth and development may result in a state of depression, psychosis, or, at least, in an iatrogenic traumatic neurosis.

ACCEPTANCE OF AN OPTIMAL BALANCE OF PASSIVITY AND ACTIVITY

As mentioned previously, the patient's acceptance of passive, receptive strivings may promote the disappearance of his psychosomatic symptoms. The therapist must evaluate the extent to which the patient's temporary regression to an oral-dependent and symbiotic situation may provide the stepping stone for further development in the direction of what can be regarded as normal passivity and relation. At the same time, the acceptance of normal or healthy patterns of activity must be related to the forms of activity and aggression regulation in which the psychosomatic patient was fixated prior to the beginning of treatment. If, during the course of psychoanalytic psychotherapy, the patient can accept normal or healthy activities and passivities much better than he did before, one may conclude that the main goal of the therapy has been achieved. This final phase of brief psychotherapy again requires that the therapist be a guide and a teacher, teaching the patient how to be active and how to be passive without unwanted strains.

Activity and passivity have frequently been related culturally to masculinity and femininity. This issue cannot be discussed in detail within the framework of this chapter, but one must keep in mind that activity is not the same as masculinity and passivity is not the same as femininity. Unfortunately, many psychosomatic patients are not aware of this, and even at this level, the therapist may contribute to a better development of the patient's feelings about his identity.

THE POSSIBILITIES AND LIMITATIONS OF PSYCHOANALYTIC PSYCHOTHERAPY

In every therapeutic process, there are three sets of variables: those of the therapist, those of the person in treatment, and those of the therapeutic process itself. From the foregoing discussion, it should be clear that analytic psychotherapy has its indications in the treatment of psychosomatic disorders. In practice, one of the greatest difficulties the therapist faces is how to determine the autonomy of the symptom in advance. An essential point to keep in mind is that psychosomatic symptoms arise only at those moments when the patient's inner tension and his related emotional instability have reached a certain level of intensity and chronicity. Although a partial diminution of his inner tension may lead to the disappearance of the bodily symptom, the question is whether this fulfills the goals of psychotherapy. Both the therapist and the patient may feel satisfied with such a result, but the danger exists that the disappearance of the symptom may be related too much to the therapist or to transference, and that the end of the therapy, with its inevitable frustrations, may induce the reappearance of the symptom, even after a so-called symptom-free interval.

The more a symptom is conflict-related, the more the possibility exists of a shift in the syndrome in the direction of the underlying psychoneurotic, mostly hysterical problems. Such a syndrome shift is frequently seen in long, continued analytic treatment or in analytic group therapy, where the last phases of treatment may be marked by a temporary reappearance of the symptom because of an increased fear of being rejected or of being left alone. In fact, this may be regarded as a fairly normal occurrence in the course of treatment. I have had experiences, however, with patients whose psychosomatic symptoms disappeared only at the end of treatment, although their related psychoneurotic problems seemed to have been resolved in the earlier phases of treatment. In these patients, one must take into account the possibility that the bodily symptom had gained its autonomy a long time before as a conditioned response that needed only a weak stimulus for it to be elicited. Even those psychoanalysts who tend to advocate psychoanalytic therapy as the only treatment method must admit that behavior therapy may have its advantages for such patients.

Although some authors have claimed that psychosomatic patients are highly disturbed patients who are characterized by severe ego splitting or weakness, one should not forget that the previously discussed activity and sthenicity of the psychosomatic patient, which may be reflected in his "psychosomatic attitude," can promote the therapeutic process. Usually the psychosomatic patient is an active co-worker in the therapeutic alliance. For patients in whom this psychosomatic attitude is closely interwoven with all their early processes of development—both on the level of cognition as well as on the level of fantasizing, feeling, dreaming, and expression—brief psychotherapy or behavior therapy is usually not sufficient to accomplish a complete and integral modification of personality functioning. For those patients whose symptom has arisen fairly recently because of a life situation in which the patient was more or less driven into a psychosomatic style of self-defense that was not present in his preceding life, however, the use of psychotherapy may be of the utmost importance, not only to ensure a rapid loss of symptoms, but also to enable the patient to learn more adequate strategies of coping, adaptation, and defense.

It is only rational, then, to expect that in general, much more can be accomplished in the setting of traditional analysis during hundreds of sessions than in the setting of brief psychotherapy, where the therapist must focus systematically on the main areas of conflicts and problems. The end of brief psychotherapy nearly always implies that a great deal is expected of the patient's capacity for self-development, self-realization, and self-analysis.

The same may be true for other forms of psychotherapy, *e.g.,* for relaxation techniques, nondirective counseling, and so on. Although to a certain extent, orthodox psychoanalysis has ignored the learning aspect of psychotherapy, the psychotherapeutic process is indeed a learning process. But how can one promote this process? The answer is that this can be achieved with the help of different techniques. A recent advance in the area of psychotherapy is the biofeedback method, which offers an important learning component due to its "mirror function." Group therapy is also an important sheltered workshop for the psychosomatic patient, where he can learn and practice communicating and expressing his emotions, fantasies, dreams, and the like, while being in actual rivalry with the other members of the group. The group members may be said to have a "mirror function" for each other.

A consideration of the contribution and the possibilities of the "mirror function" automatically leads to the question of how training in psychotherapy can be made available for the general practitioner, as well.

It is well known that a complete psychoanalytic training is open only to a minority of psychotherapists. This training may, in fact, provide the trainee with the best feedback or "mirror function" that he needs to neutralize the so-called blind spots in his own "professional" approach. Although the contribution to the personal growth of the therapist that this highly professional training may provide is beyond doubt, it does not always guarantee the superior functioning of the psychoanalyst in all the various kinds of interactional processes that general practitioners and other therapists are involved with in everyday life. Therefore, a sufficient experience with group processes—training groups, therapeutic groups, family settings, and so on—is of utmost importance for a proper training in psychotherapy, especially for those who do not have the opportunities for or who cannot afford psychoanalytic training.

With regard to a proper training method for general practitioners and other therapists, the method of Balint (3, 4) should be mentioned. Balint's method of training, in which the general practitioner can present his problem cases to a group of colleagues guided by a well-trained psychotherapist, may also contribute to a considerable, though limited, change in the personality of the doctor. The Balint training method, which originally started in London, has spread to some of the European countries in the last 20 years, especially to Holland, Germany, France, and Switzerland, but it has diffused to a lesser extent to other countries of the world. Although the Balint Society is still active in promoting the improvement of the technique and its further dissemination into the world, the claims of the social sciences—namely, that newer techniques stemming from systems theory are superior—have overshadowed this development.

Again, it ought to be mentioned that the rapid development of behavior therapy has provided the therapists with efficient tools to deal with monosymptomatic psychosocial diseases. For many psychologists and doctors, these techniques are very attractive, because they are less time-consuming and because they seem to be less demanding of the personal growth of the therapist. It seems very unlikely, however, that this trend will prove to be efficient if it is allowed to develop in isolation in the course of time.

The patient is not an instrument or a machine that can be repaired with instrumental techniques only. Although the instrumental trend in psychotherapy has already served to jar the traditional conceptions of even the most orthodox psychoanalyst, the integrative approach to medicine demands from the doctor a flexible open-mindedness regarding intricate interrelations among the cognitive processes (thinking, ideation, and imagination), the subjective feeling processes, and the behavioral processes. Of these, the last can especially be analyzed with the help of techniques modeled on those of the natural sciences.

What the suffering part of mankind is requesting today from doctors and therapists is understanding, empathy, and experience based on the best knowledge of contemporary developments in different areas of the medical and social sciences. This implies that technical skill, technically oriented encounter, is required. This need is summarized in the statement of Bettelheim: "Our hearts must know the world of reason, and reason must be guided by an informed heart" (14).

Finally, for those who are active in the practice of psychotherapy, it must be mentioned that many patients are in need of so-called combined treatment. When their complaints of bodily suffering arise from sociogenic or psychogenic factors, the therapist must especially be aware of the possibilities of the combination of psychotherapy with pharmacotherapy. The employment of such a combination may facilitate the rapid disappearance of the bodily symptom, and the dosages of the required drug can be diminished as soon as the psychic process takes a favorable course.

REFERENCES

1. Alexander F: Psychosomatic Medicine; Its Principles and Applications. New York, W. W. Norton, 1950

2. Ammon G: Psychoanalyse und Psychosomatik. München, Piper & Co, 1974

3. Balint M: The Doctor, His Patient and the Illness. London, Pitman Medical, 1956

4. Balint M: Psychotherapeutic Techniques in Medicine. London, Tavistock Publications, 1962

5. Bastiaans J: The place of personality traits in specific syndromes: cause or effect? In Wisdom JO, Wolff H: The Role of Psychosomatic Disorder in Adult Life. London Pergamon Press, 1965

6. Bastiaans J: Lernprozesse in der Psychoanalyse. Prax Psychother XVI (5) 221–239, 1971

7. Bastiaans J: Fixation points in the regulation of aggression and their meaning for syndrome formation. Proc V World Congr Psychiatry, Amsterdam, Excerpta Medica, 1971

8. Bastiaans J: Psychiatric Aspects of Migrainous Headaches. Migraine and Related Headaches. Sandoz, 1975

9. Bastiaans J: Der Beitrag der Psychoanalyse zur psychosomatischen Medizin. In Die Psychologie des 20. Jahrhunderts. Zürich, Kindler Verlag, 1976 (In press)

10. Bastiaans J: Das erste Gespräch mit psychosomatischen Patienten. In Praktische Psychosomatik. Bern, Hans Huber Verlag, 1976 (In press)

11. Bastiaans J: The optimal use of anxiety in the struggle for adaptation. In Spielberger Co, Sarason IG: Stress and Anxiety, Vol II. New York, Halsted Press, 1976 (In press)

12. Bastiaans J, Groen J: Psychotherapy of internal disease. In The Affective Contact. Amsterdam, Strengholt, 1952

13. Bastiaans J, Groen J: Psychosocial stress, interhuman communication and psychosomatic disease. In Spielberger CD, Sarason IG: Stress and Anxiety, Vol I. New York, Halsted Press, 1975

14. Bettelheim B: The Informed Heart. New York Avon Books, 1971

15. Marty P, de M'Uzan M, David C: L Investigation Psychoanalytique. Presses Universitaire, Paris, 1963

16. Winnicott DW: Transitional objects and transitional phenomena. Int J Psychoanal 34 (2) 89, 1953

10 Group Psychotherapy

WALTER BRÄUTIGAM, ALMUTH RÜPPELL

Group psychotherapy is a treatment method in which a number of patients work jointly with a psychotherapist in an attempt to overcome their somatic or psychological disturbances. Discussions in these group sessions concentrate on the patients' conflicts.

Patients may be said to suffer from *psychosomatic disease* when the origin and progress of their somatic complaints, with or without organic findings, can be said to be influenced by their life situation and biographical determinants. This category includes patients with important psychosomatic illnesses, such as bronchial asthma, ulcerative colitis, and rheumatoid arthritis, as well as those who have complaints without organic findings, such as headaches, epigastric pain, a sense of oppression, and so on.

There are several reasons why psychosomatic patients are especially suitable for group therapy:

1. Patients with somatic disorders who have received attention primarily through organically directed medicine usually have difficulty relating their complaints to psychic causes, *i.e.*, in relating their conflict situation to their life history. This difficulty reveals itself in their initial resistance to an understanding of the psychic background of their illnesses. In a group discussion with patients who face the same problems, these difficulties are more easily overcome. It is a source of relief to meet other patients with concerns similar to their own who can help them and whom they can help in return. In the course of group therapy, patients often say, "I always thought that I was all alone in having such problems." Close contact and dialog with other patients also serves to relieve the common feelings of guilt that usually are associated with a person-oriented understanding of illness.

2. Patients suffering from psychosomatic disorders tend to entrust their treatment to the doctor and to assume that they need only be patient, obedient, and confident in order to be helped. Actually, it constitutes a decided improvement in the psychotherapeutic process if the patients realize that they are participants in the process of recovery and share the responsibility for it. What patients disclose in the way of fantasies, memories, and feelings yields the material and substance for the therapeutic process. Initiative in sharing responsibility is more easily taken in the group, by following the example of fellow patients, than it is in individual therapy.

3. Patients with psychosomatic symptoms and reactions are often less capable of introspection. They are incapable of verbalizing not only their personal and autobiographical experiences, but also their feelings about others and about their relationships with them. According to investigations by Hollingshead and Redlich (8), members of lower social strata have a stronger tendency toward psychosomatic reactions. These patients are usually not among the traditional clientele of psy-

choanalysts, and classic psychoanalytic techniques often demand too much of them. In the group, however, the patient learns to speak about himself; he learns to come into contact with his needs and emotions.

SPECIFIC CHARACTERISTICS OF THE PSYCHOSOMATIC PATIENT

As early as the 1950s, Shands (14) raised a question about the difference between patients with psychosomatic and those with psychoneurotic disorders. He noted characteristic differences in the way anxiety neurotics and arthritic patients view the world. The patient with an anxiety neurosis moves in a world full of frightening possibilities. He feels isolated and dependent, and he sees the doctor as an expert and leader with whom he can establish a personal relationship as an equal. He is aware of the peculiarities of his situation, including his frequent morbid physical and psychological disturbances, and he can relate these in minute detail. The arthritic patient, although progressively more physically incapacitated, sees the future as ordered and understandable. The doctor is seen as a magic helper who will aid him. In his integral identification, he is oriented toward group norms. He is not particularly interested in his feelings, and they are not an object of analysis for him. He regards his feelings and his surroundings as things that can be taken for granted. Shands spoke of these two groups of patients as "easy" and "difficult" patients with regard to the possibility of psychotherapeutic communication with them.

Nemiah and Sifneos (12) described psychosomatic patients as "alexithymic." They are incapable of perceiving and verbalizing their differentiated, fantasy-bound moods, and they are governed by uncontrolled emotions, *e.g.,* by impulsively surfacing, mostly negative affects, such as irritation or anger. Above all, they are unable to let conflicts emerge so that they can be worked out in fantasy or imagination. Motor actions are used to abreact the emerging feelings, but these feelings are not articulated. Their inability to conceive and convey their feelings tempts the therapist to become too active and to interpret a great deal. Psychosomatic patients often react to this by further reinforcing such defense mechanisms as denial and negation.

The Parisian psychosomatic school regards the characteristic, regressive ego state, with deficient control and integration in dealing with other people (11), as a special feature of the "psychosomatic structure." A differentiation between the patient and other individuals does not take place. The relationship between closeness and psychic distance cannot be mastered. Patients who suffer from psychosomatic conditions that are characterized by excessively conformist adjustments of behavior show absolute emptiness in their relationships with others. The other person no longer exists with a representative value of his own *(relation blanche).* The patient sees the doctor as a stereotype of himself and, like himself, without contour and profile (projective reduplication). Other persons are exchangeable and possess only an instrumental value for the patient *(comportement operatoire).* The significance of outer reality cannot be internalized through linguistic symbolization *(pensée opératoire),* but it can be perceived only in its immediate instrumental meaning. Reality exists only as a copy, a sign of a predominantly superficial contact in which human interactions are adopted strategically and then dropped. The patients depend upon the actual presence of others. From the weak libidinal valence of their own self-system and other persons' diminished significance in it, it follows that in the opinion of such patients, no one can play a decisive role, not even the doctor. They want treatment to be prescribed for them, but, at the same time, they experience it as something forced upon them.

Many questions remain unanswered with regard to this description of psychosomatic patients: are there other personal features that are typical of patients with certain illnesses, such as colitis ulcerosa, or, overall, are these features also, present in all persons who react to psychic stress with bodily disturbances? It is also unknown to what extent this behavior is dependent upon inherited personality factors or upon influences of socialization, *e.g.,* those of the patient's social stratum. Most observers agree, however, that patients suffering from psychosomatic diseases, because of their difficulty in perceiving and describing their feelings, their poverty of fantasy, and their lack of linguistic symbolization, are seldom suited for individual psychotherapy.

THEORETICAL CONCEPTS OF GROUP PSYCHOTHERAPY

Theories about therapeutic groups are related, on one hand, to the influences of psychoanalysis and, on the other, to social psychology, in particular to the group-dynamic field theories of Kurt Lewin (9). Influences from both fields are usually of equal importance in the various theories of group therapy developed during the last three decades. Theoretical concepts, whether formulated or not, determine the behavior of the therapist, his interventions, and his interpretations. They also exert a large influence on the development of the group, depending on the strength of the therapist and the degree to which members of the group identify with him. There is a danger that the therapist may become too theoretical and may distance himself too much from the therapeutic process of the group and from his role in helping the group to become a working and therapeutically effective entity.

MULTIPLICITY VERSUS UNITY

Some theories about group therapy suggest that if one regards the analytical relationship already operative at the beginning of a small group, it is possible to recognize in the individuals of the group the behavioral problems described in psychoanalytic developmental and conflict theories. Theories of psychoanalysis in the group (19) deal with the personal relationships of the individual and his personality structure as these develop in the group. According to these theories, the therapist should understand and follow the psychodynamics of each individual participant, and, by means of suitable interventions and interpretations of transference, he should respond to the difficulties of each member (17). As in individual therapy, because of his salient position, a special transference gradient should exist in relation to the therapist. Free association, dream interpretation, and fantasies are promoted by a regression-stimulating group atmosphere that is concentrated on transference and the working-through process. The matrix of the group is the network of fantasies and the modes of behavior as determined by the sum total of individual structures and histories at any given time (6).

These theories conflict with the theories of the therapeutic group that regard the group as an autonomous organism, even as a living entity. According to these theories, the various contributions of the different patients are the ambivalent tendencies of a single group that speaks as one person. They represent the conflicts between instinct and psychic defense (4) in relation to disturbing and reactive themes (18). Bion (1) theorized that the group is a homogeneous entity and cites, as signs of this, certain basic attitudes through which the group relates to the therapist, *e.g.,* dependency, flight-fight, and pairing.

AHISTORICAL AND HISTORICAL GROUP THERAPIES

Theories have been put forth that concentrate entirely on the "here and now" of the present group and the social network existing among the actual individual relationships. Causality is held to lie in the present and not in the effects of the past, which can determine behavior only via the actual dynamics. Thematically, according to Ezriel (5), the influences of actual interactions and their unconscious determinants are the only objects for the therapist's diagnostic and interpretative work.

In contrast, other theories envision the understanding of the group and its efficacious interpretation as only a kind of archeological research, which must take into consideration the history of each individual as well as the history of the group as a whole. Most psychoanalytic schools suggest that the present behavior in the group should be understood as infantile or primary process behavior that is actualized by regression-stimulating influences. An exact knowledge of the personal histories and the inclusion of the experience derived from the primary group of the family should be taken into consideration if group therapy is to be effective. Theories that try to comprehend the group as a whole go back to Sigmund Freud (7). Bion's first "basic assumption of dependency" (1) is contained in Freud's theory of the primal horde and its dependence upon the primal father who possesses all women. This is certainly a characteristic of initial group sessions before the group revolts against and attacks the therapist, *i.e.*, commits "patricide." In this way, the conquered and introjected father fortifies each group member, allowing them to identify with one another. Slater (15) suggested a theory based on a sequence of phases in a group: he describes a beginning phase of ambivalent dependency; this is followed by increased contact and solidarity among the group members, which forms the prerequisite for a revolt in which the group leader is overcome. In the continuing history of the group, individual needs are elaborated and the members learn to differentiate and are able to build up an increasing autonomy.

EFFECTIVE THERAPEUTIC FACTORS IN GROUP PSYCHOTHERAPY

There are indications that the treatment process and the effective factors in group therapy are not completely identical with those of individual therapy. Viewed retrospectively by patients who have been successfully treated, a change for the better seems possible at that point when, through emotional involvement, important and up until then unconscious, unverbalized contents find expression. It is of decisive importance for the patients to be able to communicate with others: to experience being understood and accepted and not depreciated. In the group, this takes place against the background of early experience in the primal family group, which gives the actual experience in the group its value. Also viewed as positive is the possibility of receiving support from other patients: of being more and more able to recognize and accept personal conflicts with their help. To be respected by others, to be able to experience closeness and warmth, to discover in others conflicts similar to one's own—these are the elements that account for the therapeutic effect of the psychoanalytic group. It is not only catharsis which is valuable, but also the constant working-through of problems over a long period of time. Reasons for inappropriate previous behavior are worked out. The patients feel accepted in the group and experience it as a family. Of course, for these factors to become effective, there must be a high degree of togetherness, of group cohesiveness, which efficient groups possess (20).

Therapists see different aspects of the group as effective dependent upon their convictions and theoretical concepts. They tend to view both the therapist and the transference process as being very important, and they also feel that analysis of the past is significant. However, although the actual group experience must always be seen against the background of early family experience and its emotional consequences, the conscious working-through and analysis of particular early life episodes is not only less possible in the group than it is in individual therapy, but it also seems to be less important here. It may be noted that therapists who surround themselves with a charismatic, messianic aura are initially stimulating for certain group members, but, in the long run, this exerts a definitely hampering influence on the group process (10).

THE THERAPEUTIC PROCESS IN GROUPS

In a closed group, the therapeutic process characteristically takes place in three separate and distinct stages. Even ahistorical theories of the therapeutic group accept that a dimension of horizontal development occurs for the group as a whole, as well as for the individual participant, as part of the therapeutic process. The characteristic variability that forms part of every experience and every form of behavior may show itself only in the course of the group history, with its concomitant conflict patterns.

THE PHASES OF THERAPY

Initial Phase

The first group therapy session is characterized by the patients' unrealistic expectations about the therapist. Disappointment and concern about the meaning and efficacy of the therapy usually follow the euphoria of the first hours. The group members try to size up one another and the group, they try to influence each other, and they endeavor to be liked. Uncertainty abounds as to how much one should, and how much one can, reveal of oneself. Communication remains superficial, especially where there is a lack of confidence and where a tendency to flee is manifested. Characteristic of this beginning stage are the first attempts to search for a community of interests, to observe similarities, and to attempt to reach quick solutions. The first relatively long periods of silence interrupt these activities, with the result that each member may be confronted with his own fantasies and unconscious. This usually leads to increased anxiety, and the group may be experienced as a threatening and devouring power.

Central and Work Phase

This phase is characterized by the beginning of decisive work in the group. A stronger ambivalence toward the therapist emerges, and often one or more attempts at revolt occur. If a certain amount of cohesiveness exists within the group, discontent and aggression may be expressed, and quarrels among members are possible. Each individual patient must come to grips with the others by differentiating himself from the others and defining his own individuality. The special qualities of each individual, his life experiences, and his vocational and personal existence outside the group force this individuation.

Late and Terminating Phase

In this phase, a new freedom of interaction promotes a special awareness of group consciousness and cohesiveness and of the existence of common goals. Patients feel a growing trust in the value of self-revelation and in their ability to cope with the outer world with the support and help of the group. With the unavoidable end of the group and the necessary separation from the therapist, fears and hostility occur again. Often these are denied by ritualizing group embraces. Fantasies about continuing the group indefinitely emerge. Group members fantasize about living in communes and suggest weekend trips. Contacts between members may occur outside the group. If negative attitudes have not been sufficiently elaborated during the group process, they may express themselves through relapses with regard to symptoms during the period preceding separation.

UNDERSTANDING OF CONFLICTS

In the course of group work, diverse steps toward an intensified understanding of conflicts may be taken. In the beginning, the most distanced form for elaborating one's own problems is externalization. The group may speak of overcrowded traffic or of the danger of collissions, when they are actually apprehensive about the proximity of intermember quarrels. A greater closeness has been established when individual, relevant events—either from the past or from present, actual life conflicts—can be communicated and treated in the group. Above all, communicating one's childhood experiences furthers the cohesiveness of the group. If a patient, however, reports how little time his parents had for him compared to his brothers and sisters when there is a similar situation in the group at that time, then this shows that defense mechanisms are still at work. In the course of the group process, the most intense emotional involvement takes place when relevant problems in the group are discussed directly, and fears, positive feelings, and aggressions can be experienced and elaborated in a way that is typical of the patients in that group. Patients should not merely report on their conflicts in the past or with their outside environment, but instead these conflicts should occur in the "here and now" of the group. The main function of the therapist lies in making this both possible and understood.

CASE ILLUSTRATION

For six years, a 24-year-old woman hairdresser had suffered from a rectoscopically and histologically proved case of ulcerative colitis. For 33 months, she was unsuccessfully treated as an inpatient at a hospital for internal diseases. There, she had 10 to 20 bowel movements daily, with bloody and purulent mucus, loss of weight, and anemia.

Her illness began when her husband was called up for military service and she was left alone with a 3-month-old child. The husband had relations with other women and did not concern himself with her, either in terms of time or money. On the urging of her parents, after four years she divorced him and went to live with them. She is the only child of a poor family of hairdressers who have had the same business in the same house for three generations. She is dependently attached to her parents, and, although she feels she is overprotected by her mother, she cannot free herself. When she tried to move out of her parents home with her daughter and have her own apartment, she had serious relapses of colitis.

In the first psychiatric interviews, she appeared helpless and clinging. She thought of herself as a victim of circumstances and not as someone who was responsible for her own actions. At first, she saw none of the psychological aspects of her illness and had only a strong feeling of physical suffering. Although there was doubt about her capacity for psychotherapeutic treatment, she was accepted into three months of inpatient treatment and then into two years of outpatient, analytical group therapy for two hours weekly.

Despite the need to commute 50 kilometers, the patient came to the group sessions regularly. In the first weeks, she was silent but, at the same time, was listening attentively. She developed a strong emotional bond to the group. She felt secure in the group and began to identify with and take part in the lives of others and in their conflicts. However, she could speak only if called upon, and she then spoke with a quiet, monotonous voice. She experienced her situation, her life, and her own behavior as inevitable. She formed a strong transference relation to her therapist, with the magical expectation that he and the whole group would be able to change and cure her.

Slowly, she learned to differentiate between group members and between the therapist and herself. Although at the beginning of therapy she could discover no wishes and needs of her own, she slowly began to learn to express these and to make her presence felt in the group. Through further development, she managed to define herself against the others and to make her own way. Simultaneously, she disassociated herself from her parents. She became more self-reliant and realistic in her relations with men, instead of passively surrendering herself with magical expectations of deliverance as she had done previously. She finally won a differentiated and defined relationship in the group and was accepted by the group. Her opinion was of importance in the group, for she had a sense of the authenticity of her assertions and was able to say critical things without hurting others. During the first year of treatment, she still had occasional diarrhea in crisis situations. Four years after termination of treatment, she is free of symptoms, and rectoscopic examination reveals no pathological findings.

THE ROLE OF THE THERAPIST

The importance of the therapist is viewed differently in accordance with the various theories about groups. In contrast to individual therapy, the group therapist is less able to remain as an opaque projective screen, limiting himself to interpretations and remaining a technical expert and distant observer. On the other hand, he cannot completely merge with the group and become a full group member, despite the fact that under certain circumstances such group membership may fulfill both the desire for contact and the therapeutic needs of many therapists. As a therapist, his function is to maintain the working ability of the group and to further its therapeutic capacities and resources. Undoubtedly, more is demanded of the therapist in the group than in individual therapy, because he is less idealized in the former context.

To be effective, a therapist must realize that the character of the group is largely dependent upon the role model that he presents. If he acts merely as a distant observer and limits himself to interpretations, the group will show an intensified form of this behavior. If, however, he shows that he is emotionally aware and freely communicates his self-perceptions, this will also be decisive in determining the style and dynamics of the group. The therapist has a special power over the group, not only because he decides when the group session begins and when it ends, but also because he decides on the beginning and conclusion of treatment. He is also the most therapeutically knowledgeable group member. He must attempt to help if crises, threats of suicide, or relapses in illness occur, but he must not forget that the fundamental therapeutic work is up to the individual patient and the group. The group process depends upon how much each individual participates, how much he communicates about his past history and his emotions, and how much he designates the group as a place in which disturbed patterns of relationship may be actualized. The therapist must render conflicts within the group sufficiently transparent so that they can be elucidated by emotional involvement and worked through. If childhood and family experiences are simply described without corresponding experiences in the group, this may become a purely rational imparting of information, which does not further therapy.

TECHNICAL QUESTIONS:
THE SETTING IN GROUP PSYCHOTHERAPY

The setting includes all questions that deal with time variables (such as the length of sessions and of treatment), the indications for group psychotherapy, and the size and composition of a group.

INDICATIONS FOR THERAPY

Because it is not always possible to associate certain neuroses or psychosomatic illnesses with specific methods of treatment, indications for therapy alone are not sufficient to determine whether a patient will profit more from individual or from group therapy. The psychic and social particularities of the individual patient, his motivation, and the special reasons for his coming for treatment when he does are usually factors of considerable importance to weigh in deciding on a form of treatment. Criteria such as age, the severity of the situation at the onset of symptoms, the duration of the symptoms, and so forth must also be taken into account in deciding between various psychotherapeutic methods.

From our experience, we believe that group therapy is especially indicated for neurotic and psychosomatic patients whose knowledge and understanding of mental illness is minimal. Most often, these patients are members of a lower social stratum and have relatively little schooling. Also suitable for group psychotherapy are those psychosomatic patients who, because of their incapacity to verbalize and their inability to introspect, find it difficult to begin and to sustain a therapy that relies upon the capacity to verbalize relevant emotional experiences. In group psychotherapy, it is possible to observe others, to have one's own behavior reflected by others, and to participate passively by listening to and identifying or empathizing with the more active members. This allows an easier ingress into treatment for such patients.

PREPARATION FOR TREATMENT

Most therapists prefer to conduct preliminary interviews with each prospective member of the group before the first group session. Such interviews make it easier for patients to enter into therapy and also decrease the incidence of dropouts. According to most therapists, a knowledge of the patient's life history is indispensable for gaining an understanding of the patient in the group.

In these pregroup interviews, some group therapists also try to orient patients toward group psychotherapy in general and to instruct them about how they should act in the group. It is recommended that they be open and honest, for example, and that they attempt to deal with any unrealistic expectations or lack of confidence. Other therapists, especially those associated with psychoanalytic schools of thought, disapprove of such pretherapeutic, anamnestic interviews and suggestions.

Many therapists also give fairly strict instructions about social meetings outside the group. It has been demonstrated that in general, the therapeutic process is not furthered by the patients' forming subgroup without the therapist or forming pairs outside the group. This is especially true if conflicts are discussed outside the therapy sessions and are not brought up in the group itself. Such discussions constitute a definite hindrance and obstruct the group process. These outside meetings, and particularly the forming of pairs, are without exception the result of avoidance of more intense relationships with the other group participants. They are attempts to avoid entering into the group process and therefore are also attempts to avoid therapeutic progress.

SIZE AND HOMOGENEITY OF THE GROUP

The ideal size for a group is approximately eight members. In general, groups with over ten or under five members cannot be considered practical for therapeutic goals.

Therapists usually need a certain amount of preparation time in order to bring a closed group together. Closed groups that remain together show a much stronger cohesiveness than open groups with continual, short-term fluctuations among members. Since experience shows that one has to anticipate that some patients will drop out of therapy, usually before the 20th hour, the question often arises whether the vacated place should be filled. It is usually advantageous, when possible, to add useful new participants to a group traumatized by the dropping out of a member. This creates what is called a "slow-open" group. Questions regarding participants who wish to terminate therapy, as well as new admissions, must be carefully handled and discussed with the group, since they represent a substantial interference in the group's progress.

Most group therapists believe that an overly homogeneous group is less capable of therapeutic work. A numerical balance between male and female participants is recommended, and the age variance should not exceed twenty years. Group participants from different social and educational levels can, under certain circumstances, considerably further the group process. It is obstructive, however, if a group member feels completely isolated in the group because of his social status or because of his age. We strongly advise against forming a group composed solely of patients with psychosomatic diseases but recommend combining these patients with patients with neurotic disorders. It is possible to take two patients with the same disorder—for instance, two patients with ulcerative colitis—into the same group. If the group is composed entirely of depressive patients or if approximately half of the members suffer from nervous anorexia—patients who, according to our experience, are emotionally affectless, psychically distant, and weak in their contacts—the group will be ineffective and the group process will not be easily launched.

DURATION OF THE MEETING AND THE LENGTH OF TREATMENT

Although there has been considerable experimentation regarding the amount of time needed for group therapy sessions, it appears that one meeting a week for a period of 90 to 100 minutes has proved to be optimal for outpatient group sessions. During the initial phase, in order to help group members to warm up to each other and to allow the group process to unfold more easily, it has been suggested that the number of sessions per week be increased or that a block of several sessions be arranged, perhaps on a weekend.

The total duration of group treatment is usually a period of two years. This length of treatment is necessary so that insights gained within the group can be transposed into the practice of daily life, tested, and consolidated.

THE COMBINATION OF GROUP AND INDIVIDUAL THERAPY

When patients lapse into an acute crisis or experience serious relapses of their symptoms, the question often arises of whether the therapeutic process in these patients would be helped by individual consultation in addition to group therapy. Experience shows that in such crises, certain patients find individual therapy of supportive value as well as a source of narcissistic supply. Above all, it may offer an opportunity to work out those experiences from childhood and the family that are causing the present form of reaction. For the therapist, there is also the question if, in such crises, he should conduct the individual consultation himself, or if he should delegate it to another therapist. We have observed that with increasing therapeutic experience and growing self-confidence, group therapists are readier and better qualified to offer individual therapy concurrent with group therapy in the interest of the individual patient as well as of the whole group.

When individual consultation is indicated, such a change must be discussed with the patient in front of the group and worked through. This usually releases fantasies and, under certain circumstances, envy or rivalry within the group. A group with good working abilities, however, is quite capable of recognizing and accepting the fact that a member is especially ill and in need of help. The group may also be both strengthened and appeased by the knowledge that this same possibility is open for each of its members. Individual therapy sessions are sometimes followed by the patient's feeling a certain isolation in the group. The patient may be tempted to withdraw from the group and to discuss his problems only in individual therapy. It is best to be sparing in such individual consultations, and one must continually try to induce the patient to bring anything that has surfaced in the individual discussions into the group as soon as possible.

SPECIAL CHARACTERISTICS OF TRANSFERENCE AND COUNTERTRANSFERENCE REGARDING THE PSYCHOSOMATIC PATIENT

The characteristic symptoms of psychosomatic patients already described are also expressed in the manner in which these patients take part in the group process. Psychosomatic patients experience the outer world as rule-bound according to the exact patterns of their own primary family as well as of the actual family. They therefore endeavor to form the group into a fixed structure with standardized rules, and they attempt to experience it only in this way. Their relationship to the other members of the group and to the therapist is stereotyped, representing at best a superego matrix on a conformistic, undifferentiated level. According to the mechanism of projective reduplication, the patient views the other participants and the therapist as lacking in contour and psychic profile, exactly as he feels himself to lack these. Observers of the group situation who watch these patients over a long period of time generally perceive them to be impersonal, overcontrolled, rational, and stereotyped in the network of their relationships.

Therapists who work with psychosomatic patients are tempted to assume the role of a magician, a savior, a representative of normality, or even a chosen leader. Under certain circumstances, the therapist is apt to develop feelings of omnipotence and to overestimate the positive consent of the group. On the other hand, the tendency of patients to maintain a formalistic, static, and fixed climate often leads the therapist to feel exhausted, bored, or uncertain about the therapeutic process. He is then easily led into a state of aggressive resentment.

Typical processes and behavioral group patterns are often lacking in psychosomatic patients. An excessive need to cling to the fixed and actual presence exists. The desire is strong to restore what was once established, to persist in a static manner, and to relive familiar, intimate feelings. The group assumes an important protective and stabilizing function. If this lasts too long, antitherapeutic group norms are established that arrest progress. If other group members try to differentiate themselves and develop autonomy, psychosomatic patients often react with far-reaching regression and renewed somatization. Psychosomatic patients also show little ability for transfer; it is difficult for them to apply what they have experienced and learned in the group to their own lives and to let it help them.

This behavior often makes the therapist irritated, impatient, despondent, and dissatisfied.

In addition, the particularly archaic-aggressive self-destruction of these patients is difficult to overcome. This self-destruction is a fundamental reason for the lack of structural stability and cohesiveness in such a therapeutic group, which will be incapable of preserving good object representations and of demarcating itself from the outer world. The resulting, almost addictively increasing need for the actual presence of the group and the therapist, if used as a defense, leads to excessive symbiotic desires. The inability to fulfill these desires leads to a deep crisis in the patient's feeling of self-esteem. Working through such a crisis often takes a course detrimental to the group: frequently, substitutes are sought outside of the group, especially in the form of paratherapy or substitute therapy. Because psychosomatic patients need to feel that everyone is being treated uniformly, they expect interventions and interpretations to be directed to the whole group. The more strongly these interventions and interpretations, when addressed to single members of the group, stress the personality of that individual member, the more difficult they are for psychosomatic patients to endure. If too great a distance from their own experience becomes obvious, this can have a very frightening effect and is experienced as a fragmentation of the entire group process.

Another danger is that of countertransference: the therapist is always in danger of exhausting himself when dealing with psychosomatic patients. The weak emotional resonance of these patients easily leads to strong, self-sacrificing interpretative and emotional expenditure on the part of the therapist. He tends to oblige the group at the expense of his time, and he often offers individual interviews in case of a crisis. He may engage himself too strongly when such patients have their frequent emotional outbursts, and he may unconsciously even identify with them. This danger of exhaustion also exists for the other members of the group.

THEMATIC AND TASK-CENTERED DISCUSSION GROUPS

Establishing information and discussion groups can be useful not only because such groups provide a better distribution of information, but also because they improve the patients' receptive capacities and ability to comply with given orders. Above all, they offer the patient an opportunity to confront himself with his fate and help him in the psychic working out of his feelings of illness and dependency. Many doctors gather their patients together for such group sessions when they want to give information about certain regimens, *e.g.,* to discuss diet for patients suffering from liver diseases, kidney diseases, obesity, and so on. Suggestions for the use of contraceptives and information about preparation for childbirth are also given in groups in many countries. Patients in the convalescent and rehabilitation phase of illness, *e.g.,* after myocardial infarction, have also used group sessions. These groups help patients to gain an understanding of their illness, which is so often lacking, and help them to accept the restrictions imposed upon them by their illness; they ease the necessary new adjustment to life. The common fate shared among the members usually produces a strong alliance. There are general practitioners who encourage their patients in the waiting room to talk to each other, not only about their illnesses but also about their life problems. Other doctors and institutions have suggested that patients on waiting lists start groups and hold discussions at first without a therapist. Large groups of obese patients and colostomy patients have formed "self-help" associations in order to exchange information about living regimes and to create a community of patients with similar fates. The largest example of such therapeutic and task-centered self-help groups is Alcoholics Anonymous, an example of group-therapeutic development that has thrived completely independent of medical influence.

In such informative group meetings, it is important to arrive at an exchange of ideas in which patients not only listen but also ask questions and discuss their own needs and difficulties. For group discussions of this kind to be effective, it is very important that the patients communicate with each other and give each other strength and help regarding appropriate sickness behavior and the adaptation to illness. Experience has shown that there are still many useful group-therapeutic possibilities and that great opportunities exist for the use of groups in rehabilitation as well as in the prevention of many disorders.

REFERENCES

1. Bion WR: Experiences in Groups. London, Tavistock, 1968
2. Bräutigam W: Pathogenetische Theorien und Wege der Behandlung in der Psychosomatik. Nervenarzt 45:298–304 1974
3. Bräutigam W, Christian P: Psychosomatische Medizin. Stuttgart, Thieme, 1974
4. Ezriel H: A psychoanalytic approach to group treatment. Br J Med Psychol 23:59–74 1950
5. Ezriel H: The role of transference in psychoanalytic and other approaches to group treatment. Acta Psychotherapeutica [Suppl] 7: 1957
6. Foulkes S, Anthony E: Group–Therapy. New York Penguin Books, 1957
7. Freud S: Totem und Tabu. Ges. Werke, Bd. 9, Imago, London, 1946
8. Hollingshead AB, Redlich FC: Social Class and Mental Illness. New York, John Wiley & Sons, 1958
9. Lewin K: A Dynamic Theory of Personality: Selected Papers. New York, McGraw–Hill, 1935
10. Liebermann MA, Yalom ID, Miles MB: Encounter Groups: First Facts. New York, Basic Books, 1973
11. Marty R, de M'uzan M, David C: L'Investigation psychosomatique. Paris, Presses Univetsitaires, 1963
12. Nemiah JC, Sifneos PE: Affect and fantasy in patients with psychosomatic disorders. In Hill OW (ed): Modern Trends in Psychosomatic Medicine. London, Butterworth, 1970
13. Shands, HC: Psychosomatics and sociolinguistics (unpublished manuscript)
14. Shands HC: An approach to measurement of suitability for psychotherapy. Psychiatry Q, 1958
15. Slater PhE: Mikrokosmos. New York, John Wiley, 1966
16. Slavson SR: Analytic group therapy with children adolescent and adults. New York, Columbia University Press, 1951
17. Slavson SR: A Textbook in Analytic Group Psychotherapy. New York, International Universities Press, 1964
18. Stock–Whitaker D, Liebermann A: Psychotherapy Through the Group Process. London, Tavistock 1965
19. Wolf A, Schwartz EK: Psychoanalysis in Groups. New York, Grune & Stratton, 1962
20. Yalom ID: The Theory and Practice of Group–Psychotherapy. New York, Basic Books, 1970

11 Group Therapy for Specific Psychosomatic Problems

A. B. SCLARE

I was introduced in 1949 to the practice of group psychotherapy by my mentor, Professor T. Ferguson Rodger, who had been closely involved during World War II with T. F. Main, W. R. Bion, Karl Menninger, S. H. Foulkes, John Rickman, and others in the development of therapeutic community concepts in the treatment of servicemen suffering from war neuroses. Like many young psychiatric registrars, I did not take to group therapy as a duck to water. I was anxious and uncertain about my role and about the validity of the method. I referred half facetiously to this approach to patients as "gripe therapy," thus alluding to the apparent superficiality of the treatment ("just moans and groans") as well as to my own discontent.

Twenty-five years' experience with the method has brought with it a more acceptable level of personal anxiety. It has become apparent that group therapy is not merely an expedient to use in coping with the heavy demands of a busy outpatient service, nor can it be dismissed as representing the therapist's phobic avoidance of the hard slog of one-to-one psychotherapy. As in psychiatric and medical therapy generally, group therapy constitutes a treatment technique that has its indications and its contraindications. Homogeneity of psychiatric diagnosis among the patients in a therapeutic group is an important principle: a single flagrantly psychotic patient in a small group of neurotic patients may prove to be highly disruptive.

This is not the place to review the significance of group therapy in general or theoretical terms. Suffice it to say that the method has ancient roots in the Socratic discipline, in John Wesley's deployment of religious groups in the eighteenth century, and in certain educational approaches utilized by the temperance movement in the nineteenth century. J. H. Pratt in the first decade of the twentieth century utilized a didactic, group approach in helping tuberculosis patients cope with their illness (30). More recently, psychiatrists have learned much about group dynamics from the successes of Alcoholics Anonymous.

Group therapies of various brands have found their major application in the treatment of patients with neurotic and personality disorders, particularly when there is an outstanding dyssocial component in their disablement. Such techniques have also yielded benefit in the management of patients who find themselves in a variety of stressful situations involving physical illness or abnormality. Markillie (26), in an informative review, described the role of group therapy in psychosomatic disorders.

It is proposed in this chapter to review the use of group techniques—formal and informal—in the treatment or as a contribution to the management of patients in a number of stress situations that entail an important physical element. Such methods involve a varied emphasis upon such dynamic features of group therapy as emotional support and bonding, verbal catharsis, identification, idealization, transference, and insight. In some clinical situations, a pressing need exists for professional staff groups, because of the unusual or severe stresses to which they are exposed during patient care.

OBSTETRIC CARE

Pregnancy is, of course, not a disease, but it is a psychophysiological situation in which the childbearing woman is required to make many adaptations at physical, psychological, and social levels. During the past 25 years, the standard regimen of antenatal care in Western society has gradually incorporated a number of psychological principles within its code. These include 1) the provision of anatomic and physiological information about pregnancy and the confinement, 2) the use of relaxation exercises, 3) opportunities during pregnancy to "inspect the pitch," *i.e.*, to view and become familiar with the labor room and analgesic method, 4) attention to the husband's role, and 5) the maintenance of a conscious, active, participating role during pregnancy and childbirth.

Especially in regard to the first three principles, group methods of a rather informal nature are now widely practiced by doctors, nurses, and physiotherapists. There is little room for the clinical psychiatrist in the normal pregnancy situation. Macnaughton (24) believes that midwives should play a major part in antenatal educational programs. According to local circumstances and the flair of the professional leader, antenatal groups may ventilate their anxieties and doubts in an informal classroom type of situation. Information about pregnancy may be imparted to the participants by means of a "lecturette," films, sound recordings, videotapes, the use of dolls, or, and by no means least, the blackboard.

The natural childbirth movement is largely derived from the work and hypotheses of Read (32) regarding the "fear-tension-pain" syndrome in childbirth. Psychological prophylactic regimens of a more or less structured nature have been practiced for over 20 years in many countries. Informal group support and participation by the husband are important elements in this approach.

Friedman (12) observed that in many instances, nine months of "natural childbirth" techniques can scarcely neutralize a lifetime of brainwashing that has promoted fears of childbirth. He stated idealistically that the story of childbirth must be told as soon as sex education begins. Williams (40) has reported on the worthwhile experimental deployment of a teacher-and-gynecologist team in Oxfordshire, England in talking to schoolchildren about human reproduction.

BRONCHIAL ASTHMA

For many years, it has been known that the removal of asthmatic children to a new environment can lead to a marked improvement in their symptoms. It is possible that the amelioration may be partly attributable to an allergen-free atmosphere. The new and caring interpersonal milieu, however, is also likely to be a major factor. Dobbs (9) described the dramatic relief that occurred in asthmatic children from England when they were cared for at a sanatorium in Davos, Switzerland. A similar project has been conducted with success for many years at Denver, Colorado (6, 16). A risk of relapse on return home exists, however, especially in those who have had atopic eczema (9). As Meyer (27) has stated, there is accordingly a need for social aftercare in such cases.

More formal techniques of group therapy in treating patients with bronchial asthma have been established longer than in the case of other stress disorders. Although they acknowledge the stimulus gained from earlier work in America (2), the Dutch group of investigators have been in the vanguard. Bastiaans and Groen

(3), for example, have described their extensive experience with dynamic group therapy. Good practical results were achieved when the method eschewed, on one hand, the passivity of the psychoanalyst and, on the other, the didactic approach of a lecturer. The therapist should be either a psychiatrist with a good knowledge of internal medicine or a physician with psychodynamic understanding. The Dutch workers found that when asthmatic patients were treated in a group, they regularly pursued the following course: scepticism about the role of the psychotherapy, an exchange of experiences regarding their disability, criticisms of the medical profession, aggressive outbursts toward family members, the discovery of the role of stress in precipitating asthma, a discussion of group members manifesting improvement, deeper exploration of personality variables, the establishment of the group's "theories" concerning asthma, and, finally, a clearer definition of the scope and limitation of group therapy for asthmatics.

Bastiaans and Groen (3) and Groen and Pelser (15) found that among a variety of treatment methods employed in chronic asthma, a combination of group therapy and corticotropin (ACTH) administration provided the most favorable results. Long-term follow-up, however, has not been clearly documented, and this highlights a general problem in the evaluation of group therapy and, indeed, of psychotherapy as a whole.

One of the psychotherapist's "nightmares" concerns the fear of an acute asthmatic attack occurring in the course of a group therapy session. Pelser (28) warned that the likelihood of such an emergency is increased in older patients and in those with a very unfavorable marriage situation, a poor employment record, lack of motivation, or an inability to introspect.

Sclare and Crocket (34) reported the results of group therapy in treating asthma, which corroborated the work in Holland. A favorable outcome occurred especially often when the patients were selected for group therapy on the basis of a dominant psychological factor in their asthma. On the whole, however, the improvement was to be found in the area of reduced anxiety and more free emotional expression, rather than in diminished respiratory symptoms. Another management problem in chronic asthma is that of "syndrome shift," and Sclare (33) noted that a very robust style of psychotherapy carries the risk of provoking depression in the asthmatic patient.

The Netherlands Asthmatic Association has been established for the promotion of the interests of asthmatic patients. Today, it comprises some 2000 members who are either asthmatic patients or the parents of asthmatic children. One of the therapeutic activities of this association in Amsterdam has been the endeavor to discover group leaders from among the patients and to encourage these leaders to conduct, with medical supervision from time to time, their own therapeutic groups. In Rotterdam, a psychologist has been similarly employed to supervise two lay group therapists who work with asthmatic patients (29).

Jackson (18) advocated the use of individual psychotherapy as an orientation procedure before embarking on a program of group therapy with asthmatic patients. He views the objective of treatment as one of "desomatization" and surrender of the "conservation-withdrawal" defensive system (Engel, 1962), which is held to be significant in asthma. A method of encounter therapy involving limited physical contact has been described by Reckless (1972) for the treatment of an acute asthmatic attack.

ANOREXIA NERVOSA

Hamilton and Hamill (17) in Glasgow have demonstrated the value of group therapy in the treatment of patients suffering from anorexia nervosa. They were motivated to experiment with this technique on finding that girls with anorexia nervosa regularly failed to achieve personal involvement and emotional expression within the broader setting of a therapeutic community milieu. In the hospital ward environment, the patients' marked denial and dependence allowed them to perform a detached, "pseudonormal" role. It was accordingly considered that a small "all anorexia" group (six patients) might assist these patients in confronting their deeper emotional problems.

The anorexia patients in the group situation progressed through the following stages, which to some degree overlapped:

1. *Resistance:* The patients confined their observations to matters of food, weight, and the physical symptoms associated with eating.
2. *Exploration:* They began to speak about a variety of emotional reactions, *e.g.,* a sense of guilt after eating and their general oversensitivity.
3. *Emotional confusion:* They discussed their problems about decision making, the conflicts about leaving home, and their general suggestibility.
4. *Cohesion:* They became more autonomous, met together socially, and, on occasions, conducted the group session when both therapists were absent.

Concurrently with the treatment of the anorexia group, the therapists scheduled group sessions with the parents of the patients. The parents' group displayed a need at the outset to deny any emotional problems and to present a facade of a happy family. It soon emerged that despite their protestations of maintaining a close family, the parents had little awareness of their daughters' true feelings. They expressed a clear preference for the "medical model" in comprehending the nature of anorexia nervosa. The mothers initially dominated the group, but the fathers participated more as time progressed. The parents' group satisfied the dependent needs of the mothers and also served as a holding maneuver while the family achieved reorientation and maturation. It is concluded that although the cause of anorexia nervosa remains obscure, there is now good evidence that group therapy for the patients and their parents can make a useful contribution to the management of the condition.

In 1974, Mrs. Pat Hartley in England founded Anorexic Aid, a voluntary society for the mutual support of anorexics and their families. This organization holds monthly meetings in a number of British cities, and it circulates information among its members. In addition to its supportive and informative role, this group is likely to become a launching site for further research into anorexia nervosa.

OBESITY

Diet regimens, with or without drugs but supervised by a physician, are notoriously limited or transient in their results in these cases. Moreover, dropout rates from such programs tend to be high (37). Likewise, psychotherapeutic endeavors based upon psychodynamic principles (5, 10) have tended to yield undramatic results in the management of obesity. On the other hand, strong claims have been advanced in recent years by groups in Britain such as Weight Watchers, Slimline, and Silhouette and in the United States by TOPS (Take Off Pounds Sensibly). Such methods depend mainly upon positive expectation and social pressure. Unfortunately, no reports are available regarding a controlled evaluation of these techniques.

An alternative approach in the management of obese patients is that based on the deployment of learning theory. Whatever may be the multiple causative factors of obesity, this approach emphasizes that overweight individuals eat too much for their activity level. Wollersheim (41) has reported from the University of Illinois one of the few controlled studies of group therapy based upon learning principles in the treatment of overweight women. The results demonstrated the superiority of "focal treatment" that employed learning principles over nonspecific or social-pressure treatments. The method entailed instructing the subjects to keep a record of their eating behavior, which helped them to identify reinforcing stimuli related to overeating and assisted them to implement self-control techniques in accordance with their life-styles. There was no evidence of symptom substitution.

Geraghty (13) in Glasgow has employed a similar method in the treatment of overweight female subjects. His original group comprised several psychotic patients, and therefore the methods of Stuart (36) and Wollersheim (41) were simplified in order to avoid overloading them with instructions. The only instruction given to the patients was to keep a diary of what they ate. The treatment sessions maintained a lighthearted tone, encouraged the patients to develop their own style of dietary control, and prompted friendly, competitive pressure among the group members. The patients weighed themselves at home, and their reports regarding weight loss were accepted as true. The objective of treatment was a weight loss of 5 to 10 pounds per month, and the patients seemed to experience little difficulty in maintaining this rate of loss. The role of the therapist was conceived of as that of a "maintenance specialist" (38). This particular group is now constituted of only nonpsychotic overweight subjects.

RENAL DIALYSIS AND TRANSPLANTATION

The psychosocial stresses experienced by renal dialysis patients have been the subject of much interest in the medical literature in recent years (1, 7, 14, 21). The psychological reactions of children to chronic dialysis have stimulated particular attention (8, 31). Psychological problems associated with kidney transplantation have been discussed by Korsch *et al.* (23) and Bernstein (4).

Formal group work with adult or juvenile patients in renal dialysis programs has not yet been established on a firm footing. James (1976) observed that group therapy with children on dialysis may carry the risk of seriously disrupting the entirely adaptive denial mechanisms that they frequently utilize, thus rendering them dangerously aware of their bad physical prognosis. The staff of dialysis units, however, like the staff of intensive care and cardiac surgery units, tends to undergo unique and severe stresses. Accordingly, staff group sessions have been set up in a number of children's dialysis units in Europe in order to deal with the emotional reactions of the professional staff as well as to comprehend the behavior of the children.

Korsch *et al.* (23) described a sophisticated unit for children in dialysis and kidney transplantation programs in Los Angeles. An open style of communication involving the children, their parents, and the staff characterizes the unit. Families are invited to come to the unit for regular conferences while their children are being prepared for or participating in the program, as well as during the stormy posttransplantation period. It is considered that in a "high technology" situation such as dialysis or transplantation, attention to psychological factors can all too readily go by default unless a group ethos of informal patient-parent-staff interaction is clearly established.

Group sessions at weekly intervals for professional members of the dialysis team were found to be of great value by Kaplan de-Nour and Czaczkes (21). The group examined the patients' problems and their own feelings concerning the work of the unit. The principal reactions observed in the team were feelings of guilt, possessiveness, overprotectiveness, and withdrawal from patients. Demands that patients should do inordinately well on the treatment were considered to stem from such emotional reactions. Unrealistic attitudes of this nature were usefully discussed at the team meetings.

Staff groups would seem to be of proved value in those medical situations that involve a high degree of stress for nursing and medical personnel. Another instance of such stress is that occasioned by the termination of pregnancy, a situation in which Sclare and Geraghty (35) advocate discussion groups for nurses.

VOLUNTARY SELF-HELP GROUPS OR MOVEMENTS

Reference has already been made to the value of self-help associations in the fields of bronchial asthma, anorexia nervosa, and obesity. Many other similar groups for dealing with various physical disorders are becoming well established in Western society. Such movements offer the members mutual support and understanding, as well as providing an information service and an active interest in therapeutic advances and research possibilities. The disease processes that appear to lend themselves readily to the formation of self-help groups tend to be chronic, relapsing, and associated with reactions of despair and anxiety. These associations are maintained largely through internal drives generated by the sufferers themselves, but they may be further strengthened by the sponsorship of relevant medical specialists.

A good example of a well-established self-help group is the British Diabetic Association, which was formed in 1934 by Dr. R. D. Lawrence and his patient and celebrated author, H. G. Wells. Sir Frederick Banting and Dr. C. H. Best, the discoverers of insulin in 1921, became vice-presidents. The association issues a journal named *Balance,* and 120 branches and clubs are to be found in various parts of Britain. There are summer camps and special hostels for diabetic children. Advice is given regarding employment for diabetics. There are now 48 national diabetic associations, these being linked through the International Diabetic Federation. In 1968, a Professional Services Section was initiated, this being open to social workers, dieticians, and nurses. Much of the correspondence received by the association is concerned with food and diet.

Many other self-help associations have developed in a number of countries in response to the needs and stresses created by chronic, severe disorders for which there may exist no specific therapy as yet. Not infrequently, such organizations act as pioneering groups, exploring the situation, activating key individuals, and providing a lead for statutory agencies. They serve outstandingly as a forum for communications, and many members feel that they receive more information in this supportive context than they receive from doctors and nurses. This is especially true of the parents of children who have such ill-understood, uncommon conditions as muscular dystrophy, leukemia, cystic fibrosis of the pancreas, or familial dysautonomia. Some of these associations are international in their organization.

A number of self-help agencies deal with post operative problems such as ileostomy or colostomy. A Mastectomy Association has recently been formed in the United Kingdom. Such support groups do much to help patients through shared experience in their acclimatization to changes of body schema. Other groups render support to the deaf, blind, and epileptic and to the parents of spastic children. The Chest and Heart Association in Britain assists patients with various cardiothoracic disorders, including myocardial infarction, and is also involved in mounting antismoking campaigns. There is an active Migraine Trust in Britain.

In general, voluntary associations provide a source of informal communications, postal contacts by means of newsletters, hope, advice, social friendships, and contact with specialists in the field. A criticism leveled from certain quarters is that these groups attract principally a middle-class clientele and largely fail to reach those persons in the lower socioeconomic groups who are in need.

TERMINAL CARE

Until recently in Western society, the topics of death and the dying patient tended to be invested with mystery, denial, or rejection. At present, however, there is a resurgence of medical interest in the problems of the terminal patient and in the need to pay close attention to the patient's distress and to the maintenance of his human dignity. Special centers for the care of the dying have recently been established in many countries. St. Christopher's Hospice, which was founded in London by Cicely Saunders in 1967, may be fairly regarded as the prototype of these caring organizations. It has been well described by West (39), who comments, "We know that patients and staff have to learn to deal not only with each other but also with themselves."

St. Christopher's Hospice is a 54-bed facility. This is considered to be an optimum size in order to facilitate administration and to foster group dynamics of the therapeutic community type. The wise leadership, caring, and dedication of the medical director have promoted intense staff loyalty and stability. A religious ambience of an ecumenical sort pervades the institution; no atheist patient or staff member need be embarrassed.

An attitude of care and concern informs the slightest actions of the nursing staff at St. Christopher's. When a new patient arrives at the hospice, the matron or her deputy personally greets him by name inside the ambulance. This welcome sets the tone of warm acceptance that typifies the institution. The patients are not idealized but are informally befriended. The group-relatedness of staff and patients is characterized by flexibility and fluidity. The patient's family is encouraged to spend as much time as possible with the patient, to have lunch with him, and to interact with other families who are visiting. Daily group sessions involving the staff and patients are scheduled. Patients help other patients both emotionally and physically, and they sometimes even provide support for the staff. The staff members and their preschool children are remarkably interlaced with the patient group. Alcohol is available to the patients; birthday parties and Christmas celebrations are given an important place. Above all, the process of dying is viewed as an interpersonal event in which the patient remains in communication with his family and professional staff throughout. No patient need die alone or in pain.

It is to be hoped that the concept of patient-family-staff interaction can be carried out into the community. Indeed, the St. Christopher's team is already heavily involved in assisting with terminal care at home as well as in the hospice.

EVALUATION OF GROUP THERAPY

Despite a statement by Foulkes and Anthony (11) that the effects of psychotherapy are too subjectively loaded to become amenable to exact measurement, others such as Jones *et al.* (20) are willing to face this difficult issue in the case of group therapy. It certainly is understandable that nonpsychiatrists should sometimes be sceptical until they have the benefit of "proof" of the method. In principle, rating scales and questionnaires could be employed to assess the results of group therapy, but it is doubtful if these are sufficiently sophisticated in most instances.

Repertory grid techniques (25) are likely to offer a more subtle means of judging improvement. These are based on the construct theory of Kelly (22). This theory, in contrast to Freudian determinism, postulates a flexibility in the individual's mode of viewing the world and his own experience. Repertory grid assessments before and after treatment are likely to provide a worthwhile technique of evaluation.

REFERENCES

1. Abram HS: The psychiatrist, the treatment of chronic renal failure and the prolongation of life. Am J Psychiatry 126:157, 1969

2. Baruch DW, Miller H: Interview group therapy with allergic patients. In Slavson SR (ed): The Practice of Group Therapy. New York, International Universities Press, 1947

3. Bastiaans J, Groen J: Psychogenesis and psychotherapy of bronchial asthma. In O'Neill D (ed): Modern Trends in Psychosomatic Medicine. London, Butterworth, 1955

4. Bernstein DM: Emotional reactions of children and adolescents to renal transplantation. Child Psych Hum Dev 1:103–111, 1970

5. Bruch H: Disturbed communication in eating disorders. Am J Orthopsychiatry 33:99, 1963

6. Bukantz SC, Peshkin MM: Institutional treatment of asthmatic children. Paediatr Clin North Am 6:755, 1959

7. Cramond WA: The psychological problems of renal dialysis and transplantation. In Hill OW (ed): Modern Trends in Psychosomatic Medicine, Vol 2. London, Butterworth, 1970

8. Debre M, Dulong O, Raimbault G: Etude psychologique d'enfants en hemodialyse chronique. Arch Franc Ped 30:163, 1973

9. Dobbs RH: Results of treatment in Switzerland In Bronchial Asthma. London, Chest and Heart Association, 1959

10. Fenichel O: The psychoanalytic theory of neurosis. New York, Norton, 1945

11. Foulkes, SH, Anthony EJ: Group Psychotherapy, 2nd ed. New York, Penguin Books, 1965

12. Friedman DD: Motivation for natural childbirth. In Morris N (ed): Psychosomatic Medicine in Obstetrics and Gynaecology. Basel, S Karger, 1972

13. Geraghty BP: Personal communication, 1975

14. Goodey J, Kelly J: Social and economic effects of regular dialysis. Lancet 2:147, 1967

15. Groen J, Pelser HE: Experiences with group psychotherapy in patients with bronchial asthma. J Psychosom Res 4:191, 1960

16. Hallowitz D: Residential treatment of chronic asthmatic children. Am J Orthopsychiatry 24:576, 1954

17. Hamilton CM, Hamill EA: Int J Group Psychotherapy (in press)

18. Jackson M: Psychotherapy and psychopathology in bronchial asthma. Paper presented at Annual Conference of Society for Psychosomatic Research, London, 1974

19. James DS: Personal communication, 1975

20. Jones M, McPherson F, Whitaker DS, Sutherland JD, Walton H, Wolff H: Small Group Psychotherapy. New York, Penguin Books, 1971

21. Kaplan de–Nour A, Czaczkes JW: Emotional problems and reactions of the medical team in a chronic haemodialysis unit. Lancet, 2:987, 1968

22. Kelly GA: A Theory of Personality. New York, Norton, 1963

23. Korsch BM, Fine RN, Grushkin CM, Negrete VF: Experiences with children and their families during extended haemodialysis and kidney transplantation. Paediatr Clin North Am 18:625, 1971

24. Macnaughton MC: Antenatal care. Practitioner 212:633, 1974

25. Mair JMM, Crisp AH: Measurement of personality in relation to clinical practice. Br J Med Psychol 41:45, 1968

26. Markillie R: Group psychotherapy in psychosomatic disorders In O'Neill D (ed): Modern Trends in Psychosomatic Medicine. London, Butterworth, 1955

27. Meyer H: A general survey of bronchial asthma in childhood. In Bronchial Asthma: a Symposium. London, Chest & Heart Association, 1959

28. Pelser HE: Group psychotherapy with asthmatic patients. Paper presented at International Conference on Psychosomatic Medicine, Amsterdam, 1956

29. Pelser HE: Personal communication, 1975

30. Pratt JH: The class method of treating consumption in the homes of the poor. J A M A 49:755, 1907

31. Raimbault G: Psychological aspects of chronic renal failure and haemodialysis. In Berlyne GM, Giovannetti S (eds): Nephron. Basel, S Karger, 1973

32. Read GD: Childbirth Without Fear, 2nd ed. London, Heinemann, 1952
33. Sclare AB: Psychological aspects of bronchial asthma. In Bronchial Asthma. London, Chest and Heart Association, 1959
34. Sclare AB, Crocket JA: Group psychotherapy in bronchial asthma. J Psychosom Res 2: 157, 1957
35. Sclare AB, Geraghty BP: Termination of pregnancy—the nurse's attitude. Nurs Mirror 140:59, 1975
36. Stuart RB: Behavioural control of overeating. Behav Res Ther 5:357, 1967
37. Stunkard AJ: The dieting depression. Am J Med 23:77, 1957
38. Thibaut JW, Kelly HH: The Social Psychology of Groups. New York, Wiley, 1959
39. West TS: Approach to death. Nurs Mirror 139 (15): 56–59, 1974
40. Williams EA: Talking to children. In Morris N (ed): Psychosomatic Medicine in Obstetrics and Gynaecology. Basel, S Karger, 1972
41. Wollersheim JP: Effectiveness of group therapy based upon learning principles in the treatment of overweight women. J Abnorm Psychol 76:462, 1970

12

A Conceptual Model of Psychosomatic Illness in Children: Family Organization and Family Therapy*

SALVADOR MINUCHIN, LESTER BAKER, BERNICE ROSMAN,
RONALD LIEBMAN, LEROY MILMAN, THOMAS C. TODD

In the past century, the study of psychosomatic illness, which began with the simplest accumulation of clinical anecdotes, has evolved to the use of the most sophisticated techniques of laboratory and behavioral science. Speculation based on the hypothesis that certain psychological dynamics are specific to certain somatic diseases has been replaced by systematic studies of the complex interrelationships of psyche and soma. Many important contributions have been made in interpreting the mediating mechanisms whereby emotions cause bodily changes.

Unfortunately, this progress in understanding the etiology of psychosomatic syndromes has not invariably been accompanied by increased effectiveness in treatment.

It is our contention that both research and therapy in psychosomatic medicine have been severely handicapped by the prevailing conceptual model of psychosomatic illness. This linear model links, in a causal chain, the individual's life situations to his emotions and thence to bodily illness. According to this model, however, the illness is seen as contained within the individual. Consequently, research and treatment approaches are focused on the individual, and this is far too limited a target (for a review of these approaches, see Reference 9). The importance of the individual's context is recognized, but there has been a curious dearth of therapeutic attempts to modify that context. This is particularly striking in the case of children, who can be assumed to be deeply involved with some form of family group, yet the child is apparently seen, from this viewpoint, as a passive recipient of noxious environmental influences. Consequently, the general therapeutic response has been only to separate him from those influences, either by individual psychotherapy, by behavioral therapy, or by "parentectomy." All these treatment approaches place the burden of change on the patient alone.

In the past decade, we have begun to look beyond the individual *per se* to the individual in his social contexts and to the feedback processes that exist between the individual and his context. As a result, a less restricted conceptual model, which is here called the *open systems model,* is evolving. It has directed investiga-

*Abridged from *Archives of General Psychiatry* 32:1031–1038, 1975, with permission of the authors and the American Medical Association.

tors to a better understanding of psychosomatic syndromes and to the discovery of more effective treatment techniques.

THE OPEN SYSTEMS MODEL

Broadening the focus from the sick child alone to the sick child within the family redefines the nature of the pathology and the scope of therapeutic change. This shift is facilitated by a conceptual model that postulates 1) that certain types of family organization are closely related to the development and maintenance of psychosomatic symptoms in children and 2) that children's psychosomatic symptoms play a major role in maintaining family homeostasis. In the open systems model, a psychosomatic crisis is held to consist of two phases, which encompass both psychological and physiological parameters. There is first the "turn-on" phase: some family conflict situation induces emotional arousal in the child, triggering a physiological response. Then there is the "turn-off" phase, or a return to baseline levels. The turn-off phase may be handicapped by the nature of the family members' involvement with each other around the conflict. Since family interactions affect the psychophysiology of the child in the psychosomatic crisis, the pathology is seen as situated in the feedback processes of child and family. The artificial boundary between individual and context no longer handicaps therapeutic efforts. These can be directed toward the child, the family, and the feedback processes of the family system's transactional patterns in whatever combinations seem to be most promising.

In other words, family interactional patterns may trigger the onset or hamper the subsidence of psychophysiological processes, or both. The resulting psychosomatic symptoms function as homeostatic mechanisms that regulate family transactions. Therefore, therapy must be directed toward changing the family processes that trigger and maintain the child's psychosomatic symptoms as well as toward changing the use of these symptoms within the family.

It is important to note that the hypotheses we are advancing here do not imply that symptom specificity exists in relation to a given family constellation; rather, we will describe a more general type of family process that encourages somatization. Within this conceptual scheme, we do not suggest a single or simple causative factor, but we will describe instead a cluster of significant, related determinants.

THE FAMILY MODEL

Our study and treatment of families of psychosomatically ill children has led to the development of an exploratory model of the structure and functioning of such families. This model holds that three factors in conjunction are necessary for the development of severe psychosomatic illness in children. First, the child is physiologically vulnerable; that is, a specific organic dysfunction is present. Second, the child's family has the following four transactional characteristics: enmeshment, overprotectiveness, rigidity, and lack of conflict resolution. Third, the sick child plays an important role in the family's patterns of conflict avoidance, and this role is an important source of reinforcement for his symptoms.

VULNERABILITY

The diabetic and asthmatic patients that we have treated were so defined by pediatric evaluation. The presence of physiological vulnerability in cases of anorexia nervosa is debatable, but we have followed the literature in treating it as a psychosomatic disease.

It may be important to distinguish here between "primary" and "secondary" psychosomatic symptomatology. In cases with *primary* psychosomatic symptoms, a physiological disorder is already present. These include metabolic disorders like diabetes, allergic diatheses such as that found in asthma, and so forth. The psychosomatic element lies in the emotional exacerbation of the already available symptom. In the *secondary* psychosomatic disorder, no such predisposing physical disorder can be demonstrated. The psychosomatic element is apparent in the transformation of emotional conflicts into somatic symptoms. These symptoms may crystallize into a severe and debilitating illness such as anorexia nervosa.

Symptom choice may be differently determined in these two instances. Our work indicates, however, that the "psychosomatogenic" family organization described here is applicable across these varieties of psychosomatic illness.

FAMILY TRANSACTIONAL CHARACTERISTICS

The four characteristics—enmeshment, overprotectiveness, rigidity, and the lack of conflict resolution—can be observed in a family's behavior during family interaction testing (10), diagnostic interviews (6), and in family therapy sessions. They appear to be representative of a general type of family organization and functioning.

Enmeshment

A pathologically enmeshed family system is characterized by a high degree of responsiveness and involvement. This can be seen in the interdependence of relationships, intrusions on personal boundaries, a poorly differentiated perception of self and of other family members, and weak family subsystem boundaries.

In a highly enmeshed family, changes in one family member or in the relationship between two members reverberate throughout the family system. Dialogs are rapidly diffused by the entrance of other family members. A dyadic conflict may set off a chain of shifting alliances within the whole family as other members get involved.

Internal structures within a highly enmeshed family system are characteristically fluid. The boundaries that define individual autonomy are so weak that an individual's life-space is impinged upon. This may be reflected in a lack of privacy or excessive "togetherness" and sharing. ("Why do you change the furniture around in my room all the time when I'm not there?" a 15-year-old individual complains to his mother.) Family members also intrude on each other's thoughts, feelings, and communications. One family member may relay messages from another family member to a third, thereby blocking direct communication. Often there are many interruptions; family members may finish each other's sentences.

Problems of enmeshment are also reflected in the family members' poorly differentiated perceptions of each other. Parents asked to tell what they like about each of their children often can speak of them only as a group.

In enmeshed families, subsystem boundaries are weak and easily crossed. As a result, executive hierarchies are confused. Children may join one parent in criticizing the other. Often the children take inappropriately parental roles toward each other. In the absence of a clearly defined and effective parental subsystem, it is common for the parents to work at cross purposes in relation to the children. A parent may frequently enlist a child's support in struggles with the other parent.

Overprotectiveness

In families with a psychosomatically ill child, the family members show a high degree of concern for each other's welfare. This concern is not limited to the identified patient or to the area of illness. Nurturing and protective responses are constantly elicited and supplied as family members interact. A sneeze sets off a flurry of handkerchief offers; complaints and queries about fatigue or discomfort punctuate the flow of communications. Critical remarks and demands are often accompanied by pacifying behaviors. Signs of distress frequently cue family members to the approach of dangerous levels of tension or conflicts. A mother's weeping as she anticipates the father's criticism, for example, may galvanize the children into distracting behavior. A symptomatic child's emotional outburst may elicit comforting and help to avert an exploration of the family conflicts.

The family members' perceptions of each other are structured around protective concerns, particularly when there is a sick child. (When family members are asked to tell what pleases them and displeases them the most about each other, they may, for example, reply: "I like it when you don't overdo." "I like it when you rub my chest." "I don't like it when he gets sick all the time.") In such families, the parents' overprotectiveness retards the children's development of autonomy and competence. (A father tells his two adolescent diabetic daughters, "If Mommy and I could only take the needles for you, everything would be all right.")

In turn, the children, particularly the psychosomatically ill child, feel great responsibility for protecting the family. For the sick child, the experience of being able to protect the family by using his symptoms may be a major reinforcement for the illness.

Rigidity

The pathologically enmeshed families are heavily committed to maintaining the status quo. In periods when change and growth are necessary, they experience great difficulty. When a child in an effectively functioning family reaches adolescence, for example, his family will be able to change its rules and transactional patterns in ways that allow for age-appropriate increased autonomy while still preserving family continuity. The family of a psychosomatically ill child, however, operates like a closed system. When events requiring change occur, family members insist on retaining accustomed methods of interaction. Consequently, avoidance circuits must be developed, and a "symptom bearer" is a particularly useful detouring route. When the family's low threshold of tolerance for conflict is approached, the sick child becomes ill, allowing the family members to detour their conflict via concern for him. The family reinforces his development of deviance and rewards its continuance, because of its usefulness in maintaining the pathogenic system's precarious equilibrium.

As a result of their inappropriately summoned homeostatic mechanisms, these families live in a chronic state of submerged stress. Issues that threaten change, such as negotiations of individual autonomy, are not allowed to surface to the point where they could be explored. Typically, these families present themselves as normal and untroubled except for the one child's medical problem. They deny any need for change in the family.

Lack of Conflict Resolution

The rigidity and overprotectiveness of the family system, combined with the constant, mutual impingements characteristic of pathologically enmeshed transactional patterns, make such families' thresholds for conflict very low. Often a strong religious or ethical code buttresses and provides a rationale for avoiding conflict.

As a result, there can be no explicit negotiation of differences. Problems are left unresolved, to threaten again and again, and continually activate the system's avoidance circuits.

Each family's idiosyncratic structure and functioning dictate their ways of avoiding conflict resolution. One spouse is often an "avoider." The nonavoider brings up areas of difficulty, but the avoider always manages to detour confrontation that would lead to the acknowledgement of conflict and, perhaps, to its negotiation. A man may simply leave the house, for example, when his wife tries to discuss a problem.

Other families bicker continuously, but the constant interruptions and subject changes typical of an enmeshed system obfuscate any conflictual issue before it is brought to prominence. Other families simply deny the existence of any problems whatsoever.

The four transactional characteristics typical of families with psychosomatically ill children—enmeshment, overprotectiveness, rigidity, and the lack of conflict resolution—provide the context for using illness as a mode of communication.

THE USE OF THE SICK CHILD

The third condition postulated in this family model is that the sick child plays an important role in the family's conflict-avoidance system and that this is an important source of reinforcement for his symptoms.

The results of our experimental work—which employed a controlled interview designed to elicit parental conflict in the index child's presence—suggest that there are characteristic patterns of conflict-related behavior that involve the child and affect him in different ways. Families commonly move into several of these patterns in the course of the interview, but one tends to predominate. These conflict-avoidance patterns have been grouped according to whether they facilitate or handicap "turn off."

Three patterns of involvement seem to handicap the turn-off phase severely and therefore are related to psychosomatic illness. In the first two patterns—triangulation and parent-child coalitions—the spouse dyad is frankly split. The child is openly pressed to ally with one parent against the other. In *triangulation,* the child is put in such a position that he cannot express himself without siding with one parent against the other. Statements that impose coalition—such as, "Wouldn't you rather do it my way?"—are used in the attempt to force the child to take sides. (One demonstrative father, for example, was finally able to express his covert criticism of his wife, accusing her of coldness to the children. Both parents then pressed their anorectic daughter to say whether she preferred her father's ways and wanted her mother to change. Stuck between the two adults, she was unable to speak.)

In the second pattern, *parent-child coalition,* the child tends to move into a stable coalition with one parent against the other. The role of the excluded parent varies to the degree that he tries to disrupt the coalition. (A mother was unable to express her rage that was due to her husband's refusing to protect her from his mother's attacks. Their asthmatic son was highly involved as the mother's protector, and he could state her complaints. He urged his father to protect her from her mother-in-law. The father tried to persuade his son to reject the mother's "childish" demands, but the wheezing boy maintained his adult stance.)

In the third type of pattern, called *detouring,* the spouse dyad is united. The parents submerge their conflicts in a posture of protecting or blaming their sick child, who is defined by them as the only family problem. In several such families, the parents required that the children reassure them that they were good parents, or that they join them in worrying about the family. The parents occasionally vacillate between their concerns for the child and exasperation over the burdens he imposes by "not trying to help himself." In most cases, parental concerns absorb the couple, so that all signs of marital strife or even minor differences are suppressed or ignored.

It is important to note that these patterns of involvement are not intended to represent a classification of families. They describe transactional sequences that occur in response to family conflict. Such sequences often occur in the transactions of effectively functioning families; they fall within the wide range of methods used to cope with conflict. Families in the normal range, however, can shift into other modes of conflict confrontation and negotiation. The rigid families with psychosomatically ill children are more likely to engage in maladaptive sequences again and again. Since they are usually operating under conditions of stress and tension, the child is frequently involved in his role as an "avoider circuit."

To summarize, we hypothesize that the family with a psychosomatically ill child is characterized by the transactional patterns of enmeshment, overprotectiveness, rigidity, and lack of conflict resolution. The sick child is involved in parental conflict. We have been testing this model in three ways. First, we are comparing the interactional characteristics of families with psychosomatically ill children with those families who have nonpsychosomatically but chronically ill children. Second, we have designed a structured family interview that permits the physiological assessment of the family members' responses to psychological family stress. The assessment of "turn on" and "turn off" is of particular interest. We will present our data in these two areas in other publications. In this chapter, we will address ourselves to our third test: the examination of whether changing the specified family behavior patterns through structural family therapy results in improved management and significant alleviation of the child's psychosomatic symptoms.

FAMILY THERAPY PROGRAM—METHODS AND RESULTS

Over the past seven years, our team has been involved in an interdisciplinary research project designed to identify the elements of family structure and functioning that are related to the development and reinforcement of psychosomatic symptoms in children. A concomitant program of family therapy oriented toward changing these elements of family organization has treated children with anorexia nervosa (3, 6, 7), children with superlabile diabetes (psychosomatically triggered recurrent ketoacidosis) (1, 8), and children with intractable asthma (2). Almost all these children were seriously ill at the time of referral. The anorectic group had suffered a mean weight loss of 30%, the diabetic group had an average of twelve hospitalizations a year, and most of the asthmatic group were steroid dependent. All cases reported were diagnosed as psychosomatic and referred for family therapy upon the basis of independent pediatric criteria rather than upon psychiatric evaluation.

Hospital admissions for the *superlabile diabetic* group were occasioned by severe bouts of ketoacidosis; chronic acetonuria cases were diagnosed on the basis of daily urine testing as well as of symptoms. In all cases, careful screening and control studies were carried out under pediatric supervision to rule out other physiological disorders and instances of insulin omission. Similar criteria were applied during follow-up.

Similarly, in the case of *asthmatic* patients, independent pediatric assessment by members of an allergist team documented the physiological severity of the illness and the necessity for special treatment (*i.e.,* steroid therapy) prior to psychiatric referral. School loss for the diabetic and asthmatic patients was determined on the basis of a pediatric chart review and was directly related to the incidence of medical symptoms; improvement in this area reflected true symptom remissions.

Table 12-1. PRESENTING CHARACTERISTICS OF PSYCHOSOMATIC PATIENTS

DIAGNOSIS	NUMBER	SEX	AGE AT REFERRAL	PRESENTING PROBLEMS
Superlabile diabetes	13	9 F 4 M	10–18 years (median, 13)	Eight cases of severe, relapsing diabetic acidosis: 6–35 hospital admissions in period of 6 months to 4 years preceding psychotherapy (average of one hospital admission per month). Five cases of chronic acetonuria: lethargy, headaches, nausea and vomiting, frequent school absence, occasional hospital admission to evaluate poor diabetic control during periods of 12–36 months prior to psychotherapy.
Intractable asthma	10	5 M 5 F	6–16 years (median, 12)	One case grade 2, seven cases grade 3, and two cases grade 4 (Pinkerton scale of clinical severity of asthma [11]; grade 1 mildest, grade 4 most severe rating). Eight of these cases were steroid dependent. Duration of illness prior to psychotherapy: 1–12 years (median, 8 years).
Anorexia nervosa	25	24 F 1 M	9–17 years (median, 14)	Percentage of body weight loss: 18%–56% (median weight loss, 30%). Duration of illness prior to psychotherapy: 1–27 months (median, 6 months).

Table 12-2. FAMILY THERAPY AND FOLLOW-UP OF PSYCHOSOMATIC PATIENTS

DIAGNOSIS	DURATION OF TREATMENT	DURATION OF FOLLOW-UP	FOLLOW-UP STATUS
Superlabile diabetes	2–15 months family therapy (median, 7 months)	15 months to 6½ years (median, 2½ years)	Eight relapsing cases: five cases, no admissions during follow-up; three cases had four admissions in 3½ years, one admission in 3 years, and two admissions in 6 years, respectively. Five chronic acetonuria cases: in all cases, significantly improved diabetic control; minimal school absence in two cases, two hospital admissions in 2½ years in one case.
Intractable asthma	5–22 months family therapy (median, 8 months)	1–3 years (median, 2 years)	Seven cases grade 1; two cases grade 2 (Pinkerton scale of clinical severity of asthma [11]; grade 1 mildest, grade 4 most severe rating). One case showed complete remission for past 17 months, was discharged by allergist.
Anorexia nervosa	7–25 inpatient days 2 months to 1 year family therapy (median, 7 months)	5 months to 4 years (median, 2 years)	Three patients dropped the program (two immediately, one after 10 months). Twenty-one recovered; one fair recovery of weight (weight gains returned to normal levels, no food problems, school, peer, and family adjustment satisfactory).

Anorectic patients were diagnosed solely on the basis of medical criteria—severe weight loss, amenorrhea, and so on—after other medical conditions were ruled out. In evaluating recovery, the major emphasis again was placed on pediatric criteria (*e.g.,* weight gain). The only psychiatric evaluation of recovery is seen in the clinical assessment of the anorectic group, and this was based on behavioral rather than psychological data.

Families were referred to the study group and for family therapy by the pediatricians, and they were free to receive treatment without participating in the study, or to refuse referral and remain in pediatric care only. Pediatricians and family therapists worked in close collaboration throughout the treatment period. The results of this combined pediatric and family-therapy treatment approach have been highly encouraging (Tables 12-1 and 12-2).

Dramatic improvement or remission of the psychosomatic symptoms has been achieved in most of these cases. We believe that the effectiveness of our therapeutic procedures can be traced to the use of the open systems model of psychosomatic illness in the development of therapeutic strategies. This conceptualization directs the therapist's attention toward the context in which the psychosomatic event was initiated and is maintained, and the therapeutic strategies will thus be directed toward modifying that matrix.

DEVELOPMENT AND MAINTENANCE OF PSYCHOSOMATIC SYMPTOMS

The open systems model explicitly differentiates the symptom choice, the precipitating event, and the maintenance of the symptom in its current manifestation.

SYMPTOM CHOICE

Symptom choice is related to the family history and organization. Frequently, other members of a family have psychosomatic complaints. Hypochondriacal fears and excessive concern with bodily functions are common. In the secondary psychosomatic disorders, symptom choice may relate to the family members' excessive preoccupation with normal areas of bodily functions. In families with an anorectic child, other family members often worry about table manners, become overly concerned with diet, have food fads, and so on. In the primary psychosomatic conditions, a child with a physiological vulnerability grows up within a family system that uses his illness as a point of concentration, as a method of diffusing system stresses, or both. The allergic diathesis of asthma, for instance, is a true physiological condition. Only some of the children thus affected, however, grow up in a family that encourages and maintains psychosomatic responses. It is this group who develops attacks that challenge medical management. In the primary cases, in other words, symptom selection is determined by the physical illness; in the secondary cases, symptom selection is idiosyncratic for each family. In contrast to workers who follow psychodynamic theories, we are less concerned with the specifics of symptom selection, and, in our approach, the analysis of the symptom does not form a basis for therapy.

We have found that in both primary and secondary cases, the child grows up in a family organization that provides fertile ground for the development and utilization of the symptom. The child's autonomy is curtailed by the other family members' intrusive concern. Areas of his psychological and bodily functioning remain subject to the control of others long after they should have become automatic or unattended. This control is maintained under the cloak of concern and protection, and it therefore cannot be challenged without impugning the motives of the concerned member.

A denial of self for others' benefit and the placement of a high value on self-sacrifice and family loyalty are characteristic of the context in which the child develops. Family members make their wishes known indirectly and "unselfishly" ("I want this because it is good for you"). Initiative and competence in areas not dictated by the family become acts of betrayal. The concern for mutual accommodation without friction produces an environment in which differences are submerged.

PRECIPITATING EVENT

This pattern of family homeostasis—with its emphasis on loyalty, protection, and the avoidance of conflict—is challenged at different stages in the development of the family and of particular family members, particularly in those normal developmental crises in which family members must make life decisions about issues that threaten the stability of the family unit. This unavoidable disequilibrium is frequently the *precipitating event* for the psychosomatic episode. All the family members are mobilized to protect the system and to protect or coerce the member whose distress or need for change is threatening the accustomed transactional patterns. The child, feeling the stresses within the system, responds with symptoms that may be utilized as a detouring mechanism. The family unites in concern and protection, and thus it rewards the symptom.

At each crossroad where a family member meets conflicting demands from the familial and extrafamilial, the stress in the family may be expressed in psychosomatic terms by the sick child. A psychosomatic episode will, therefore, have different characteristics at different periods of a family's life, because the family context in which the child experiences his illness is organized around different life tasks.

The developmental stages of the family in treatment have consequences for the selection of treatment strategies. When working with families in which the identified patient (IP) is a preadolescent child, for instance, the therapist will help to increase the parents' sense of competence and support their executive function. When working with families in which the IP is an adolescent, however, the therapist will challenge the parents to grow up, too, so that they can support the child's right to explore the extrafamilial world. In each instance, the therapist will encourage an age-appropriate differentiation of the child.

SYMPTOM MAINTENANCE

Once it has appeared, the psychosomatic symptom becomes embedded in, but also changes, the family organization. Challenged by the chronicity, the unpredictability, and the life-threatening quality of the illness, the family members respond by increasing their protective control of the sick child and by establishing a strong dependency on the pediatrician. The concentration on the symptomatic child maximizes his self-appraisal as a patient, with the consequent utilization of his illness as a significant coin for interpersonal transactions. Parents and siblings feel exploited by the demands of the "child and his illness" and increase their controlling protection. The child feels protected though scapegoated, and he increases his dependency on the parental members. If this process continues for a significant period of time, the child may be rendered incompetent in many areas of life functioning, and he may consequently increase his dependent demands.

The change in family organization goes beyond the dynamic needs of detouring family conflict. The family feedback to the child's symptoms becomes an autonomous process that maintains the symptom.

Initial therapeutic strategies that challenge these processes may sometimes result in rapid improvements of the child's symptoms and a further clarification of the family's dynamics. The therapist may concentrate, for example, on the manipulative aspect of the child's behavior, pointing out how the child controls family transactional patterns. A child who has been seen as weak and sick and in need of family protection is relabeled as a disobedient child who is using his illness to control the family. The parents will then develop a demanding attitude that evicts the child psychologically from his roles in the enmeshed system. As a result of the maneuver (which may seem unfair), the child moves from an "I am sick" stance to a stance of "I am controlling the situation." This increases the distance between the child and the family by enhancing his autonomy.

Such a maneuver also challenges the family's conflict-avoidance patterns. The child and parents begin to enter into areas of conflict, and these become the center of therapy. This strategy has been successful in treating a number of cases of anorexia, where the child's control of his symptom is more apparent. In other cases, the strategy of concentrating on the behavior of other siblings, who transitionally become the sick members, serves initially to move the child out of the central position. Intertwined with these strategies, the basic therapeutic procedure is directed toward changing the four characteristics of the family system that were described previously: enmeshment, overprotection, rigidity, and the lack of conflict resolution.

CONCLUSIONS

It is beyond the scope of this chapter to describe the many particular therapeutic techniques employed; these have been elaborated upon elsewhere (2–7). Rather, our concern has been to outline the therapeutic approach in relation to the open systems family model developed earlier.

Our experience with therapy for many families with psychosomatic children supports our impression that when the family organization is changed, the psychosomatically ill child improves significantly. These conclusions are based not only on the results reported in Tables 12-1 and 12-2, but also on our work with other psychosomatic conditions, *i.e.,* psychogenic vomiting, headaches, gastrointestinal disorders, and so forth.

Independent documentation of the changes in our patients' family organizations must await the final analyses of the data from our current study. We believe, however, that the evaluation of family therapy outcomes, as indicated by pediatric improvement as well as by improvement in other adjustment problems, offers support for the hypotheses underlying the goals and strategies employed in our approach.

We have explored the significance of a theoretical model in framing a method for research and treatment. A conceptual model maps the areas for exploration, but it tends to limit the data collected to those that fit within the framework of the model. Psychosomatic medicine has been handicapped by the use of an inadequate model that focuses on the individual and does not take into account the transactions in a patient's life context. This excluded area in the traditional model may account for much of the inadequacy of previous treatment techniques.

It has been suggested that the open systems model of psychosomatic illness is a more effective guide to exploration and therapy. This circular model does not preclude work with physiological mediating mechanisms, or with pharmacological and biofeedback intervention techniques based on a better understanding of these mechanisms. These techniques may be easily incorporated into the open systems framework.

Among the points that have been highlighted in our presentation is the claim that interventions that modify the life context of the psychosomatically ill patient seem to achieve a faster and more sustained remission of symptoms than do interventions that focus exclusively on the individual. The need for prolonged hospitalization for nonphysiological reasons disappears, because the patient will move from the controlled institutional environment to a natural environment that is changing according to therapeutic goals. The model of the psychosomatogenic family pinpoints dysfunctional areas within the child's most significant life context, thereby shortcutting much of the necessary exploration as well as opening areas for intervention. This knowledge of the family organization and functioning that predisposes to psychosomatic problems can also be used in preventive programs.

REFERENCES

1. Baker L, Minuchin S, Milman L, Liebman R, Todd T: Psychosomatic aspects of juvenile diabetes mellitus: a progress report. Israel J Med Sci (in press)

2. Liebman R, Minuchin S, Baker L: The use of structural family therapy in the treatment of intractable asthma. Am J Psychiatry 131: 535–540, 1974

3. Liebman R, Minuchin S, Baker L: An integrated treatment program for anorexia nervosa. Am J Psychiatry 131: 432–436, 1974

4. Liebman R, Minuchin S, Baker L: The role of the family in the treatment of anorexia nervosa. Child Psychiatry 13: 264–274, 1974

5. Minuchin S: The use of an ecological framework in the treatment of a child. In Anthony EJ, Koupernik C (eds): The Child in His Family. New York, John Wiley & Sons, 1970, pp 41–57

6. Minuchin S: Families and Family Therapy: A Structural Approach. Cambridge, Harvard Press, 1974

7. Minuchin S, Baker L, Liebman R, Milman L, Rosman B, Todd T: Anorexia nervosa: successful application of a family therapy approach (abstr). Pediatr Res 7:294, 1974

8. Minuchin S, Baker L, Rosman BL, Liebman R, Milman L, Todd TC: A conceptual model of psychosomatic illness in children. Arch Gen Psychiatry 32: 1031–1038, 1975

9. Minuchin S, Barcai A: Therapeutically induced family crisis. In Masserman J (ed): Science and Psychoanalysis, Vol 14. New York, Grune & Stratton, 1969, pp 199–205

10. Minuchin S, Montalvo B, Guerney BG, Rosman BL, Schumer F: Families of the Slums: An Exploration of Their Structure and Treatment. New York, Basic Books, 1967

11. Pinkerton P, Weaver CM: Childhood asthma *in* Modern Trends in Psychosomatic Medicine. Edited by O. Hill. London, Butterworths, 1970

13 Hypnosis

GEORGE PETERFY

The use of hypnosis for therapy always did and still does arouse more controversy, both among the professionals and in the general public, than probably any other form of treatment. This, though regretable, seems to be inevitable. An aura of unrespectability still clings to the use of hypnotism, and this is not surprising if one witnesses the eager crowds drawn to the performances of stage hypnotists.

Hypnosis is probably the oldest form of treatment, and it may have been practiced from the beginning of time by shamans, witch doctors, and so forth. There are many accounts of the use of hypnosis throughout history. In China, Wang Tai —"the father of Chinese medicine," whose works are still used—wrote in 2600 B.C. about medical treatment using incantations and mysterious passes over the patient, leaving no doubt about the hypnotic value of these actions. In 1500 B.C., the Hindu *Vedas* mentioned the use of hypnosis, and the Ebers Papyrus, which is over 3000 years old, described a method very similar to the one being used today. As always, we find that everything we are doing today, the Greeks have already done and sometimes so much better. Regarding the use of hypnosis, I feel that Hippocrates' statement about the art of medicine, that "nothing should be omitted in an art which interests the whole world, especially something which may be beneficial to suffering humanity and which does not risk human life or comfort," still cannot be matched.

In the Bible, both in the Old and in the New Testament, there are many references to the use of suggestion and hypnosis in the treatment of diseases that today would be classified as conversion hysteria or psychosomatic disorders. In medieval times, kings healed by the "royal touch." Unfortunately, kings, charlatans, religious leaders, and those dabbling in the occult arts of witchcraft, sorcery, and black magic have all been intrigued by the potentialities of hypnosis and have attempted to use it to further their own ends.

The contemporary status of hypnosis is accurately illustrated by C. L. Hull's statement: "All sciences alike have descended from magic and superstition, but none has been so slow as hypnosis in shaking off the evil associations of its origin."[6] In some countries—in the U.S.S.R., for example—the application of hypnosis is favored and widely practiced due to the Pavlovian teaching regarding the therapeutic value of cortical inhibition, whereas in other countries, the use of hypnosis as a mode of treatment has only recently been approved. The Canadian Medical Association, for instance, approved of hypnosis only in 1963.

THEORIES OF HYPNOTISM

Of the countless theories proposed in an attempt to explain the mechanisms of hypnosis, the majority fall into one of the three following groupings.

129

THE PSYCHOANALYTIC SCHOOL

Freud (5) hypothesized the existence of an erotic and submissive component, according to which the subject is involved in a submissive love relationship with the therapist, but without sexual involvement. Recently, Kubie and Margolin (7) attempted to combine the psychoanalytic and Pavlovian theories. They proposed that during the induction phase, the patient becomes progressively more oblivious of external stimuli, except for those produced by the hypnotist. This is explained by assuming a central zone of cortical excitation surrounded by a zone of inhibition. The psychological interpretation of this would be a dedifferentiation between the ego and the external world, represented by the therapist. As a result, the patient is unable to distinguish between the self and the outside world, regresses to an infantile state, and attributes to the hypnotist the role of the parent.

THE PAVLOVIAN SCHOOL

This school theorizes that hypnosis is a state of partial inhibition, a state between wakefulness and sleep, with the word "partial" referring both to the intensity and the topography of the inhibition. The remaining waking thoughts in the cortex make it possible to establish contact between the patient and the hypnotist (9).

THE SCHOOL INFLUENCED BY EXPERIMENTAL PSYCHOLOGY

Bernheim (2), at the turn of this century, categorically stated that there was no such thing as hypnosis, only suggestibility. Barber's works (1) follow the same line. His brilliantly controlled scientific experiments—which attempted to prove that hypnotic phenomena do not exist and that the physiological changes that are supposedly induced through hypnosis can be produced in the waking state in predisposed patients—are contradicted in many other, just as brilliantly written articles. Weitzenhoffer (11), for example, is convinced that a "hypnotic state" exists that includes "something else," which has been commented upon by many hypnotists throughout the centuries but which still cannot be defined.

Personally, I cannot say that I adhere to any of the above-mentioned theories, although my views are closest to the Pavlovian school. The results of animal experiments show that hypnosis represents a form of self-protective behavior as a result of a change in the animal's relationship to his surroundings, and it is characterized by the inhibition of motor activity (3). During hypnotherapy with humans, a similar mechanism is present, and a psychobiological substratum quite definitely exists. This appears to be substantiated in experiments where the physiological and biochemical changes under various hypnotic stresses were studied (4, 8).

CHARACTERISTICS OF THE HYPNOTIST AND THE SUBJECT

From times immemorial, the personality of the hypnotist has been highly intriguing. Despite all the lingering mysticism with which it surrounds itself, no scientific evidence exists to support the notion that a hypnotist must have a specific character trait in order to be competent in his work. Just as in any other field of the medical profession, knowledge, skill, and experience supply the most important components. I am convinced that a person can be an excellent hypnotist without any flamboyant qualities. Probably in no other branch of medicine is it easier to lose the correct perspective of one's limitations and to begin playing God. If the physician falls into his own trap by enjoying this role—so similar to that of many faith healers and political leaders—he can do great harm.

No conclusive evidence has yet emerged, despite extensive work, that correlates the capacity to be hypnotized with sex, race, physical or psychological factors, economic status, or whatever. Clinical experience shows that some people cannot be hypnotized at all, whereas others go almost immediately into a trance. For all intents and purposes, the important fact remains that a great majority of patients can be hypnotized to some degree and certainly enough for the purpose of treatment. The widespread misconception that a hysterical or weak character is a prerequisite for being hypnotized should be dispelled. On the contrary, it is widely accepted among hypnotists that "normal" people are easier to hypnotize than are neurotics.

TECHNIQUES OF HYPNOSIS

In principle, there are basically two kinds of hypnotherapy: therapy *by* hypnosis and therapy *under* hypnosis.

The first, therapy by hypnosis, implies that the curative effect is achieved by the hypnotic state itself. Prolonged sessions from 1½ to 24 hours are used, during which therapeutic suggestions may be given from time to time. The second and more common kind, therapy under hypnosis, utilizes short sessions, commonly of 30 to 60 minutes' duration, with the emphasis being placed on direct suggestion and the use of persuasion.

Before attempting hypnosis, it is essential to discuss with the patient any questions he may have regarding the treatment. The few minutes required for this might be important in determining the results of the treatment, since patients often have fears, superstitions, or moral objections toward hypnosis, some of which they are ashamed to mention.

After this introduction, a few suggestibility tests—such as the pendulum, handclasp, body-sway, or hand-levitation tests—are begun. If the outcome of these tests is satisfactory, hypnosis may be attempted. There are many ways of inducing hypnosis, and I do not feel that any of the mentioned methods have any specific advantage, although I use the hand-levitation method developed by Erickson and described by Wolberg (12). A good practice is to get familiar with the one method that best suits the therapist. Books on the subject to be recommended are Weitzenhoffer's *General Techniques of Hypnotism (10)* and Chertok's *Hypnosis (3)*.

INDICATIONS FOR HYPNOTHERAPY

From what has been stated, it is not surprising that psychosomatic disorders constitute the most promising area of medicine for the use of hypnotherapy. This is not only supported by long-standing empirical clinical observations, but it is also corroborated more and more by the results of basic scientific research. If hypnosis can produce physiological changes that are measurable with the most modern electronic, biological, and biochemical methods, then hypnosis may be able to alter the physiological conditions produced by emotional factors.

RESPIRATORY DISORDERS

Hypnosis can be used with dramatic results in treating hyperventilation by decreasing anxiety. It can also be applied with good results in ticlike coughing and psychogenic air hunger. The most important psychosomatic illness of the respiratory system is bronchial asthma, including its acute and more severe form, status asthmaticus, both of which respond well to hypnosis.

Most investigators agree that a conditional bronchial spasm is the common end result of a complexity of physical and emotional mechanisms, and it is felt that the hazards involved in the use of steroids provide sufficient reason to recommend hypnosis as a treatment, if not at least as an adjunct to the treatment of asthma.

The use of hypnotherapy is exemplified by the following case*:

Case 1. A 26-year-old, single male, who suffered from asthmatic attacks from the age of 10, was recently seen in my office. At the age of 16, he had been treated successfully at the psychiatric department of a children's hospital. For the past few years, he had been taking daily as many as 10 to 12 tablets of a theophylline-ephedrine-barbital preparation (Tedral), and he used one or two vials of an epinephrine-containing spray (Vaponefrin) a day. Because of the epinephrine ingredient, the patient had become quite dependent on his spray, and he was in a constantly hyperactive condition. Reluctantly, he accepted the advice to submit to hypnotherapy, and after the first hypnotic session, both he and his family noticed a decrease in the frequency of his asthmatic attacks. After six sessions, treatment was terminated. The patient was completely free of asthma for the first time in his life, and he was able to discontinue his medications for at least the three months in which I had contact with him following the termination of treatment. Apparently, both the relaxing and anxiety-relieving effects of hypnosis and the direct reconditioning orders ("your breathing will be perfectly normal," "you shall be free of any difficulty in breathing," "you will not have any asthmatic attacks," "you will not need any medication," and so forth) were responsible for the removal of the symptoms.

CARDIOVASCULAR DISORDERS

The connection between the various cardiac arrhythmias and their precipitating emotional factors is well known. Good results have been reported in their treatment by hypnosis. Equally, the connection between emotional factors and attacks of angina pectoris hardly needs to be emphasized. Both in angina pectoris and in postcoronary syndrome, a decrease in anxiety and the alleviation of fear by relaxation are highly important and can secure many symptom-free years in the cardiac patient's life.

Case 2. A 24-year-old, single, legal secretary had suffered for the past three years from various psychophysiological symptoms, including palpitations and atrial paroxysmal tachycardia. Despite reassurances by cardiologists and negative ECG results, her symptoms had increased in both frequency and intensity until she was finally forced to give up her job. After three months of 30-minute hypnotic sessions, at first five times a week and later decreasing to twice weekly, she became completely free of symptoms. She got a better job and her whole life changed. She is now seen twice a month for a 10-minute session of hypnotherapy, but even this is tapering off. No substitute symptom has emerged.

Case 3. A 53-year-old male manager of a large company consulted me six years ago on account of elevator phobia and claustrophobia. At the age of 50, he had developed angina pectoris, and after several cardiological examinations, including ECGs, he was placed on nitroglycerine therapy, which proved ineffective. After three months of hypnotherapy combined with relaxation exer-

---

*Due to limited space, I have chosen from my practice case histories that illustrate positive results achieved by hypnotherapy. In spite of careful screening, results with other patients were less successful and there were occasional failures.

cises and direct suggestions, his symptoms disappeared. He occasionally sees me for mild, acute anxiety attacks and phobic symptoms, but he has had no more attacks of angina.

GASTROINTESTINAL DISORDERS

The gastrointestinal tract has rightly been called the "sounding board of the emotions." The patient who has had repeated, complete, physical and roentgenographic examinations with negative results, but who still has so-called functional bowel problems, is well known to all practitioners. The statement, "I have always had a nervous stomach," is heard repeatedly in every doctor's office. In these conditions, the main emphasis in treatment is on alleviating anxiety and tension and teaching the patient to relax. The treatment of peptic ulcer with hypnotically induced relaxation has shown good results. This also applies to other conditions, such as vomiting, diarrhea, and irritable colon.

Case 4. A 28-year-old, single nurse had been referred by the Surgical Department for consultation regarding a decision between conservative or surgical treatment. She had, during the past seven years, suffered five recurrent, bleeding episodes of duodenal ulcer. As the patient was reluctant to undergo surgery, she was accepted for hypnotherapy. For the next five years, with 30-minute sessions twice a week, the patient enjoyed perfect health, did not have a single relapse, and did not need to follow any diet or take any medication. Treatment was discontinued when the patient left for another part of the country. She began work in a small community, where she was unable to find anyone to treat her with hypnotherapy. Within one year, she had two exacerbations of the ulcer with severe bleeding, and she subsequently had to undergo subtotal gastrectomy.

METABOLIC DISORDERS

The treatment of obesity will be dealt with in Chapter 24. Several patients have been successfully treated for this disorder with hypnotherapy. The method used is based on classic Pavlovian conditioning. All food, except the prescribed diet, is associated through conditioning with disagreeable tastes and odors to produce aversion. All patients had tried numerous remedies prior to hypnotherapy, which had been either unsuccessful or with only temporary success. If patients are selected carefully (the most important factors being motivation and persistence), about 80% of them will achieve their ideal weight with three to five sessions per week for 6 to 12 months. Unfortunately, if they drop out of treatment, many regain their weight in roughly the same amount of time as it took them to lose it. The majority of patients, however, have been able to hold close to their ideal weight over many years or decades, fluctuating 10 to 20 pounds, when they continued with about one session of hypnotherapy every week or two.

Case 5. The patient came under treatment 13 years ago. She was then 30 years old, and she had been slim in childhood and adolescence. After her boyfriend left her at the age of 18, she started gaining weight and gradually reached 280 pounds. She maintained this weight until the commencement of hypnotherapy, except for a few occasions when she lost 40 or 50 pounds on different diets and medications, always regaining what she had lost within a short period of time. At the beginning of her treatment, she was hospitalized for seven months with a regimen of daily hypnotherapy, a 500-calorie diet, and exercise. She lost 150 pounds and reached her ideal weight of 130 pounds by the time of discharge. She has remained slim ever since, with a few minutes of hypnotherapy once or twice a week.

NEUROLOGICAL DISORDERS

It is worthwhile to try hypnotherapy with patients suffering from headaches. A fair number of them respond to it favorably. Cluster headaches, atypical facial neuralgia, migraine headaches, and tension headaches also fall into this category. The aim of the treatment is to decrease the patient's tension and to raise his pain threshold. Hypnotic relaxation alone can decrease or terminate the headache. If the patient can achieve a more relaxed and less tense life-style, it is sometimes possible to eliminate recurrent headaches.

Case 6. The patient, a single, 28-year-old secretary, was referred by a neurologist after all available migraine headache remedies had been exhausted. She had suffered from migraine, just as several other members of her family had done, from the age of 16, and she used to have five or six severe attacks a month, which greatly interfered with her work. The headaches usually became more frequent and intense in her premenstrual period. The patient complained of premenstrual tension, menstrual cramps, and nausea. All these complaints vanished after six months of hypnotherapy, and the migraine headaches became less severe. During the past four years, the patient has had only three or four attacks a year, and she has been able to maintain this condition with one 15-minute session every second week.

GENITOURINARY DISORDERS

Female Disorders

The psychosomatic approach to gynecological disorders will be dealt with in Chapter 27. Good results have been obtained with hypnotherapy in the treatment of functional amenorrhea, primary dysmenorrhea, and functional uterine bleeding. Hypnotherapy has also been successfully employed in the treatment of premenstrual tension when other therapies have failed, and it is used as an adjunct to estrogen treatment in dealing with menopausal symptoms.

Some highly selected patients suffering from frigidity are amenable to relaxation and direct conditioning under hypnosis.

Case 7. A 30-year-old, married, executive secretary complained that she had never experienced orgasm, neither before nor during her eight years of marriage. She mainly blamed herself, but felt that she might have a chance with another man. She became emotionally involved with someone at her place of work and started fantasizing about having sexual intercourse with him. It was obvious that she loved her husband and regarded her marriage as above average in quality. She realized that if she became sexually involved with the man who attracted her, the outcome would probably be a renewed experience of frigidity. She was treated for six months with 30-minute hypnotherapy sessions three times a week. Under hypnosis, she was encouraged to fantasize about amorous and sensual sex play with the man to whom she felt so attracted. Direct orders were given regarding relaxation and "letting things happen." Orgasm was never suggested, only relaxation and a warm, sensual feeling during sex play and penetration. After three months, the patient started experiencing orgasm under hypnosis. After the first orgasmic experiences, she completely lost interest in her putative lover and started fantasizing about her husband. Shortly thereafter, during sexual intercourse with her husband, she experienced orgasm more and more frequently. During the past ten years, contact has been kept with this patient, and she is seemingly getting along very well.

Male Disorders

I agree with the widely held opinion among professionals that hypnosis is not a useful treatment for erective impotence. Ejaculatory impotence and ejaculation praecox, however, are both amenable to hypnotic treatment.

Case 8. A 45-year-old business man had for the past four years suffered from complete ejaculatory impotence. His wife had left him because of his sexual dysfunction. He masturbated two or three times a day. He had had several physical checkups, and each time he had been found healthy. His male hormone levels were normal. Women had always been attracted to him; sometimes he had two or three dates per week. In desperation, he went to a doctor, who for six months treated him with hormone injections to no avail. In fact, he completely lost all sexual desire. When he came for hypnotherapy, he discontinued the hormone treatment, and within one month, his sexual desire and erective ability returned. Short hypnotic sessions were started at a rate of five times at first, and later, three times a week. After three months of treatment, he came back after a weekend and reported excitedly that he had had sexual intercourse successfully three times with a divorcee, whom he had known for only ten days. Thereafter, he was equally successful with several other partners, and he was contemplating marriage to the latest one. He has a good chance of not relapsing, even after treatment has been terminated.

DERMATOLOGICAL DISORDERS

Among patients suffering from skin disorders who were treated with hypnotherapy, the treatment of those suffering from pruritus vulvae has been particularly successful.

Case 9. A 45-year-old married female had suffered from severe genital pruritus since she entered her menopause three years earlier. She had failed to respond to local treatments or to estrogenic hormone administration. It became obvious that the patient believed that with the termination of her menstrual periods, she stopped being a woman, and that she felt very uneasy about having sexual intercourse with her husband. Her pruritus became a legitimate excuse for avoiding intercourse. After three months of hypnotherapy with relaxation, reeducation, and direct suggestions, a marked decrease of her symptoms was achieved. She resumed sexual relations with her husband, and without any further treatment, her pruritus completely disappeared.

SUMMARY AND CONCLUSIONS

Hypnosis is no panacea, but, if judiciously applied, there is a place for it in one's medical armamentarium. It can bring temporary or permanent relief to many patients who suffer from psychosomatic ailments.

Hypnotherapy, just like other forms of behavior therapy, has been criticized by Freudian psychoanalysts on the ground that it removes the symptoms but leaves the underlying problem untouched. As this underlying problem resurfaces, it is argued, the patient develops substitute symptoms. Clinical practice, however, has often shown that this is by no means the case. Even if some patients should develop substitute symptoms, the original symptoms can, in many cases, be replaced by less unpleasant ones.

The advantages of hypnotherapy include the short duration of the treatment and its usually immediate and recognizable results. Another reason for using hypnosis is based upon the insufficient number of trained persons doing psychotherapy and the length and expense of their training, whereas the technique of hypnosis can be learned quite easily in a short period of time.

The dangers of hypnosis have been greatly overestimated. Hypnosis should not be used in patients with moderate to severe depression, suicidal tendencies, or paranoid trends, nor where there is a persistent history of acting out. Homosexual panic, activation of psychosis, and the worsening of depressive and suicidal behavior have been observed after injudicious hypnotherapy. These possibilities, however, are not greater, but actually smaller, than in other forms of psychiatric treatments, and they can be avoided by a careful psychiatric evaluation of prospective patients. The main criteria to be considered in selecting patients for hypnotherapy include the absence of serious psychotic or neurotic disturbances in the patient, and the lack of grounds for suspecting that the lifting of defenses might do more harm than good. A well-founded expectation, based on clinical judgment, that the patient will function well after the target symptom is removed, is essential in deciding whether or not to use hypnotherapy.

In my practice, I do not combine hypnotherapy with pharmacotherapy. The only medication the patient takes is what the patient's physician may have prescribed for the disorder, and this is tapered off in dosage or discontinued only after consultation with that doctor as the patient's condition improves.

It is hoped that with the gradual acceptance of behavior therapy, hypnosis will also become an accepted treatment modality for both psychiatrists and medical specialists, and that it may be practiced, not as a last resort, but in well-selected cases as a worthwhile first trial.

REFERENCES

1. Barber TX: Physiological effects of "hypnosis." Psychol Bull 58:390, 1961
2. Bernheim H: Suggestive Therapeutics. New York, Putnam, 1902
3. Chertok L: Hypnosis. New York, Pergamon Press, 1966
4. Cleghorn JM, Peterfy G, Pinter EJ, Pattee CJ: Verbal anxiety and the beta adrenergic receptors: a facilitating mechanism? J Nerv Ment Dis 151:266, 1970
5. Freud S: Group Psychology and the Analysis of the Ego. London, Hogarth Press, 1940
6. Hull CL: Hypnotism and Suggestibility—An Experimental Approach. New York, Appleton-Century-Crofts, 1933, p 18
7. Kubie LS, Margolin S: The process of hypnotism and the nature of the hypnotic state. Am J Psychiatry 100:611, 1944
8. Peterfy G, Pinter EJ: Some physiological aspects of emotional stress. In Lissak K (ed): Hormones and Brain Function. New York, Plenum Press, 1973, pp 459–474
9. Svorad D, Hoskovec J: Experimental and clinical study of hypnosis in the Soviet Union and the European socialist countries (bibliography). Am J Clin Hypn 4:36, 1961
10. Weitzenhoffer AM: General Techniques of Hypnotism. New York, Grune & Stratton, 1957
11. Weitzenhoffer AM: The nature of hypnosis, Part I. Am J Clin Hypn 5:295, 1963
12. Wolberg L: Medical Hypnosis, Vol I, The Principles of Hypnotherapy. Vol II: The Practice of Hypnotherapy. New York, Grune & Stratton, 1948

14 The Behavior Therapies

G. TERENCE WILSON

The historical roots of behavior therapy can be traced back to the beginning of this century and even before, but it was not until the 1950s that it emerged as a systematic, alternative approach to the prevailing psychodynamic model of treatment. An important landmark was the publication in 1958 of Wolpe's book *Psychotherapy by Reciprocal Inhibition* (13), which introduced a number of behavioral techniques based upon the conditioning principles of Pavlov and Hull, as well as upon his own research on the elimination of experimentally produced neurotic reactions in animals. The pioneering clinical studies of Wolpe and his associate, Lazarus, in South Africa, laid the groundwork for the contemporary practice of clinical behavior therapy with adults. At the Maudsley Hospital in London, Eysenck and his students, emphasizing the principles of modern learning theory, provided a decisive impetus to the scientific approach to the analysis and treatment of abnormal behavior. In the United States, the influence of Skinner and the development of the experimental analysis of behavior helped establish observable behavior as worthy of study in its own right, rather than considering it as merely a symptom of a presumed underlying psychic illness. Procedures utilizing operant conditioning principles were soon extended to the modification of an entire range of psychiatric disorders, particularly those of children and institutionalized adults (12).

In these early attempts to generalize from conditioning studies in the experimental laboratory to the therapeutic situation, there was an understandable tendency to oversimplify complex clinical phenomena. During the 1960s, the necessity of going beyond the emphasis on conditioning principles was highlighted by Lazarus' broad-spectrum behavioral approach (7), which recognized the wider determinants of clinical disorders. In what has been perhaps the most comprehensive formulation of behavior therapy, Bandura (1) has stressed the central regulatory role of cognitive mediational processes. These include vicarious learning (modeling), self-control functions, and cognitive restructuring. Within this social learning framework, man is viewed not as a passive reactor to external, environmental forces or to psychic pressures. Behavior, as well as psychosomatic functioning, are not affected automatically, but they are mediated by the way in which environmental events are cognitively transformed. People have the capacity for self-directed behavior change, and the development of self-control procedures that promise them enhanced personal mastery over physiological conditions and social situations represents the most significant feature of the behavior therapies.

Behavior therapy is based on a model in which abnormal behavior is seen, not as symptomatic of an underlying quasi-disease process, but as the way in which a person has tried to cope with the stress and difficulties of living in a changing and increasingly more complex physical and social environment. Accordingly, treatment is concerned with the direct application of social learning principles rather than with indirectly "working through" presumed underlying personality conflicts. Above all else, behavior therapy is characterized by the explicit specification of treatment procedures and their rationale, critically testable hypotheses, and an insistence on rigorous standards of proof and objective measures of outcome.

BEHAVIORAL ASSESSMENT

Behavior therapists reject the use of psychodynamic trait theory in describing people and their problems. It is assumed that the individual is best understood by determining what he thinks, feels, and does in particular life situations. Behavioral assessment hinges on two main questions: 1) What are the psychosomatic and environmental factors that are *currently* maintaining the disorder? 2) Which technique or combination of techniques might most effectively and efficiently produce improvement? In a detailed clinical guide to assessment, Lazarus (8) stresses the multimodal examination of the patient's difficulties. More specifically, the therapist explores the patient's overt behavior, affective responses (*e.g.,* anxiety), sensory reactions (*e.g.,* muscle tension or tachycardia), imagery (*e.g.,* negative self-image), cognitive processes (*e.g.,* self-defeating verbalizations), and interpersonal relationships (*e.g.,* assertion), as well as whether appropriate medication might be indicated. The acronym BASIC ID (derived from *B*ehavior, *A*ffect, *S*ensation, *I*magery, *C*ognition, *I*nterpersonal, and *D*rugs) provides a mnemonic for covering these seven separate yet interrelated modalities.

A common misconception about behavior therapy is that it represents a superficial approach in which only symptoms are modified. In fact, behavior therapy necessarily addresses itself to *all* the causes of psychological problems; the difference between the behavioral and psychodynamic approaches lies in how "underlying causes" are conceptualized. Psychodynamic formulations favor historical and hypothetical unconscious determinants of behavior; behavior therapy emphasizes the learning contingencies and the social-influence processes that are currently governing the problem under consideration. An inadequate behavioral assessment will lead to an incomplete treatment program and might well result in a rapid relapse of symptoms or apparent "symptom substitution."

Consider, for example, the alcoholic who seeks some control over his excessive, destructive drinking patterns. Ascertaining circumstances under which he drinks heavily would be part of a complete behavioral assessment. It might be found that he becomes inebriated when feeling depressed. The conditions that govern his depression must then be gauged. If the patient consistently becomes depressed after fighting with his wife, therapy would have to be expanded to restructure a more meaningful marital relationship. Failure to do this, while perhaps focusing exclusively on the problem drinking *per se* (*e.g.,* by using aversion conditioning methods), will result in the very real possibility of relapse or of the patient's adoption of some other self-defeating pattern of behavior in trying to cope with an unhappy marriage.

TREATMENT METHODS

Behavior therapy has been applied to the full range of psychosomatic and psychiatric disorders (10). Rather than attempting a sketchy overview of these diverse applications, the specific use of behavioral assessment and treatment methods in clinical practice will be selectively illustrated with reference to three widespread classes of psychosomatic problems: sexual dysfunction, obesity, and cardiovascular disorders.

SEXUAL DYSFUNCTION

The behavioral approach emphasizes that human sexual inadequacy is a function of the patients' ignorance of the physiology of sexual functioning and their faulty learning of negative emotional reactions, rather than being a result of physical or intrapsychic disease. Sexual dysfunction can be caused by certain physical conditions and general illnesses (*e.g.,* diabetes), just as a loss or diminution of sexual responsiveness might be associated with primary psychotic states. These cases are relatively rare, however, and in most instances, it is some combination of performance-related anxiety, the lack of social-sexual skills and knowledge, or the unavailability of a sexually reinforcing partner that is responsible for the development and maintenance of sexual problems. The absence of an emotional attachment for one's sexual partner may also result in sexual difficulties, particularly in women. The person may be in love with someone else, or hostility might exist as the result of interpersonal conflict.

Masters and Johnson's rapid therapy program (9) is an example of the direct behavioral treatment of sexual dysfunction. The treatment is basically an *in vivo* desensitization procedure in which fear of failure or performance anxiety is gradually extinguished under nonthreatening conditions. Both marital partners are required to participate in therapy, since Masters and Johnson consider that the "relationship between the partners is the patient," even if only one member of the couple is dysfunctional. This requirement reflects the concern with establishing effective patterns of both sexual and interpersonal communication. A dual-sex therapy team is used for several reasons. It eliminates the feeling of being "ganged up" on by the patient who is in the minority of the two-to-one sex ratio that occurs with a single therapist. It is assumed that only a therapist of the same sex can fully understand the sexual difficulties of a patient, and the possibility of getting biased information is reduced, because the "games people play" to impress the other sex are minimized. Finally, the presence of a co-therapist obviates the development of any transference between the patient and the therapist of the opposite sex. This would interfere with the primary goal of therapy, namely, the facilitation of intricate emotional communication between the partners themselves.

Following a detailed assessment of the patient's problem, an intensive educative process focuses on correcting faulty attitudes and misconceptions about sex. Initially, all sexual behavior between partners is prohibited. Thereafter, the therapists direct them to engage in a carefully graduated program of mutually pleasant sensual and sexual involvement, which is called "sensate focus." This provides an opportunity for the partners to learn to feel and think sensuously by giving and getting physical pleasure, first by nongenital contact and then by specific genital stimulation. The purpose is to abolish a preoccupation with goal-oriented performance and to demonstrate that sexual gratification does not necessarily depend on orgasm through coitus. As sexual arousal spontaneously occurs during these experiences, the treatment is oriented toward the specific form of sexual inadequacy in question. In cases of impotence, for instance, when erection occurs, the woman uses a "teasing technique" in which she manipulates the penis to erection and then relaxes with her partner until the erection disappears. She then repeats the procedure several times, thereby desensitizing the male's fear of losing an erection and not regaining it during sexual interaction. Therapy continues with the woman facilitating nondemanding intromission (by assuming the superior coital position), followed by progressively more virorous thrusting until orgasm occurs.

The methods of Masters and Johnson are only part of the behavioral approach to sex therapy. Effective treatment often requires that nonsexual sources of sexual inadequacy be eliminated using a broader range of behavioral techniques. Lazarus (7) describes the case of an impotent man whose social learning history revealed that his domineering mother had taught him to fear and revere all women. As a result, he was overly submissive and dependent on his wife, and he was unable to assert himself on any issue. While he resented being bossed around, he dreaded the criticism or rejection that might follow his giving vent to his feelings; he also believed that such disclosure would be unmanly. Using the principles of Ellis's rational-emotive approach (5), the patient's irrational beliefs, which led him to regard women as objects rather than people, were actively disputed and corrected. In addition, a brief regimen of assertion training was employed to equip the patient with the necessary social skills to confront his wife constructively and to express his genuine feelings without anxiety, guilt, or a destructive display of aggression. This was accomplished through the use of behavior rehearsal. First, the patient was encouraged to role-play how he would normally cope with an unreasonable demand by his wife. The therapist then modeled a more appropriate, alternative response, in which he honestly asserted his own legitimate rights. The patient repeatedly rehearsed this novel mode of responding, while the therapist provided feedback on both nonverbal (*e.g.,* eye contact) and verbal components of his performance. His wife's possible reactions to this newfound assertiveness were discussed, and rehearsal techniques were used to prepare the patient to deal with tears, interruptions, denials, and counterallegations. An example of the latter was as follows:

"I feel that when you order me about and treat me like a child I ought to tell you how I really feel . . . instead of acting like an obedient puppy dog. And most important of all, when you go ahead and make plans for me without consulting me, and especially when you yell at me in front of your parents, maybe I should quit acting as if I didn't mind and let you know how strongly I really react inside. What I am getting at is simply that in spite of my love and affection for you, I would really rather be unmarried than be a henpecked husband like my father . . ." (7)

Instructed to put this training into practice, the patient reported that although she was a little upset, his wife agreed to restructure the relationship. That night, he felt very close to his wife and had "very good sex."

In those cases where sexual dysfunction is a conditioned avoidance response maintained by sex-specific anxiety, the use of imaginal systematic desensitization has been shown to be effective. In this technique, the patient is first trained how to relax through a procedure in which he alternately tenses and relaxes different muscle groups in a systematic fashion so as to become aware of the buildup of tension and to acquire the ability to let go and relax both mentally and physically. The patient is then instructed to imagine a hierarchy of anxiety-eliciting scenes, ranging from mildly stressful to very threatening items, while deeply relaxed. If anxiety is experienced at any point, the patient is asked to cease imagining the item, restore relaxation, and then repeat the item until the anxiety is extinguished. A modified version of this technique, in which relaxation is induced through the intravenous administration of a 1% solution of sodium methohexital, has been used to treat orgasmic dysfunction successfully in women.

Techniques such as cognitive restructuring, assertion training, and systematic desensitization have been widely used to treat phobic and other stress-related psychosomatic disorders, such as asthma, hypertension, tension headaches, anorexia nervosa, and peptic ulcers.

Among the many sexual disorders successfully treated by behavior therapy are premature ejaculation and primary orgasmic dysfunction. The treatment for the former is similar to that for impotence. The woman, in the superior coital position, manually stimulates the penis almost to the point of ejaculatory inevitability and then ceases all stimulation or squeezes the penis on each side of the coronal ridge, with the result that the urge to ejaculate disappears. With repeated practice, the male is able to maintain increasingly longer erections. The progression then moves from the woman inserting the penis into her vagina while remaining motionless, to gradually more vigorous pelvic thrusting. If, at any point, the male senses that he is going to ejaculate, the woman withdraws and ceases stimulation as before. This simple procedure soon enables a couple to engage in intercourse for 15 minutes or longer, and many women who have never achieved orgasm because their partner ejaculated prematurely find themselves completely responsive and climax for the first time. If orgasmic dysfunction persists, the woman may be directed to engage in a graduated sequence of masturbation exercises, at first in private and then in the presence of her partner, which are designed to facilitate orgasm. It must be stressed that this is an adjunctive procedure that should be part of a comprehensive behavioral treatment program for orgasmic inadequacy.

OBESITY

Obesity is not an illness *per se,* but it is a serious medical problem. It shortens the life span, it increases the vulnerability to a wide range of physical illnesses, especially cardiovascular ones, and it has adverse psychological effects due to interfering with social, sexual, and occupational activities. In contrast to his earlier conclusion that neither medical nor psychological methods of treatment had been shown to be effective in treating obesity, Stunkard (11) has recently observed that behavior therapy has been demonstrated to be successful in producing weight loss. The fundamental assumption on which behavioral methods are based is that whatever its root causes (which undoubtedly involve genetic and physiological factors that are as yet imperfectly understood), obesity is primarily a function of inappropriate *eating habits.* Simply stated, obese individuals take in a greater number of calories than they expend through exercise. Accordingly, the therapeutic task is to alter inappropriate food habits by teaching the obese person how to develop self-control. Specific diets are not prescribed, but well-balanced, nutritious meals are recommended.

The first step in developing self-control strategies is to pinpoint the various discriminative, eliciting, and reinforcement stimuli that affect eating behavior. Intensive, problem-focused interviews with patients are supplemented by requiring them to keep detailed daily records of the amount, nature, time, and circumstances of their eating. As is typical of all behavioral assessment, the question of why the patient overeats is not pursued; rather, the behavior therapist seeks answers to questions beginning with the words "when," "what," "how," and "with whom." These records also provide continuous feedback about the efficacy of the program and how it might be improved. *Counting and recording calories consumed* on a daily basis has been shown to be an effective treatment method in its own right, and it should provide the foundation on which all behavioral procedures are built.

A second major aspect of the treatment program is the modification of the stimulus control of eating. The patient is instructed how to narrow the wide variety of cues that prompt eating. Meals are to be eaten only at predetermined times, in a particular room, and at a specific table with distinctively colored napkins and tablecloth. Eating in other places, at other times, or in conjunction with other activities, like reading or watching television, is prohibited. Additional examples of eliminating cues associated with eating would include keeping only necessary nutritional foods, which require preparation, in the house, and going food-shopping—and thus coming into contact with the most tempting, food-related stimuli that advertisers can devise—only after a full meal and with just sufficient money to purchase the necessary food items according to a list that has been previously compiled.

Eating behavior is directly modified. Obese people tend to eat more rapidly than individuals of normal weight. In order to interrupt the chain of eating responses, which are usually run off in automatic fashion, the patient is told to eat "like a gourmet." This entails finishing chewing and swallowing his last bite before putting any more food on the fork, eating very slowly while savoring and attending very closely to the food in his mouth, and introducing short breaks during a meal by placing the cutlery down and simply sitting at the table for a time without eating.

Most importantly, the patient is taught how to reinforce himself, contingent on the gradual development of more healthy eating behavior. Behavioral programs are designed to promote gradual, rather than dramatic, weight loss (1 to 2 pounds per week) so as to avoid intense levels of deprivation that can precipitate unwanted eating. In severely obese people, it might take weeks and even months before the impact of the program becomes sufficiently discernible and therefore reinforcing. Consequently, other sources of reinforcement have to be provided to maintain the self-controlling activities initially; these include reassurance and encouragement from the therapist (and, hopefully, from others of significance in the client's natural environment) and, most importantly, self-reinforcement by the client. A particularly relevant class of reinforcing events that patients can arrange for themselves includes any high-probability behaviors, such as reading or watching television, which, according to the Premack principle, can strengthen less probable behavior by being made contingent upon it.

Competing responses are encouraged as a way of coping with urges to eat. Feelings of tension, anxiety, depression, or frustration, which often trigger eating, can be counteracted by training in relaxation skills. A multifaceted treatment approach is especially vital with "binge eaters." In such cases, eating functions as a self-defeating means of coping with strong emotional conflicts, as alcohol sometimes does in the alcoholic. The use of cognitive restructuring to overcome feelings of personal worthlessness, as well as assertion training to establish more constructive means of emotional expression and social skills, are often necessary.

Finally, as with other addictive disorders like alcoholism and cigarette smoking, there exists the definite possibility that the patient will relapse after successful treatment unless explicit methods are employed to insure the generalization and maintenance of treatment-produced improvement. Two major procedures are particularly recommended. Specific "booster" sessions,which provide feedback and reinforcement (especially from a treatment group) for continuing to implement self-control strategies, should be systematically scheduled following the termination of the initial therapy program. The patient's spouse or other family members might be involved in the treatment program and counseled in ways to support the patient's attempts to maintain successful weight control in the home environment.

CARDIOVASCULAR DISORDERS

The behavioral treatment of disorders such as hypertension, migraine, and cardiac disease has been largely limited to the clinical application of biofeedback procedures, which have been critically reviewed by Blanchard and Young (4). Clinically significant decreases in blood pressure (as much as 80% of the baseline level in terms of diastolic pressure) in hypertensive patients have been demonstrated. Briefly, the typical procedure involves providing the patient with both visual and auditory feedback that is contingent upon the desired response, *i.e.,* a small blood pressure change in the direction away from a specified, criterion, blood pressure value on each heart beat. In one study, patients were additionally reinforced with small financial incentives as their blood pressure began to decrease. Unfortunately, there is little evidence of the stability of these changes when the feedback is withdrawn, nor is there substantial evidence of the degree to which these therapeutic changes transfer to situations outside of the laboratory. Neither is it clear that the effects that have been obtained are attributable to the instrumental conditioning of blood pressure *per se,* or whether biofeedback procedures are merely elaborate means for teaching relaxation.

Migraine headaches have been treated with a combination of skin-temperature feedback, which increases warmth (blood flow) in the hand, and a form of relaxation produced through autogenic training. Initial results are encouraging, but they should be accepted with reservation until confirmed by evidence from better-controlled research. Interestingly, electromyographic (EMG) feedback-assisted relaxation training, which has proved effective in eliminating tension headaches, appears to be ineffective in the treatment of migraine.

Specific cardiac arrhythmias, such as sinus tachycardia and premature ventricular contraction (PVC), have been successfully treated with biofeedback. With respect to the latter condition, hospitalized patients were given feedback about beat-by-beat changes in their heart rate. A visual signal indicated when their heart was responding according to the particular training schedule being used, such as the speeding or slowing of the heart rate, alternating speeding and slowing, or maintaining the heart rate within a certain range. The last schedule provided the patients with feedback about the occurrence of PVCs. In one study, four of eight patients showed lasting and generalized reductions in PVCs at follow-up 3 to 21 months after treatment, while a fifth patient was able to recognize their occurrence and control them by resting at home. Subsequent examination revealed that two of the patients who did not respond favorably had extremely diseased hearts, which suggested that a bodily organ cannot be excessively damaged if operant feedback is to have any ameliorative effects. The third unsuccessful patient was discovered to fear an improvement in the heart problem, since this would entail losing disability benefits and returning to work. It is very probable that this patient actively sabotaged the treatment program, which raises an important clinical consideration. Even if biofeedback can modify important physiological activity, it will be most successful as part of a multifaceted behavioral treatment program that would take into account other relevant maintaining variables, such as the wider functional significance to the patient of his being either physically or psychologically disabled.

A caveat must be issued about biofeedback methods in general. Variously hailed as "behavioral medicine" and "autonomic behavior therapy," they have generated what Birk (3) has called a kind of "furor therapeuticus"—an unbridled optimism and a frenzy of publication unconstrained by careful scientific evaluation. Much of the research has been conducted with normal, volunteer subjects, and with few exceptions, such as those noted above, it has produced results that are statistically but not always substantively significant. Systematic studies controlled for subject expectancies and placebo effects have yet to be carried out. Finally, comparative outcome studies are necessary in order to show that alternative therapies, which might require less in the way of expensive and sophisticated physiological recording apparatus, are not equally effective.

CONCLUSION

Behavior therapy is now an accepted part of the clinical establishment. A task force of the American Psychiatric Association has recently concluded that behavior therapy has reached a stage of development where it has ". . . much to offer informed clinicians in the service of modern clinical and social psychiatry" (2). It has become a genuinely interdisciplinary field, attracting researchers and practitioners from the ranks of both clinical psychology and psychiatry. Behavior therapy continues to develop and expand at a furious pace (6). A salutary feature of the contemporary behavioral therapy scene is that exaggerated claims of its efficacy have been replaced by a more cautious optimism. Therapeutic strategies have become more sophisticated and are increasingly applied to the most complex psychosomatic disorders. Most important, however, is the increase in controlled, experimental evaluation of the efficacy of therapeutic methods.

REFERENCES

1. Bandura A: Principles of Behavior Modification. New York, Holt, Rinehart & Winston, 1969

2. Behavior Therapy in Psychiatry. Washington DC, American Psychiatric Association, 1973

3. Birk L (ed.): Biofeedback: Behavioral Medicine. New York, Grune & Stratton, 1973

4. Blanchard EB, Young, LD: Clinical applications of biofeedback training. Arch Gen Psychiatry 30:573–589, 1973

5. Ellis A: Humanistic Psychotherapy. New York, McGraw–Hill, 1973

6. Franks CM, Wilson GT (eds): Annual Review of Behavior Therapy: Theory and Practice, Vol 3. New York, Brunner/Mazel, 1975

7. Lazarus AA: Behavior Therapy and Beyond. New York, McGraw–Hill, 1971

8. Lazarus AA: Multimodal behavior therapy: treating the "basic id". J Nerv Men Dis 150:404–411, 1973

9. Masters WH, Johnson VE: Human Sexual Inadequacy. Boston, Little, Brown and Co, 1970

10. O'Leary KD, Wilson GT: Behavior Therapy: Application and Outcome. Englewood Cliffs, Prentice–Hall, 1975

11. Stunkard AJ: New therapies for the eating disorders: behavior modification of obesity and anorexia nervosa. In Franks CM, Wilson GT (eds): Annual Review of Behavior Therapy: Theory and Practice, Vol 1. New York, Brunner/Mazel, 1973

12. Ullmann LP, Krasner L: Case Studies in Behavior Modification. New York, Holt, Rinehart & Winston, 1965

13. Wolpe J: Psychotherapy by Reciprocal Inhibition. Stanford, Stanford University Press, 1958

15 Autogenic Therapy

W. LUTHE, S.R. BLUMBERGER

One of the important assumptions of autogenic therapy is that nature has provided man with homeostatic mechanisms not only to regulate fluid and electrolyte balance, blood pressure, heart rate, wound healing, and so on, but also to readjust more complicated functional disorders that are of a mental nature. In autogenic therapy, the term "homeostatic self-regulatory brain mechanisms" is often used (33, 34, 42). This concept assumes that when a person is exposed to excessive disturbing stimulation, (i.e., either emotional or physical trauma), the brain has the potential to utilize natural biological processes to reduce the disturbing consequences of the stimulation (i.e., neutralization). At the mental level, some of this self-regulatory neutralization or recuperation occurs naturally during sleep and dreams.

The techniques developed and used in autogenic therapy have been designed to support and facilitate the natural self-healing mechanisms that already exist. Thus, the emphasis is not on trying to control the natural system, but rather on helping natural systems utilize their inherent potentials of self-regulatory adjustment more fully.

In contrast, there has been a tendency in American medicine to overemphasize symptomatic treatment and to overlook the unity of the individual. This "left hemispheric" (11, 29) approach has resulted in a preference for easy, clear-cut, mechanical solutions: e.g., inject, operate, or prescribe more medication.

Autogenic therapy has always viewed the mind and body as a unit, and it approaches mental and bodily functions simultaneously. Autogenic methods permit the adaptation of the treatment program to the individual. Of practical importance is the fact that patients learn to do most of the therapeutic work by themselves at home, and that the most frequently used clinical method—autogenic standard training—can be applied in groups ranging from elementary school children to the elderly. In certain disturbances such as sleep disorders (31) or examination anxiety (34), significant improvements within two weeks or less are not exceptional. Often patients are freed from their reliance on tranquilizers and hypnotics. The degree of dependence on the physician is kept at a low level. In addition, the therapist who employs autogenic approaches is able to make more efficient use of his time than with most other psychotherapeutic methods.

Figure 15-1 illustrates the various methods that can be applied in autogenic therapy. *Autogenic training* is the foundation for all other approaches and is therefore the most important and widely used technique. Of the many methods, the use of autogenic training alone is sufficient for the majority of treatment situations. In 10% to 20% of patients, however, because of the history or the nature of the disorder, a more intensive method called *autogenic neutralization* may be necessary. *Meditative exercises, autogenic modification,* and *graduated active hypnosis* are less frequently employed and are reserved for

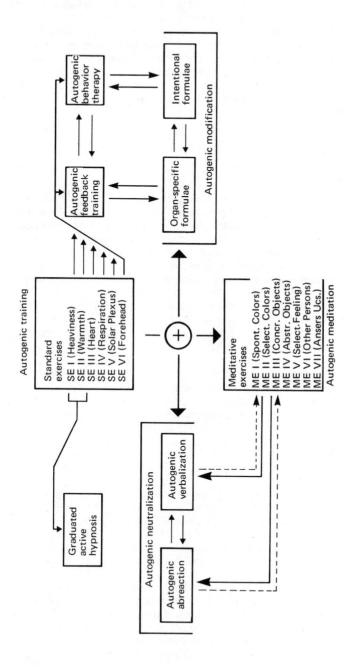

Fig. 15-1. Methods of autogenic therapy. Combinations of methods and procedural interactions among the various approaches available for the treatment of psychosomatic disorders are illustrated.

special situations. *Autogenic feedback training* and *autogenic behavior therapy* are relatively new techniques that are the result of interdisciplinary interaction.

Combinations of the methods available provide effective and flexible treatment techniques for many organic, psychosomatic, and psychiatric disorders, as well as for the psychophysiological effects of mental and bodily stress. Table 15-1 illustrates some of the physiological changes that have been observed in psychosomatic patients treated with autogenic approaches. Table 15-2 summarizes the medical and psychosomatic disorders for which autogenic methods have been used, either solely or as an adjunct to the medical treatment. Table 15-3 indicates some other special clinical situations where autogenic approaches have been successfully applied.

AUTOGENIC TRAINING

STANDARD EXERCISES

Autogenic training (AT) is the most frequently applied treatment technique that a patient can carry out himself by using passive concentration upon certain combinations of psychophysiologically adapted stimuli. Passive concentration on autogenic standard formulas can be so tailored that a measurable, normalizing influence upon various bodily and mental functions will result (42).

Psychophysiologically, autogenic training is based on three main principles: 1) mental repetition of topographically oriented verbal formulas for brief periods (*e.g.,* 30 seconds); 2) mental activity known as "passive concentration" (24, 42); and 3) reduction of exteroceptive and proprioceptive afferent stimulation (specific training postures). The mental practice periods are always terminated in three consecutive steps by briskly flexing the arms, taking a deep breath, and opening the eyes.

The verbal formulas are organized into *six standard exercises* (SEs) that are physiologically oriented (42). The content of these formulas is focused on the general topics of heaviness and warmth in extremities, calm and regular function of the heart, self-regulation of respiration, soothing warmth in the upper abdominal area, and agreeable cooling of the forehead. Occasionally, a complementary exercise, called the "first space exercise" (SP-I) (29, 30), is taught prior to beginning work with the orthodox series of standard exercises.*

Passive Concentration

The patient's attitude while repeating a formula in his mind is conceived of as "passive concentration." It entails a casual attitude during the performance of a task and complete indifference about the result. Any goal-directed effort, active interest, or apprehensiveness must be avoided. The effectiveness of passive concentration on a given formula depends on two other factors, namely 1) the mental contact with the part of the body indicated by the formula and 2) keeping up a

*The first space exercise (SP.-I) has only recently been adapted from Fehmi's biofeedback procedure and used with patient's in AT[30]. It involves the sequential imagination of spaces between symmetrical parts of the body. The pattern of formulas is as follows: "I imagine the space between my eyes" . . . (about a 5 sec. interval) . . . "I imagine the space between my ears" . . . (5 sec. interval) . . . "I imagine the space between my shoulders" . . . (5 sec. interval) . . . and so on for elbows, wrists, hands, fingers, knees, heels, feet, toes, and legs. The aim is to more specifically mobilize (non-dominant) right hemispheric functions. The theoretical importance of the issue of laterality in the etiology and treatment of a wide variety of disorders is discussed in the section on "Autogenic Neutralization".

Table 15-1. EXAMPLES OF PHYSIOLOGICAL CHANGES IN PSYCHOSOMATIC
PATIENTS PRACTICING AUTOGENIC METHODS*

NATURE OF ORGAN AND FUNCTION	NATURE OF CHANGE	NATURE OF DISORDER
Cardiovascular Functions		
Heart rate (HR)	Decreased (Increased)	Sinus tachycardia (Sinus
Heart rhythm	Normalization	bradycardia)
Blood pressure	Decreased	Certain arrhythmias
	Increased	Essential hypertension
		Forms of hypotension
ECG†	Elevation of depressed ST segment and/or increase of T wave (independant of changes in HR)	ST depression, lowering of T wave; angina pectoris, myocardial infarction, "coronary prone persons"
Peripheral circulation	Increased	Intermittent claudication
Skin temperature	Increased (also amplification of the effects of certain vasodilatory drugs)	Buerger's disease, Raynaud's phenomenon, scleroderma, frostbite, cold feet, acrocyanosis
Rectal temperature	Decreased	Nonspecific effect
Diuresis	Increased	Nonspecific effect
Respiratory Functions†		
Respiratory frequency	Decreased	functional disorders, bronchial asthma, (pulmonary tuberculosis)
Respiratory amplitude (thorax)	Increased	
Respiratory amplitude (abdomen)	Increased	
Duration of inspiration	Increased	
Duration of expiration	Increased	
Inspiration/expiration ratio	Increased	
Vital capacity	Increased	
Oxygen consumption	Decreased (faster recuperation)	After muscular work
	Increased (RV decrease)	At rest
Gastrointestinal Functions		
Esophagus†	Better filling of hiatus hernia, wider opening of cardia	Hiatus hernia, spasms of the esophagus, cardiospasm
Stomach‡	Initial, transitory, sharp reduction of motor activity (atonic phase, up to several minutes). Gastric contractions more ample and energetic, peristalsis more regular, emptying more complete, transport enhanced Improved passage into	peptic ulcer, duodenitis, Gastric discomfort, pyloric spasms, stress-related hypermotility, postlaparotomy complaints

(continued)

Table 15-1. EXAMPLES OF PHYSIOLOGICAL CHANGES IN PSYCHOSOMATIC
PATIENTS PRACTICING AUTOGENIC METHODS* (continued)

NATURE OF ORGAN AND FUNCTION	NATURE OF CHANGE	NATURE OF DISORDER
Gastrointestinal Functions (continued)		
	efferent loop, decreased hypermotility and pH	Gastrectomy
Duodenum	Enhanced transit and enterogastric reflex, better filling	Duodenal ulcer
Jejunum	More regular and efficient transport functions (better filling, sharper contours)	—functional disorders
Colon†	Increased blood flow, activation of peristalsis, normalization of bowel movements	Irritable colon, chronic constipation, flatulence
Endocrine and Metabolic		
Blood and urinary glucose	Decreased	Stress-related elevation
Insulin requirement	Decreased	Diabetes mellitus
Protein-bound iodine (PBI)	Increased	"Low normal levels" (subjects without iodine deficiency)
PBI, total iodine (TI), serum total iodine (STI)	Decreased	Functional thyroid disorders; elevated or high-normal levels
Serum cholesterol	Decreased	Elevated or high-normal levels (hereditary and pathological factors excluded)
Cortisol	Decreased	Elevated or high-normal levels
Reproductive System		
Dilatation phase	Shorter	Obstetrics; delivery
Number of contractions	Decreased	—delivery
Duration of labor	Decreased	—delivery
Pain	Decreased	Independent of intensity of contraction
Plasma cortisol levels	Decreased	—delivery
Central Nervous System		
Muscular action potential (EMG)	Decreased	Cerebral palsy, proctalgia fugax
Patellar response	Decreased	Psychosomatic patients
T reflex (Achilles tendon)	Decreased	—
H reflex (tibial nerve)	Decreased	—
Microvibration (minor tremor)	Decrease in frequency	—
Conditioned motor response	Decrease in amplitude	("Proportional response")
Motor expression	Normalization	Writer's cramp, speech disorders

Table 15-1. EXAMPLES OF PHYSIOLOGICAL CHANGES IN PSYCHOSOMATIC
PATIENTS PRACTICING AUTOGENIC METHODS* *(continued)*

NATURE OF ORGAN AND FUNCTION	NATURE OF CHANGE	NATURE OF DISORDER
Central Nervous System (continued)		
Galvanic skin response (GSR)	Increase in resistance	—psychosomatic and neurotic patients
EEG, §Paroxysmal	Facilitated	Neurotic patients, epilepsy
phenomena	Increased	(psychomotor, grand mal,
Autogenic discharges	Prolonged	temporal lobe, petit mal)
Alpha-frequency	Condensation (main	—
spindles	frequency)	
Alpha band	Increase (main frequency)	—
Alpha abundance	Decrease	—
Alpha voltage		
Cortical evoked potentials,		
Variability (AVER) during AT	Decreased	Long-term trainees
Maximum vertical range (AVER)	Decreased	—long-term trainees
Electrooculography (EOG),		
Variability	Decreased	Schizophrenia
Amplitudes	Decreased	—schizophrenia
Intraocular pressure	Decreased	Glaucoma (primary)
Anxiety	Decreased	Neuroses, schizophrenia, phobias
Ego strength, ability to concentrate	Increased	Schizophrenia

*Results with normal subjects have not been included in this table
†Organ-specific formulas were also used in addition to the standard exercises.
‡Standard exercise V is contraindicated for most gastrointestinal disorders.
§For details of the EEG research, see Reference 24.

steady flow of filmlike (verbal, acoustic, or visual) representations of the autogenic formula in one's mind. Passive concentration on a formula should not last more than 30 to 60 seconds in the beginning. After several weeks, the exercise may be extended to three to five minutes, and after a few months, up to ten minutes and longer.

The Reduction of Afferent Stimuli

At the beginning, the exercises are easier to practice in a quiet room with a moderate temperature and reduced illumination. Restricting clothing should be loosened or removed. The body must be relaxed and the eyes closed before the mental exercises are begun. Three distinctive postures have been found adequate: 1) the horizontal posture, 2) the reclined armchair posture, and 3) the simple sitting posture. All three training postures require careful consideration of a number of physiologically important points (42). When certain details are not observed, disagreeable side effects or aftereffects and an ineffective performance of the exercises have been reported.

Table 15-2. MEDICAL AND PSYCHOSOMATIC APPLICATIONS OF AUTOGENIC METHODS

TYPE OF DISORDER	SPECIFIC APPLICATION
Cardiovascular	Certain cardiac arrhythmias, ischemic heart disease, angina pectoris, recovery phase of myocardial infarction, hypertension, hypotension, disorders of peripheral circulation, blushing, functional cardiovascular complaints
Respiratory	Bronchial asthma, tuberculosis
Gastrointestinal	Functional disorders of deglutition, food allergy, dyspepsia, irritable colon, constipation, hemorrhoids, peptic ulcer, some biliary disorders, ulcerative colitis, anorexia nervosa, obesity
Genitourinary	Functional disturbances of micturition, sexual dysfunction
Musculoskeletal	Rheumatoid arthritis, various arthralgias, degenerative joint disease, nonarticular rheumatism, low back syndrome
Endocrine and Metabolic	Diabetes mellitus, functional thyroid disorders, certain lipid disorders
Neurological	Headache and migraine, tics, tremors, facial spasms, blepharospasm, neuralgia, phantom-limb pain, brain injuries, epilepsy, recent cerebellar ataxia, cerebral palsy, parkinsonism

Table 15-3. SPECIAL CLINICAL APPLICATIONS OF AUTOGENIC METHODS*

Certain dermatological disorders and gynecological disorders
Ophthalmology (adaptation to blindness, glaucoma, certain cases of strabismus)
Surgery (reduced preoperative stress, improved postoperative recovery, postlaparotomy complaints)
Dentistry (reduced tension in dental chair, improved adaptation to prostheses)
Modification of reaction to pain
Pregnancy and delivery

*For psychiatric applications—*e.g.,* schizophrenia, phobic neurosis, and obsessive neurosis —see Reference 34.

Beginning AT.

When AT is started with passive concentration on the formula, "my right arm is heavy,"* about 40% of trainees readily experience a feeling of heaviness in the

*For a right-handed person formula sequence is slowly expanded, week by week, in this pattern: My right arm is heavy (RAH) . . . RAH . . . RAH . . . RAH . . . My left arm is heavy (LAH) . . . LAH . . . LAH . . . Both arms are heavy (BAH) . . . several repetitions . . . My right leg is heavy (RLH) . . . LLH . . . BLH . . . Arms and legs are heavy (A&LH) . . . Neck and shoulders are heavy (NSsH) . . . My right arm is warm (RAW) . . . LAW . . . BAW, RLW, LLW, BLW, A&LW. See Luthe W (ed): *Autogenic Therapy (Vol. I): Autogenic Methods,* for important details on these and the other four standard exercises 42.

forearm. About 10% of trainees, however, never experience a sensation of heaviness. Therefore, patients should be told that the experience of heaviness is of no importance and that the "heaviness" formula functions merely as a technical key to bring about many different functional changes that one may or may not feel. For the patient, it is also important to know that the exercises are effective as long as they are performed correctly, even if one does not feel any changes. Distractions are normal. No effort should be made to stop these and other self-starting and self-terminating training symptoms (*e.g.,* sensory, motor, ideational, visual, and vestibular phenomena).

The effectiveness of the patient's technique and the progress of the therapy can be monitored by the patient's training symptoms and by physiological and psychological tests. The blood pressure and heart rate should be assessed initially as well as periodically during the course of therapy, because about 3% of the population responds paradoxically to AT with progressively increasing blood pressure. Such unpredictable developments are a contraindication for continuation of the method. Table 15-4 lists other nonindications and contraindications for AT.

Although the approach seems quite simple, significant problems can be encountered if the treatment is applied in a mechanical manner and is not tailored to the individual reactions of the patient, *e.g.,* by helping the patient successfully deal with a chronic inability to cry, or by adapting the formula pattern and the duration of exercises (Fig. 15–2).

ROLE OF THE PATIENT

The patient participates actively in his treatment and assumes major responsibility for the treatment work. It is up to him to practice as many brief sets of exercises scattered throughout the day as possible (less than three sets of three exercises are inadequate). In order to monitor training symptoms and other details of the practice pattern, the patient is asked to make notes on his experiences during the exercises at least twice a day.

During the initial psychosomatic evaluation, the following procedures are recommended: 1) the joint elaboration of a personal history written by the patient at home, 2) a complete list of traumatic events and accidents (intoxications, procedures involving inhalation anesthesia, loss of consciousness, drowning, suffocation, panic situations, or traumatizing medical procedures), and 3) a list of wishes. The initial evaluation includes a physical examination, appropriate laboratory tests, and, if possible, clinically oriented psychological tests.

ROLE OF THE THERAPIST

The information obtained during the initial evaluation helps the therapist to understand and evaluate the onset of occasional autogenic discharges (*e.g.,* crying spells, anxiety, headaches, pain, or nausea) that may be disturbing. Usually, these self-regulatory phenomena are transitory and subside. A careful, differential diagnostic evaluation is required, however, since certain symptoms (*e.g.,* epigastric pain) may be secondary to undiagnosed, latent, pathological processes. Autogenic training should not be applied to persons whose state of health is unknown or when a differential diagnosis of training symptoms cannot be carried out.

In the process of instructing the patient how to practice autogenic exercises, the therapist acts primarily as a technical guide providing supervision. Since the therapeutic effectiveness of the approach is not based on insight, transference, inter-

Table 15-4. NONINDICATIONS AND CONTRAINDICATIONS FOR AUTOGENIC
TRAINING

Nonindications
Severe mental deficiency
Acute schizophrenic reaction
Insufficient motivation
Children below the age of five
When state of health is unknown
When differential diagnosis of training symptoms (*e.g.,* of pain) is not possible

*Contraindications**
Doubtful or impending myocardial infarction
During and directly after acute myocardial infarction with complications†
Repeated significant paradoxical increase in blood pressure during AT
Paranoid reaction showing an increase of delusions during or after AT
Involutional psychotic reaction
Dissociative reaction (*e.g.,* fugue, amnesia, or stupor) unless close clinical
  supervision is available
Diabetes mellitus when the patient's cooperation is unreliable or when careful
  monitoring of the blood sugar is not possible
Hypoglycemia when the differential diagnosis is incomplete or when the patient's
  cooperation is unreliable

---

*Relative contraindications for the use of particular autogenic formulas may be found in
References 33 and 34.
†Based on clinical studies of 35 patients, Koleshao, Savitsky, and Sapchenko insist that AT
should be used as an adjunctive approach in the treatment of acute myocardial infarction
in intensive care units.

pretations, or dream analysis, the therapist has considerable leeway to adapt his
management to the actual needs of the patient (*e.g.,* supportive, directive, passive,
or active).

Patients often need explanations why, from a homeostatic point of view, it is
advisable to avoid situations that would further accumulate anxiety stimuli. For
instance, the avoidance of violent films, risky sports, attendance at funerals, or
visits to dying persons might be suggested to a person who has an overload of
anxiety or aggression. The techniques used to communicate these suggestions
include confrontation, "paradoxical intention" (10), and support.

HOLISTIC CONCEPT OF AUTOGENIC THERAPY

To the autogenic therapist, the level of functional harmony is of central importance; it is determined both by a person's adaptation to environmental demands
and by adaptation to inner realities that evolve from his genetic constellation and
the consequences of his life experience. In other words, the assumption is that
reaching and maintaining a desirable level of inner harmony and living in favorable
agreement with the "authentic self" means 1) the recognition of the genetically
and otherwise given limits of functional possibilities, 2) the use of the circumstances of life to promote development in agreement with the biologically determined potential (*i.e.,* self-realization) 2) and 3) the avoidance, reduction, or elimination of those stimuli and circumstances that are known to produce
harmony-disturbing effects.

Practically, the development of inner harmony with the "authentic self" is accomplished in several ways. Autogenic training plays the key role by mobilizing self-regulatory homeostatic forces, *i.e.,* by a shift to a trophotropic state that is diametrically opposed to stress like states. The patient, through the combination of autogenic techniques, not only experiences functional adjustments (*e.g.,* a reduced anxiety level), but also develops increased sensitivity as to "what is good" and "what is not good" for his system.

THE ROLE OF MEDICATION

Since autogenic therapy aims at restoring and supporting natural homeostatic functions as quickly and effectively as possible, the reduction or elimination of psychopharmacological agents—particularly diazepam, trifluoperazine, barbitu-

Fig. 15–2. Formula patterns used in a hypertensive patient. Because of frequent feelings of restlessness, increasing distractions and irritability, the intermittent practice of telegram-style (*i.e.,* only one or two mental repetitions per formula) exercises (*e.g.,* 1–4 min, about 10 × day) was used. The deviation of blood pressure components and other complaints (*e.g.,* anxiety, marked aggressive feelings, heavy smoking, heavy drinking, unsatisfactory sexual relations, chronic sleep onset insomnia, difficulties in coping at work, inability to cry) began to improve during the second week, and progressively normalized or disappeared within 6–12 weeks.

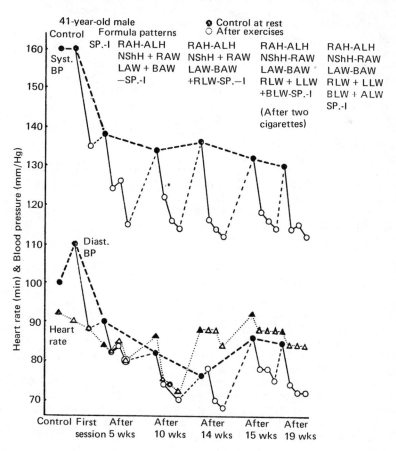

rates, amphetamines, and monoamine-oxidase inhibitors—that tend to interfere with this process is important. Among the various families of psychopharmacological agents, certain drugs have been found to interact better with AT than others. The agents that have been observed (34) to interfere the least with the homeostatic action of AT include the anxiolytics chlordiazepoxide and meprobamate, the antidepressant imipramine, and the neuroleptics chlorpromazine and promazine.

Reduction in medication is the rule in a variety of disorders, *e.g.,* in chronic bronchial asthma, constipation, epilepsy, hayfever, essential hypertension, primary glaucoma, migraine, sleep disorders, and certain disorders of cardiac rhythm. Particularly important in the management of diabetic trainees is that a progressive lowering of insulin requirements occurs as their experience in the practice of AT increases.

AT AND OTHER "RELAXATION RESPONSE" PROMOTING APPROACHES

There is general agreement that different methods, such as transcendental meditation (TM), various forms of Yoga, Zen meditation, progressive relaxation (3, 16), certain approaches of heterohypnosis (37) and autohypnosis (20, 23), certain biofeedback techniques (9, 12, 13, 38, 39), and certain approaches in behavior therapy (48), can contribute desirable elements for the improvement of mental and physical health through the elicitation of a "relaxation response" (2).

In comparing the various technical elements among these approaches, we find in addition to the common basic elements—*e.g.,* the nature of the mental device, a passive attitude, a decreased muscle tonus, a quiet environment, and a trained instructor (2)—there are psychophysiologically important differences in procedural details—*e.g.,* hetero-instructed versus self-instructed, topographic versus nontopographic, directive versus nondirective, symptomatic versus nonspecific, and verbal versus nonverbal techniques. Each of these procedural details may exert therapeutically desirable, undesirable, or relatively nonspecific effects, depending on the patient's history and actual functional situation. This leads to the question: who should practice what technique, in what manner, for how long, and under what kind of treatment control?

In certain specific situations, *e.g.,* in cases of intractable pain or hyperemesis gravidarum, "monosymptomatic" approaches may be the method of choice. In hyperemesis gravidarum, for example, symptomatic treatment with heterohypnosis is the best approach. The symptomatic treatment of headache by heterohypnosis or biofeedback (35) could however, be a serious technical error when, for example, the headache is a homeostatic signal calling for the release of a suppressed need for crying.

AT AND THE DROPOUT RATE

In private practice, the dropout rate for AT may be as low as 1%, whereas outpatient services may find an outright rejection of 20% to 30% (40). The highest rate of early dropout (69%; $N = 83$) in outdoor service treatment was reported in groups of young (*i.e.,* below the age of 26) male patients suffering from essential hypertension (18, 33). This is significantly higher than the average AT dropout rate (36%; $N = 326$) in the same clinic (40).

In medically supervised evening courses (one evening for seven weeks) involving heterogeneous groups of adults, about 40% to 50% dropped out within six weeks (19). About the same rate has been noted in groups of interns and residents participating in postgraduate training courses (W. Luthe).

The long-term dropout rate is equally variable. Most frequently, patients tend to forget to practice AT because they feel well and are unaware of the necessity of continuing the method to support their homeostatic functions. In 1250 psychosomatic patients (750 with cardiovascular disorders), Laberke reported that 10% dropped out early, 90% practiced regularly for one year or less, 80% for up to two years, 60% for up to three years, and 50% for longer than three years (22).

One of the AT-related variables that can easily motivate the patient to discontinue the method is the repeated experience of disagreeable training symptoms, *e.g.,* the feeling of spinning, dizziness, the feeling of losing consciousness, headaches, nausea, massive motor discharges, or disturbing images. Since such transitory phenomena are largely related to a history of accidents, traumatic events, and certain medical procedures (*e.g.,* electroconvulsive therapy, intoxication, suffocation, or inhalation anesthesia), it is most important that the therapist knows the case history and prepares and supports the patient accordingly.

Another variable that tends to interfere with the motivation to practice AT is an accumulated and suppressed need for crying. When the patient is not helped to "relearn" how to cry (*e.g.,* by role playing for five minutes twice a day) or continues to suppress the need to cry, then frequent frontal or other headaches, pains in the neck, spine, or joints, and other psychophysiological reactions may continue and discourage the patient from practicing AT.

Similarly, it is important to manage patients correctly who may have a disturbing overload of aggression, by, for example, introducing autogenic verbalization (to be discussed subsequently) or by using Luthe's "creativity mobilization technique" (4, 32).

AT AND LONG-TERM FOLLOW-UP

Autogenic methods are not a panacea and cannot be successful with patients who continue daily patterns of life that are saturated with exposure to situations that disturb their mental and physical homeostasis.

The patient's understanding and willingness to adjust his way of life to the actual homeostatic capacity of his system and to respect the adaptational exigencies arising from internal and external sources are decisive factors in both short-term and long-term outcome. In bronchial asthma, for example, 70% ($N = 150$) of Schenk's patients maintained stable improvement over follow-up periods lasting up to seven years (41); 30% showed slight or no improvement, or gave up. Other reports on asthmatic patients, with follow-up periods of 6 to 50 months, note that 61% to 66% ($N = 300$) remained symptom-free, 25% had significant improvement, and 9% to 13% gave up or did not improve significantly (33). In two groups of patients with angina pectoris (21), one group ($N = 30$) relied on medication only and suffered four infarctions within one to four years, while there was no myocardial infarction in a comparable group ($N = 31$) that practiced AT in addition to medication during the same period.*

Generally, the less favorable results have been noted with the use of autogenic standard exercises in patients who have a history of severely disturbing accidents or other traumatizing events. To obtain good results with such patients, it is often necessary to use AT in combination with autogenic abreaction (to be discussed).

AUTOGENIC MODIFICATION

Autogenic modification consists of two complementary approaches (Fig. 15–1): 1) psychologically oriented "intentional formulas" (IF) and 2) physiologically ori-

---

*Follow up data from other clinical areas are presented and discussed in Luthe W (Ed): Autogenic Therapy, Vol. II and III 33, 34

ented "organ-specific formulas" (OSF) (42). Both approaches are designed to utilize the peculiar psychophysiological nature of the autogenic state as a functional vehicle for obtaining specific, desirable effects that were not obtained through the regular standard exercises. For example, when chronic constipation has not improved sufficiently after ten weeks of AT, the formula, "my lower abdomen is warm," may be added to the end of the series of SEs in order to stimulate organ-specific activation of peristalsis in the colon and to increase blood flow in the colon wall (24, 33). Or, when the regular practice of AT does not readjust anxiety-dream-related awakening within two months, desirable readjustments of the patient's dream behavior and sleep pattern may be obtained by adding the IF*: "In my dreams I remain passive and go along with (the message of) my brain" (31).

AUTOGENIC MEDITATION

The practice of the seven meditative exercises (see Fig. 15–1) is not indicated if a trainee has difficulty in maintaining an adequate level of passive concentration over long periods (*e.g.,* 30 to 50 minutes) or if there is evidence of disturbing autogenic discharges (42). Occasionally, however, the visuo-imaginary components of the meditative exercises have been successfully used in the management of specific psychosomatic problems, either in combination with autogenic behavior therapy techniques (28, 44, 47) or as a complementary approach in psychoanalytic therapy.

AUTOGENIC NEUTRALIZATION

The hypothesis that there exist biological self-regulatory brain activities is not new. One of the elements that distinguishes autogenic therapy from other forms is the assumption that the patient's own system knows best how certain functional disturbances came about and how to reduce their disturbing effects (neutralization).

Observations of spontaneous training symptoms or autogenic discharges that occur during the autogenic state indicate that they have no apparent relationship to the content of the formulas. Detailed studies of these discharges showed that they occurred in great variety and had a unique profile for each patient. Often, there was a close relationship to the patient's complaints, his clinical condition, and certain events of his past. In some ways, they resembled the phenomena described during "sensory isolation" or during certain stages of sleep (*e.g.,* motor discharges or dreams) as well as the responses obtained by direct electrical stimulation of cortical and subcortical structures (36). It was therefore hypothesized that the autogenic state facilitates spontaneous discharges from certain parts of the brain that have a need for "unloading," and that this discharge activity is one of the therapeutic factors at work during AT. On the basis of this hypothesis, two different techniques of autogenic neutralization—*autogenic abreaction* (AA) (25, 26) and *autogenic verbalization* (AV) (42)—were developed to enhance the therapeutic effect of AT by giving the brain a better opportunity to neutralize and release whatever it needs to discharge.

*For technical details governing the indications, contraindications, relative contraindications and a variety of procedural aspects, see Luthe W (Ed) Autogenic Therapy, Vol. I—VI 24, 25, 26, 33, 34, 42

AUTOGENIC ABREACTION

If an increasing number of disturbing phenomena are noted during AT, the introduction of AA may be necessary. Restlessness, vestibular discharges (such as unpleasant dizziness and marked body image distortions), pain, headaches, bursts of anxiety, repeated episodes of disagreeable somatesthetic sensations, inability to continue the exercises, massive interference from intruding thoughts, and the frequent appearance of differentiated visual phenomena are some of the autogenic discharges that indicate a particular homeostatic need to unload more systematically and to neutralize accumulated disturbing material.

Clinical observations have shown that certain events in a patient's history have particularly damaging effects and therefore increase the likelihood that AA will be necessary. These factors include life-threatening accidents (especially when followed by unconsciousness), inhalation anesthesia, near drowning, severe drug intoxications (*e.g.,* unconsciousness following an overdose), sexual deviations (*e.g.,* homosexuality), and anxiety-provoking forms of religious education.

The technique of AA (25) includes the following elements. The patient is asked to shift mentally from the initial use of passive concentration on autogenic formulas to a spectatorlike attitude called *passive acceptance*. The mental shift comes during or after a two- to three-minute period of repetition of the "heaviness" formulas. In the autogenic state and with this "carte blanche" attitude of passive acceptance, the patient verbally describes, without restriction, everything that he experiences. The description may include sensory, motor, visual, intellectual, auditory, olfactory, affective, or vestibular phenomena. Both the patient and the therapist must observe and respect the therapeutic *principle of noninterference*. Interventions are limited to the management of resistance and should only be made after it repeatedly becomes obvious that the neutralization is blocked from proceeding in a direction already indicated by the patient's self-regulatory elaborations. The period of description should be prolonged until a sufficient level of neutralization is reached. The AA is terminated in the usual three-step sequence by flexing the arms, taking a deep breath, and opening the eyes. The entire AA is tape-recorded by the patient, and, as soon as possible after the session, he types a verbatim transcript. After reading it aloud (verbal reexpression during an unaltered state of consciousness), he includes a commentary (feedback and integration). The patient carries out unsupervised AAs at home as soon as he has acquired a satisfactory level of competence with the technique.

When autogenic abreaction is applied, it is important that the patient practices the standard exercises regularly and demonstrates that his therapeutic cooperation is reliable. The notes on his training symptoms during AT usually provide a good indication of his motivation. Unless it is practical to carry out a large portion of the therapy in the office, AA should not be started with patients who do not seem to have the motivation to work intensively on their own.

During a typical AA session, the therapist may initially assist and heteroverbalize the "heaviness" formulas. The patient begins to describe his experiences as soon as he notices the onset of training symptoms. If an inexperienced patient does not begin to talk by the end of the "heaviness" sequence, the following supportive formula may be added: "And you now imagine yourself in a meadow, and tell me how the meadow looks today or whatever else you see, or feel, or think." It must be made clear to the patient that the supportive "meadow image" is merely another stimulus (like "heaviness"), and that no mental effort should be made to obtain or maintain it.

An AA may last 15 to 150 minutes, and it is important that the patient keeps describing until the pattern of homeostatic elaborations indicates that nothing further is happening and he feels quite comfortable. If such a self-regulatory ending is not reached and premature termination cannot be avoided, however, it is possible to minimize any disagreeable aftereffects (*e.g.,* headaches, depressive feelings, anxiety attacks, nightmares) by ending the AA during a positive or relatively neutral phase.

A few observations and theoretical issues deserve special mention. On the surface, it may seem that the technique simply involves the pairing of a relaxed "trophotropic" state with a continuous, uncensored description of spontaneous elaborations (*e.g.,* sensory, motor, vestibular, visual, ideational, or affective) to thereby produce neutralization. This explanation, however, is an oversimplification of the complex and unique dynamics observed. The elaborations are often symbolic, primary-process, and dreamlike, and they seem to be closely related to nondominant, right hemispheric functions (29).

The emphasis on right hemispheric activity observed during AA is in keeping with the hypothesis that part of the transmission from one hemisphere to the other can be selectively and reversibly blocked. Bogen and Bogen proposed that "certain kinds of left hemisphere activity may directly suppress certain kinds of right hemisphere action. Or, they may prevent access to the left hemisphere of the products of right hemisphere activity" (6). Similarly, Galin considered "the hypothesis that in normal intact people mental events in the right hemisphere can become disconnected functionally from the left hemisphere (by inhibition of neuronal transmission across the corpus callosum) and can continue a life of their own. This hypothesis suggests an neurophysiological mechanism for at least some instances of repression, and an anatomical locus for the unconscious mental contents" (11). The corollary of this theory is that a functional imbalance or inhibition between the two hemispheres participates in the development of psychodynamic and psychosomatic disorders. One can further hypothesize that AA facilitates communication between the two cerebral hemispheres and allows repressed, primary-processlike, disturbing material (presumably right hemispheric) to become integrated into logical, analytical, verbal awareness (largely a left hemispheric function) (29). The result is a reduction in the disturbing potency of traumas (neutralization or resolution of intrapsychic conflict).

During AA, the patient's homeostatic brain mechanisms may automatically select and control the release of disturbing material, adapt the process of neutralization to the patient's level of tolerance, modify and repeat certain themes until sufficient neutralization is achieved, shift to other "pressure areas" once neutralization of a given theme is sufficiently advanced, neutralize negative transference, and signal that the neutralization of certain themes is terminated.

Accidents and Traumatizing Events.

Extensive clinical experience with AT and particularly with AA indicates that the damaging effects of accidents and traumatizing medical procedures (*e.g.,* inhalation anesthesia or electroconvulsive therapy), particularly in conjunction with artificially induced alteration or loss of consciousness, have been underestimated. The neglect of this type of medical problem may stem from the fact that no detectable neurological lesions are involved and no approach, other than autogenic therapy, has the tools to cope with the disruptive psychophysiological effects. Thus, these patients are often dismissed as malingerers with a "compensation neurosis."

The effects of such physical traumas tend to become functionally linked to other unrelated events and thereby aggravate existing problems (*e.g.,* homosexuality (5) or psychosomatic disorders). Since the experience and its consequences are nonverbal, exploration of this field is difficult or impossible by verbal approaches alone. During AT and AA, some patients may transitorily have feelings of being about to lose consciousness, unpleasant vestibular phenomena (spinning, dizziness, falling, and so on), and unpleasant physical sensations in a previously injured area of the body, which are accompanied by anxiety.

At first, self-regulatory brain mechanisms often neutralize such traumatic events by disintegrating the reality features into puzzlelike bits. Then, after many repetitions, the pieces of the puzzle gradually begin to take shape and increasingly realistic confrontations with the underlying traumatic event become possible. Although the effects of such traumas are never completely eliminated, a substantial reduction in their disturbing potency is possible and is usually accompanied by improvement in the patient's disorders.

AUTOGENIC VERBALIZATION

Autogenic verbalization is a more limited method of neutralization (42). This approach differs from autogenic abreaction in that it does not involve a "carte blanche" attitude, but rather it focuses on a predetermined specific topic such as aggression, anxiety, or obsessive material. For instance, in the autogenic state, after the "heaviness" formulas, the patient is instructed to verbalize all the things that make him angry and is encouraged to keep expressing his aggression. A typical verbalization consists of many repetitions of the same theme, and it usually lasts 10 to 40 minutes. The patient practices the method at home. For the correct use of this technique, it should be emphasized that he must verbalize continuously until he is certain that his mind is "empty" and there is nothing more to say. If a verbalization is cut short, the disturbing affect may remain mobilized, and disagreeable aftereffects may ensue (*e.g.*, headaches, anxiety, irritability, or chest pain). The approach is particularly useful when there has been a recent acute disturbance. Close supervision of patients using autogenic verbalization is important, because the incorrect use of the technique may spontaneously convert into unwanted, complicated processes of autogenic abreaction.

GRADUATED ACTIVE HYPNOSIS

In contrast to all other autogenic methods (see Fig. 15–1), the combination of AT with elements of the orthodox techniques of hypnosis (20) aims at obtaining a shift to hypnotic states. The method emphasizes the exclusive use of self-instruction, *i.e.*, self-hypnosis (23). After about two weeks of preparatory practice of the first and second standard exercise, the hypnotic element of eye fixation (sometimes in combination with monotonous auditory stimuli, *e.g.*, provided by a metronome) is added in order to promote the shift to a hypnotic state. Then, after a preparatory technical discussion, the patient continues to use regularly "the self-induced hypnotic state exercises" for implanting, by mental repetition, sloganlike phrases that are designed to support specific, therapeutically desirable developments. Kretschmer (20) recommended this approach for the treatment of neurotic patients or those having personality disorders with strong obsessive-compulsive components and also as a complementary method to "problem focused" analytical psychotherapy, *i.e.*, *zweigleisige Standardmethode*, or the "double-track standard method" (23).

AUTOGENIC BEHAVIOR THERAPY

Behavior therapists who were interested in finding a more satisfactory alternative to Jacobson's "progressive relaxation" (PR) technique (3, 16) initiated the use of behavior therapy techniques (*e.g.,* systematic desensitization) together with autogenic methods (*i.e.,* autogenic behavior therapy, or ABT). To support the different phases of systematic desensitization effectively, preparatory periods of intensive practice of standard exercises (*e.g.,* five to eight sets of SE I and SE II per day for two weeks) are most frequently used. Other ABT procedures may include the frequent practice of the partial exercise "my neck and shoulders are heavy," the case-adapted use of meditative exercises when the therapeutic procedures are intended to emphasize work with visual imagination (*e.g.,* preparatory visual rehearsal), the occasional use of intentional formulas when additional support in a specific functional area is needed, or the use of autogenic verbalization when massive overloads of aggression (or anxiety) require "deflation" before (and during) systematic desensitization (28).

The substitution of AT for PR led independent investigators to conclude that ABT 1) augments the effects of traditional behavior therapy with PR, 2) affects in unit time a more substantial improvement in stress defenses, 3) augments the degree of defense against extrapsychic pressures, 4) facilitates the conditioning routine, and 5) provides improvements in personality dynamics that are different from the removal of a symptom or a symptom complex. It was also found with ABT that fewer cases fail to respond adequately, that there is no abrupt termination of therapy by patients who continue AT, and, finally, that AT "supplies essential therapeutic ingredients at present missing from traditional behavior therapy methods" (14).

The combination of autogenic therapy with techniques of behavior therapy can provide faster treatment results in specific areas, *e.g.,* with food allergies, phobic reactions, writer's cramp, contact dermatitis, cold-induced dermatitis, muscular dystrophy, cerebellar ataxia, and collagen disease. Results of this combination of therapies when applied to 208 patients with these disorders showed that 84% were significantly improved or cured (12% failures) over follow-up periods of 6 to 30 months. (1, 14, 15, 28, 43–47).

AUTOGENIC FEEDBACK TRAINING

The combination of biofeedback techniques with autogenic approaches (27) began around 1965 under the influence of Gardner Murphy at the Menninger Foundation with the work of Green, Green, and Walters (12, 13). As in autogenic behavior therapy (28), independent investigators hypothesized that the use of biofeedback combined with AT would yield better results than the use of biofeedback alone.

A variety of studies involving, for example, the control of migraine, blood pressure, or heart rate, supported or confirmed this assumption (6, 9, 35, 38, 39). In a one-year follow-up study of 23 patients with migraine or tension headaches or both, Pearse *et al.* (35) found that a five-day, intensive, autogenic feedback training program involving the regulation of hand temperature was successful in 82.4%. Cowings, Billingham, and Toscano, in searching for a means to control the debilitating effects of motion sickness *e.g.,* in space flight, found that groups of subjects who used biofeedback together with AT to control multiple autonomic responses simultaneously—*i.e.,* the heart rate, respiration rate, and the blood volume pulse of the face and hands—withstood the stress of Coriolis acceleration significantly better than did control group subjects (7, 8). Available findings in the area of autogenic feedback training show that the combination of biofeedback and AT is a powerful tool in learning to control voluntarily a variety of bodily functions. Although this appears to be very encouraging—from a mechanistic point of view—for symptomatic treatment, further research is needed to clarify certain questions. Some of these questions are related to the occasional observations that specific functional disturbances may occur after successful learning of the voluntary control of autonomic functions by means of biofeedback, *e.g.,* of local blood flow regulation, paresthesia, or spermatogenesis (27). Such functional disturbances may mean that "forceful," nonhomeostatic interferences with homeostatically controlled functions can lead to undesirable disturbances of specific sectors of the human system.

REFERENCES

1. Abe T: Behavior therapy and blepharospasm, hyperhydrosis, Raynaud's symptom of collagen disease, myasthenia gravis, ataxia, dystrophia muscularis and Schilder's disease. Jap J Psychosom Med 11:2:31–33, 1971
2. Benson H, Beary JF, Carol MP: The relaxation response. Psychiatry 37:37, 1974
3. Bernstein DA, Borkovec TD: Progressive Relaxation Training. A Manual for the Helping Professions. Champaign, Ill, Research Press, 1973
4. Blumberger SR: Similarities between autogenic approaches and W. Luthe's "Creativity Mobilization Technique". Rome, Proc 3rd Congr Int Coll Psychosom Med & 2nd Int Symp Autogenic Therapy, Vol IV, 1976
5. Blumberger SR, DeRivera JLG: Homosexual dynamics studied with autogenic abreaction and psychotherapy of analytic orientation. Rome, Proc 3rd Congr Int Coll Psychosom Med & 2nd Int Symp Autogenic Therapy, Vol IV, 1976
6. Bogen JE, Bogen GM: The other side of the brain III: the corpus callosum and creativity. Bull Los Angeles Neurol Soc 34 (4): 191–220, 1969
7. Cowings PS, Billingham J, Toscano BW: Learned control of multiple autonomic responses to compensate for the debilitating effects of motion sickness. Rome, Proc 3rd Congr Int Coll Psychosom Med & 2nd Int Symp Autogenic Therapy, Vol IV, 1976
8. Cowings PS, Toscano BW: Psychosomatic health: simultaneous control of multiple autonomic responses by humans. A training method. Rome Proc 3rd Congr Int Coll Psychosom Med & 2nd Int Symp Autogenic Therapy, Vol IV, 1976
9. Diamond S, Franklin M: Autogenic training and biofeedback in treatment of chronic headache problems in adults. Rome, Proc 3rd Congr Int Coll Psychosom Med & 2nd Int Symp Autogenic Therapy, Vol IV, 1976
10. Frankl V: Paradoxical intention: a logotherapeutic technique. Am J Psychother 14:520, 1960
11. Galin D: Implications for psychiatry of left and right cerebral specialization. Arch Gen Psychiatr 31:4, 572–583, 1974
12. Green E: Biofeedback for mind-body self-regulation: healing and creativity. In Shapiro D, Barber TX, Dicara LV, Kamiya J, Miller NE, Stoyva J (eds): Biofeedback & Self-Control 1972. Chicago, Aldine, 1973, pp 152–166
13. Green EE, Green AM, Walters ED: Voluntary control of internal states: psychological and physiological. J Transper Psychol II (1): 1–26, 1970
14. Haward LRC: Reduction in stress reactivity by autogenic training. In Luthe W (ed): Autogenic Training. Correlationes Psychosomaticae. New York, Grune & Stratton, 1965
15. Ikemi Y, Nakagawa S, Kusano T, Sugita M: The application of autogenic training to "psychological desensitization" of allergic disorders. In Luthe W (ed): Autogenic Training. Correlationes Psychosomaticae. New York, Grune & Stratton, 1965
16. Jacobson E: Progressive Relaxation, 2nd ed. Chicago, University of Chicago Press, 1944
17. Klumbies G, Eberhardt G: Results of autogenic training in the treatment of hypertension. In Lopez-Ibor JJ (ed): IV World Congress of Psychiatry, Madrid, 5–11, IX, 1966. Int Congr Series No. 117, pp 46–47. Amsterdam, Excerpta Medica, 1966
18. Koleshao AA, Savitsky VV, Sapchenko GV: The use of autogenic training in the complex treatment of patients with myocardial infarction in the ward of intensive therapy. In Romen AS (ed): Psichicheskaya Samoregulyatsiya. Alma Ata (USSR), 1974
19. Körmendy E: Psychische Störungen und Autogenes Training. Erfahrungen mit dem Autogenen Training in einer Volkshoch-schule. Rhein Ärztebl 18:541–546, 1975
20. Kretschmer E: Medizinische Psychologie, 8th ed. Leipzig, G Thieme Verlag, 1945, pp 264–266
21. Laberke JA: Über eine psychosomatische Kombinationsbehandlung (mehrdimensionale Therapie) bei sogenannten inneren Krankheiten. Münch Med Wochenschr 94 (35): 1718–1724, 94 (36): 1809–1816, 1952
22. Laberke JA: Klinische Erfahrungen mit dem Autogenen Training bei Herz- und Kreislauferkrankungen. In Luthe W (ed): Autogenic Training. Correlationes Psychosomaticae. New York, Grune & Stratton, 1965, pp 201–206

23. Langen D: Die gestufte Aktivhypnose, 2nd ed. Stuttgart, G Thieme Verlag, 1967

24. Luthe W: Autogenic Therapy. Research and Theory. New York, Grune & Stratton, 1970

25. Luthe W: Autogenic Therapy. Dynamics of Autogenic Neutralization. New York, Grune & Stratton, 1970

26. Luthe W: Autogenic Therapy. Treatment with Autogenic Neutralization. New York, Grune & Stratton, 1973

27. Luthe W: Autogenic feedback training. Jap J Hypn 18:2: 3–15, 1973

28. Luthe W: Autogenic behavior therapy (1965–1972) Jap J Hypn 19:23–29, 1974

29. Luthe W: Hemispheric specialization and autogenic therapy. Rome, Proc 3rd Congr Int Coll Psychosom Med & 2nd Int Symp Autogenic Therapy, Vol IV, 1976

30. Luthe W: On the development of space exercises in autogenic training. Rome, Proc 3rd Congr Int Coll Psychosom Med & 2nd Int Symp Autogenic Therapy, Vol IV, 1976

31. Luthe W: The dream formula. Rome, Proc 3rd Congr Int Coll Psychosom Med & 2nd Int Symp Autogenic Therapy, Vol IV, 1976

32. Luthe W: Creativity Mobilization Technique. New York, Grune & Stratton, 1976

33. Luthe W, Schultz JH: Autogenic Therapy. Medical Applications. New York, Grune & Stratton, 1970

34. Luthe W, Schultz JH: Autogenic Therapy. Applications in Psychotherapy. New York, Grune & Stratton, 1970

35. Pearse BA, Walters ED, Sargent JD, Meers M: Exploratory observations of the use of an intensive autogenic feedback training (IAFT) procedure in a follow-up study of out-of-town patients having migraine and/or tension headaches. Topeka, KS, Accreditation (BA) Study, Washburn University, 1974

36. Penfield W, Jasper H: The Functional Anatomy of the Brain. Boston, Little, Brown, 1954

37. Ruch JC: A study of self-hypnosis under alternative procedures. Diss (PhD), Stanford, Stanford University, 1972

38. Sargent JD, Green EE, Walters ED: Preliminary report on the use of autogenic feedback training in the treatment of migraine and tension headaches. Psychosom Med 35:129–135, 1973

39. Sargent JD, Walters ED, Green EE: Psychosomatic self-regulation and tension headaches. Semin Psychiatry 5 (4):411–428, 1973

40. Schaeffer G: Das autogene Training in einer medizinischen Poliklinik. In Luthe W (ed): Autogenes Training. Correlationes Psychosomaticae. Stuttgart, G Thieme Verlag, 1965, pp 215–222

41. Schenk T: Das autogene Training in der Behandlung von Asthmakranken. Psychotherapie 3:148–150, 1958

42. Schultz JH, Luthe W: Autogenic Therapy. Autogenic Methods. New York, Grune & Stratton, 1969

43. Takaishi N, Hosaka M, Minami R, Kaneko Z: Systematic desensitization therapy by the use of autogenic training. Jap J Hypn 12 (1):24–28, 1968

44. Uchiyama K: Effects of autogenic training relaxation in the systematic desensitization treatment. Jap J Counsel Sci 3 (2):65–75, 1970

45. Uchiyama K: The efficacy of behavior therapy for anthropophobia: systematic desensitization with autogenic training. Clin Psychiat (Jap) 48 (7):57–61, 1972

46. Uchiyama K: A study on writer's cramp: treatment by systematic desensitization with autogenic training. Bull Clin Consult Psychol 13:1–2, 1973

47. Ujimori H, Uchiyama K: The amplitude's fluctuation of the plethysmogram under images of anxiety situation. Study on AT relaxation 5. Bull Clin Consult Psychol 10:85–94, 1970

48. Wolpe J: Psychotherapy by Reciprocal Inhibition. Stanford, Stanford University Press, 1958

16 Biofeedback and Biocybernetics

JOSEPH D. SARGENT

At the first annual meeting of the Biofeedback Research Society in 1969, the term *biofeedback* was officially coined as the shortened version of "biological feedback." Continuous monitoring of physiological performance became possible with the advances in electronic technology after World War II, and this development allowed the assessment of moment-to-moment changes in bodily functions in such subjects as astronauts in space flight and patients in coronary care units. Such physiological information relayed back to the physician or other professional personnel forms the basis for decisions regarding the management of the individual being monitored, the latter being unaware of the basis for these decisions. Biofeedback, in contrast, concerns itself with the antithetical concept, in which the subject, furnished with his own physiological data, makes decisions concerning his own welfare with relatively little outside intervention.

Man from his earliest days has been oriented and sensitive to the outside world, since his survival depended on his alertness to external dangers. His perception of internal derangement, however, begins to assume importance only in times of illness or when he is under unusual physiological or psychological stress, such as in adaptation to high altitudes or to periods of sleep deprivation.

THE MECHANISM OF BIOFEEDBACK

The course of events in perception is diagrammed in Figure 16-1. The perception of an external event *(a)* brings about a cognitive and affective response through simultaneous activitation of the cortical and limbic systems *(b)*. This, in turn, stimulates the hypothalamus *(c)*, which, via the pituitary-hormonal axis and the autonomic nervous system *(d)* evokes a somatic response *(e)*. Under normal conditions, most of us have little conscious awareness of these somatic responses. A monitoring instrument can provide the subject with information regarding the direction and magnitude of such responses and helps him to observe objectively the internal event *(f)*. Certain features presented in Figure 16-1 are of special interest: first, the cognitive and affective responses *(b* and *h)* have conscious and unconscious components that are defined by the presence or absence of awareness; second, there is an ongoing interaction between the hypothalamus *(c)*, the pituitary-hormonal axis and autonomic nervous system *(d)*, and the somatic response *(e)*.

The monitoring instrument that feeds back objective data *(f)* allows the subject to correlate the direct perception of the internal event with the objective data *(g)*. This is well illustrated by a subjective change of sensation in the hands *(g)* associated with an observable and measurable rise in the reading on a temperature trainer *(f)* as the blood flow increases in response to vascular dilatation *(e)*. Simultaneously, with the direct perception of this physiological change *(g)*, there are cognitive and affective responses via the cortical and limbic systems *(h)*. Eventu-

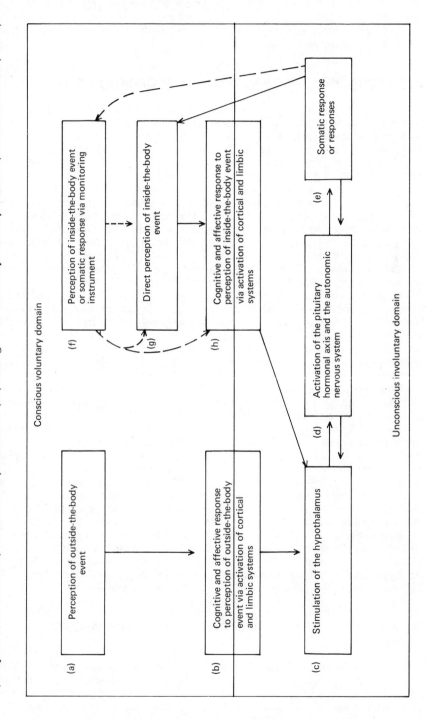

Fig. 16-1. Biofeedback and biocybernetic concepts in relation to physiological functioning. Please see text for explanation. (Adapted from Green E, Green A: In Jacobson N (ed): Being Well Is a Responsibility. London, Tiernstone Book, 1975)

Conscious voluntary domain

Unconscious involuntary domain

(a) Perception of outside-the-body event

(b) Cognitive and affective response to perception of outside-the-body event via activation of cortical and limbic systems

(c) Stimulation of the hypothalamus

(d) Activation of the pituitary hormonal axis and the autonomic nervous system

(e) Somatic response or responses

(f) Perception of inside-the-body event or somatic response via monitoring instrument

(g) Direct perception of inside-the-body event

(h) Cognitive and affective response to perception of inside-the-body event via activation of cortical and limbic systems ally, as the subject learns to rely entirely on direct perception *(g)* with its cognitive and affective response *(h)*, the need for the monitoring apparatus is gradually eliminated (dashed lines in Figure 16–1). The steps *(c, d, e, g,* and *h* form a closed circle, the *biocybernetic loop*.

BIOFEEDBACK IN THE TREATMENT OF MIGRAINE HEADACHE

The use of biofeedback is illustrated by the application of peripheral vasodilatation training in the management of migraine headache. The patient with migraine has a direct perception of an alteration in his internal environment with the onset of the headache and its associated symptoms *(e* and *g)*. This perception, when registered in the central nervous system, generates morbid thoughts and sensations *(h)*, which affect the equilibrium established between the hypothalamus *(c)*, the pituitary-hormonal axis and the autonomic nervous system *(d)*, and the somatic response *(e)*. This altered equilibrium, in turn, influences the patient's awareness of his somatic symptoms. Thus, the biocybernetic loop is established. How can the clinician intervene to break this cycle? Admittedly, the treatment of the disorder with drugs, surgery, psychotherapy, behavior-modification techniques, or other modalities has hitherto yielded dubiously beneficial results at best and, more often, only failures. Mindful of the new developments in biofeedback technique, what use can the migraine sufferer possibly make of it?

The literature in the past decade has provided some evidence demonstrating a tendency to abnormal vasomotor tone in the blood vessels of the hands in patients with migraine (1, 2, 9). One is not ordinarily aware—and this includes the patient with migraine—of the state of change of tonus in local vascular structures. Such an individual, however, can gain knowledge of the altered local circulation by learning to use a temperature trainer. Further, he can be trained by various means to raise the skin temperature of the hand, and if he succeeds in doing so by as little as 1.5°F, he becomes aware of a change in the sensation in the hand, which includes warmth, a sense of fullness, and even throbbing. Such experience can be obtained by the patient early in the learning process only when he is thoroughly relaxed and without symptoms. The ultimate goal, of course, is for the patient to apply the acquired skills under conditions of stress and, most importantly, during the earliest phase of a headache episode, for it is then that peripheral vasodilatation induces the sensory changes in the hand, and the control of the migraine attack can be achieved. The properly trained individual, after learning to affect such sensory responses rapidly (in a matter of seconds), can bring about an amelioration in the severity or a complete subsidence of the headache in a few moments. A clinical observation worth emphasizing is that a full-blown headache (or an equally severe episode) can recur within a few minutes after the patient discontinues his concentration techniques for peripheral vasodilatation. Often this technique must be repeated at frequent intervals over a number of hours to keep the headache under control until its tendency to recur has subsided. Such a phenomenon has been noted particularly in the early stages of training.

RELATIONSHIP OF BIOFEEDBACK TO OTHER THERAPEUTIC MODALITIES

The techniques that are useful in creating the new biocybernetic loop include the use of autogenic training phrases, the repetition of biofeedback exercises at home and in the laboratory, the relaxation of skeletal muscles, suggestion, and, perhaps, an altered stage of consciousness. The particular type of imagery used by the patient is a matter of individual choice, and the type of effective imagery varies greatly from person to person; for some, no imagery is needed. Biofeedback is helpful in the learning process, since it provides the patient with objective data so that he does not have to depend entirely on subjective feelings.

Two important questions may arise here: First, what specially acquired physiological skill can eventually prove to be most useful in helping, for example, the migraine patient? Koppman *et al.* (13) have shown that good results in the control of migraine can be obtained by constriction of the superficial temporal artery. Clinical experience shows that the headache will subside as long as the examiner occludes that artery on the ipsilateral side of the pain. Second, once a specific physiological skill has been acquired, what combination of behavioral techniques will result in acquiring physiological skills in the shortest time for the largest number of patients? Biofeedback can be central in any such training, since, if appropriately chosen, it will help the patient in achieving the perception of the relevant physiological response.

There are four general methods that have been used to bring about an awareness of, and changes in, adverse internal physiological functioning. The first is by means of altering the state of consciousness through changes in cerebral functioning, so that a person has access to, and control of, the less conscious realms of his mind. Such techniques include autogenic training, transcendental meditation (TM), hypnosis, self-hypnosis, states of free association, and biofeedback electroencephalographic (EEG) training. Second, simple relaxation of the skeletal musculature allows one to be aware not only of tension in strained muscle, but also of internal organ functioning. Examples of this are provided by progressive relaxation exercises, autogenic training, and biofeedback electromyographic (EMG) training. A third way to influence internal functioning is simply to change a person's conscious, observable mode of coping. Such methods include systemic desensitization, operant conditioning, assertiveness training, and classical conditioning. A fourth method involves the cortical control of the autonomic nervous system, which may be acquired, for example, by biofeedback training in peripheral vascular control. This technique, which is useful in controlling some aspects of the autonomic nervous system, depends greatly on what somatic response is to be monitored. Thus, for the resistance of air flow in cases of asthma to be altered, modifications in the smooth musculature of the airway passages are required, and, in this instance, the monitoring of skin temperature in the hands may not be particularly helpful.

I know of no published data that show what happens simultaneously in skeletal muscle, brain functioning, and other portions of the autonomic nervous system when a particular somatic response is subjected to modification. An effective biofeedback technique for altering the autonomic nervous system may need to utilize, in the training phase at least, techniques from the first three methods in order to bring its function under cortical control. Eventually, all four general methods for bringing about awareness and changes in adverse physiological functioning have a final common pathway: the integration of psychosomatic responses to create a state of well-being in the patient.

CLINICAL USES OF BIOFEEDBACK

As yet, biofeedback is not a tool to be applied indiscriminately to any and all human afflictions without some circumspection. Many authorities in the field have called for controlled clinical studies (14, 15), and I am in total concurrence with this viewpoint, since anything less will only result in discredit to the field and, worse yet, the loss of valuable time. So far, no controlled, clinical studies with significant numbers of patients have been published, and, from an ethical viewpoint, there are no biofeedback systems that could be construed as practical, proven approaches to any medical or psychological condition. Many biofeedback systems are under investigation, but, in my view, they are only experimental, not practical, applications in medical practice.

Some of the most convincing work in the experimental application of biofeedback has been in the treatment of neurological disorders. Sterman (19), in working with four poorly controlled epileptics, showed that through prolonged training, these patients demonstrated a significant reduction in seizure activity. Johnson and Garton (12) demonstrated the value of EMG feedback in a 6- to 18-month training period for retraining weakened muscles in 10 hemiplegics. Blanchard and Young, in a review article, concluded that "the work on EMG feedback for muscle retraining has established the therapeutic effect of biofeedback training" (4). Budzynski and his colleagues (6) have shown the value of EMG training in handling tension headaches in 18 subjects in a controlled study, but no one has, as yet, reported any supporting, controlled studies that contain larger numbers of subjects.

My work in treating migraine headaches led to a noncontrolled study with 74 patients who were observed from 270 days to more than 3 years in some cases. Of these, 55 had a reduction in headache activity of 26% or more, as determined by the criteria of frequency and severity of headaches (16). These results suggested a trend that was good enough for us to embark later on a controlled, clinical study.

One of the areas of great interest for physicians has been the application of biofeedback to cardiovascular problems. Engel and his colleagues have been the most active in this area; his work has been with premature ventricular contractions (21), paroxysmal atrial tachycardia (7), and Wolff-Parkinson-White syndrome (5). Again, some positive results have been accomplished clinically with a limited number of patients. Hypertension has also been investigated in a relatively small number of patients, but the conclusions have been confusing. Some of the earliest workers in this area, such as Benson *et al.* (3) and Schwartz and Shapiro (18), have been the most active in employing biofeedback techniques.

Raynaud's disease has been of some interest to researchers in the applications of biofeedback, since it is a condition for which there is no established medical treatment. The results, once again, are sketchy, and the reports involve only a few cases (17, 20). Our informal study of eight such patients, who were observed for several months to two years, showed four to be markedly improved and four to have done poorly using peripheral vasodilatation. This, too, is an area that needs systematic investigative work.

The management of gastrointestinal problems, such as hyperacidity (22), fecal incontinence (8), and irritable colon (10), by biofeedback techniques is now only in a nascent stage. The same thing can be said for investigations in metabolic and endocrine disorders such as diabetes mellitus.

Studies using biofeedback techniques in conjunction with a number of treatment modalities have investigated its usefulness for several other medical and psychological problems, but all this work is still very preliminary.

REFERENCES

1. Appenzeller O: Vasomotor function in migraine. Headache 9:147–155, 1969

2. Appenzeller O, Davison K, Marshall J: Reflex vasomotor abnormalities in the hands of migrainous subjects. J Neurol Neurosurg Psychiatry 25:447–450, 1963

3. Benson H et al.: Decreased systolic blood pressure through operant conditioning techniques in patients with essential hypertension. Science 173:740–742, 1971

4. Blanchard E, Young L: Clinical applications of biofeedback training: a review of evidence. Arch Gen Psychiatry 30:515, 1974

5. Bleecker E, Engel B: Learned control of cardiac rate and cardiac conduction in the Wolff–Parkinson–White syndrome. N Engl Med 288:560–562, 1973

6. Budzynski T, Stoyva J, Alder C, Mullaney M: EMG-biofeedback and tension headache: a controlled outcome study. In Birk L (ed): Biofeedback Behavioral Medicine. New York, Grune & Stratton, 1973

7. Engel B, Bleecker E: Application of operant conditioning techniques to the control of cardiac arrhythmias. In Obrist P et al. (eds): Contemporary Trends in Cardiovascular Psychophysiology. Chicago, Aldine–Atherton, 1974

8. Engel B, Nikoomanesh P, Schuster M: Operant conditioning of rectosphincteric responses in the treatment of fecal incontinence. N Engl Med 290:646–649, 1974

9. French E, Lassers B, Desai M: Reflex vasomotor responses in the hands of migrainous subjects. J Neurol Neurosurg Psychiatry 30:276–278, 1967

10. Furman S: Intestinal biofeedback in functional diarrhea: a preliminary report. J Behav Ther Exp Psychiatry 4:317–321, 1973

11. Green E, Green A: Biofeedback, research and therapy. In Jacobson N (ed): Being Well is a Responsibility. London, Tiernstone Book, 1975

12. Johnson M, Garton W: Muscle re-education in hemiplegia by use of electromyographic device. Arch Phys Med Rehab 54:320–325, 1973

13. Koppman J, McDonald R, Kunzel M: Voluntary regulation of temporal artery diameter by migraine patients. Headache 14:133–138, 1974

14. Melzack R: The promise of biofeedback: don't hold the party yet. Psychol Today 9: 18–22, 81–82, 1975

15. Miller M: Biofeedback: evaluation of a new technic. N Engl J Med 290:684–685, 1974

16. Sargent J, Taylor J, Coyne L, Thetford P, Walters E, Segerson J: Progress report in the psychosomatic self-regulation of migraine headaches. Presented at Kansas Regional American College of Physicians, 1975 (in press)

17. Schwartz G: Clinical applications of biofeedback: some theoretical issues. In Upper D, Goodenough D (eds): Behavior Modification with the Individual Patient. Proceedings of the Third Annual Brockton Symposium on Behavior Therapy. Hutley, Roche, 1972

18. Schwartz G, Shapiro D: Biofeedback and essential hypertension: current findings and theoretical concerns. In Birk L (ed): Biofeedback: Behavioral Medicine. New York, Grune & Stratton, 1973

19. Sterman M: Neurophysiological and clinical studies of sensorimotor EEG biofeedback training. In Birk L (ed): Biofeedback: Behavioral Medicine. New York, Grune & Stratton, 1973

20. Surwit R: Biofeedback: a possible treatment for Raynaud's disease. In Birk L (ed): Biofeedback: Behavioral Medicine. New York, Grune & Stratton, 1973

21. Weiss T, Engel B: Operant conditioning of heart rate in patients with premature ventricular contractions. Psychosom Med 33:301–321, 1971

22. Welgan P: Learned control of gastric acid secretions in ulcer patients. Psychosom Med 36:411–419, 1974

17 **Pharmacotherapy**

ARNOLD J. MANDELL

Prompt prescription of the appropriate phenothiazine by a discerning internist or general practitioner treating a patient who shows the early signs of psychotic decompensation demonstrates both the increased sophistication of the generalist and the remarkable specificity of some of the newer antipsychotic agents. An internist's intuitive sense of incipient depression in a fastidious middle-aged woman and his use of tricyclic antidepressant therapy may also be considered a tribute to the advances in clinical and basic pharmacotherapy. Such instances, however, are more rare than they ought to be. Ironically, in spite of the accumulation of knowledge in this field, the rationale for the clinical applications of many psychotropic drugs are left largely to the advertising media. One of the intentions of this chapter is to provide a practical alternative guide for doctors who do not regularly treat psychiatric patients but who do treat patients whose problems have psychic components.

When a doctor in general or internal medical practice is confronted with a patient having psychological symptoms, or having phenomena that the patient insists need pharmacological medication, it is essential that he make informed and judicious decisions about both the patient and the drug before starting treatment. One problem intrinsic to making such discriminations results from the exploitation of language in the drug advertisements; it is difficult for the nonspecialist to decide, on the basis of what is written, whether a particular drug is indicated or not. A drug suggested for use in treating "depression" might "help" half the people in the United States or it might help only 0.001%, depending upon the operational definition of the word "depression." Likewise, such words as "anxiety," "irritability," "combativeness," "resistance to psychotherapy," and untold others have become vague vehicles through which marketing directors—and doctors as well—can express their personal bias relative to the use of psychotropic agents.

More importantly, a very sensitive aspect of the doctor-patient relationship can be lost by the simple dismissal of the patient's psychological problems through the prescription of agents that are admittedly relatively harmless in themselves.

THE NEUROTIC PATIENT

The neurotic people who come forth with medical complaints are numberless. So common are they that, out of frustration and impatience, many doctors keep in contact with them for as brief a period as possible and readily prescribe psychotropic drugs for them. What is required is *more* contact to distinguish the neurotic from the incipient psychotic patient. The latter will benefit from the proper use of antipsychotic agents; the former, who often requests medicine and accounts for most of the licit psychoactive drug traffic, may be a less than ideal candidate for therapy with the so-called minor tranquilizers, which he or she may ask for by their proprietary names (*e.g.,* the glycerol derivatives, the diphenylmethane derivatives, the benzodiazepine derivatives, or various other compounds that are usually represented to be sleeping medicines). Despite what one may read in the advertisements in the throwaway journals, the efficacy of some of these agents is far from established. Several double-blind studies have indicated that tranquilizers are no better than small, carefully controlled doses of barbiturates for temporary amelioration of mild neurotic symptoms. Moreover, some side effects and sequelae associated with the use of barbiturates have not been considered relevant to understanding the minor tranquilizers, because they belong to a different chemical family. From the standpoint of clinical phenomena, however, the two families of drugs do not differ greatly. After moderate to high doses of the minor tranquilizers, there can be withdrawal excitement, even convulsions. Overdoses of minor tranquilizers produce respiratory and cardiovascular failure, much as the barbiturates do.

Most self-declared candidates for this kind of treatment are afflicted with chronic disturbances of living that are not going to be altered easily; once begun, a drug habit tends to remain with them. What they, and apparently many of their physicians, do not seem to realize is that, in addition to building up a psychological dependency on drugs as a way of coping with problems, many tranquilizers, and stimulants as well, leave effects upon withdrawal that simply intensify the subjective phenomena that led to the request for "something to help" in the first place. Thus, a depressed housewife who requests an amphetamine ostensibly to help her diet may find that her subjective feelings of depression and lethargy increase when her prescription lapses. A person who attempts to cope with anxiety with minor tranquilizers runs the risk of incorporating them regularly into his living style, along with incurring the shakiness and irritability that emerge when even low doses of these agents are discontinued.

Brief interpersonal therapy, family consultations, and referrals to psychiatrists, psychotherapists, psychologists, or self-help groups are probably better courses of action than the prescription of a tranquilizer. Furthermore, anxiety and depression are often effective warning signals that indicate the patient needs to work on his attitudes or rearrange his environment. Obtunding such affective messages with drugs, particularly if the patient is likely to remain in the situation and therefore continue to require the medicine, does not have the kind of rationale that belongs with good medical practice.

There is, on the other hand, a spectrum of circumstances in which the use of psychotropic drugs *is* indicated. A number of sound, relatively conventional indications exist for the use of certain psychotropic agents, and, in the following, I will add to those a compendium of unconventional pharmacotherapeutic maneuvers that I and some others are finding useful in treating certain patients.

CONTROL OF ABERRANT BEHAVIOR

The clinical situations where a practitioner might be confronted with a patient whose behavior is extremely erratic are potentially legion; a patient might become paranoid as a result of ingesting amphetamine indiscriminately, an alcoholic might go into delirium tremens, an elderly man who has become disoriented after eye surgery might jump out of his bed late at night, and so on. When the requirement for the patient-drug interaction is the immediate control of severely disordered behavior, the drug of choice is one of the phenothiazines—chlorpromazine, promazine, thioridazine, or chlorprothixene—which is usually given in high doses. These so-called high-dose phenothiazine derivatives bring erratic behavior under control by reducing the patient's initiative and motor activity, regardless of the cause of the disorder. In urgent situations, their "disadvantages"—*e.g.,* motor inhibition, depression, some impairment of intellectual function, and, occasionally, reduction of motivation—are almost irrelevant.

There is no standard dose of the phenothiazines. Sensitivity varies markedly from person to person with regard to the reduction of psychotic symptoms and the development of extrapyramidal and cardiovascular side effects; moreover, the sensitivity is independent of the clinical state of the patient. It is best to titrate the dose to control the patient's aberrant mentation or behavior without unduly impairing his motor function. Psychiatrists do not agree whether the phenothiazines should be continued after the remission of an acute episode or discontinued upon remission and reinstituted upon relapse. The socioeconomic situation of the patient and the likelihood of his returning for help, should he need it, would determine the choice of long-term treatment in some cases.

PREVENTION OF PSYCHOTIC EPISODES

General practitioners are frequently the only doctors to see patients whose personalities are reasonably well compensated most of the time, but who have what we might call "borderline" or incipient psychotic tendencies. Often, it becomes the general physician's responsibility to be aware when an individual's thoughts, feelings, or behavior become peculiar and indicate a need for intervention. For example, a patient who reports that the pain radiates from in front of him to behind him through his knee, or that his glasses need to be changed because of the bizarre colors and distorted shapes he's seeing, may be prevented from further decompensation, and even show marked improvement, if the practitioner recognizes these signs of incipient psychosis and starts drug treatment.

Doctors in every medical specialty can usually come to recognize characteristic sets of such somatized mental symptoms. The drugs of choice in such cases are those phenothiazines that impair motility the least, *i.e.,* the fluorinated and piperazine derivatives, as well as the thioxanthenes and butyrophenones. Patients can sometimes be brought back from the brink of psychosis with brief supportive psychotherapy and low doses of these agents. These often are people who usually avoid contact with psychiatrists or other mental-health specialists precisely because they are worried that their fear that they are insane will be confirmed; frequently, their general physician is their only source of help.

There are other patients who chronically lack affect, spark, or ambition. In their inertia, they may be experiencing psychotic mentation without emotional upset. Such people can benefit from higher doses of the same phenothiazine derivatives that have been mentioned as indicated for incipient psychosis. Because these drugs tend to promote motility rather than retard it, their effects may be more consistent with a program of active rehabilitation. Studies during the past few years have demonstrated that in terms of modifying psychotic symptoms, little difference is found among the antipsychotic drugs if the doses are equalized for their differential potency. Because of their different effects on such parameters of adaptive function as motility, mood, or intellectual function, however, it may be appropriate to choose a particular subgroup of phenothiazine derivatives for a specific clinical situation. The long-term use of the low-dosage, high-potency phenothiazines or phenothiazine-type drugs for the chronically inert psychotic may be one such example.

DEPRESSIVE PATIENTS

Amphetamines or other stimulants are frequently prescribed for lethargic depression, but one's tolerance to them develops rapidly, and their withdrawal can precipitate depression; the rationale for their use in such cases is as tenuous as that for using minor tranquilizers to treat neurosis. People who use amphetamines ostensibly to lose weight but who are in fact addicted to the drug number in the millions. Although in ordinary doses amphetamines probably do not have significant physiological side effects, their use in a psychotherapeutic treatment strategy is irrational. The clinical experience of many doctors is that intolerable circumstances in a patient's marriage, business, or social roles may be made tolerable by the patient's regular ingestion of amphetamines, but again, one can argue that their use, in addition to creating permanent drug habits, takes away the motivation for the patient to change his situation or himself. Interpersonal intervention might be more constructive; this may take the form of brief supportive psychotherapy by the doctor, family consultation by the general physician, or referral to a psychiatrist, a psychologist, or any of several kinds of self-help groups.

LITHIUM THERAPY IN AFFECTIVE DISORDERS

Although lithium carbonate has been used in the treatment of extreme mood disorders in Europe, particularly in Scandinavia, for nearly twenty years, it has been used generally in the United States for less than a decade. Early clinical reports indicated that it specifically eliminates mania and prevents its recurrence; later reports indicated that cyclic psychotic disorders characterized by intermittent depression and mania can be prevented by instituting lithium carbonate treatment during the periods of remission or mania. Now it appears that almost all recurrent mood disorders as well as some recurrent episodes of acute schizophrenia are preventable with this agent if appropriate lithium levels are maintained in the blood for a sufficiently long time. Adequate prophylaxis requires levels in the range of 0.6 to 0.8 mEq per liter, and the levels must be monitored periodically. Ongoing management in some cases may become the responsibility of the patient's personal physician. Because of the length of treatment that is necessary before lithium's prophylactic effect becomes maximal, patient compliance with the regimen is sometimes difficult to maintain; the drug temporarily takes away one's "spark."

Another area in which lithium treatment may be applicable is in controlling episodes of sporadic violence. If temporal-lobe epileptic foci, which lithium would make worse, can be ruled out, then the administration of lithium might be helpful in preventing such episodes. Researchers have used lithium to treat prisoners who had been locked in individual maximum security cells; within a couple of months, these men, who had had to exercise in solitary because otherwise fights would break out, had a basketball league functioning.

Our experience in treating binge drinkers with lithium suggests that this drug reduces the frequency of episodes of compulsive drinking. We almost routinely use disulfiram, tricyclic antidepressants, and lithium along with group therapy and Alcoholics Anonymous for all our alcoholic patients. The early statistical results are promising.

PSYCHOPHARMACOLOGY AND TARGET SYMPTOMS ALTERATIONS

A common type of depressive patient tends to be overweight, undermotivated, full of inertia, and covertly angry. Such a person is probably in a difficult intrapsychic or environmental situation. Thus, when considering drug treatment, the doctor is again faced with the possibility of creating a chronic drug pattern and failing to help the patient change himself or his life. The physician in this case should realize that rearrangements in one's psychosocial environment are often motivated by feelings of dissatisfaction. Monoamine-oxidase inhibitors have been tried in the treatment of such patients. Those of the hydrazine family yielded poorer results in populations of depressed patients than the tricyclic agents did; several studies have shown them to be no better than a placebo. Moreover, subacute yellow atrophy of the liver can occur, even though rarely, with the use of the hydrazine-type monoamine-oxidase inhibitors, and some clinical psychopharmacologists avoid their use for that reason. Monoamine-oxidase inhibitors other than hydrazine derivatives—e.g., (tranylcypromine or pargyline)—do not produce liver disease, but moderate to high doses of these agents can cause marked episodic hypertension and cardiovascular potentiation if the patient ingests medicine or foods (such as cheese or wine) that are high in tyramine.

Certain interesting observations began to come to light when it was noticed that the treatment of a major psychiatric disorder with a drug might subtly alter facets of a patient's behavior. In other words, not only were there changes in the target symptoms (e.g., in the major psychopathology, the sleep disorders, the suicidal depression, and so forth); other factors were changed as well. Such observations have led to a number of unconventional uses of psychopharmacological agents in patient management. Although little has been written on this topic, I suspect that many practitioners may have discovered such subtle pharmacological stratagems on their own. Most are probably embarrassed about sharing them for fear that someone else could not duplicate the results. I would like to introduce some of these esoteric pharmacotherapeutic techniques here.

a) Overweight, lethargic, passive-aggressive people are difficult to motivate. Klein (5) has found that tiny amounts of monoamine-oxidase inhibitors, e.g., 10 mg a day, are useful in helping overweight, underachieving teenage girls. I use pargyline, a nonhydrazine compound that is listed in the *Physicians' Desk Reference* as an antihypertensive agent, not as a psychiatric drug. It is the most potent monoamine-oxidase inhibitor on the market, and it has the least side effects. People with high blood pressure may take as much as 60–80 mg pargyline per day; in the 10-mg range, there is no danger of a patient's getting too much tyramine in his blood as a result of eating cheese or drinking wine. Gradually, a more energetic, assertive, aggressive personality will emerge in the therapeutic relationship; arguments, for example, may occur. Parents will complain that their child is being too assertive or too active. In long-term work with people who have certain kinds of personality deficits, it is good to let them experience a new way of life, rather than allowing them to continue experiencing themselves as they have been—failing and unable to change. Such patients can begin to restructure their psychosocial environment, since they are now perceived differently by those around them. Within a year or two, their body images can also change dramatically.

A regimen of small doses of a monoamine-oxidase inhibitor will also provide startling remission in a large percentage of cases of what we call *hallucinogen burn-out syndrome*. This is exemplified by the chronic LSD freak whose affect is flat and whose thoughts are disorganized; he wants to go back to school, for instance, but he is having trouble "getting it together." As a result of his treatment, however, his parents may start complaining that they want their old freak back: his new self is argumentative, and he always wants the car.

A third unusual use of the monoamine-oxidase inhibitors is for the "borderline" patient, the one who suffers from pseudoneurotic schizophrenia, which is characterized by pananxiety and panneurosis. With the administration of a monoamine-oxidase inhibitor, a tightening of secondary-process thinking occurs in some of these people, particularly when the inhibitor is given in conjunction with low doses of a phenothiazine like trifluoperazine or haloperidol. It might seem that such patients would benefit from phenothiazine therapy alone, but they sometimes have difficulty accepting the subjective effects of the ataractics. In our clinic at The University of California, San Diego, we often initiate treatment by using a monoamine-oxidase inhibitor to promote this tightening of secondary-process thinking before we add a low dose of phenothiazine to the regimen.

Please realize that I am trying to jostle your preconceptions. The changes in personality that I am describing take a month or longer to appear. They do not occur in every case. Each time we give a drug to an individual, we are experimenting, and, as clinicians, we have to pay close attention to what happens. As we become more familiar and more comfortable with the use of psychotropic drugs, we learn to operate with much more subtle nuances of human behavior.

b) Many a general practitioner would find familiar the woman who is fastidious to the point of fussiness, hard working, and conscientious; during late middle age, she begins to develop insomnia and lose weight; she engages in almost constant intrapunitive ruminations. She could stay that way the rest of her life, or she may progress into a syndrome of psychotic depression. She and others like her benefit markedly from the administration of tricyclic antidepressants—imipramine, desmethylimipramine, amitriptyline, or nortriptyline. Such a patient usually experiences a somatic focus of discomfort, and the sensitive general physician is presented with an opportunity that no psychiatrist would have until much later in the course of her disease. The agitated depressive patient often resists psychotherapy, and the general practitioner or nonpsychiatric specialist might be able to exploit the medical context in which she consults him to initiate the use of a tricyclic antidepressant drug in conjunction with brief but regular counseling.

Klein (5) has distinguished patients with phobias that respond to monoamine-oxidase inhibition from those with phobias that respond to tricyclic antidepressants. Someone whose phobia does not impair his autonomy—who is not clinging to a doctor, a wife, or a mother for secondary gain—is more likely to benefit from treatment with the monoamine-oxidase inhibitors. On the other hand, someone who is too afraid to let go of his doctor's hand is more likely to benefit from the administration of a tricyclic. The issues of attachment and separation may or may not be dynamic determinants in anxiety and depression, but the use of tricyclics clearly reduces the fear of separation. Children who are phobic about going to school suffer acutely from separation anxiety and they can be helped significantly with imipramine in doses of 50 mg per day or less.

Some psychiatrists are now using tricyclic antidepressants for patients undergoing the emotional trauma of divorce and find that it facilitates a reduction in psychosomatic symptoms, depression, sleep loss, and the pain of the detachment. Certain patients regress in intensive psychotherapy, not into depression, but into an exaggerated dependence on the therapist or on the physician who is treating their chronic complaints, and this can be thinned out with the use of tricyclics. Some people get into trouble constantly by forming overly dependent, clinging, sadomasochistic relationships, but their life-styles can be altered by therapy utilizing the tricyclics. Again, these changes happen with relatively small doses of the drugs, and they happen gradually.

Tricyclic antidepressants may be the best drugs we have for the treatment of enuresis. They have proved to be more effective than atropine in such cases. They reduce stage IV sleep, or deep sleep, when all the so-called pathologies of sleep occur, such as teeth-grinding, head-banging, sleepwalking, and bed-wetting. By reducing stage IV sleep, the tricyclics eliminate the enuresis. I do not recommend giving more than 25 to 50 mg per day to a child. This treatment fits our preferred dynamic strategy of letting the patient experience a new way of being; we can say to the child, "You're not doing that any more. See, you don't have to do it." When his self-concept is improved and he has a record of success, the drug treatment can be stopped.

The Minnesota Multiphasic Personality Inventory (MMPI) results with antisocial young people, or adolescents who are acting out, show a relatively high incidence of occult depression. Some theorists have said that such acting out might represent a desperate effort on the patients' part to treat their depressions with the thrill of chaos or the externalization of anger. It might thus seem bizarre to treat someone with antidepressant medication whose behavior is already agitated, but we found the use of tricyclics to be remarkably helpful for some refractory patients in this group.

Another type of patient for whom the tricyclics might be helpful includes those who have severe dermatological conditions. A child with a skin disease is itchy and uncomfortable; his mother is supposed to help, but she is not able to do anything to relieve him. He thus feels helpless and is mad at her. The physician may also find himself in the same situation with regard to a patient who has a permanent disfigurement.

To achieve a gradual, subtle increase in autonomy for a patient, it is important to remember that one is not dealing with a full-blown endogenous depression. The dosage may start with 25, 50, or 75 mg of the antidepressant per day; it does not take very much. This subtle, pervasive effect has incredible ramifications; to appreciate this, one need only reflect on the control that his own attachment needs and separation anxieties exert over his judgment and mobility.

The physician may have to deal with side effects, in treating patients with these antidepressants, but he should consider the case carefully before letting concerns about the effects on the autonomic nervous system deter him from using tricyclics.

ROLE OF LABORATORY RESEARCH IN PSYCHOPHARMACOLOGY

The fact that these now somewhat esoteric applications of psychotropic drugs were born of empirical clinical observations must not detract from the importance of the laboratory research that may be developing the base to elevate such exquisite manipulations from the esoteric to the scientific, a base provided by a better knowledge and understanding of the functions of the important neurotransmitters in the brain. In the laboratory, we have been continuously learning more about the effects of therapeutic psychotropic agents on the synthesis, binding, release, and degradation of these transmitters and about the relationships of these drugs to specific neurophysiological systems. In the near future, we can hope that both sources of knowledge will nourish the emergence of comprehensive rationales for psychotropic drug treatment.

The following example may serve to illustrate this interaction between research and clinical application: Not long ago, I was called to see a patient suffering from hyperexcitement, hallucinations, hyperactivity, and peculiar twitching motor movements caused by an overdose of a monoamine-oxidase inhibitor. A similar case had been treated with barbiturates, and that patient died. On the basis of laboratory research, we knew what the probable state and actions of the neurotransmitter amines in the brain would be under those circumstances, and that the phenothiazines would block their access to and passage through the neural membranes. The second patient was treated with phenothiazines and lived.

The general or nonpsychiatric physician will have to forsake overly optimistic or vague detail men and advertisements as sources of information about psychotropic agents. The effects of these agents are diverse among people and pervasive in individuals; their intelligent use requires perceiving and experiencing each patient under care. In its logic and comprehensibility, the basic science of the actions of these drugs is approaching our scientific knowledge of the kidneys or the glands. To remain current with these developments, the practitioner, whatever his specialty, should read reviews of psychopharmacology in dependable journals and take workshops when they are available.

REFERENCES

1. Cooper JR, Bloom FE, Roth RH: The Biochemical Basis of Neuropharmacology, 2nd ed. New York, Oxford University Press, 1974

2. Freedman AM, Kaplan HI, Sadock BJ (eds): The Comprehensive Textbook of Psychiatry. II. Baltimore, Williams & Wilkins, 1975

3. Grenell RG, Gabay S (eds.): Biological Foundations of Psychiatry. New York, Raven Press, 1976

4. Klein DF (with Howard A): Psychiatric Case Studies: Treatment, Drugs, and Outcome. Baltimore, Williams & Wilkins, 1972

5. Klein DF, Davis JM: Diagnosis and Drug Treatment of Psychiatric Disorders. Baltimore, Williams & Wilkins, 1969

6. Kline NS (ed): Factors in Depression. New York, Raven Press, 1974

7. Mandell AJ: Psychoanalysis and psychopharmacology. In Marmor J (ed): Modern Psychoanalysis. New York, Basic Books, 1968

18 Morita Therapy

TOMONORI SUZUKI, RYU SUZUKI

Morita therapy is a method for treating neurosis that has been practiced in Japan for over fifty years. It was developed by Professor Shōma Morita (1874–1938). This chapter provides a general description of this form of psychotherapy.

MORITA'S THEORY OF *SHINKEISHITSU*

Morita held that most cases of neurasthenia develop from a character disposition which he called *shinkeishitsu*. He excluded from this concept those patients with a neurasthenic state secondary to physical fatigue, those with immature and hysterical character traits, and those with extreme compulsive behavior. According to his definition, *shinkeishitsu* is characterized by introversion, extreme self-consciousness, perfectionism, and the excessive desire to live fully. Those with this character disposition tend to have feelings of anxiety about themselves when their living environment is changed and when they undergo even minor psychic traumas.

Morita called these feelings of anxiety "hypochondriacal dispositions," and he thought they were related to the genesis of neurosis in two ways: 1) he assumed that feelings of anxiety were a preexisting condition for the development of neurosis and 2) when precipitating events occur, the person with *shinkeishitsu* characteristics pays attention to his anxiety and endeavors to escape from it. The more attention such a person pays to his anxiety, the more sensitive and anxious he becomes, thus creating a vicious cycle. Morita called this dynamic process "psychic interaction." During the course of this obsession with his psychic conflict *(toraware),* the patient expresses his anxiety in terms of psychic or somatic symptoms.

It should be noted, however, that this psychic conflict is not an unconscious psychological process, such as those revealed in psychoanalysis, but rather it is conscious. As a rule, in Morita theory, neither unconscious mechanisms nor the history of the patient is considered. In recent years, however, Doi has done work from a psychodynamic point of view and has pointed out the importance of *amae,* that is, the need to depend on and to presume upon another's love, both in mother-child relationships and in subsequent interpersonal relationships. He explains the preconditional anxiety on which *toraware* (obsession) develops as that induced by a crisis involving *amae* (dependency). Although such psychic immaturity related to the patient's life history may be found in Japanese *shinkeishitsu* patients, we should not ignore the possibility of hereditary influences on the character disposition from which the neurosis develops.

INPATIENT MORITA THERAPY

CONTRACT ON ADMISSION

The majority of patients who come to our Morita therapy clinic have tried various kinds of therapies, but in vain. Usually they have read about Morita therapy and therefore have some general idea of the Moritist approach on their first visit. It may be said, then, that the therapy has already begun before a patient comes to the clinic. If he has not yet read any book on Morita therapy, the therapist recommends that he do so.

We always try to make a *verbal contract* with the patient who wishes to be admitted. We tell him that it is acceptable for him to have doubts about Morita therapy or to be reluctant to undertake it. We point out that since he has already tried to resolve his anxiety or his neurotic symptoms by himself and has not succeeded, why not try Morita therapy? He is instructed to follow our therapeutic rules even though he has doubts about the result. If the patient agrees to these requests, then the basis of the therapeutic relationship has been established. Morita therapy is made possible not by coercion, but by agreement. Morita himself did not make a clear verbal contract with his patient, but we find that in modern Japan, a patient participates in the treatment more actively with an agreement than he does without it.

The therapist advises the patient to clear up all outstanding social or personal obligations prior to his admission to the hospital. It goes without saying that a complete physical examination is made, particularly in cases of hypochondriasis or anxiety neurosis.

THE MILIEU OF MORITA THERAPY

Morita recognized that a patient could not freely change his awareness of anxiety by will power or by focusing on what ought to be; however, by involving the patient in a therapeutic milieu, the vicious cycle of psychic interaction could be broken.

The therapeutic milieu of the Morita hospital is quite different from that of an ordinary mental hospital. It is a place where the one-to-one relationship between the therapist and patient is dominant. Some have suggested that in Morita therapy, the therapist plays the role of an authoritative father to the patient, but we think that the therapist-patient relationship more clearly resembles that of teacher and student. This relationship is complemented by other relationships, such as those with part-time therapists, nurses, and other inpatients. Generally, the hospital has the atmosphere of a school for therapeutic training. It also has something of a homelike quality. It is important that *shinkeishitsu* neurosis be considered not as morbid, but as an acceptable character disposition. The patient will discover this for himself as he progresses.

In addition, a patient finds himself in the midst of many other patients who suffer from the same or similar symptoms. He discovers that he is not the only person suffering from these problems. The nonverbal atmosphere of the hospital seems to influence the patient as powerfully as verbal persuasion does. The ideal number of inpatients seems to be from 15 to 20. If the therapist is engaged full-time in the hospital life, more patients—up to about 30—may participate.

ISOLATED BED REST

The first phase of inpatient Morita therapy is isolated bed rest. The patient is required to lie quietly in bed for a week. He is not allowed to engage in any activities, such as reading, smoking, talking, or getting up except when he eats or goes to the bathroom. He may think about anything, feel anything, or fall asleep. The therapist meets him briefly once a day to check on his condition. In this situation, deprived of all means of diversion and distraction, the patient is forced to confront his anxiety directly. All his psychic energy is concentrated on his preoccupations and obsessions. Usually he tries to avoid or to escape his anxiety as he has done previously, but without success. He is forced to immerse himself in the vicious cycle of attention and sensitivity until the anxiety reaches its peak. Eventually, after a sustained period, he comes to accept his anxiety as it is and to identify himself with his anxiety. This experience of "being totally in the now," or of accepting what he is, is the crucial point in Morita therapy. The patient can then recognize that he does not need to fight his anxiety or to regard it as something morbid. It is to be stressed that the emergence of this attitude of nonopposition is brought about not by the patient's willing it, but because of some natural, autonomous attitude of acceptance innate to the human psyche.

There are some patients whose vicious cycle is dramatically broken and whose anxiety symptoms are resolved during this isolated bed-rest phase, but for the majority of patients, the change is less complete and the bed-rest phase serves to lay the foundation for the attitude of acceptance. This phase of therapy also serves as a period in which the *shinkeishitsu* type of neurosis is differentiated from other types of neurosis and from psychiatric disorders such as borderline psychosis, schizophrenia, and so on.

THE WORK THERAPY PHASE

The work therapy phase begins as soon as the patient has completed the bed-rest phase. Light work activities—such as raking leaves, making envelopes, and house cleaning—are assigned for several days. During this transitional period of light work, the patient remains in the hospital milieu with little concrete direction from the therapist. Although initially he may wonder what to do, he gradually begins to participate in the therapeutic milieu and to be spontaneously involved in his current activity. From the fifth or sixth day after completing bed rest, the patient is assigned more and more strenuous activities, *e.g.*, cutting wood, planting grass and flowers, cooking, and looking after pets. The tasks are individualized by the therapist, who knows the patient's physical and mental condition.

The patient is advised not to talk about his symptoms to the other patients. He is instructed to immerse himself in his present work. Distractions interrupt his spontaneity and hinder his work activities. His work activities may appear trivial and worthless to the patient, especially if he evaluates them intellectually. Nevertheless, the patient is advised to involve himself in these activities while suspending his evaluation of them. Work activities are not prescribed for the purpose of distraction from anxiety symptoms. When the patient is totally involved in his present work, he assumes the orientation of being in the "here and now." Through this experience, his attitude changes gradually and naturally to one in which he no longer struggles obsessively against his anxiety symptoms.

After the twentieth or thirtieth day of the work phase, when he is truly involved in his work activities, he is allowed to go shopping, to read, and to do other work activities.

Until about the fortieth day, the patient is advised to refrain from seeing his family or friends and from talking with them by telephone. This helps his change of perspective occur more rapidly, which it will do in an isolated situation away from his usual personal relationships.

The minimum criterion of discharge is that the patient has reached the point where he is able to engage in his necessary daily activities despite anxiety symptoms. About 83% of the patients are discharged when they arrive at this level. The remaining 17% have progressed to a state in which they take no notice of their anxiety symptoms and have developed a positive orientation toward living life fully.

The inpatient period usually ranges from 60 to 120 days.

THE DIARY

In Morita therapy, the patient's diary is a very important means of communication between the patient and the therapist. After the bed-rest phase, the therapist advises the patient to write in a diary every evening. The therapist reads the diary notes, makes written comments, and returns the diary to the patient the next day. Initially, the patient tends to write about his symptoms or his thoughts concerning the therapy, but, as he enters into the milieu and as his fixed, obsessive, and stagnated awareness begins to flow normally, he comes to write about how and what he discovered and achieved during his work activities. At the same time, emphasis on his complaints and symptoms decreases. The patient who continues to complain about his symptoms is advised to stop complaining and to write about his activities.

In addition, nearly every day a group session is held during which the therapist comments on various diaries and answers questions that are meaningful to the patients. Communication between the therapist and patient is usually not a general discussion, but rather it consists of direction or guidance about how the patient is expected to behave himself in the therapeutic milieu.

"NO RESPONSE" THERAPY (*FUMONRYOHO*)

The neurotic patient invariably complains of his symptoms and asks the therapist how to cure his neurosis. At first, the Morita therapist answers his questions with the advice to live in the present. If the patient asks repeatedly, the therapist does not reply any further. He ignores such questions and continues to instruct the patient to apply himself to the tasks awaiting him. When the patient is left to work in the therapeutic milieu without getting attention for his complaints, his interest turns toward his tasks. The technique is called *fumonryoho*, that is, "no response" therapy. It cannot be employed in the outpatient clinic, where verbal communication is dominant, nor can it be applied to a patient who does not trust his therapist. In addition, the therapist himself may find it difficult to practice this technique at first, but he gradually develops this ability with experience. The application of this "no response" technique may be misunderstood by the patient as being unkind, but it is purposefully carried out for the patient's own benefit.

GUIDANCE AFTER DISCHARGE

As stated above, the inpatient period of Morita therapy is relatively short. When discharged, the majority of the patients have not yet been completely cured of their neurosis, but they have only arrived at the level of being able to engage themselves in their necessary daily activities despite their anxiety symptoms. Psychotherapeutic guidance is offered, therefore, to ex-patients to help them progress further.

In our clinic, some ex-patients are readmitted for one weekend a month, during which they live the same hospital life as before. Some have done this as many as ten times. During this post-discharge period, many patients lose their symptoms completely. In addition, bimonthly psychotherapeutic meetings for guidance are held with a variety of people in attendance. There are ex-patients representing various stages of treatment, and outpatients are present as well, including some who were treated by Morita himself 40 or 50 years ago. Further, a quarterly bulletin is issued for the purpose of publishing the therapists' comments and advice to ex-patients as well as to nonneurotic readers living all over Japan.

By these various methods, we reinforce and develop the patients' basic orientation that was acquired during the inpatient period.

OUTPATIENT MORITA THERAPY

Whereas inpatient Morita therapy can produce inner changes that are reflected in the patient's behavior in a relatively short period, the outpatient approach takes a much longer time to bring about positive changes. This is because it is carried out only through verbal communication. In the outpatient clinic, after taking the patient's history and listening to his problem or symptoms, the therapist explains the Moritist view regarding the mechanism of neurotic development, and he advises the patient to take an alternative attitude that will disrupt the vicious cycle caused by his anxiety.

The main points of outpatient psychotherapy are as follows:

1. A patient who complains of somatic symptoms is given a careful physical examination.
2. The patient is instructed to accept his anxiety rather than attempt to ignore it.
3. The patient is directed not to complain of his neurotic symptoms to his family or friends. It is better if they do not listen or reply to his complaints.
4. A person who is suffering from social phobias (*e.g.,* anthropophobia) should not engage himself in mental rehearsals of threatening situations. This is because the rehearsal process creates anticipatory anxiety. Rather, in the Moritist approach, a patient is directed to accept his tension and dare to engage himself in activity. This is necessary, even though he may feel uncomfortable and anxious.
5. When the patient forces himself to carry out his necessary daily activities, he gradually becomes involved in his present tasks. His character is strengthened. Rather than trying to fight his anxiety as something abnormal, he comes to affirm and accept this part of himself.
6. Those suffering from strong secondary depressive states need supplementary pharmacotherapy.

Mildly neurotic patients can be successfully treated with Morita therapy on an outpatient basis. Patients who have been unsuccessfully treated with other kinds of therapy often achieve a satisfactory inner change. It usually takes many outpatient sessions for them to do so, however.

INDICATIONS FOR MORITA THERAPY

Morita therapy is a treatment mode that is suitable for *shinkeishitsu* type neurotics, including those who suffer from obsessive neurosis, hypochondriasis, or anxiety neurosis. Morita therapy is inappropriate for patients with hysterical character traits and for those who are poorly motivated. Other types of neuroses similar to *shinkeishitsu, e.g.,* depressive neurosis, may be treated effectively by a combination of Morita therapy and pharmacotherapy. Patients with marked compulsive behavior may be treated successfully if Morita therapy is applied less intensively and if the patient is led into the therapeutic milieu more gradually. The Morita approach is useful in treating those who suffer from somatic symptoms as well as those who manifest psychological symptoms. The somatic symptoms from which *shinkeishitsu* type neurotics often suffer include headaches, dizziness, malaise, insomnia, tinnitus, epigastric discomfort, indigestion, constipation, diarrhea, urinary frequency, palpitations, choking feelings, and so on. Patients whose main complaints were about such somatic symptoms constituted approximately 41% of those who were admitted to our hospital.

As a rule, Morita therapy is applied to people aged 15 to 40. The younger the patient is, the better the outcome is likely to be. Occasionally, patients over 50 years old are treated with relative success.

CASE HISTORIES OF PATIENTS TREATED BY MORITA THERAPY

Case 1. This patient was male, unmarried, and 22 years old at admission. At age 16, he began suffering from headaches. He withdrew from school for one year. During the next three years, he was thoroughly examined, with negative findings, and he was treated with drugs, psychotherapy, and electroshock, but without success. After barely graduating from high school, he was engaged for three years in a dangerous job at a huge dam construction. Here, he attempted to gain self-assurance and to stop worrying about his headaches. When he was 22 years old, he was hospitalized for two months. On the fifth day after the period of bed rest he wrote, "I am confused because I doubt whether Morita therapy is effective for me. I suffer from severe headaches, but I was given a comment in my diary that I should not complain of them and should engage in the present activities no matter how I might feel."

On the 33rd day, the patient wrote, "I work at tasks, one after the other, though I still have headaches as before. I don't know why, but I am cheerful and pleasant."

On the 56th day, he wrote, "If I pay attention to myself, I become aware of the headaches. To my surprise, I tend to forget the headaches and I am capable of fully engaging in my activities." Thus, the change in his perspective occurred rather gradually during the hospitalization period. After discharge, he entered a university, and he is now working as a leading member of a camera company. In 1974, 18 years after discharge, he stated during one of our group sessions, "When I worked on the site of the dam construction, I was always thinking about my headaches and whether they were more or less severe. While I was in the hospital, this obsession with my symptom disappeared rapidly."

Case 2. Another male patient was married and 29 years old at the time of his admission. His first attack of palpitations and sensations of suffocation occurred at age 27, at a time when he was exhausted. After having frequent attacks of palpitations, he was examined thoroughly and was diagnosed as suffering from a "cardiac neurosis." He underwent autogenic training for eight months, but without success. He was shocked profoundly by the successive deaths of his two superiors from cardiac diseases, and he was completely disabled for a year. He had feelings of being choked, even when he was in the bathroom. When he was referred to us, he was so anxious that he needed assistance from his doctor to undertake even a 40-minutes drive for a visit.

He endured the isolated bed rest with difficulty and tended to complain of his symptoms quite frequently. During the work phase, he became better, and he went to work in a rose garden, one kilometer away from the hospital. On the 60th hospital day, his mother died. The therapist persuaded him that he should attend her funeral by himself, though he hesitated to do so. At Tokyo Station, which he reached with much difficulty, he had an attack of palpitation which made him feel unable to go further. He wrote in his diary, "I felt that I would be laughed at by other people if I returned from there to the hospital. Therefore, though I was suffering from palpitation, I desperately got on the train. After that, I was forced to endure the pains for the two hours and thirty minutes' trip to my home town." His attitude toward his symptoms changed rapidly after he passed through this experience.

The patient was discharged on the 90th day. The next day after discharge, he began work at his company. He said at a group session one year later, "Even now, whenever I suffer from palpitation, I feel my pulse as I used to, but I continue to do things, which needed to be done, and treat the palpitation as acceptable." Four years after the discharge, he said, "I live my life fully. Even when I have palpitation, I don't feel anxious because of it."

THE MEANING OF "CURE" FOR SHINKEISHITSU NEUROSIS

Morita therapy aims not merely at symptom removal, but rather at a basic change of attitude that transcends anxiety symptoms.

The first step involves changing the patient's inner conflict through the experience of being in the "here and now." By accepting his anxiety, the patient develops a positive perspective toward his present life. The psychic energy that has been misdirected toward his inner conflict is redirected toward realizing a fruitful life, and the patient gains experiential insight into his psychic conflicts. The Morita therapist helps the patient to take this first step. Thereafter, inner changes promote the spontaneous development of the patient's ability to understand his character traits as being acceptable. Because he is able to live life more fully, he develops a stable, positive self-concept.

Morita himself made no attempt to bring about an alteration of the basic *shinkeishitsu* character. It is believed, however, that a basic change in personality structure can be accomplished, beginning with a radical impatient experience, although practice indicates that such a change in personality structure is impossible during a relatively short hospitalization period. If one were to observe patients over a longer period of time than Morita himself could do, such basic changes would be observed.

INVESTIGATION OF THE EFFECTIVENESS OF MORITA THERAPY

Several Morita therapists have studied the effectiveness of this therapy. These therapists clinically evaluated treatment success or failure at the time of discharge. Since this method did not deal with the problem of recurrence, we carried out a follow-up investigation, starting in May 1966, of patients who had been discharged for at least six months.

A questionnaire was sent to 888 ex-patients who had been treated at the Suzuki clinic. These patients had been hospitalized, diagnosed as neurotics of the *shinkeishitsu* type (or related to the *shinkeishitsu* type), and treated for one to six months during the period of June 1952 to December 1965. We questioned them about their current adjustment, and we were able to differentiate four levels of adjustment:

1. The ex-patient who is generally unaware of any anxiety symptoms and lives an active daily life.
2. The ex-patient who, though aware of some symptoms, is not unduly concerned about them. (In the case of anxiety neurosis, for example, he is aware of palpitation, but he is not greatly worried about it and lives an active daily life.)
3. The ex-patient who feels anxious about his symptoms but still finds he is able to live a normal life.
4. The ex-patient who, because he feels anxious about his symptoms, cannot live a normal life.

Of the 888 questionnaires sent, 601 questionnaires were answered and returned by the ex-patient himself, 9 were answered and returned by the ex-patient's family, 214 were not returned, and in 64 cases, the mail could not be delivered because of a change of address.

Among the 815 delivered questionnaires, 181 cases (22.0%) belonged to category 1, 218 cases (27%) to category 2, 179 cases (22%) to category 3, and 237 cases (29.0%) to category 4. We made the severe assumption that the unanswered cases were category 4, *i.e.*, not cured of their neurosis. The clear *shinkei-shitsu*-type neurotic constituted 78.8% of the returned sample, and the rest were neurotics with depressive or, to use Kretschmer's term, "sensitive," tendencies. If we consider the cases belonging to categories 1 and 2 as cured of neurosis, they account for 48.5% of all the delivered questionnaires. If the cases belonging to categories 1, 2, and 3 are considered as improved, they account for 70.1%.

It should be mentioned that most of the patients who visit our clinic come when they find it difficult to live a normal life because of their inner conflicts.

We further asked patients evaluated as cured (*i.e.*, in categories 1 and 2) at what time they stopped noticing their anxiety symptoms and began to act constructively and productively. There were 340 responses, which showed a mean period of 27.5 months from the date of admission.

MODIFICATIONS OF MORITA THERAPY

Thus far we have discussed orthodox, inpatient Morita therapy as well as its outpatient approach. The issue of modifications of this form of therapy will be discussed briefly. Some authors have cast doubts on the effectiveness of inpatient Morita therapy for the modern Japanese. Kelman (3) expressed doubts about the future of Morita therapy, because he considered the hierarchical authoritarian system of Japan, which is currently changing, to be an essential underlying feature. Reynolds (6) pointed out some "new trends in Morita psychotherapy" and wrote that these changes in technique paralleled changes in the Japanese sociocultural context.

Inpatient Morita therapy, however, definitely still works in present Japan. If the therapy is begun with a clear verbal contract, we have found that it works well for voluntary patients. It does seem to us that present patients have a little more difficulty entering into therapy than those of 20 years ago did. We have examined the reasons that patients have given for discontinuing Morita therapy. In our hospital, about 7% to 8% of the inpatients broke off therapy during the period from 4 to 15 days after admission. Four-fifths of them stated that they terminated because of strong doubts that they would be cured by this therapy or because they thought that they could adhere to the same therapeutic principles in their homes as in the hospital. The rest broke off therapy because they could not bear the "pain" and difficulty involved in the treatment.

We believe that patients suffering from severe neurosis can be successfully treated in a relatively short time only by means of inpatient Morita therapy. Moritist principles are being applied in modified forms outside the hospital to treat those with mildly neurotic tendencies. An example of this newer approach is found in the *Seikatsu-no-hakken-kai* (literally: "Group for the Discovery of Life"). Group discussions are held once a month by this organization, and quarterly workshops have been opened for Moritist work activities and group meetings. Monthly bulletins are issued to educate the group members.

Certain transcultural issues have been brought up involving Morita therapy. It has often been said that Western people are primarily rationalistic and that they tend to struggle against nature. In contrast, the Oriental point of view has been described as naturalistic and passive with regard to nature. It has been suggested by some that the Moritist approach is applicable only to Oriental people. It is clear, however, that during the last 40 or 50 years, Japanese people have been strongly influenced by Western rationalism. Moreover, it might well be said that obsession and psychic conflict of the *shinkeishitsu* type occurs when a person takes a rationalistic and idealistic attitude toward his feelings of anxiety. We believe, therefore, that the same kind of problem exists both in modern Japan and in Western countries. If this is indeed the case, the principles of Morita therapy ought to be effective in the treatment of Western neurotic patients, too.

We would like to stress two points that have been overlooked in discussions that have questioned the usefulness of Morita therapy outside Japan. First, it is necessary that the patients have sufficient knowledge about Morita therapy prior to beginning therapy. In Japan, as would be the case in any country, it is difficult for the patient to enter into therapy if he is not adequately informed. Second, the patient must voluntarily try the Moritist approach after having had no success with several other forms of treatment. The patient must be highly motivated toward the therapy.

Leonhard (5) and Kumasaka (4) have stated that isolated bedrest cannot be employed with individualistic Western neurotic patients, because they cannot endure this "isolation hell." The experience of two American researchers, however, who tried isolated bed rest for seven days in our clinic was not as painful as had been feared before the experiment, although, of course, they were not neurotic patients. If the two previously mentioned conditions of information and motivation are fulfilled, it is probable that the Western patient could complete the period of isolated bed rest. Some modification of Morita therapy, may have to be made for Westerners. We consider that verbal communication has to be stressed more, and that "no response" therapy might not work for Western people. It should again be stressed that the patient's change of perspective occurs spontaneously, not by intellectual interpretation. It comes about as the result of his changed bheavior under the therapeutic regulations of the hospital milieu.

We are indebted to D. K. Reynolds, Ph.D., and T. Yamaguchi, M.D., for their advice on the translation and contents of this article.

REFERENCES

1. Chang SC: Morita therapy. Am J Psychother 28:208, 1974

2. Doi, T The anatomy of dependence Kodansha International Ltd Tokyo, New York & San Francisco 1973

3. Iwai H, Reynolds DK: Morita psychotherapy: the views from the West. Am J Psychiatry 126: 1031, 1970

4. Kelman H: Psychoterapy in the Far East. Prog Psychother 4: 296, 1959

5. Kumasaka Y: Discussion: Morita therapy. Int J Psychiatry 1: 641, 1965

6. Leonhard K: Die japanische Morita-Therapie aus der Sicht eigener psycho-therapeutischer Verfahren. Arch Psychiatry Nervenkr 207: 185, 1965

7. Reynolds David K: Morita Psychotherapy. Berkeley, University of California Press, 1976

19 Yoga

N. S. VAHIA, DINSHAW R. DOONGAJI

The word *Yoga* is derived from the Sanskrit word *Yuj,* meaning to unite. Patanjali's treatise on Yoga (20) is of practical value to medicine, inasmuch as it presents methods for the development of harmonious functioning of the personality through increasing self control and decreasing the impact of environmental influences. Although these methods were formulated about 2500 years ago, they remain useful even today, since they can be applied to modify psychophysiological functions and social behavior without the constant need for a therapist, electronic devices, or psychoactive drugs.

CONCEPTUAL FOUNDATIONS OF YOGA

Ordinarily, man's attention is directed toward the world he perceives through his sense organs and to which he responds. His behavior is thus greatly modified by environmental influences. These environmental stimuli, his responses to them, and the resultant feedback maintain a constant involvement with the changing environment, and his feeling of well-being depends upon his ability to cope adequately with the environment for resultant gains. Constant effort, however, is needed to cope with changing reality, due to one's fear of loss of adequate adjustment with the passage of time. Even when one is adequately adjusted, the craving for more happiness may lead to more effort. When a person's coping ability is inadequate, however, the impact of external feedback disorganizes his personality functions, which results in disturbances in his psychological, physiological, or social well-being.

Thus, dependence on external factors makes a person vulnerable to a greater or lesser degree of tension, and he is therefore liable to psychological disintegration. This dependence on external sources for well-being is due to a failure to realize that one pays a heavy price for any resultant gains, namely, the propensity to disorganization. If one could develop greater self-control, one's mental and physical faculties and social behavior would be less vulnerable to external stress.

Unlike the environment, the self cannot be immediately perceived (21). It can, however, be conceptualized as an internal but independent observer of all behavior, psychological, physiological, and social. Patanjali's argument is that all changes in one's activity can be observed not only by others, but also by one's self. If the changes in all aspects of the personality in response to a changing environment can be objectively observed and controlled, and if the resultant behavior under self-control is not preoccupied with the environmental feedback, then the impact of external sources cannot disturb personality function. Undisturbed by such feedback, one's behavior under self-control is free from internal and external conflicts and therefore is free from tensions, fluctuations, and the danger of disorganization.

TECHNIQUES OF YOGA

Patanjali (20) has recommended many methods for the development of self-control, but the one that has been found useful in the prevention and treatment of stress disorders consists of eight measures: *Yama, Niyama, Asana, Pranayama, Pratyahara, Dharana, Dhyana,* and *Samadhi.*

Yama and *Niyama* provide guidelines for interpersonal relationships. *Asana, Pranayama,* and *Pratyahara* are meant for the control of the voluntary nervous system and visceral functions. *Dharana* and *Dhyana* are helpful in the control of thought processes. *Samadhi* is a state during which one can observe and maintain harmony among all personality functions.

YAMA AND NIYAMA

A sense of satisfaction derived from the optimal use of one's abilities, rather than from the resultant gains, makes one less vulnerable. To achieve such satisfaction, one's behavior should be primarily motivated by an urge to utilize one's abilities with a sense of dedication. In the absence of external preoccupation, the assessment of one's abilities may be objective and realistic. Aggression for personal gain is out of question, since it leads to tension and involvement with the environmental feedback. The important gain derived from such behavioral modification is that the gratifying or frustrating nature of feedback may still result in corresponding happiness or unhappiness, but it should not be allowed to make enough impact so as to disorganize one's capacity to function.

ASANA, PRANAYAMA, AND PRATYAHARA

Asanas are different types of postures involving bodily movements of different groups of muscles. These postures are to be maintained in a steady and relaxed state, with minimum effort, for a given length of time. Both the agonist groups of muscles as well as their antagonists should be relaxed. Many *Asanas* require rhythmic bodily movements that involve flexion, extension, lateral movement, or rotation of the spine. These movements are to be performed as slowly and as gently as possible and without tension. The eyes are kept closed while the various postures are maintained to minimize the influence of the surroundings. A gradual decrease in muscle tension occurs, and the individual feels happy and invigorated rather than exhausted.

Pranayama is meant for the control of visceral functions. The practice begins with the control of respiration. Each phase of *Pranayama*—respiration, inspiration, retention of breath, and expiration, as well as the period between expiration and the next inspiration—is controlled. The duration of each phase of *Pranayama* and the number of *Pranayamas* are gradually increased by practice. *Pranayama* is also performed in a relaxed posture and with the eyes closed.

Pratyahara is an integral part of *Asana* and *Pranayama.* As the body reacts to external stimuli by changes in the muscles or in visceral activity, any disturbing influence in the surroundings or any intruding extraneous thought is actively resisted during the practice of *Asana* and *Pranayama,* since these would retard the individual's attempts to gain internal control. Ideas involving anger or fear, for instance, would affect the tone of the voluntary musculature or the visceral activity, which in turn would interfere with the practice for acquiring control over bodily functions. It is therefore recommended that during these practices, one should maintain one's attention or concentration on either bland imagery (*e.g.,* blue sky or flowing water) or on a part of the body such as the forehead or the precordium.

DHARANA AND DHYANA

When the voluntary and autonomic functions are under control, it becomes comparatively easy to control the thought processes.

The self, as the inner observer and controller of all activity, cannot be perceived (21). A symbol representing this unchanging, inner, independent self is therefore used as an object for concentration. This symbol could be a sound or a word which is selected by the patient with the help of the therapist. It might also be a religious symbol such as a mantra, the image of a deity or of a prophet, the word "OM," the sign of the cross, or a crescent and a star. It could be a symbol with a nonreligious connotation, such as a flower, the sky, the calm sea, or flowing water. Whatever the imagery, it should be constant and consistent during each session.

In the beginning, even though the selected symbol is very appealing to the patient, his attempt to concentrate on it is disturbed by numerous other thoughts. These may be thoughts about present problems, real or imagined fears about his inability to achieve desired goals, or the fear of loss of whatever he has achieved. Initially, the patient is unable to maintain his concentration for more than a few seconds. He is then made to realize that similar distractions were responsible for his anxiety, depression, bodily pains, or visceral symptoms. Through practice, he gradually increases his ability to avoid distractions and to maintain continuous concentration to the degree where his sense of time is also lost. The improved concentration in his chosen field of activity will help him to focus his abilities on the tasks of his choice, which in turn will improve his feeling of well-being.

SAMADHI

When one's personality functions are under self-control and free from the constant need for coping with external factors, the resultant harmony of mental, physical, and social behavior takes place almost effortlessly. This state of internal and external harmony is described as *Samadhi.*

STUDIES IN THE TREATMENT OF NEUROSES AND PSYCHOSOMATIC DISORDERS

It has been thought that the methods of Yoga might be useful in the treatment of mental and physical illnesses, and studies were conducted in the psychiatric services of the King Edward VII Memorial Hospital, Bombay. The details of the technique and the results of these studies have also been reported elsewhere (25–29.)

Our preliminary studies showed that Yoga methods were most effective for patients with psychoneurosis and psychosomatic disorders. They were not suitable for manics, depressives, schizophrenics, and sociopaths, and in fact, with schizophrenic patients these methods often increased their tendency toward autistic thinking and withdrawal from reality. The mentally retarded were also not treated with this therapy for obvious reasons.

Asthma was the only psychosomatic disorder that could be treated, since only with this disorder were there a sufficient number of referrals.

THERAPEUTIC METHODS

Initially, each patient was individually interviewed and the general outline of treatment was explained. There were daily treatment sessions for six days a week, each session lasting for one hour. Patients were instructed to attend the session after an overnight fast. Six weeks was considered the minimum period necessary for assessment. Therapy was initiated with training in the practice of *Asana,* which was demonstrated by the therapist. The *Asana* consisted of sitting in a relaxed manner with arms and legs folded and eyes closed. The patient was instructed to relax all his muscles until the adopted posture was comfortable and the whole body was relaxed.

After the patient had learned to practice this *Asana* correctly, he was instructed in the next one. He was instructed to lie down in a supine position with his hands parallel to his body, his legs spread slightly apart, and his eyes closed, simulating and maintaining the cadaveric posture. Subsequently, he was taught four other *Asanas,* which involved flexion, extension, lateral movements, and rotation of the spinal column. These *Asanas* were to be performed as gently and as slowly as possible and with minimum effort, so that the patient felt exhilarated rather than exhausted after their performance.

Next, the patient was initiated into the practice of *Pranayama,* or breathing practices. He was instructed to close one nostril and inhale air from the other nostril. This was done as slowly as possible. He then closed both nostrils and paused for as long as he comfortably could. This was followed by exhalation from the other nostril, again performed as slowly as possible. The patient next closed both nostrils and paused for as long as he comfortably could before starting another cycle with the next inspiration. The duration of each phase of this cycle and the number of *Pranayamas* were timed, and both the duration of each phase and the number of cycles were increased gradually over a period of time.

While the patient was learning these techniques, it was explained to him that the relaxed performance of *Asana* and *Pranayama* would be disturbed by extraneous thoughts. He should therefore attempt to maintain concentration on some bland imagery, such as blue sky or flowing water, during these practices *(Pratyahara).* The *Asanas, Pranayamas,* and *Pratyaharas* were taught during the first two weeks.

After acquiring proficiency in the above practices, the patient was taught to practice *Dhyana* and *Dharana.* Sitting in a relaxed posture, he was asked to select an object or a symbol that appealed to him to concentrate on. He soon found that his concentration was distracted by internal and external stimuli, *e.g.,* noises from his immediate environment, aches and pains in different parts of his body, muscle fatigue, or intruding thoughts about the past, present, or future. Doubts about the effects of the treatment and a desire to terminate the sitting often occurred at this stage. Later, the disturbing thoughts were of immediate problems, past experiences, guilt due to misbehavior, or fear of the future. Anger, fear, hatred, jealousy, craving for power and prosperity, or excessive love and affection were other common sources of distraction. The patient gradually learned to be less preoccupied and disturbed by these as he gained greater voluntary control over his thought processes.

Whenever the patient had difficulty maintaining such control, it was explained to him that his inability to concentrate showed that although he thought that his thoughts were under his control, in actual fact they were controlled by external factors because of his need for resultant gains. Such explanations helped the patient learn to maintain concentration for longer periods and with less effort. He also found that concentration was accompanied by relief of his mental and physical symptoms and an increase in his functioning capacity.

RESULTS

Three studies were carried out. The value of Yoga therapy in those patients who had failed to respond to other treatment had been assessed initially. Because the initial results were encouraging in the treatment of psychoneurosis (29), a further study involving a greater number of patients was performed.

First Study

The trial period was six weeks long, since the number of dropouts was found to increase when the duration was longer. The global improvement of the patients was arbitrarily rated by the clinicians as 25, 50, 75, or 100 on the basis of the opinions of the patients, their relatives, and the physical therapist; an improvement over 50 was considered satisfactory. Improvement was seen in 70% of the patients who were treated for six weeks, which suggested that the treatment compared favorably with psychoanalytic psychotherapy, eclectic psychotherapy, and behavior therapy (25). The comparison with other therapies, however, was not very significant, because it did not take into account the differences in the diagnostic criteria used, differing periods of treatment, varying assessment methods, as well as other variables (7, 23).

Second Study

Two psychiatrists, working independently, diagnosed the patients studied as suffering from neurosis. These patients were randomly distributed into two groups. The index group was treated with Yoga therapy, while the control group was treated with placebo or "pseudo Yoga"; all other variables were the same for both of these groups. Placebo tablets were given to both groups of patients.

With the patients who were treated by "pseudo Yoga" therapy, no attempt was made to teach them to develop control over their voluntary or autonomic functions or their thought processes, but these patients mechanically performed practices similar to *Asana, Pranayama, Dharana,* and *Dhyana.* They were taught postural practices that involved sitting up, lying down, or bodily movements. General instructions to relax were given, but no attempt was made to ensure that the practice of *Asana,* for example, was free from tension and was steady and effortless. The breathing practices that were prescribed to the control group consisted of deep inspiration and deep expiration. They were not instructed to resist internal or external distractions *(Pratyahara).* After the practice of mock *Asana* and *Pranayama,* they were to sit in a relaxed posture with closed eyes for a length of time, and they were then asked to write whatever thoughts came to their minds. They were reassured that they would gradually recover. The entire study was double blind.

The results of the psychological tests of the 15 patients on Yoga therapy (index group) and the 12 patients on "pseudo Yoga" therapy (control group) showed that there was a significantly greater improvement in the index group (27).

Third Study

The value of Yoga therapy was compared with drug therapy as it is commonly used in treating psychoneurosis (33). In the drug-therapy group, a combination of amitriptyline and chlordiazepoxide was used. A senior psychiatrist interviewed each patient on drug therapy at weekly intervals and adjusted the dosage of these drugs for optimal response. The index group was treated with Yoga therapy. There were 35 patients who received Yoga therapy and 41 patients, who received drug therapy.

Taylor's Manifest Anxiety scale, the Hamilton Depression Rating Scale, and Bell's Social Adaptation Rating Scale were used, and no significant differences were found in the initial scores on all three scales. Both groups showed improvement at the end of six weeks of treatment, but the improvement in the level of anxiety and social adaptation was significantly greater in patients receiving Yoga therapy as compared to those on drug therapy. The decrease in the level of depression in either group was not significant (1).

DISCUSSION

The World Health Organization (WHO) defines *health* as physiological, psychological, and social well-being, and not merely the absence of disease or infirmity (32). This definition has been criticized by Lewis (15) as being idealistic but impractical. He felt that it would be difficult to find such a healthy person in contemporary society. According to Jus (12), the concept of health would vary from country to country, and it would depend upon social expectations. He has argued that "health" should be a unitary concept which can be applied in different countries without modifications; therefore, social well-being should not be considered as a basic requirement for health.

Patanjali (20) maintained that WHO's definition of health is neither impractical nor idealistic. However, as long as man's behavior is under dual control—both by the self (which is constant) and by the environment (which is constantly changing)—it is difficult to expect it to be always in harmony with both control systems. Perfect health, in his view, can be maintained only by the internal control of behavior and freedom from the need to cope with a constantly changing external environment.

Psychophysiological investigations (11, 13) have shown that the interaction between man and his environmental stimuli results in arousal of the cortical, autonomic and peripheral nervous system which varies in intensity from individual to individual. Different bodily systems are involved in the level of response. When a person is moderately aroused by external stimuli, his behavior is adaptive, but, when the environmental influences are severely stressful, chronic, or abnormal, there is a higher state of arousal. Under such conditions, the subject is less able to adjust to repetitive stimuli. His ability to adapt diminishes and the state of hyperarousal becomes self-perpetuating. Chronic states of high arousal are associated with dysfunctions of the viscera which may lead to pathological changes over a period of time. Rational treatment of such disorders would thus include methods for decreasing the hyperarousal state at all levels. Lang and Sternbach (14), for example, recommend such a multidisciplinary approach. Patanjali's methods may help admirably in bringing about decreases in the state of arousal at three levels, namely, the cortical, autonomic, and peripheral levels.

Acquisition of self-control is the main objective of many therapies. According to Strupp (22), it is the sole aim of the deep psychotherapies. One of the major problems in behavior therapy is the progression from external control of behavior (33) to self-control. Psychotherapy, behavior therapy, biofeedback, and drugs have customarily been employed to help the patient to acquire self-control. These methods may allow the patient to develop a greater ability to cope, but they may simultaneously increase his dependence upon them (4). This has been shown to be true, for example, with the deep psychotherapies and with drugs. Operant conditioning techniques improve the patient's response patterns largely by modification of his environment. Biofeedback techniques do not modify the factors responsible for visceral dysfunction, neither do they increase the patient's own capacity for internal control. Thus, though the aim is to achieve self-control, what happens in actual practice is that such techniques prolong the patient's dependence on external agencies. In this respect, critical assessments of the value of these therapies have not been encouraging (3, 6–10, 17, 18, 23, 24).

Chhina (5) and his colleagues have reported evidence that Patanjali's methods are useful in the development of self-control. They reported that subjects show an increased control over autonomic activity and a decrease in arousal; these observations are consistent with those of other workers (2, 16, 19). A decrease in the activity of peripheral and autonomic functions and a corresponding decrease in the level of anxiety with improvement in the performance capacity have been reported to occur with the use of the allied technique of transcendental meditation (TM) (30).

The possibility exists that the improvements reported with the use of the techniques of Yoga may largely be due to faith (4, 8, 9), because of cultural factors, and the prevailing attitude of acceptance of yogic practices in India. Similar encouraging results might not be obtained if such studies were repeated in different cultures. It is our belief, however, that any therapeutic procedure that decreases the state of arousal of the cortical, autonomic, and peripheral nervous systems and simultaneously improves the subject's psychological and social behavior must be culture-free to a great degree. Extensive studies in countries around the world, which would employ sophisticated experimental designs and advanced electronic instrumentation, are needed to establish the precise value and limitations of Patanjali's concept of Yoga as a therapeutic technique.

REFERENCES

1. Balkrishna V, Sanghavi LD, Mistri PP, Rana K Doongaji DR, Vahia NS: Comparison of results of psychophysiological therapy with drug therapy in psychoneurosis (to be published)
2. Bhatnagar OP, Ganguly AK, Ananthraman V, Gopal KS: Influence of yogic training on thermoregulation. Proc Int Union Physiol SciXI: 378, 1974
3. Blanchard EB, Young LD: Clinical application of biofeedback training: a review of evidence. Arch Gen Psychiatry 30 (5): 573–589, 1974
4. Calestro EM: Psychotherapy faith healing and suggestion. Int J Psychiatry 10 (2): 83–113, 1972
5. Chhina GS: The voluntary control of autonomic responses in yogis. Proc Int Union Physiol Sci X: 103, 1974
6. Conn JH: The decline of psychoanalysis. JAMA 228 (6): 711–712, 1974
7. Eyesenck HJ: The effects of psychotherapy. Int J Psychiatry 1 (1): 97–143, 1965
8. Fish JM: Psychotherapy and Faith Healing: in Placebo Therapy: San Francisco, Jossey-Bass 1973, pp 1–9
9. Frank JD: The restoration of morale. Am J Psychiatry 13(3): 271–274, 1974
10. Gelder MG, Bonaoft JHJ, Gath DH, Johnston DW, Mathews AM, Shaw PM: Specific and nonspecific factors in behaviour therapy. Br J Psychiatry 123 445–463, 1973
11. Hill D: Summing Up. Physiology, Emotion and Psychosomatic Illness, Ciba Foundation Symposium 8 (new series). North Holland, Amsterdam, London. Elsevier, Excerpta Medica, 1972, pp 401–408
12. Jus A: Social system and criteria of health as defined by the World Health Organization. Am J Psychiatry 130: 125–131, 1973
13. Lader M: Psychophysiological Research and Psychosomatic Medicine. Physiology, Emotion and Psychosomatic Illness. Ciba Foundation Symposium 8 (new series). North Holland, Amsterdam, London, New York, Elsevier, Excerpta Medica, 1972
14. Lang PJ, Sternbach RA: Psychophysiology of emotion. In Greenfield NS, Sternbach RA (eds): Handbook of Psychophysiology. New York, Holt, Rinehart & Winston, 1972, p 639
15. Lewis A: Health as a social concept. Br J Sociol 4: 109–124, 1953
16. Lobo RJ, Michailov MCH, Iyenger V, Zonevia VT, Neu E: On psychological effects of Hatha yoga. Long time group teaching. Proc Int Union Physiol Sci XI: 378, 1974
17. Malan DH: The outcome problem in psychotherapy research. Arch Gen Psychiatry 29 (6): 719–729, 1973
18. Mechanic D: Mental Health and Social Policy. Englewood Cliffs, Prentice-Hall. Cited by: Slater E: The psychiatrists in search of a science. III. The depth psychologies. Br J Psychiatry 126: 205–224, 1975
19. Mookerji SM: Impact of yoga training in some psychological norms. Proc Int Union Physiol Sci XI: 378, 1974
20. Patanjali: Yogasutra. In Swami Vivekananda (ed): Raja Yoga. Calcutta, Advaita Ashrama, 1966, pp 123–286
21. Ryle G: Self Knowledge: The Concept of Mind. New York, Hutchinson's University Library, 1949, pp 154–198
22. Strupp HH: Specific versus nonspecific factors in psychotherapy and problems of control. Arch Gen Psychiatry 23 (5): 393–401, 1970
23. Strupp HH, Bergin AE: Some empirical and conceptual basis for coordinated research in psychotherapy. Int J Psychother 7 (2): 18–90, 1969
24. Torrey EF: The Mind Game : Witchdoctors and Psychiatrists. New York, Bantam Books, 1973
25. Vahia NS, Doongaji DR, Deshmukh DK, Vinekar SL, Parekh HC, Kapoor SN: A reconditioning therapy based upon concepts of Patanjali. Int J Soc Psychiatry 18: 61–66, 1972
26. Vahia NS, Doongaji DR, Jeste DV: Value of Patanjali's concepts in the treatment of psychoneurosis. In Arieti S, Chrzanowski G (eds): New Dimensions in Psychiatry—A World View. New York, John Wiley & Sons, 1975, pp 293–304
27. Vahia NS, Doongaji DR, Jeste DV, Kapoor SN, Ardhapurkar I, Ravindra NS: Further experience with the therapy based upon concepts of Patanjali in the treatment of psychiatric disorders. Int J Psychiatry 15: 32–37, 1973

28. Vahia NS, Doongaji DR, Jeste DV, Kapoor SN, Ardhapurkar I, Ravindra NS: Psychophysiological therapy based on the concepts of Patanjali—a new approach to the treatment of neurotic and psychosomatic disorders. Am J Psychother 27: 557–565, 1973

29. Vahia NS, Vinekar SL, Doongaji DR: Some ancient indian concepts in the treatment of psychiatric disorders. Br J Psychiatry 112: 1089–1096, 1966

30. Wallace RK: Transcendental meditation: a wakeful hypometabolic physiologic state. Proc Int Union Physiol Sci X:69, 1974

31. Wheatley D: Evaluation of psychotropic drugs in general practice. Practitioner 827–829, 1971

32. World Health Organization Report. I: 1–2, 1947–1948

33. Yates AJ: Future trend. In Behaviour Therapy. New York, John Wiley & Sons, 1970, pp 408–423

20 A Social Ecological Perspective on Medical Disorders*

RUDOLPH H. MOOS

A physician advises a harried executive with high blood pressure to spend a week in the country. A pediatrician recommends that an underdeveloped, neglected child be sent to a foster home. A social worker encourages an asthmatic client to seek a job with more human contact. A cardiologist urges an administrator to delegate some of his responsibilities to others in his office. Each of these workers is influenced by the belief that the patient's environment has important effects on his physiological processes. In addition, their recommendations reflect the assumptions that one can distinguish different types or dimensions of environmental stimuli, that these dimensions can have distinctive influences on physiological processes, and that the effects of these dimensions may differ from one individual to another.

The idea that the physical and social environment influences health and disease has a long and varied history. The classical psychosomatic point of view asserts that the emotional experience of an individual can affect his bodily functions, his health status, and the onset, course, and treatment of his diseases. According to this viewpoint, the link to the environment is provided by emotional experiences, since these are aroused by the characteristics of the environment in which people live. Such considerations have resulted in a greater interest in the role of the environment in medical disorders, as well as in attempts to develop a social or ecological perspective toward psychosomatic processes (12, 18).

A social ecological approach is joined with the traditional concerns of human ecology through its emphasis on the measurement of objective physical characteristics of environments and on the short-term evolutionary and adaptive consequences of these environments. It joins with the traditional concerns of the behavioral sciences, particularly psychology and sociology, in its emphasis on the importance of the social environment and in its consideration of the environmental impacts on such psychological variables as self-esteem and personal development. It is linked to traditional concerns in psychiatry, medicine, and epidemiology in its focus on dysfunctional or pathological reactions (*e.g.,* illness, accidents, suicide, or crime) and their relationship to environmental variables. A social ecological approach provides a distinctive point of entry through which human environments and their impacts on human functioning may be studied (26).

In accordance with this broad conceptualization, we have identified six methods by which the characteristics of human environments have been studied. These methods have focused on 1) ecological dimensions, which include geographical and meteorological factors as well as architectural and physical design variables;

*Preparation of this chapter was supported in part by NIMH Grant MH16026, NIAAA Grant AA02863, and Veterans Administration Research Project MRIS 5817–01.

2) behavior settings; 3) dimensions of organizational structure and functioning; 4) dimensions identifying the collective personal or behavioral characteristics of the inhabitants of a particular environment (*i.e.,* the human aggregate); 5) variables relevant to the functional analyses of environments in terms of social reinforcement contingencies; and 6) psychosocial characteristics and organizational climate, in particular, the perceived social climate. The dimensions relevant to each of these six methods have important impacts on individual behavior and on disease processes (11, 24).

The relevance of a social ecological perspective for understanding environmental influences on disease processes can be illustrated by focusing on psychosocial characteristics and organizational climate. The social-climate perspective assumes that environments have unique "personalities," just as people do. Social environments can be characterized with a great deal of accuracy and detail. Some people are more supportive than others; likewise, some social environments are more supportive than others. Some people feel a strong need to control others; similarly, some social environments are extremely rigid, autocratic, and controlling. Order, clarity, and structure are important to many people. Correspondingly, many social environments strongly emphasize order, clarity, and organization.

Recent research has shown that vastly different social environments can be described by common or similar sets of dimensions: relationship dimensions, personal development or personal growth dimensions, and system maintenance and system change dimensions. These broad categories of dimensions are similar across many environments, although vastly different settings may impose unique variations within the general categories (22, 23). The dimensions identified in work and family settings are illustrated in Table 20-1.

Relationship dimensions identify the nature and intensity of personal relationships within the environment. They may be used to assess the extent to which people are involved in the environment, the extent to which they support and help each other, and the extent to which there is spontaneity and free and open expression among them. Involvement and cohesion, for example, reflect the extent to which people actively participate and are emotionally concerned with others in the setting. Support reflects the extent of concern for others in the group, the intensity of efforts to aid one another with personal difficulties and problems, and an emphasis on open and honest communication.

Personal development dimensions indicate the basic directions along which personal growth and self-enhancement tend to occur in a specific environment. They include, for example, autonomy and responsibility (the extent to which people are encouraged to be self-sufficient and to make their own decisions), achievement-orientation (the extent to which different types of activities are cast into an achievement-oriented or competitive framework), and moral or religious emphasis (the extent to which ethical and religious issues are emphasized). Other personal growth goals include competition, academic achievement, self-understanding, task-orientation, and the like.

System maintenance and system change dimensions represent the extent to which the environment is orderly, clear in its expectations, controlling, and responsive to change. Clarity in a work milieu, for example, assesses the extent to which workers know what to expect in their daily routines and how explicitly rules and policies are communicated. Clarity in a classroom refers to the emphasis on following a clear set of rules and on the students' knowledge of what the consequences will be if they do not follow these rules. The degree of social control and of the responsiveness to change are clearly relevant to—and clearly discriminate among—most social settings. An additional and important dimension that may be identified in work environments is work pressure.

These dimensions represent the salient characteristics of a wide variety of social settings and are related to important measures of outcome such as morale and

Table 20-1. SOCIAL ENVIRONMENTAL DIMENSIONS OF WORK AND FAMILY SETTINGS

SETTING	RELATIONSHIP	PERSONAL DEVELOPMENT	SYSTEM MAINTENANCE AND SYSTEM CHANGE
Work	Involvement Peer cohesion Staff support	Autonomy Task orientation	Work pressure Clarity Control Innovation Physical comfort
Family	Cohesion Expressiveness Conflict	Independence Achievement- orientation Intellectual-cultural orientation Recreational orientation Moral-religious emphasis	Organization Control

satisfaction, objective indices of treatment outcome, and other behavioral and attitudinal criteria. Their derivation from the individual perceptions of environmental influences, rather than from "objective" stimulus factors, is important in light of the evidence that individual differences in defenses and coping strategies can affect physiological responses to the "same" situation. In the following sections, we will briefly illustrate the relevance of these social environmental factors to medical disorders in relation to 1) the onset and causes of disease, 2) the utilization of medical care, and 3) the course of disease and the outcome of treatment.

THE ONSET AND ETIOLOGY OF DISEASE

Behavioral characteristics have been shown to be strong risk factors in many diseases, most notably cigarette smoking in lung cancer and the type-A behavior pattern, obesity, lack of exercise, and cigarette smoking in coronary artery disease. Environmental factors are associated with each of these high-risk behaviors. People who smoke, for example, are more likely to work in responsible and highly pressured jobs, to associate with others who smoke, to have parents who smoke, and so on. Ecological analysis indicates that cigarette smoking is a source of ego strength, facilitates social interaction, and helps to cope with the demands of an achievement-oriented stressful life (20).

Rosenman and Friedman have identified a behavior pattern that they believe is associated with a high risk for coronary artery disease. The coronary-prone behavior pattern, designated "type A," is characterized by extreme aggressiveness, competitiveness, and ambition along with feelings of restlessness and, in particular, a profound sense of time urgency. Type-A persons are engaged in "a relatively chronic struggle to obtain an unlimited number of relatively poorly defined things from the environment in the shortest period of time." Rosenman and Friedman believe that the contemporary Western environment encourages the development of this pattern. They also believe that the pattern represents the interaction of environmental influences and individual susceptibilities, and they argue that it may not occur if a type-A individual is removed to a type-B setting (9).

Caffrey (3, 4) has shown that it is possible to rank environments according to the degree to which their "atmospheres" encourage type-A behavior. He had three physicians rate 14 Benedictine and 11 Trappist monasteries using paired comparison methods. Caffrey showed that groups of monks that had a higher proportion of type-A individuals living in type-A environments and consuming a high fat diet also had the highest rates of coronary disease (3, 4). The dimensions of responsibility and work pressure include the sorts of environmental influences that encourage the sense of time urgency experienced by the individual with a type-A personality. The association of responsibility and work pressure with coronary artery disease has gained considerable support elsewhere in the literature (8, 17).

Another finding supports the hypothesis that responsibility and work pressure may have a cumulative noxious effect. Air traffic controllers, who work under extreme time pressure and with the responsibility for hundreds of lives, were shown to have a higher risk and an earlier onset of hypertension and peptic ulcers than a control group of second-class airmen. Most of the excess incidence was found in the younger age groups, which implies that the diseases begin at an earlier age among the controllers. The risk of developing hypertension was greater among those working at towers and centers with high traffic densities. There was also a striking difference in the prevalence of peptic ulcer at towers and centers where conditions of high stress were found, compared to those where lower stresses were present (5).

Certain types of liver disease, as well as several other diseases, are related to alcoholism and "problem-drinking" behavior. Although many studies have attempted to characterize the personality characteristics of alcoholics, recent evidence indicates that environmental factors predominate among the correlates of alcohol-related problems, and, in fact, that alcohol consumption may be as much a property of social contexts as a property of individuals. Specific characteristics of the social setting that have been implicated in the development and maintenance of "problem-drinking" behavior include the psychosocial equilibrium between an individual and his environment, the degree to which the family models favor the use of alcohol to solve problems, as well as general family, occupational, and social group influences. Certain social environmental dimensions—such as family conflict, work responsibility and pressure, and a lack of moral or religious emphasis—appear to be associated with drinking problems (1).

Gout has been related to extravagent living, particularly the overconsumption of rich food and drink. Serum uric acid levels are higher in the upper and middle social classes than they are in the lower social classes. High levels have also been noted in achievement-oriented individuals, *e.g.,* the drive, achievement level, and professional accomplishment of university professors has been related to their serum uric acid levels (2). The drive for achievement is itself strongly influenced by social environmental characteristics, such as the climate created for motivating achievement, the opportunities for verbal development, the nature and amount of assistance provided in overcoming academic difficulties, the intellectual level in the environment, and the kinds of work habits expected of the individual (34).

Holmes and his colleagues (10) developed the Social Readjustment Rating Scale (SRRS), which consists of different life events that were scaled according to the amount of "readjustment" they were judged to require, *e.g.,* the death of a spouse, 100 life change units (LCU); divorce, 73 LCU; marital separation, 65 LCU; and so on (see Table 1–1, Ch. 1). They found that clusters of life events that required changes in ongoing life adjustment were associated with the onset of tuberculosis, heart disease, skin disease, and hernia (10). Thus, the social environmental dimensions of responsibility, achievement-orientation, competition, work pressure, and life change are related to the onset of illness.

THE UTILIZATION OF MEDICAL CARE

Medical sociologists have demonstrated that most people who have physical or psychological symptoms and who complain of various illnesses do not seek help from health professionals. Some people, however, overutilize health services.

Various social environmental factors have been related to the utilization of health care. Some impressive relationships exist, for example, between the social environments of military basic-training companies and their sick-call rates, *i.e.*, the degree to which the enlisted men use the health-care services. The characteristics of companies with high sick calls include an emphasis on order and organization that borders on extreme restrictiveness. In these units, the men are kept busy, but with tasks they perceive to be repetitious and boring. Relatively strict officer control is emphasized, and the enlisted man's personal status is deemphasized. The men feel that they are ridiculed in front of others, that the officers do not help orient them to the company, and that they never know when an officer will ask to see them. One way to adapt to this kind of noxious social environment is to become ill (23).

Similar findings were obtained in a study of nine high-school classrooms. Classrooms in which student medical absences were high were also characterized by competition, strict teacher control, and a lack of emphasis on task-orientation. Thus, perhaps not surprisingly, students stay away from classes that they perceive to be restrictive and difficult, even if they feel that they learn more in these classes (24).

Complaints about physical symptoms, which are related to the use of health services, are exacerbated in certain social environments; for example, complaints about physical symptoms were found to be more numerous than expected from students living in groups that were low in involvement, support, and student influence (*i.e.*, in which the students felt a lack of control over the milieu) but high in competition. These studies indicate that the use of health-care services may be closely related to the social environment in which an individual functions.

The extent to which a person adopts the "sick role" may also be related to the social environments within his work and family settings. Settings in which work pressure is high and in which there is a high degree of conflict are likely to foster sick-role behavior. Dalton (6) has pointed out the role of family environmental factors and emotional stress in her observation that mothers who are in either the menstrual or premenstrual phase of their menstrual cycle are more likely to bring children with minor symptoms, such as colds and coughs to pediatricians. The patients' social and cultural milieu has a profound effect on his reaction to and interpretation of pain and other bodily symptoms, as well as on his use of health-care facilities (21).

THE COURSE OF ILLNESS AND THE OUTCOME OF TREATMENT

Personal and background factors are related to the speed with which the disease progresses, the remission or exacerbation of symptoms, the success of rehabilitation, and so on. Patients who are reasonably well defended, who are able to control their impulses, who do not manifest an abnormally high degree of anxiety, depression, or dependency, and who are somewhat confident and socially outgoing often remain able to function well despite evidence of objective illness.

Unfortunately, there is as yet very little information about the social environmental factors that promote impulse control, confidence, extroversion, positive mood, and so on. We do know that psychological support is strongly related to these factors. Mutual understanding or empathy on the part of stroke patients and their families, for example, is related to the patient's rate of rehabilitation (28). Patients with intractable duodenal ulcer or other intractable diseases who scored higher on a scale of environmental deprivation (which included such factors as emotional impoverishment within the family and in other social relations) tended to have a poorer outcome following surgery (33). Prospective studies have indicated that a fatal outcome after open-heart surgery is more frequent in those patients who feel depressed or hopeless before surgery (15).

In this connection, many studies have shown that providing a patient with information and a supportive doctor-patient relationship can facilitate his postsurgical recovery. Giving patients such information and encouragement regarding their impending operation may not only facilitate their postoperative recovery, but may reduce their length of hospital stay as well (7). In one study, nurses were trained to create an atmosphere in which the mothers of children admitted to a hospital for tonsillectomy would be supportive, and feel free to express their anxieties and to request information and emotional support. Children whose mothers were in the experimental group adapted better to hospital routines and procedures, showed better inhospital postsurgical recovery, and had more rapid posthospital recovery than did those children whose mothers were in a control group (31).

Although only a few studies have been carried out, there is evidence that the social environment may affect the outcome of pharmacotherapy programs and posthospital recovery rates in psychiatric and other illnesses (14). In addition, social environmental factors affect the patients' compliance with treatment regimens as well as their reactions to physicians' waiting rooms and to unusual hospital environments, such as intensive care and cardiac care units, isolation units, and recovery rooms (16).

The family environment is probably the most important mediator between background characteristics and posthospital adjustment. One aspect of the family environment that may vary with social factors is the attitude toward the hospitalized individual once he returns home; lower class families, for example, are more reluctant to accept a person back after he or she has been hospitalized (27). Even while the patient is still in the hospital, families in lower classes visit and correspond with their relatives less frequently than families of middle-class patients do. The expectations about the returning patient's functioning are generally more pessimistic the lower the socioeconomic level of the family. Former patients are likely to expect more of themselves in homes in which their family members have high expectations for them.

THE INTERACTION OF PERSONALITY AND SOCIAL ENVIRONMENTAL VARIABLES

The social environment may be viewed as a system of stimuli exerting influence on the individuals within that environment. Many of these influences or pressures can be categorized as relationship dimensions, personal development dimensions, or system maintenance and system change dimensions. Although individuals are sufficiently alike and the environmental stimuli sufficiently potent so that the individuals within a given environment can make reliable and consistent judgments about the magnitude of a given dimension, the social stimuli do not act directly on the individual. Rather, it is his *perception* of the social environment—as mediated by personality variables, role and status relationships, and his behavior within the environment—which affects him directly and, in turn, affects his personality and behavior.

There are two main ways in which individual variables and social environmental variables can interact which lead to different physiological responses:

1. Given the same social environmental pressures, two individuals may perceive different levels of the same dimension. A suspicious person, for example, might perceive little support in an office that is seen as very supportive by his less suspicious co-workers. In time, of course, this individual might very well come to receive less support than his peers, thus confirming his perceptions.
2. Given similar perceptions, two individuals may still differ in their affective and adaptational responses to these perceptions. Person A and person B, for example, may work in an office that both perceive as offering little support. Person A has a loving wife and children, many friends, and a history of interpersonal successes. Person B is recently divorced and has long regarded himself as an interpersonal failure. It is likely, then, that A and B would differ in their emotional responses to the office environment as well as in their resources for coping with or defending against the emotions aroused.

Sapira and his co-workers (30) presented films depicting two types of doctor-patient interaction to hypertensive and normotensive patients. In one film, the doctor was rude and disinterested in the patient, whereas in the other, he was relaxed and warm. The responses to the films, as measured in terms of blood pressure and pulse rate, were stronger in the hypertensive group than in the normotensive group. More important, in interviews following the films, the normotensive subjects clearly differentiated between the behavior of the good doctor and that of the poor doctor, whereas the hypertensive subjects did not. Thus, hypertensive persons may perceptually screen out potentially noxious stimuli as an adaptive response to a hyperreactive pressor system.

In practice, it is often difficult or impossible to distinguish an individual's perception of a situation from his defenses or coping strategies. Without attempting to differentiate perceptual factors from coping factors, however, it is possible to point to a number of studies that illustrate the interaction of personality and environmental variables. Several studies, for example, demonstrated that certain psychological defenses—especially denial—are associated with reduced 17-hydroxycorticosteroid secretion in what one would expect to be extremely stressful situations (19).

Katz and his colleagues (13) assayed 17-hydroxycorticosteroids in 30 women with breast tumors several days before biopsy was to be performed to determine if the patients had breast cancer. The subjects showed a broad range of values for adrenocorticosteroid secretion, none of them remarkably high. In addition, the subjects were extensively interviewed to determine their patterns of coping and the "adequacy of ego-defenses." Patients who used one of the three defensive patterns that the authors labeled "stoicism-fatalism," "prayer and faith," and "denial with rationalization" experienced considerably less disruption as judged by both the steroid hormone secretion rates and the psychiatric rating scores.

CONCLUSION

In conclusion, social ecological factors may have pronounced effects on human physiological processes. It is difficult at this point to make definite statements about the specific kinds of effects associated with different psychosocial stimuli, given the diversity of the populations, variables, and settings considered. It does appear, however, that the social stimuli associated with the relationship dimensions of support, cohesion, affiliation, and involvement generally have positive effects, such as enhancing normal development and reducing the recovery time from illness, for example. Personal development or system maintenance and system change dimensions—such as responsibility, work pressure, and change—can increase the likelihood of stress and disease.

People are more satisfied and tend to perform better when the relationship dimension areas are emphasized. They are also less likely to drop out, be absent, and report that they are sick. People also tend to do better in environments that emphasize the personal growth dimensions, but some personal costs may be involved. Students learn more, but are absent more often, in classrooms that emphasize competition and difficulty. Patients do better in treatment programs that emphasize autonomy and practical orientation. Students learn more in universities that emphasize independent study, high standards, criticism, and breadth of interests. Greater responsibility and greater work pressure, however, may have certain negative physiological concomitants, *i.e.*, greater arousal and an increased probability of cardiac dysfunction. Such effects probably also occur in patients who are pushed out of hospitals, as well as in students who are pushed to the limits of their performance capacities.

One might argue that most of the above-mentioned physiological changes could be subsumed under the rubric of "stress" and that the evidence merely indicates that too little support and clarity, or too much responsibility and change, may lead to stress responses. Individuals perform best within a restricted range of levels of the social environmental variables. The physiological changes could represent the concomitants of adaptive efforts that take place when a perceived social environmental dimension is not of optimal magnitude. Rather than labeling the process with the global term "stress," however, it may be more fruitful to attempt to understand the specific physiological effects of distinct social environmental dimensions. Evidence exists that different affective states are associated with distinguishable psychophysiological responses. Social-milieu dimensions might thus relate differentially to different physiological effects. This is in accordance with the notion of stimulus specificity, *i.e.*, that distinct stimuli (or situations) tend to evoke characteristic psychophysiological responses (29).

The measurement of the perceived social climate is relevant to the question of congruence between the person and his environment. Social environmental profiles could enable the clinician, physician, or social worker who is familiar with the probable physiological effects of various configurations of dimensions to aid their clients in making prudent choices or in effecting beneficial changes in their social milieus. A more complete understanding of social environmental dimensions could enable clinicians to predict which environments would be adverse or beneficial for particular patients and to suggest specific and limited changes in environments where individuals suffer from particular symptoms. The systematic measurement of social climates could thus become an important aspect of the work of the diagnostician.

We are beginning to understand how environments actually function. We can identify some important dimensions that allow discrimination among environments and are differentially related to human functioning. We can begin to identify certain coping and adaptive mechanisms that are related to the successful handling of environmental pressure and stress (25). Given this information, we will soon be in a position to enhance environmental competence by teaching people how to create, select, and transcend their environments (24).

There is a need for environmental "educators" or "managers," *i.e.*, people who help individuals or organizations maximize the utilization of their existing environments (32). Environmental educators could teach people about their environment, how to conceptualize its component parts and their interrelationships, and, most important, how to understand and control its potential impact on their everyday lives. Such information would be useful for physicians who wish to help their patients maximize the health-enhancing potential of their community settings.

REFERENCES

1. Alcohol and Health: New Knowledge. Washington DC, Department of Health, Education and Welfare, Government Printing Office, 1974

2. Brooks J, Mueller E: Serum urate concentrations among university professors. J A M A 195: 415–418, 1966

3. Caffrey B: Reliability and validity of personality and behavioral measures in a study of coronary heart disease. J Chronic Dis 21: 191–204, 1968

4. Caffrey B: Behavior patterns and personality characteristics related to prevalance rates of coronary heart disease in American monks. J Chronic Dis 22:93–103, 1969

5. Cobb S, Rose R: Hypertension, peptic ulcer and diabetes in air traffic controllers. J A M A 224: 489–492, 1973

6. Dalton K: The Premenstrual Syndrome. Springfield Ill, C C Thomas, 1964

7. Egbert L, Battit G, Welch C et al.: Reduction of postoperative pain by encouragement and instruction of patients: a study of doctor–patient rapport. N Engl J Med 270: 825–827, 1964

8. French J, Caplan R: Organizational stress and individual strain. In Marrows A (ed): The Failure of Success. New York, American Management, 1973

9. Friedman M: Pathogenesis of Coronary Artery Disease. New York, McGraw–Hill, 1969

9A Friedman, M, Rosenman R: Type A Behavior and Four Heart. New York, Alfred A. Knopf, 1974.

10. Holmes T, Masuda M: Life change and illness susceptibility. In Dohrenwend BS, Dohrenwend B (eds): Stressful Life Events. New York, John Wiley & Sons, 1974

11. Insel P, Moos R: Health and the Social Environment. Lexington Ma, DC Heath, 1974

12. Jenkins C: Social and epidemiologic factors in psychosomatic disease. Psychiatr Ann 2:8–21, 1972

13. Katz J, Weiner H, Gallagher T, Hellman L: Stress, distress and ego-defenses. Arch Gen Psychiatry 23: 131–142, 1970

14. Kellam S, Goldberg S, Schooler N et al.: Ward atmosphere and outcome of treatment of acute schizophrenia. J Psychiatr Res 5: 145–163, 1967

15. Kimball C: Psychological responses to the experience of open heart surgery. Am J Psychiatry 126: 348–359, 1969

16. Kornfeld D: The hospital environment: its impact on the patient. Adv Psychosom Med 8: 252–270, 1972

17. Liljefors I, Rahe R: An identical twin study of psychosocial factors in coronary heart disease in Sweden. Psychosom Med 32: 523–542, 1970

18. Lipowski ZJ: Psychosomatic medicine in a changing society: some current trends in theory and research. Compr Psychiatry 14: 203–215, 1973

19. Mason J: A review of psychoendocrine research on the pituitary adrenal cortical system. Psychosom Med 30: 576–607, 1968

20. Mausner B: An ecological view of cigarette smoking. J Abnorm Psychol 81: 115–126, 1973

21. Mechanic D: Social psychologic factors affecting the presentation of bodily complaints. N Engl J Med 286: 1132–1139, 1972

22. Moos R: Evaluating Treatment Environments: A Social Ecological Approach. New York, John Wiley & Sons, 1974

23. Moos R: Evaluating Correctional and Community Settings. New York, John Wiley & Sons, 1975

24. Moos R: The Human Context: Environmental Determinants of Behavior. New York, John Wiley & Sons, 1976

25. Moos R (ed): Human Adaptation: Coping with Life Crises. Lexington Ma, DC Heath, 1976

26. Moos R, Insel P (eds): Issues in Social Ecology. Palo Alto, Mayfield, 1974

27. Myers J, Bean L: A Decade Later: A Follow-Up of Social Class and Mental Illness. New York, John Wiley & Sons, 1968

28. Robertson E, Suinn R: The determination of rate of progress of stroke patients through empathy measure of patient and family. J Psychosom Res 12: 189–191, 1968

29. Roessler R, Engel B: The current status of the concepts of physiological response specificity and activation. Int J Psych Med 5: 359–366, 1974

30. Sapira J, Scheib E, Moriarty R, Shapiro A: Differences in perception between hypertensive and normotensive populations. Psychosom Med 33: 239–250, 1971

31. Skipper J, Leonard R: Children, stress and hospitalization: a field experiment. J Health Soc Behav 9: 275–287, 1968

32. Sommer R: Design Awareness. San Francisco, Rinehart Press, 1972

33. Thoroughman J, Pascal G, Jarvis J, Crutcher J: A study of psychological factors in patients with surgically intractable duodenal ulcer and those with other intractable disorders. Psychosom Med 29: 273–278, 1967

34. Wolf R: The measurement of environments. In Anastasi A(ed): Testing Problems in Perspective. Washington DC, American Council on Education, 1966

Part IV
Specific Disorders

21 Psychotherapeutic Management of Bronchial Asthma

PETER H. KNAPP

Bronchial asthma is a lifelong, often life-threatening disorder, in which a chronic disposition interacts with a variety of life circumstances to produce a variable and fluctuating pattern of illness. Its cause is not clear; presumably there is a genetic predisposition, although recent studies—particularly the striking investigation by Edfors-Lubs (7) of 7000 pairs of twins from the Swedish twin registry—show a much smaller concordance rate, and presumably a smaller biological component, than had previously been postulated. This study found symptom-specific concordance rates in monozygotic (MZ) twins to be 19% for asthma and 25% for all allergic disorders; in three-quarters of the cases, environmental factors must have had an overriding influence.

Recent biological evidence suggests that there are mechanisms whereby emotional conflicts can influence the pulmonary processes involved in asthma. These mechanisms may be operative at several levels: at the level of the hypothalamus and limbic system; at the level of the autonomic nervous system, where both parasympathetic and sympathetic activity may exacerbate or minimize immunological factors; and at the peripheral tissue level, where higher influences converge on receptors and the activities of the cyclic nucleotides (18). Experimental and clinical evidence suggests that psychological factors can influence pulmonary function in asthma either adversely or beneficially. This chapter will consider the variety of psychological approaches that have been used in the treatment of this disorder. First, however, a word of caution is in order regarding some of the more strictly medical aspects.

MEDICAL ASPECTS OF BRONCHIAL ASTHMA

The popular picture of an individual who is essentially well except for the occurrence of severe paroxysms in which he gasps for breath is largely a fiction. Hyperreactivity of the pulmonary tree may well be a lifelong trait in asthmatics, and some degree of pulmonary impairment tends to be chronic and persists between acute episodes, which themselves usually represent the peak of slower moving waves. Asthmatic congestion is caused by a combination of bronchospasm, edema, and hypersecretion in variable admixture. It builds up slowly, leading to a low-grade inflammatory thickening of the bronchial walls and a plugging of the bronchiolar lumens. The changes, which are present even in the acute disease state and certainly in the more chronic forms, cannot be rapidly and magically dissipated by any type of intervention. Indeed, anecdotal accounts have described patients in status asthmaticus who were treated by force of suggestion (*e.g.,* hypnosis) and then, feeling subjectively better, slipped off to sleep and to death, much as older clinicians warned they might if given morphine (14).

Medical management of this physiologically treacherous disease has undergone crucial developments as a result of the discovery that steroids have a powerful, presumably nonspecific, antiinflammatory action in cases of asthma. It has proved to be one of the disorders that respond dramatically to steroid treatment. Adrenocorticotropic hormone (ACTH), which was used in the earliest days of steroid therapy, was soon replaced by cortisone and its more concentrated synthetic congeners. The effects of steroid medication are profound: the symptoms of severe asthma can be strikingly ameliorated, if not in minutes, at least in hours and days. Sustained status asthmaticus is no longer a terrifying and uncontrollable crisis. The long-term consequences of steroid medication, however, are more problematical. More often than not, the underlying asthmatic process persists. The side effects of continued steroid administration—abnormal fat distribution, osteoporosis, the propensity for peptic ulceration, cataract formation, and hypertension—are distressing. It is difficult to be sure of a total reduction, rather than merely a delay, in the malignant consequences of the disease itself. In children, for instance, some estimates indicate that mortality rates have been even higher following the introduction of steroids than they were before (29).

These long-term effects become obscured in the glow of symptomatic relief that steroids bring; it is difficult to persuade patients, and many physicians for that matter, to attempt the difficult task of reducing them. The weaning process is complicated by the fact that large doses of steroids cause physiological suppression of natural pituitary-adrenal stimulation, so that a state of physiological dependence develops. Withdrawal is characterized by weakness, lassitude, apathy, and, in addition, often severe asthmatic relapse. The gradual reduction of exogenous steroids to a level approaching that produced by the body and and an increase in the period between doses (as in alternate-day treatment) are aids to the weaning process. Naturally, they succeed best when the disease process is not too severe and, perhaps, only when a high degree of determination is present on the part of both the patient and the therapist.

The use of topical steroids via inhalation is a possible further aid. It is limited, however, because systemic absorption, though less than when the drug is taken orally, still takes place, and it is difficult to predict the amount that will occur. During the past five years, a further advance has resulted from the introduction in Great Britain of beclamethasone diproprionate (Propaderm), a potent topical steroid administered by inhalation that has negligible systemic absorption. Rapidly accumulating experience with this drug suggests that many asthmatics can be maintained with its use, that they show minimal evidence of side effects or adrenal suppression, and that once the physiological dependence has been broken, a substantial number of patients may be enabled to do without steroids all together (10, 19, 27).

All these considerations have important implications for the total management of the asthmatic patient and for the role played in this management by psychotherapy. *Accurate medical and pathophysiological assessment of an asthmatic patient is essential.* The treating physician must know whether he is dealing with a mild and easily reversible disorder or with a stubborn, intractable, widespread pulmonary process. It follows from what has been said about drug treatment that the treating physician must also be alert to the symptomatic well-being that is achieved only by a large, suppressant dosage of steroids. Not only is an initial diagnostic assessment essential, but so is the continued evaluation of the course of the disease.

Thus, in almost all instances where the asthma involves significant impairment, *if psychotherapy is to be undertaken, it must be in conjunction with sound medical and allergic management.* At times, the psychological aspect of treatment can be encompassed by a medical specialist who has particular talent or who has had special training. Far less often, if ever, is the mental-health specialist equipped to assume responsibility for the medical aspects of treating a severely asthmatic patient. Joint therapy thus becomes necessary in most cases. Such a venture calls for close collaborative communication in order to minimize the patient's inevitable misunderstanding or even his unconscious exploitation of the differences between the two therapists.

PSYCHOTHERAPEUTIC APPROACHES TO THE TREATMENT OF ASTHMA

A wide variety of psychotherapeutic modalities have been applied to this difficult disorder. They include predominantly biological methods, particularly the use of psychotropic drugs; suggestive measures; behavior modification approaches; and psychotherapy in the more traditional sense, that is, interpersonal verbal therapy, which in turn may be subdivided into group, family, and individual approaches.

PSYCHOTROPIC DRUGS

Although the use of some of these has provided a measure of subjective relief, none—including amphetamine and the major phenothiazinelike tranquilizers—has been demonstrated to help asthmatic dysfunction significantly.

The tricyclic antidepressants may provide a possible exception to this statement. Experimentally, these agents have been found to exert a bronchodilatory effect in animals (3) as well as in some acute cases in humans (23). Early clinical reports also suggest that they have some effectiveness (11, 25, 32). It seems unlikely that these drugs will prove to have a dramatic effect on the established syndrome of asthma, but they remain a possible supplement to antiasthmatic regimens. Their own action may be pluralistic. The anticholinergic and antihistaminic properties of these compounds are well known; so are their effects in blocking catecholamine uptake. It is conceivable not only that they could act in a nonspecific way on depressed moods, but also that their augmentation of catecholamine action and their anticholinergic effects might have beneficial peripheral and even central effects.

SUGGESTION AND HYPNOSIS

The earliest experimental evidence bearing on the role of suggestion in treating asthma was the report in 1886 of Sir James MacKenzie, who described "rose asthma" (acute coryza, congestion, and wheezing) in a young woman who was disturbed by the sight of a paper rose under glass (22). Without evidence of reversible obstructive effects in the airways, of course, this remains a suggestive anecdote. Sporadic, increasingly sophisticated attempts to repeat this observation followed. The most successful of these was the recent series of experiments carried out by Luparello, McFadden, Lyons, and co-workers (21, 24). These authors performed whole-body plethysmographic studies on 40 subjects exposed to aerosolized saline. It was suggested to the subjects that the vehicle was an allergenic precipitant to which they had previously been found sensitive. Approximately half of their subjects responded with a clear-cut, relatively rapid reduction in airway conductance. This response was reversed when the saline was administered with the suggestion that it was a bronchodilator. Atropine blocked the bronchoobstructive effect, which implied vagal mediation.

This classic experiment has not been replicated. The systematic attempt to do so by Weiss *et al.* (35) with children was unsuccessful, possibly because it was difficult to involve these subjects in the experiment to the same degree as adults and possibly because the instrument used in the measurements was the relatively insensitive Wright peak-flow meter.

The use of direct suggestion with therapeutic intent has not been explicitly studied in asthma, but hypnosis has. This modality has its own complexities. The most dramatic evidence pertaining to its ability to influence allergic reactions is that provided by Black (4). He employed selected subjects who were capable of entering a deep hypnotic trance, and he observed marked amelioration of asthmatic symptoms in one chronic, severe, asthmatic patient. He also reported a highly significant shift in the Prausnitz-Küstner induced allergic response in that patient, as well as in a number of other hypnotized volunteers. The selection of subjects may have been a crucial factor. Black screened large numbers of individuals in order to obtain a final group who were capable of going into deep trance states. Phillip *et al.* (28) reported that the effect of suggestion on the forced-expiratory volume ($FEV_{1.0}$) was more marked in a group of ten intrinsic asthmatics than it was in a group of ten extrinsic asthmatics, where both groups were defined by their response to skin tests. White (36), who used a relatively insensitive instrument to assess pulmonary function, attempted to influence asthmatics suffering from clinical attacks. The patients reported subjective relief but provided no objective evidence of improved pulmonary function.

It is possible that hypnotherapy, when applied as a long-term treatment modality, may have cumulative benefits. Falliers (8) studied 120 asthmatic patients, using 115 control subjects who also suffered from asthma. The experimental group was treated with brief, rapid-induction hypnosis at weekly intervals. The control subjects were treated with suggestion to promote body relaxation. Both groups showed improvement, but the female patients showed significantly more improvement with hypnosis. By the end of a year, 59% were better and 8% worse in the hypnotized group, in contrast to the control group figures of 43% better and 17% worse ($p < 0.05$). One patient died in each group. It is not possible to exclude a general "physician interest" effect in this study, and one would want to know more about the exact characteristics of the populations involved. Nevertheless, this represents a beginning in the study of an important treatment modality.

Relaxation, as a form of quasi-suggestive therapy, has also been tried in the treatment of asthma, largely with children. Studies by Alexander *et al.* (1, 2) demonstrated that some effects, mostly in mild cases, resulted from relaxation instructions, which were relayed to the subjects in different ways. The approach has a certain rationale. Clinically, many asthmatics report that if they can only attain a state of "relaxation," then their tightness, wheezing, and congestion will improve. Although Alexander's results of controlled studies are promising, the effects observed are of short duration; it will be necessary to wait for further evidence before we can fully assess the clinical import of this approach.

BEHAVIOR MODIFICATION

A number of therapists have attempted to use the general paradigm of conditioning and have concentrated upon specific behavioral observation and instruction. Most prominent among these approaches has been the use of "desensitization," modeled after classical Pavlovian conditioning. The method attempts to ascertain, by means of a careful history, the psychosocial events that may act as triggering stimuli of asthma and to render these stimuli inert by a graduated revival of them in the patient's mind or, sometimes, in his actual experience. A variant of this method is to induce "reciprocal inhibition" by exposing the patient simultaneously to other stimuli with a presumed opposite action.

Successful treatment of individual cases using desensitization has been reported by Walton (34), Cooper (5), and Sergeant and Yorkston (30). Moore (26) extended these observations in a controlled study in which systematic "desensitization" was compared with two other treatment modalities: simple suggestion and a relaxation therapy. She studied 12 subjects, six of them children, and used a balanced incomplete block design, so that two forms of treatment were given to each patient and each of three treatments could be compared across eight subjects. All three forms of treatment led to some subjectively reported improvement. Significantly more improvement in the peak airflow, the physiological measure used, was found in the group that received behavioral modification therapy. The strength of this study lies in the fact that the patients were their own controls. A major share of the variance, however, was contributed by two subjects, who received reciprocal inhibition as the first treatment given to them and who improved markedly after it. It is possible that individual differences in the small group of subjects still played a major role. Few details were given about the initial status of the patients or the severity of their illness. The study needs replication, but it is nonetheless a landmark for systematic, controlled investigations into the therapeutic approaches in this area.

Operant conditioning has been used as another form of behavioral modification. Several observers have remarked on the fact that the classical or Pavlovian form of conditioning, in its pure form, requires extraordinarily stable laboratory conditions, and even when these have been obtained, its result proves to be a tenuous phenomenon, which readily disappears in "extinction" trials. An alternative approach, which employs a model perhaps more applicable to the human clinical situation, is that of operant conditioning. In this paradigm, the organism actively invokes a response to gain desired reinforcement. Conceivably, this type of behavior resembles that of the child who "thinks himself into asthma," in order to get a manifestation of the love he craves or to avoid some fantasied danger.

Vachon (33), using a forced oscillation method, obtained a second-by-second computer analysis of respiratory resistance. Subjects were instructed to keep a red light on, which had been programmed to flash when their resistance decreased below a critical level. He worked with two groups of mildly asthmatic patients without symptoms (15 in one group and 13 in the other), all of whom showed elevated airway resistance at rest. Both groups of experimental subjects exhibited a "learned" drop in airway resistance. They differed significantly from a control group of comparable mildly asthmatic subjects who were exposed to the same situation but given purely random reinforcement; this group showed no change. Careful analysis of the tidal volume measurements showed that the decrease in resistance was attributable to alterations of the bronchi and not to a shift in lung volume nor to changes in glottal contraction. The total net changes were modest, however. It remains to be seen whether their extent can be increased, and whether they can be shown to persist over time and be clinically significant.

A similar approach was tried by Kahn *et al.* (13), who attempted to induce asthma by exposing children to psychological stimuli and then to "countercondition" them, helping them "learn" bronchoconstriction by selectively reinforcing increases in the vital capacity, as measured by the $FEV_{1.0}$. This procedure was repeated on an intensive schedule and was then extended over six months in a series of refresher sessions. The group of children thus treated showed reductions in the frequency of asthmatic "attacks," the number of emergency hospital visits, and the amount of medication taken. These reductions were significantly greater than the reductions shown by a comparison group that was matched for a number of variables. It is not clear, however, that the comparison subjects received the same overall amount of interest and attention. Data demonstrating the effects of conditioning *per se* are lacking. Other authors (6) have been unable to obtain evidence of operant conditioning using a similar method, and they argued that Kahn's results may represent the effect of a general suggestive factor.

GROUP THERAPY

Groen (12) reported the results of experience with intensive group therapy in 1960 in the Netherlands. The program involved weekly meetings with patients and an extensive supportive medical and milieu regimen. Patients were categorized into three groups according to treatment: 1) treatment of symptoms only, 2) symptomatic treatment plus steroid treatment, and 3) both of the previous plus group therapy. "Improvement" rates were 17% in group 1, 28% in group 2, and 73% in group 3. The percentages of those determined to be "worse or dead" were ranked in the reverse order. The large number of variables involved as well as the difficulty in knowing the initial and final pathophysiological levels make this energetic endeavor difficult to assess.

FAMILY THERAPY

Liebman, Minuchin, and Baker (20) have reported the successful use of family therapy with seven chronic asthmatic children, ages 8 to 15, and four of them boys. All the children were reported initially to be dependent on steroid medication, and they required frequent additional treatment and emergency hospital visits. Six of them had had prior individual counseling. The authors found the parents to be "overdependent, especially on physicians" and, at the same time, "overly involved with the patients," so that they then became "manipulated" by the episodic crises of the illness. The psychiatrist, working with a pediatrician, treated the family as a whole. He taught specific breathing exercises and gave instruction both in the emergency treatment of asthmatic symptoms and in the uncovering of pathogenic relationships. The authors reported that for all seven patients, this program resulted in a marked reduction in the number of hospital visits, a cessation of the need for positive-pressure breathing as well as of desensitization regimens, and, most important, the discontinuance of steroids. If such striking results can be replicated in another sample of comparably ill patients, this form of treatment will be established on an impressive basis.

LONG-TERM PSYCHOANALYTICALLY ORIENTED PSYCHOTHERAPY

This method was applied to the original series of 26 adults and children reported by French and Alexander (9). They described substantial improvement in their series, but they did not give detailed physiological data or follow-up results. The approach has also been applied to severely incapacitated patients by Knapp *et al.* (15–17), Sperling (31), and others. To date, however, the necessary long-term follow-up studies are lacking. One can argue logically that such a long-term approach is indicated if one accepts the clinical evidence offered by these authors that an early disturbance occurred in the mother-child relationships and that hidden "primitive" conflicts are present in many asthmatic patients. Regardless of the exact formulation, the asthmatic patients who seek psychotherapy—or for whom it is recommended—are often chronically incapacitated and have major emotional problems. The therapist is necessarily involved in a long-term relationship with them.

Most observers feel that the classical psychoanalytic approach must be modified for asthmatic patients, as it must be for many individuals suffering from serious personality disturbances. In severe cases of asthma, it is often possible to find manifestations of "borderline" psychoticlike disturbances, although these may be masked by many effective areas of functioning. Different strategies are possible within a general psychoanalytic framework, such as the more nurturant and empathic approach advocated by some, or the more confrontative and active attack on the defensive and gratifying "use" of symptoms by the patient that is advocated by Sperling (31). Perhaps the most useful concept is that of therapeutic alliance. This must be established by meeting the patient where he or she is psychologically, which often means meeting many of his or her primitive needs. The bond is supportive, but once it has been established, one can often move— to a varying degree according to the patient's psychological resources—toward more interpretative therapy that seeks to understand many of the meanings of the illness.

PRACTICAL MANAGEMENT OF ASTHMA

How can these abstract views and as yet inconclusive findings best be translated into practical guidelines for the primary treating physician? I suggest the following somewhat arbitrary principles.

A *strong personal relationship,* based on the natural style of the doctor, is particularly important for the asthmtic patient, whose disease inevitably makes him anxious and to some extent dependent, although he may struggle against these attitudes. In such a relationship, the therapist should be reassuring in his overall attitude, but he should not necessarily give reassurance about specific points, as such specific reassurance is often proved false. He should be supporting and available, since the distress of the asthmatic patient often can only be allayed by the knowledge that medical help is never far off. He should be concerned about complaints that may seem trivial, because to the patient they are serious, even when (or, perhaps, especially when) they arise partly out of anxiety.

Reinforcement of independent efforts on the part of the patient may provide the antidote to the excessive dependence that such an initially supportive relationship might seem to foster. It involves sharing the responsibility for the management of his illness with the patient and giving positive reinforcement to his efforts at requiring less and less immediate medical help. One further suggestion may be helpful, although its scientific merits are still obscure: this is the use of physical exercise to a progressively expanded level of tolerance. It may be helpful physically and is certainly helpful psychologically.

Weaning from medication, especially, though not exclusively, from steroids, follows logically. It must be a true weaning, but one that respects the patient's need for relief from discomfort. Alternate-day administration of medication now seems solidly established as being both physiologically and psychologically useful. When the dosage is lowered, relapses must be expected. Often, the therapist has to take a very long range, but optimistic, try-and-try-again attitude. Beclamethasone, as mentioned earlier, may be invaluable in this effort.

Communication must be encouraged: let the patient talk, and remember that communication goes in two directions. The doctor must listen carefully. I recall visiting a distinguished colleague, himself a gifted natural therapist. After he had asked a frightened girl about her interim history, he routinely ordered a skin test for dog dander; she had told of having an attack of asthma on visiting her sister, who had a dog. What he failed to hear was that the attack had developed while she was driving to the sister's home. If his ear had been more finely tuned, he might have entertained at least a suspicion of autosuggestion!

A *genuine open-minded curiosity about the role of psychological factors should be maintained.* If one denies the possibility of their existence, one cannot see the evidence pointing to them, however obvious it may be. Once such evidence has emerged, it is not necessary to point it out immediately to the patient. In fact, doing so too soon is undesirable: he will only feel it as an accusation. If the connection between his psychological state and his illness is genuine and strong, and if the atmosphere in which it is elicited is inquiring and nonjudgmental, then this connection will emerge and become so clear that the patient will discover it himself. That is what really counts.

In short, the prescription is for eclectic office management. Its core is a positive, caring, doctor-patient relationship that offers support to the patient. Reinforcement is used to encourage the patient's independence. Understanding is directed toward causal patterns. When possible, the family is included to broaden the scope of understanding and to extend the pattern of reinforcement so that it comes from the whole social milieu surrounding the patient. Psychiatric consultation or referral may help in treating the most difficult and disturbed cases, but the majority of asthmatic patients can and should be managed, as they have been in the past, by primary physicians who are sensitive to the psychological issues they present.

REFERENCES

1. Alexander AB *et al.:* Systematic relaxation in asthmatic children. Psychosom Med 34 (5):38, 1972

2. Alexander AB et al.: Systematic flow rates in asthmatic children: relationship to emotional precipitants and anxiety. J Psychosom Res 16(6): 405–410, 1972

3. Avni J, Bruderman I: The effect of amitiyptyline on pulmonary ventilation and the mechanics of breathing. Pharmacologia (Berlin) 14: 184–192, 1969

4. Black S: Mind and Body. London, W Kimber, 1969

5. Cooper AJ: A case of bronchial asthma treated by behavior therapy. Behav Res Ther 1: 357, 1964

6. Danker PS, Miklich DR et al.: An unsuccessful attempt to instrumentally condition peak expiratory flow rate in asthmatic children. J Psychosom Med Res 19(3): 209–215, 1975

7. Edfors–Lubs ML: Allergy in 7000 twin pairs. Acta Allergol (kbh) 26: 249–285, 1971

8. Falliers CJ: Treatment of asthma in a residential center—a 15 year study. J Allergy 28: 513, 1970

9. French TM, Alexander F: Psychogenic factors in bronchial asthma. (Monograph) Psychosom Med 4: 2–94, 1941

10. Godfrey S, Konig P: Asthma treatment with the aerosol steroid beclamethasone diproprionate. Ann Allergy 33: 150–154, 1974

11. Goldfarb AA, Venutolo F: The use of an antidepressant drug in chronically allergic individuals. Ann Allergy 21: 667, 1963

12. Groen J: Experience with and results of group therapy with bronchial asthma. J Psychosom Res 4: 191, 1960

13. Kahn AU, Staerk M, Bonk C: The role of counterconditioning in the treatment of asthma. J Psychosom Res 18(2): 89–92, 1974

14. Knapp PH, Mushatt C, Nemetz SJ: Asthma, melancholia, and death. I. Psychoanalytic considerations. Psychosom Med 28: 114–133, 1966

15. Knapp PH, Nemetz SJ: Personality variations in bronchial asthma: a study of 40 patients: notes on the relationship to psychosis and the problem of measuring maturity. Psychosom Med 19: 443–465, 1957

16. Knapp PH, Nemetz SJ: Sources of tension in bronchial asthma. Psychosom Med 19: 443, 1957

17. Knapp PH, Nemetz SJ: Acute bronchial asthma. I. concomitant depression and excitement and varied antecedent patterns in 406 attacks. Psychosom Med 22: 42–56, 1960

18. Knapp PH, Vachon L, Mathe S: Psychosomatic aspects of bronchial asthma: a Review. In Weiss EB, Segal MS (eds): Bronchial Asthma, Its Nature and Management. Boston, Little, Brown & Co (in press)

19. Lal S, Harris DM, Banlla KK: Comparison of beclamethasone diproprionate aerosol and prednisone in reversible airway obstruction. Br Med J 3: 314–317, 1972

20. Liebman R, Minuchin S, Baker L: The use of structural family therapy in the treatment of intractable asthma. Am J Psychiatry 131(5): 535–540, 1974

21. Luparello RJ, Stein M, Park, CD: Effect of hypothalamic lesions on rat anaphylaxis. Am J Physiol 207: 911–914, 1974

22. MacKenzie JN: The production of "rose asthma" by an artificial rose. Am J Med Sci 91: 45, 1886

23. Mattila MJ, Muittari A: Modification by imipramine of the bronchodilator response to isoprenaline in asthmatic patients. Ann Med Int Fennica 57: 185–187, 1968

24. McFadden ER Jr, Luparello T, Lyons HA et al.: The mechanisms of action of suggestion in the induction of acute asthma attacks. Psychosom Med 31: 134–43, 1969

25. Meares RA, Mills JE et al.: Amitriptyline and asthma. Med J Aust 2: 25–28, 1971

26. Moore N: Behavior therapy in bronchial asthma—a controlled study. J Psychosom Res 9: 257–277, 1967

27. Morrow–Brown J, Storey G, George WHS; Beclamethasone diproprionate: a new steroid aerosol for the treatment of allergic asthma. Br Med J 1: 585–590, 1972

28. Philipp, RL, Wilde GJS, Day JH: Suggestion and relaxation in asthmatics. J Psychosom Res 16: 193, 1972

218

29. Schneer HI: The death of an asthmatic child. In The Asthmatic Child: Psychosomatic Approach to Problems and Treatment. New York, Hoeber, Harper & Row, 1963

30. Sergeant HGS, Yorkston N: Verbal desensitization in the treatment of bronchial asthma. Lancet 3121, 1969

31. Sperling M: A psychoanalytic study of bronchial asthma in children. In Schneer HI(ed): The Asthmatic Child. New York, Harper & Row, 1963

32. Sugihara H, Ishihara K, Noguchi H: Clinical experience with amitriptyline (Tryptanol) in the treatment of bronchial asthma. Ann Allergy 23: 422, 1965

33. Vachon L: Visceral learning of respiratory resistance. Psychosom Med 24: 471, 1971

34. Walton D: Application of learning theory to a case of bronchial asthma. In Eysenck HJ (ed): Behavior Therapy and the Neuroses. London, Pergamon Press, 1960

35. Weiss HH, Martin C, Riley J: Effects of suggestion on respiration in asthmatic children. Psychosom Med 32:(4) 409–415, 1970

36. White H: Hypnosis in bronchial asthma. J Psychosom Res 5: 272, 1961

22 Cardiovascular Disease

STEWART WOLF

Evidence that the highest neural centers are involved in cardiovascular phenomena has been available from time immemorial. More recent systematic studies of the effects of symbolic stimuli—*i.e.,* circumstances without intrinsic force but having a peculiar meaning for the individual concerned—have shown them to be capable of arousing a multitude of cardiovascular responses, including changes in heart rate, heart rhythm, and peripheral vascular function. Such psychosomatic phenomena are actuated by central regulators of autonomic activity and neurohormonal effects.

Among the cardiovascular disorders most clearly related to, or complicated by, psychosomatic mechanisms are palpitations and decreased exercise tolerance (with or without changes in the force or velocity of cardiac contraction), cardiac arrhythmias, certain electrocardiographic changes, essential hypertension, myocardial infarction, angina pectoris, and sudden death. Moreover, the alterations in electrolyte and water balance that are associated with emotional stress may aggravate congestive failure in those persons with already damaged hearts (6).

Successful therapeutic strategies have utilized the general principles outlined in the following pages as well as special approaches tailored to what is known of the temperamental characteristics that cluster in certain cardiovascular diseases.

PALPITATIONS AND REDUCED EXERCISE TOLERANCE

A common syndrome, one that resembles the "neurocirculatory asthenia" or "soldier's heart" of World War I, is characterized symptomatically by palpitation, lack of stamina, and often breathlessness. Physiologically, it is akin to the situation that prevails after prolonged bed rest or in persons who are "out of condition." Exercise tolerance is reduced because of an inordinate increase in pulse rate and cardiac output, together with insufficient cardiorespiratory coordination and often the failure of the normal drop in peripheral vascular resistance that accompanies exercise. Simple reassurance and an opportunity to talk over problems may be all that the patient requires, although in addition a graded program of exercise may be helpful.

Case 1. A 24-year-old housewife complained of palpitations, tightness in the throat, pain in the left chest, difficulty in breathing, and light-headedness. When she was 22, three years after the death of her father of coronary disease, her mother, who was unable to live harmoniously with her elder daughter, came to live with the patient. The older woman, a diabetic, was rigid, demanding, and untidy. The patient found her mother's behavior increasingly irritating. She could neither chastise nor modify her. She was deeply dependent on her, however, and she prided herself on tolerating her mother when her sister had been unable to do so.

220

In this setting of conflict and anxiety, her palpitations began, and they continued to occur until she came to the hospital. At her first visit, her exercise tolerance, as estimated from her pulse rate, was considerably impaired. During the time the patient was observed in the clinic, successive tests of exercise tolerance were made. The second test was made a few days after the sudden death of the patient's mother, to which she reacted with considerable guilt and depression. Although her resting heart rate was lower on this day, the exercise tolerance was more impaired than it had been on the previous day. During the interviews that followed, the patient was able to talk more freely about her relations with her parents and brother. She gained some understanding of her emotional development and, in addition, was reassured concerning the condition of her heart, as her symptoms had made her anxious about this. In the three months following the death of her mother, the patient gradually improved and became free of symptoms. Her exercise tolerance was then found to be normal.

The patient remained completely well for another seven months. At this time, she arranged for her husband to obtain work at her factory, and she intended to resign from her own job and have a baby. Her boss, who had obliged her by employing her husband, hinted that he would discharge him if she left the company. The patient felt frustrated and tense, but she was unable either to express her feelings to the boss or to leave her job. In this setting, she had a return of the former symptoms, though in a milder degree. Although her resting pulse rate was only slightly higher than it had been, her exercise tolerance was impaired and continued to be so for some months thereafter.

WORK OF THE HEART

It is evident that the work of the heart cannot be estimated with any degree of accuracy by means of reference to the amount of physical exertion actually undertaken. If the subject is "in training," his cardiovascular efficiency will be such that a relatively great load may be carried on with a minimum of work. On the other hand, whether he is in training or not, the heart may be called upon to work hard when the subject is sitting or reclining and contemplating, consciously or unconsciously, some troublesome personal problem. Pertinent to the work of the heart under these conditions is the adrenergic inotropic effect on the myocardium that is secondary to activity in the cardiac sympathetic nerves or to adrenomedullary secretion.

Theorell *et al.* (9) compared more than 2800 ballistocardiographic tracings made serially over a period of two or more years in 65 individuals who had suffered a well-documented myocardial infarction in the past with an equal number of individually matched controls. They found a striking correlation between the ejection velocity (as calculated from the IJ wave) and the prevailing emotional state in both the patients and the controls. In both naturally occurring life situations and in stress interviews, aggressive attitudes were associated with an accelerated ejection velocity, while attitudes of withdrawal and defeat were accompanied by slower ejection velocities. The alteration in contractile force that is responsible for the changes in ejection velocity presumably reflects differences in adrenergic activity by the sympathetic nerves of the heart.

ARRHYTHMIAS

A wide range of cardiac arrhythmias may be precipitated by stressful life experiences. Even those arrhythmias related to myocardial ischemia or other local disturbances in the myocardium appear to result from a disturbed balance of extrinsic neural control of the heartbeat. Engel and his associates (3) have been able to control atrial and ventricular arrhythmias by the techniques of biofeedback. The frequency of premature ventricular contractions (PVCs) may also be reduced during intense mental concentration (11). Stevenson *et al.* (7) found that patients with a variety of cardiac arrhythmias were notably anxious and insecure, some of them actually timorous. The psychotherapeutic approach to patients with cardiac arrhythmias has therefore emphasized measures directed at reducing anxiety, reassurance, sympathetic listening, and counseling.

Measures to combat anxiety that have been successful in reducing the frequency of cardiac arrhythmias have included transcendental meditation (TM) and other techniques, as well as reassuring talks with a physician in which problems and conflicts are discussed. Anxiolytic drugs are recommended only in situations of acute anxiety. The withdrawal of such agents after chronic administration may lead to a recrudescence of arrhythmias. The most helpful drug for relatively long-term use is propranolol in a dosage sufficient to block the cardiac effects of circulating catecholamines, but not so high as to interfere with neurotransmitter function in the sympathetic nerves to the heart.

Case 2. A 52-year-old bartender was brought to the emergency room of a hospital because of a sudden, severe, substernal pain associated with palpitation, dyspnea, and orthopnea. The symptoms had been present for approximately four hours when the patient was first seen by the physician. At that time, the patient appeared pale and weak and was perspiring profusely. His extremities were cold, and his pulses were difficult to feel. The heart rate was 150 beats per minute, and the beats appeared to be irregular. There were rales at both lung bases, but there were no other significant findings except for a blood pressure of 90/75 in both arms. An electrocardiogram revealed atrial flutter with a shifting block. The patient was rapidly digitalized. Several hours later, the rhythm was found to be atrial fibrillation. The following morning, he was in normal sinus rhythm and free of complaints. An exhaustive study of this patient failed to reveal any evidence of structural heart disease.

During the next 18 months, he had several such attacks. Some were treated in other hospitals, where attempts were made to discover an underlying heart disease. With one of the episodes, he had a grand mal seizure, but there were no significant neurological findings following the attack. The results of lumbar puncture showed the spinal fluid to be unremarkable. An electroencephalogram made several days after his seizure showed a normal pattern. Several examiners attempted to uncover personality conflicts in this patient that might have been of significance in producing the acute arrhythmias, but it was very difficult to get him to talk about himself.

Finally, through his brother, it was ascertained that the patient had been questioned concerning a neighborhood crime several days before the initial attack. This investigation had apparently been suddenly terminated, because of the intervention of a politically influential beer distributor. The beer distributor had then attempted to induce the patient to dispense the distributor's beer exclusively. When the owner of the tavern was unwilling to make this change, our patient was "caught in the middle." The first attack had occurred when the patient was at work, and it coincided with the distributor's entering the tavern to check up on the types of beer sold. All subsequent attacks could be traced to similar encounters with this beer salesman. The patient finally acknowledged the whole story, with evident relief. He was greatly strengthened by the understanding support of the physician. Thereafter, he was observed in the clinic for six months, and no further recurrences were noted.

HYPERTENSION

A study of personality adjustment among patients with hypertension did not delineate any characteristic personality "type," but it did yield strikingly similar data regarding the subjects' values, attitudes, and way of life (10). By and large, the hypertensive patients had grown up feeling the need to excel but, at the same time, to avoid conflict or overly vigorous self-assertion. These strivings, often opposed as they were, frequently led to dilemmas, and they were manifested by wary, tentative, and noncommital attitudes with respect to important interpersonal relations and major endeavors in life.

In this study, the treatment of hypertension consisted of encouraging the patient to discuss his life, his problems, and his early relations with his parents, siblings, and others. Unconscious material was elicited from dreams and associations. The patient was allowed to express hostility as freely as he would, and the doctor consistently maintained a supporting, friendly attitude. Frequently, other members of the family were seen, and their support was enlisted if possible.

In all, 14 of 114 closely observed patients became and have remained normotensive. All the individuals initially displayed the usual evidence of essential hypertension, including blood pressure readings consistently higher than 160/94, but none had signs of primary renal disease, endocrine tumor, or congenital vascular anomaly. Since, however, we can only know what the level of blood pressure is when it is being measured, it is possible only to say that when we first came in contact with these 14 subjects, their blood pressure readings were consistently above normal. In each, in association with a changed attitude and orientation, the readings became normal and stayed so, except for transitory reactions to specific stimuli. This change took place without surgery and without drugs.

Case 3. A 50-year-old municipal employee had been born into a restrained family, where the domineering mother never allowed him to express anger. He grew

Table 22-1. LOSS OF EVIDENCE OF HYPERTENSION IN 14 PATIENTS

CASE	SEX	AGE WHEN DISCOVERED	KNOWN DURATION OF (YEARS)	TOTAL PERIOD OF OBSERVATION (YEARS)	DURATION OF NORMAL B.P. TO TIME OF LAST OBSERVATION (YEARS)
1	M	34	12	7	3
16	M	25	4	4	3
17	M	17	1	5	4
18	F	40	10	6	2
21	M	23	1	7	6
26	F	41	15	6	2
29	M	47	2	8	4
43	M	38	1	6	5
44	M	23	7	6	5
47	M	31	½	5	4
67	F	33	3	6	4
68	M	45	½	4	3
108	M	48	1	3	2
113	M	23	1	2	1

up earnest and compliant, in contrast to his independent, self-reliant older brother who did well in business. At age 36, he married a school teacher, temperamentally similar to his mother, who emphasized his limitations, made him take speech training, and refused to divulge the amount of her salary to him. She and his mother were not congenial; he observed, "I was caught between two strong women." His hypertension was first recognized when his job as a meter inspector, which he had held for 28 years, was threatened because of political change.

In the clinic, he was given strong reassurance and support, and he was encouraged to express his feelings freely. Moreover, long discussions of his recollections and of his relations to his mother were undertaken. His wife was called in and her support was enlisted. As he became increasingly relaxed and self-confident during treatment, he was successful in defying his boss at work, and he noted that his wife was "softening up." His blood pressure remained normal for the next four years, except for brief episodes of elevation associated with specific threats. On one occasion, his blood pressure rose to 165/110 during a discussion of his more successful brother. On another occasion, a less marked rise in blood pressure occurred following a psychological testing procedure that he felt revealed inadequacies in him.

CORONARY HEART DISEASE

Coronary atherosclerosis may exist, even in advanced form, without making its presence known through the occurrence of symptoms or a limitation of exercise tolerance. On the other hand, angina pectoris, congestive heart failure, myocardial infarction, and fatal cardiac arrhythmias may be directly attributable to coronary atherosclerosis. The precise distribution of the atheromas may be a crucial factor; so, too, may be the ability of the coronary arteries to dilate under appropriate circumstances. There is evidence correlating the vasomotor behavior of the coronary arteries to emotionally stressful experiences, as well as less clear evidence that relates the atheromatous process itself to psychosomatic mechanisms. In any case, the whole range of manifestations of coronary heart disease offers significant opportunities for a psychotherapeutic approach.

ANGINA PECTORIS

Angina, which is clearly precipitated by emotionally stressful events, has yielded dramatically to a diverse collection of surgical procedures, exercises, and drugs including, notably, placebos. Psychotherapy that is not camouflaged in one of the above more tangible maneuvers has not been significantly successful in the treatment of angina.

CONGESTIVE HEART FAILURE

A condition of limited cardiac reserve with susceptibility to congestive heart failure may be aggravated by tachycardia, arrhythmias, changes in myocardial metabolism or the force and velocity of cardiac contraction, coronary vasoconstriction, increased peripheral resistance, or other peripheral disturbances, such as increased salt and water retention by the kidneys. All these mechanisms have been shown to be reactive in an individual's response to meaningful life experiences. Attitudes of withdrawal and emotional depression appear to be particularly associated with a diminished force and velocity of cardiac contraction (9). Depressive moods may also be associated with renal salt and water retention and with resistance to diuretic therapy (6).

Psychotherapy in such cases is therefore best directed at relieving the depressed state. Antidepressants have a place here, but they should be employed only for brief periods. More lasting benefit in resolving the depressive features associated with congestive heart failure has been obtained through reassuring contacts with the physician that offer opportunities for the patient to review interpersonal relationships, his goals, and his aims in life. Often, discussions with spouses or bosses and colleagues at work have helped to encourage a patient, which in turn has alleviated the fluid and electrolyte retention associated with depressive moods.

The converse, hyperdynamic state of the cardiovascular system also appears to increase the susceptibility to congestive heart failure in a person with an already damaged heart. Here, the psychotherapeutic effort should be directed toward alleviating anxiety, reducing agitation and tension, and restoring confidence.

MYOCARDIAL INFARCTION

Myocardial infarction has been shown to occur most typically under circumstances of emotional drain, *e.g.,* in association with bereavement or after unusual challenges associated with frustration and disappointment (2). This striking emotional setting for such an important and widespread disease led the author to compare the coronary-prone person with Sisyphus, the mythological king of Corinth, who, when condemned to Hades, was required to push a huge stone up the side of a hill. Each time he was near the top, it would roll down again; thus he was required to continue to labor without ever experiencing a sense of achievement. Friedman and Rosenman (4) have elegantly documented the association between myocardial infarction and their so-called type-A behavior pattern, in which the person is found to have aggressive drives and an overwhelming sense of the pressure of time. One should also emphasize the aspect of lack of satisfaction, however, the joyless devotion to hard work has been considered characteristic of "coronary" patients since Osler's observations.

The most desirable time to initiate psychotherapy in cases of coronary heart disease would be before the infarction occurs. Groover (5), in a study of the incidence of myocardial infarction among Air Force personnel at the Pentagon, reported suggestive evidence that myocardial infarction might be avoided at periods of special susceptibility by removing the subject from his daily work responsibilities, allowing him to rest, and providing him with sedation and strong reassurance.

THE ACUTE PHASE

There is highly persuasive evidence that the cardiac arrhythmias associated with acute myocardial infarction are mediated reflexively via central neural connections, and that these in turn may be influenced by impulses from the frontal lobes. Such interactions, especially in the presence of fright, may result in serious bradycardia that can lead to fatal cardiac arrest or ventricular arrhythmias culminating in ventricular fibrillation. Hence, there is a rationale for the prompt administration of anxiety-reducing drugs, such as morphine, during the acute phase. Reassuring behavior on the part of the medical attendants may be of equal life-saving importance.

THE PERIOD IN INTENSIVE CARE

The potentially pathogenic nature of coronary care units has been observed. The heart of the patient who has had a recent myocardial infarction may display exaggerated responses in anxiety-provoking circumstances. The events taking place on the ward, the presence of visitors, or contacts with nurses and other personnel may touch off such abnormal responses. It is important, therefore, that an ambience of competent solicitude, reassurance, and emotional support is provided in the coronary care unit.

CONVALESCENCE

The period when the patient is in the hospital offers an opportunity for more individualized psychotherapy as well as for instituting those changes in goals and plans that are appropriate to his recovery and his maintenance of well-being. Often the physician must contend with an attempt at denial by his patient, who may refuse to recognize the gravity and implications of his experience. A period of reactive depression may ensue later, or, alternatively, an attitude of bravado and impatience with restrictions may develop. This is a time when the presence of an alert and receptive listener may be of great help to the patient. When suppressed or repressed anxieties, self-doubts, anger, and the like finally find expression, the way is clear for the physician to engage the patient in a thoughtful analysis of his career goals and other objectives in life, in planning a reasonable and workable approach to them, and in making whatever changes in his pattern of life that may be required.

Regular physical exercise has been found to be a "morale builder" in many people and to have considerable effect in boosting an individual's sense of well-being and capability. Before discharge, a patient should be counseled concerning a prudent program of gradually increasing exertion, the gradual resumption of his normal sexual activity, and the avoidance of sudden, violent exercise, at least until complete recovery is judged to have occurred.

POSTCONVALESCENCE

Whether or not the physician maintains contact with his patient through periodic visits, and, if so, how intense the contact should be, are decisions that depend upon the individual features of the case and the needs of the patient.

PROPHYLAXIS

Certain prophylactic principles that are applicable specifically to coronary artery disease, as well as to psychosomatic disorders in general, derive from a social environment that is stable, reasonably predictable, and supportive.

Little attention has been accorded factors that may sustain the person, protect him against abandonment, and reduce his stress and thus the likelihood of illness. It has been widely accepted that the probability of coronary atherosclerosis, myocardial infarction, and sudden death is enhanced not only by obesity, hypertension, and diabetes, but also by a way of life that includes a high consumption of animal fats, cigarette smoking, and little muscular exercise, together with a pattern of behavior characterized by tireless striving and "doing things the hard way" without commensurate satisfactions. Hence, these aspects of life-style are collectively referred to as "risk factors."

Social forces that may counteract the effects of such "risk factors" were encountered in studies of the Italian-American town, Roseto, Pennsylvania. The death rate from myocardial infarction in Roseto was found to be less than half that of surrounding towns (8). The outstanding features of the community are its close family and community ties, the respected status of the elderly, and a stable, unambiguous male-female relationship in which the man is automatically conceded the primary position (1). The studies in Roseto illustrate that social stability and mobility are not necessarily antithetical; like a ship underway, the community is stable with respect to certain buffetings, but yet it moves forward. Thus, Roseto has been economically prosperous in comparison to its neighbors and innovative with respect to community projects. An unusually high percentage of high school entrants go on to graduation, and a similarly unusual percentage of them complete a four-year college course. It is tempting to speculate that the oft-proposed relationship between health and self-esteem, self-confidence, and optimism has a sound scientific basis. In any case, it seems appropriate to supplement our focus on emotional stress with attention to the forces that counteract stress and sustain the person.

REFERENCES

1. Bruhn JG: An epidemiological study of myocardial infarctions in an Italian–American community. J Chronic Dis 18: 353, 1965

2. Bruhn JG, McCrady KD, duPleissis AL: Evidence of "emotional drain" preceding death from myocardial infarction. Psychiatr Dig 29: 34–40, 1968

3. Engel BT, Melman KL: Operant conditioning of heart rate in patients with cardiac arrhythmias. Pav Soc J 1967

4. Friedman M, Rosenman R: Association of specific overt behavior pattern with blood and cardiovascular findings. JAMA 169: 1286, 1959

5. Groover ME: Clinical evaluation of a public health program to prevent coronary artery disease. Trans Coll Phys 24: 105, 1957

6. Schottstaedt WW, Grace WJ, Wolff HG: Life situations, behavior patterns and renal excretion of fluid and electrolytes. JAMA 157: 1485–1488, 1955

7. Stevenson IP, Duncan CH, Ripley HS: Variations in the electrocardiogram with changes in emotional state. Geriatrics 6: 164, 1951

8. Stout C, Morrow J, Brandt EN, Wolf S: Unusually low incidence of death from myocardial infarction. Study of an Italian–American community in Pennsylvania. JAMA 188: 845–849, 1964

9. Theorell T, Blunk D, Wolf S: Emotions and cardiac contractility as reflected in ballistocardiographic recordings. Pavlovian J 9(2): 65–75, 1974

10. Wolf S, Cardon PV, Shepard EM, Wolff HG: Life Stress and Essential Hypertension. Baltimore, Williams & Wilkins, 1955

11. Wolf S, Goodell H: Behavioral Science in Clinical Medicine. Springfield Ill, C C Thomas, 1976

23

Anorexia Nervosa

HILDE BRUCH

The condition of self-inflicted starvation, in the absence of recognizable organic disease, is usually diagnosed as *anorexia nervosa* in the English-speaking world; in the German literature, it is referred to as *Pubertaetsmagersucht*. These names, which focus on the most dramatic aspects of the disorder, may actually describe two essentially different syndromes. It is of decisive dynamic significance whether a patient is preoccupied with body size and a relentless pursuit of thinness due to a phobic avoidance of being fat, or whether the patient's eating function itself is disturbed for a variety of reasons, with true loss of appetite as a result.

The term *anorexia nervosa* is a misnomer for the classic syndrome; *Magersucht*, the mania to be thin, comes closer in its meaning to the key issue. This preoccupation with body size is a late step in the abnormal development of individuals who have lived their lives in dread of being "a nothing." By the time the abstinence from food begins to take place, they may have been engaged for years in a desperate but futile struggle to establish a sense of control and identity. Concern with control —with being in charge of one's own body and leading one's own life—is the basic psychological issue in classic or *primary anorexia nervosa*.

It is essential to distinguish this genuine syndrome from an atypical form in which the eating function itself is disturbed as a result of a variety of underlying causes, for which no common denominator has been found. Much of the confusion about the causes and the treatment of this condition has resulted from the failure to differentiate between the primary form and the atypical picture. Anorexia nervosa used to be so rare that until recently, few doctors had observed more than an occasional case. The incidence of anorexia nervosa, however, is increasing, and thus the delineation of these different clinical pictures has become possible.

HISTORY OF THE CONCEPT OF ANOREXIA NERVOSA

Since the description of anorexia nervosa a little more than 100 years ago, a certain atmosphere of controversy has attached itself to the discussion. Lasègue (13) considered some hysterical disturbance in the digestive tract to be the starting symptom, and he accordingly named the condition *anorexie hystérique*. Gull (11) attributed the want of appetite to a "morbid mental state—I believe, therefore, that its origin is central and not peripheral," and he coined the term "anorexia nervosa." Both authors emphasized the absence of somatic disease. Gull also commented on the restless hyperactivity seen in patients with this disorder.

In spite of the short history of our knowledge of anorexia nervosa and the rarity of this disorder, there exists an amazingly large literature, which is characterized by considerable disagreement. The whole issue became even more confused when Simmonds (19), a pathologist, reported in 1914 that he found destructive lesions in the pituitary gland of an emaciated woman who had died following delivery. The whole approach changed and every case of malnutrition was then explained as due to some endocrine deficiency, which resulted in increased vagueness about what was to be diagnosed as anorexia nervosa. At present, there is renewed interest in possible endocrine and neurophysiological factors, and studies have been carried out with greatly refined laboratory techniques. It is not yet possible, however to establish whether such hormonal deviations are the cause or the result of the malnutrition (3, 10).

When, during the 1930s, a psychological syndrome of anorexia nervosa was differentiated from so-called Simmonds' disease, psychoanalytic thinking dominated the field. Investigations focused on exploring the disturbed eating, the "oral" component, in the hope of explaining the whole complex picture through one psychodynamic formulation. The high point of this approach is represented by a paper published in 1940 that claimed, "psychological factors have a certain specific constellation centering around the symbolization of pregnancy fantasies involving the gastrointestinal tract" (22). Even today, "fear of oral impregnation" is still looked for as a casual factor.

There has been a definite change in the whole approach to this disorder since about 1960, when reports about larger patient groups began to appear. There now exists a convergence of opinion that the true anorexia nervosa syndrome must be differentiated from unspecific types. Such reports have come from such geographically scattered countries as England, Sweden, Australia, Russia, and Italy (8, 9, 12, 15, 16, 17, 20, 21). The somatic picture in both forms looks deceptively alike; amenorrhea is associated with severe weight loss and various signs of malnutrition. Primary anorexia, however, is characterized by an intense interest in food and extreme hyperactivity, whereas in the atypical form, loss of appetite, fatigue, and indolence are common (5).

PRIMARY ANOREXIA NERVOSA

In this form, the patient's need to be thin, the fear of gaining weight, overshadows all other symptoms. The basic psychological issue is a frantic effort to establish a sense of control and identity. The manifest picture is usually preceded by a year or two of behavior changes and mood disturbances. It is this form that has been found to be occurring with increasing frequency (5).

Characteristically, the disorder has its onset close to puberty, with a second peak occurring at around 18 years of age. In the primary group, the occurrence of the disease during prepuberty is not uncommon; this seems to be the characteristic time when it occurs in male patients. Although the atypical picture usually develops somewhat later, it may be seen in pubescent girls. The age of menarche is within the normal range in both groups. Amenorrhea is characteristic, although it is a somewhat less consistent finding in the atypical group. The decisive differences between the groups are found in the psychological constellation.

As previously mentioned, the leading dynamic issue in the genuine syndrome is the "fear of fatness." The angry refusal to eat serves to maintain an extreme degree of thinness. In evaluating the underlying problems, a clear-cut distinction must be made between the issues of the developmental impasse that results in anorexia nervosa and the secondary, even tertiary, problems and complications that develop in the wake of it. The failure to make this distinction has led to much confusing misinformation in the older reports on the behavior of the patients and on family attitudes.

The true syndrome is amazingly uniform, although distinctive differences may exist in the way the basic problems manifest themselves in individual patients. Three areas of disordered psychological functioning can be recognized: first, there is a disturbance in body image and body concept of delusional proportions; second, one may observe an inaccurate and confused perception and cognitive interpretation of stimuli arising in the body, with inaccurate hunger awareness being the most pronounced deficiency; third, a paralyzing sense of ineffectiveness is found that pervades all the patient's thinking and activities. Further, specific family transactions and developmental patterns are found to be associated with this disorder.

BODY IMAGE DISTURBANCES

Of pathognomonic significance is the vigor and stubbornness with which the patient's often gruesome emaciation is defended as normal and right (5). The true anorectic has a skeletonlike appearance, actively maintains it, and denies its abnormality. In the atypical syndrome, in which the same pitiful degree of emaciation may be reached, the patients will complain about their weight loss and sickly appearance.

The patient's misperception of her size may be expressed by her interpretation of the increasing weight during puberty and of the developing curves as excessive and "too fat." Since anorectic patients uniformly say that they dieted because they felt they were "too fat," it has often been assumed that anorexia nervosa is preceded by an obese phase. In my observations, this is true in only a fraction of the cases, probably not more than 15% to 20%, and in these, only mild degrees of overweight have been noted.

Patients who make progress in therapy will express bewilderment about their inability to see themselves realistically. One girl admitted, "I really cannot *see* how thin I am. I look into the mirror and still cannot see it. I know that I am thin because when I feel myself, I feel nothing but bones." A realistic body image is a precondition for recovery in cases of anorexia nervosa. Patients will gain weight for a variety of reasons, but no real or lasting cure is achieved unless the misperception of their body image is corrected. Such a change occurs during psychotherapy as the patients develop awareness of their own identity. It can also be brought about through direct confrontation with their starved appearance, although there is no evidence that it occurs faster or is more effective when induced by this means.

Another disturbance is the failure to experience their body as being their own. Not uncommonly, anorectic patients, as well as their families, conceive of the whole illness as something "that happened," not as something that the patients actively do in their efforts to extricate themselves from family enmeshment. As they come to recognize their problems, many will confess that they felt that they were hurting their parents by not eating, but they may have been completely unaware that they themselves were undergoing the ordeal and misery of starvation.

MISPERCEPTION OF BODILY FUNCTIONS

The symptom that arouses the most concern, compassion, frustration, and rage in others is the anorectic's refusal to eat. This abstinence from food is the origin of the name *anorexia*. Although there is no true loss of appetite, the awareness of hunger in the ordinary sense seems to be absent. This failure to recognize the signs of nutritional need and the confusion with regard to hunger awareness are part of the essential underlying personality disturbances and are closely related to other developmental deficits. Although their gastric activity is similar to that observed in normal subjects and although they are able to sense the contractions, these patients will deny feeling hungry (18). They are also significantly inaccurate in identifying the amounts of food that are introduced into their stomach (7).

In spite of their stubborn refusal to eat, anorectic patients are frantically preoccupied with food, continuously talk about it, collect recipes, and prepare meals for others and force them to eat, while they refuse to eat even a bite. Most develop unusual, even bizarre, highly individualistic food habits, becoming more and more specialized in what they permit themselves to eat. They will usually allow themselves some small amount of protein-rich food, whereas carbohydrates and fats are avoided as if they were poison. They will eat more and more slowly, taking hours to finish even the smallest meal. It is noteworthy that dawdling and continuous preoccupation with food may be commonly observed during starvation for external reasons.

Anorectic individuals will complain of feeling "full" after a few bites of food or even a few drops of fluid. Some will feel "full" by watching others eat, or having "people eat for me." This sense of fullness appears to be a phantom phenomenon involving a projection of memories of formerly experienced sensations. In the advanced stages of emaciation, a true loss of appetite may result from the severe nutritional deficiency, which seems similar to the complete lack of interest in food in the late stages of starvation during a famine.

In some patients, the abstinence from food is alternated with enormous eating binges, which are usually started without an awareness of hunger and are often followed by self-induced vomiting. Although such patients identify with the abstinent phase, they experience the overeating as a submission to something that overwhelms them; they are terrified by this loss of control. Even those who do not indulge in binge eating fear that they may not be able to exercise control over their eating if they dare to relax their rigid discipline. In their fight against fatness and to remove unwanted food from their bodies, many resort to self-induced vomiting and enemas, or the excessive use of laxatives and, increasingly often, of diuretics, which may result in serious disturbances in their electrolyte balance.

Another characteristic manifestation of these patients' falsified body awareness is their *hyperactivity,* which may take the form of walking by the hour or doing calisthenics to the point of exhaustion. Patients who continue in school will spend long hours on their homework, intent on having perfect grades. This often precedes the abstinent phase and hyperactivity. Denial of fatigue persists until the emaciation is far advanced. The subjective feeling is that of not being tired, of wanting to do things. This stands in marked contrast to the lassitude, fatigue, and avoidance of any effort that are signs of chronic food deprivation, which patients in the atypical group regularly complain about.

One might also consider the failure of sexual functioning and the absence of sexual feelings as falling within the area of perceptual and conceptual deficits, although the possibility that some form of gonadal failure contributes to the loss of sexual interest continues to be discussed. Other bodily sensations, such as temperature awareness or sensitivity to pain, are also incorrectly recognized or responded to. Anorectics appear to be deficient in identifying emotional states as well, and they describe their feelings of anxiety or other emotional reactions with a limited vocabulary. Even severe depressions may remain masked and unexpressed.

THE SENSE OF INEFFECTIVENESS

The discovery that anorectic patients are characterized by this deep sense of ineffectiveness—which is associated with the conviction of acting only in response to the demands of others, of not doing anything because one wants to—came as a surprise in view of the vigorous and stubborn defiance with which anorectics present themselves. It also stands in contrast to the reports of unusually good, even perfect, early development. These youngsters had been the pride and joy of their parents, and great things were expected of them. Detailed inquiry will reveal, however, that they had functioned with robotlike obedience. Parents find it difficult to recognize that such extreme conformity is a cover-up for serious problems, self-doubt, and an inability for self-assertion.

It has always been puzzling that commonplace events or trivial remarks seem to precipitate this very serious illness. Frequently, the patient undertakes the drastic dieting when faced with new experiences, such as going to camp or a new school (in the younger group), or, later on, entering college. In these new situations, they feel in some way at a disadvantage, and this is expressed as a fear of being "too fat" or not athletic enough. When the planned lower weight is reached, it is "not enough," because much more than weight loss has been expected, and being and staying thin becomes a goal in itself. Since no manipulation of the body and its size can possibly provide the experience of self-confidence, self-respect, or self-directed identity, the patient's pursuit of thinness becomes more frantic, the amounts of food smaller and smaller, and the aimless activity to "burn off calories" more hectic.

FAMILY TRANSACTIONS

As puzzling as the nearly uniform reports about the trouble-free childhood of the older patient are the descriptions of their families as "happy." The literature on the family background in anorexia nervosa is particularly unsatisfactory, since most of the earlier reports refer to a variety of clinical pictures and deal with the disturbed patterns after the condition has existed for some time (5).

The distribution of patients according to socioeconomic status appears to have some significance, since similar findings are reported from different countries. In my own group, more than half were of upper-class background and very few came from the lower class. Atypical anorexia develops more often in patients from the middle or lower classes. The success-, achievement-, and appearance-orientation of such wealthy families appears to be related to the patient's frantic search for something that earns them "respect."

The families are of small size, but in only a few instances are such patients "only" children. The position of the patient's being the first of two girls appears relatively often, and there is a conspicuous paucity of sons among these families. The age of the parents at the time of the birth of the later anorectics was about 30 years; about half the patients were first-born children.

The families appear to be stable, with few broken marriages, and the parents will emphasize the "happiness" of their homes. It is only through extended contact that it can be recognized that underlying the apparent marital harmony, there is a deep disillusionment with each other, with secret competition regarding who is the better parent. The mothers are often women of achievement or career women frustrated in their aspirations, who are conscientious in their conception of motherhood. They are subservient to their husbands in many details, without truly respecting them. The fathers, despite a social and financial success that is often considerable, feel in some sense "second best." They appear to be enormously preoccupied with outer appearances in the physical sense of the word, admiring fitness and beauty, as well as expecting proper behavior and measurable achievements from their children.

The later anorectic patients were well cared for as children. They were exposed to many stimulating influences in education, the arts, athletics, and the like, but this was done without encouraging or reinforcing initiative or self-expression. Thus, reliance on their own inner resources, ideas, or autonomous decisions has remained undeveloped. Pleasing compliance has been their way of life, offering a facade of normalcy, which turns into indiscriminate negativism when adolescence demands independence instead of conforming obedience.

Evidence of a disregard of the patient's needs and emotions can be readily recognized in the ongoing transactions as observed in conjoint family sessions.

Parents will focus on the patient's weight loss as the only complaint, and they will stress the nuisance value of the illness. Many appear to be impervious to the emotional needs and reactions of the patients, in the past as well as in the present. Even the weight loss may not arouse their concern until it is far advanced; in one instance, the patient herself asked the family physician to tell her parents that she was seriously sick.

A DEVELOPMENTAL MODEL

In order to visualize how a child fails to develop an adequate sense of self-effective-ness, one must conceive of the child's personality development as being related, from birth on, to two forms of experiences. A child's behavior may be differen-tiated into that *initiated* in himself and that which occurs *in response* to external stimuli. Sufficient, appropriate responses to those clues that originate in the child are essential for normal development, in addition to the stimulation from the environment. This principle applies to all areas of development. How it operates can be observed in the feeding situation, which is also the area in which there is most interaction between mother and child in the first year of life. If the mother offers food in response to signals that indicate nutritional need, the growing child will gradually develop a definite concept of "hunger" as a sensation distinct from other tensions or needs. If, on the other hand, a mother's reaction is continuously inappropriate—be it neglectful, oversolicitous, inhibiting, or indiscriminately per-missive—then the outcome for the child will be a perplexing confusion, and he will not learn to differentiate among his being hungry, his being sated, and his suffering from some other discomfort (5).

Not only this confusion in hunger awareness, but many other deficits develop out of such inappropriate interactions as well. If the parent's responses to child initiated clues are continuously inappropriate or contradictory, the child will grow up unable to experience himself as being in control of his body and its functions, *i.e.*, he will lack the conviction of living his own life. Such deficits in basic psychic orientation can be recognized as core issues in cases of primary anorexia nervosa.

The early feeding histories of such patients, which were reconstructed in great detail, are conspicuous in their blandness. The mothers reported with pride that the child never gave them any trouble and ate exactly what was put before him. Some would report how they always "anticipated" their child's needs, never per-mitting him to feel "hungry." Since these mothers are reasonably well-informed about a child's needs, the outer picture may be that of a normal, well-nourished, and well-functioning child.

ATYPICAL ANOREXIA NERVOSA

In contrast to the strong similarities in the dynamics of cases of primary anorexia nervosa, no general picture can be drawn for the atypical group (5). In the latter, the loss of weight is incidental to some other problems, frequently complained of, or valued only secondarily for its coercive effect. Often, a desire to stay sick in order to remain in the dependent role is found in these patients, in constrast to the struggle for an independent identity that is found in the primary anorectic group. Assignment to the atypical group is based on the absence of the character-istic features of the primary syndrome that were just described; the illness is as serious and difficult to treat, however, as the primary form.

The atypical form may occur in chronic neurotic disorders, or it may be part of schizoid reactions. Such patients will be more disturbed in their sense of reality, and they misinterpret the whole function of eating; they often have a delusional fear of vomiting, or they may refuse food as being unworthy. Characteristically, they are apathetic and indolent and show no signs of hyperactivity or perfectionistic striving. They usually are indifferent toward their emaciation, and they certainly will not express pride in it.

ANOREXIA NERVOSA IN THE MALE

Anorexia nervosa in the male is conspicuously less frequent than in females, and the literature on it is even more ambiguous and contradictory (5). One finds statements that typical anorexia nervosa does not occur in the male, or, that it is not different from that observed in the female. If one approaches the syndrome in psychiatric terms, as I have done here, then the condition does occur in males and, when the therapist is confronted with the same psychological constellation and issues as found in the female patients, it should be diagnosed as such. As in females, anorexia nervosa in the male is not a uniform condition, and both the primary and the atypical form are observed. The atypical form shows divergent pictures, whereas boys in the primary group, like their female counterparts, have many features in common, with the relentless pursuit of thinness being the leading symptom. Although they seem to have been doing well, in reality they are engaged in a desperate struggle to become "somebody" and to establish a sense of differentiated identity.

It is probably of significance that in my series, the boys who developed primary anorexia nervosa were still in prepuberty. Other authors have also reported that typical anorexia nervosa in the male occurs mainly in young patients (5). Its rarity may well be related to the psychobiological effect of the male sex hormones. The characteristic slavelike attachment of the patient to the mother is more apt to develop in a girl, but even when a boy has functioned with the same robotlike obedience, his pubescence will flood him with hormones that evoke powerful new sensations and more aggressive impulses, which will make a new type of self-assertion possible. Once a boy is caught in the vicious cycle of self-starvation and distorted body experience, however, endocrine treatment appears ineffective, even disturbing. Such treatment becomes of value only after the underlying psychological problems have been clarified.

TREATMENT OF ANOREXIA NERVOSA

Treatment of this disorder involves two distinct tasks that must be integrated: 1) the restitution of normal nutrition and 2) the resolution of the underlying psychological problems, including the disturbed patterns of family interaction. Anorexia nervosa has always been considered a condition that offers difficult and frustrating treatment problems, and death or continued invalidism may not be an infrequent outcome. Recently, a series of optimistic reports have appeared in the literature that stress success with producing a gain in weight. By whatever method this is achieved, however, weight gain alone is an unreliable sign of progress. Relapses are frequent, and the case histories with fatal outcomes illustrate the fallacy of considering the restitution of weight alone a cure (4).

Claims of successful treatment have been made in the past for a great variety of methods, ranging from implantation of the pituitary gland, insulin injection, and electroconvulsive shock therapy, to the use of psychotropic drugs. The latest claim of invariable success in providing rapid weight gain has been made for treatment by means of behavior modification (1). The principle employed is to make conditions extremely uncomfortable for the patient, and various privileges are granted only as reward for weight gain; in such a "nonpampering" environment, weight gain is the patient's only escape. This method usually accomplishes a substantial weight increase, which, however, is frequently lost soon after the patient is discharged or escapes from the hospital. The patients I have seen had experienced the program as brutal coercion and had become depressed, even suicidal. Their family interactions, social relations, and eating patterns had also deteriorated (6).

Equally enthusiastic are the claims made for the value of family therapy, whereby the family conflicts are supposedly resolved during a few dramatic sessions, after which the patient resumes eating (2, 14). Family therapy seems to be an effective approach for treating young patients soon after the onset of the condition, but it is less effective after the illness has existed for any length of time and for those with serious psychiatric problems. In these cases, too, the disengagement and redirection of malfunctioning forces in the family is essential, but the deficits in the psychic development of the patient require individual psychotherapeutic help. A certain degree of nutritional restitution is a prerequisite for effective psychotherapy, and the course of the illness may be unnecessarily prolonged if the therapist indulges in the unrealistic expectation that the patient's weight will correct itself once the unconscious meaning of the refusal of food and the sexual conflicts have been made conscious. Such an exclusive focus on symbolic aspects is associated with the traditional psychoanalytic approach, which has been found to be singularly ineffective in treating anorexia nervosa.

In the treatment of this disorder, the psychotherapeutic results are closely linked to the pertinence of the psychodynamic understanding (5). According to the theoretical model presented here, the patients' deficits in the sense of active self-awareness and their conviction of ineffectiveness are the core issues, and patients need help with these aspects as well as with the underlying identity problems. The aim of therapy must be to encourage the patients to become active participants in the treatment process by evoking their awareness of impulses, feelings, and needs originating within themselves. With the repair of at least some of the cognitive distortions, they can learn to rely on their own thinking, become more realistic in their self-appraisal, and become capable of living as self-directed, competent individuals who can enjoy what life has to offer and no longer need to manipulate their body and its functions in this bizarre way.

REFERENCES

1. Agras WS, Barlow DH, Chapin HN, Abel GG,Leitenberg H: Behavior modification of anorexia nervosa. Arch Gen Psychiatry 30: 279–86, 1974

2. Barcai A: Family therapy in the treatment of anorexia nervosa. Am J Psychiatry 128: 286–90, 1971

3. Boyar RM, Katz J, Finkelstein JW, Kapen S, Weiner H, Weitzman ED, Hellman L: Immaturity of the 24-hour luteinizing hormone secretory pattern. N Engl J Med 291: 861–865, 1974

4. Bruch H: Death in anorexia nervosa. Psychosom Med 33: 135–144, 1971

5. Bruch H: Eating Disorders: Obesity, Anorexia Nervosa, and the Person Within. New York, Basic Books, 1973

6. Bruch H: Perils of behavior modification in treatment of anorexia nervosa. JAMA 230: 1419–1422, 1974

7. Coddington RD, Bruch H: Gastric perceptivity in normal obese and schizophrenic subjects. Psychosomatics 11: 571–79, 1970

8. Crisp AH: Some aspects of the evolution, presentation and follow-up of anorexia nervosa. Proc R Soc Med 58: 814–20, 1965

9. Dally P: Anorexia Nervosa. New York, Grune & Stratton, 1969

10. Garfinkel PE, Brown GM, Stancer HC, Moldofsky H: Hypothalamic–pituitary function in anorexia nervosa. Arch Gen Psychiatry 32: 739–744, 1975

11. Gull WW: Anorexia nervosa. Trans Clin Soc London 7: 22–28, 1874

12. King A: Primary and secondary anorexia nervosa syndromes. Br J Psychiatry 109: 470–79, 1963

13. Lasègue C: On hysterical anorexia. Med Times 2: 265–66, 367–369, 1873

14. Liebman R, Minuchin S, Baker L: The role of the family in the treatment of anorexia nervosa. Am J Child Psychiatry 13: 264–274, 1974

15. Russell GFM: Anorexia nervosa: its identity as an illness and its treatment. In Price JH (ed): Modern Trends in Psychological Medicine. London, Butterworth, 1970, 131–164

16. Selvini MP: L'Anoressia Mentale. Milano, Feltrinelli, 1963

17. Selvini MP: Self-Starvation: From the Intrapsychic to the Transpersonal Approach to Anorexia Nervosa. London, Chaucer, 1974

18. Silverstone J, Russell GFM: Gastric "hunger" contractions in anorexia nervosa. J Psychiatry 113: 257–63, 1967

19. Simmonds M: Ueber embolische Prozesse in der Hypophysis. Arch Path Anat 217: 226–228, 1914

20. Theander S: Anorexia nervosa. A psychiatric investigation of 94 female patients. Acta Psychiatr Scand [Suppl] 214: 1970

21. Ushakov GK: Anorexia nervosa. In Howells JG (ed): Modern Perspectives in Adolescent Psychiatry. Edinburgh, Oliver & Boyd, 1971, 274–289

22. Waller JV, Kaufman MR, Deutsch F: Anorexia nervosa: a psychosomatic entity. Psychosom Med 2: 3–16, 1940

24 Psychobiological Factors in Obesity

HENRY A. JORDAN,
LEONARD S. LEVITZ, GORDON M. KIMBRELL

The treatment of obese patients has always been difficult. Even though some promising techniques are now becoming available, such treatment is still hampered by an old problem: the distinct separation of biological and psychological approaches. We can easily classify almost all diagnostic and treatment approaches to obesity as being primarily biological or primarily psychological in orientation. When a new drug or metabolic treatment for obesity is evaluated, rarely does the investigator report on the psychological parameters that may be involved. Similarly, psychiatrists and psychologists—whether they use classical psychoanalysis, group therapy, or behavior modification techniques—rarely report or evaluate the biological concomitants of their treatment. Any practicing physician who is involved in the treatment of obesity recognizes that obesity is a complex disorder that encompasses both biological and psychological problems. What seems indicated is a framework in which the physician can consider and integrate these factors.

Our hope is that this chapter will provide a beginning to this process of integration. Regardless of the treatment modality used, it is essential that we understand both the biological and psychological factors affecting the obese patient. Furthermore, we must consider these factors not only as they exist at a single point in time, but also as they interact during the entire natural history of the disorder. Biological and psychological determinants are found to interact in the causation of obesity, in the maintenance of excess adipose tissue, during attempts at weight reduction, and in the maintenance of reduced body weight. Whether one is using diets, starvation, behavior modification, surgery, drugs, or psychotherapy, the therapist must try to achieve an integrated treatment involving all the determinants of a patient's obesity.

EVALUATION OF THE OBESE PATIENT

A preliminary step toward an integrated approach was taken at the Conference on Obesity held in 1973 at the Fogarty International Center, National Institutes of Health. The purpose of this conference was to assemble systematically the current information relevant to obesity. As a result, a problem-oriented classification system was developed that focuses attention on the variety of determinants that contribute to the cause of obesity and influence treatment decisions. Table 24–1 summarizes the portion of this classification system that deals with the medical, familial, and weight-history factors to be considered in the evaluation of the obese patient.

As in the evaluation of any disorder, an accurate history is required. In evaluating obesity, the history should include detailed information regarding any family history of obesity and related problems, as well as a detailed account of the patient's weight history. The age of onset of a patient's obesity, for example, has both biological and psychological implications. Recent work by Hirsch and Knittle (4) has shown that individuals with obesity of juvenile onset have more fat cells than those with adult onset. We have known for a long time that obesity of juvenile onset is more difficult to treat, and we now have insight into the biological nature of this phenomenon. Although hypercellularity may help to explain this increased résistance to treatment, the emotional disturbances that are found more frequently among those patients whose onset occurred in childhood are probably a product of these patients' having been obese during critical periods of their psychological development.

After a detailed history is taken, the physical examination is conducted. All too often, especially in the case of the hyperobese patient, an accurate weighing is not made during the examination. Accurate weight is a valuable piece of information, and there is no justification for its omission. Table 24–1 also indicates laboratory studies that should be done if indicated by the case history and physical examination.

One of the strengths of the original Fogarty problem-oriented approach was its acknowledgment of the importance of socioeconomic, nutritional, and psychological factors in the evaluation of obesity. The inclusion of this kind of information was a major step forward, but a more detailed elaboration seems indicated. The evaluation of socioeconomic and nutritional factors must include information not only about the patient himself, but also about the environment in which he lives. The psychological aspects must include not only intrapsychic events, but a variety of other factors that influence the patient's behavior, emotions, and cognition. Thus, a complete evaluation of obesity must include an appraisal of the patient's life-style, daily routine, past experiences, cultural background, aspirations, and priorities concerning weight and weight loss.

We have found it helpful to organize the inquiry concerning these macrosocial and experiential factors into the following categories. Examples of the kind of questions that should be answered are provided.

1. Early feeding and parental attitudes toward food and weight
   Examples: A. What was the role of food in the family?
             B. How much did the parents attempt to control eating and weight?
             C. Was food used for reward and punishment?
2. History of psychological or psychiatric disturbance and treatment
   Examples: A. When and for what reason was treatment undertaken?
             B. Were there any untoward effects in previous attempts at weight loss, *e.g.*, depression, anxiety, or body-image disturbance?
3. Socioeconomic status and education level
   Examples: A. Is the patient's occupation conducive to overeating and underactivity?
             B. What foods and activities are readily available at the patient's socioeconomic level?
4. Current psychological functioning
   Examples: A. Are there any significant life changes or crises at present or anticipated in the near future, *e.g.*, changes in health, marital status, occupation, and so on?
             B. Are there any acute or chronic disturbances in mood?

Table 24-1. A PROBLEM-ORIENTED APPROACH TO OBESITY: RECOMMENDED DATA
BASE OF FACTORS RELEVANT TO OBESITY IN MAN*

I. Familial background (genetic or environmental)
   A. Obesity with juvenile onset
   B. Obesity with adult onset
   C. Diabetes mellitus
      1. overt
      2. suspected (history of large birth weights)
   D. Hyperlipidemias, types III–V
   E. Accelerated arteriosclerosis and coronary or cardiovascular disease
   F. Specific endocrine disorders associated with obesity

II. Functional profile
   A. Gestation
      1. duration
      2. maternal health and nutrition
      3. birth weight
   B. Age of onset of obesity
      1. in infancy
      2. prepuberal or puberal
      3. adult years
      4. during pregnancy
      5. not known
   C. Rate of progression
      1. weight
         At end of grade school:
         At end of high school:
         At graduation from college:
         At marriage (age):
         At other landmarks:
      2. present dynamic phase
         Rate of gain or loss in past month:
         Rate of gain or loss in past year:
      3. present static phase
         Duration of plateau weight:
      4. history of episodes suggesting hypoglycemia during fasting
   D. Age of onset of puberty

III. Pharmacological agents and drugs
   A. Endocrine
      1. oral contraceptive
      2. iatrogenic insulin excess
      3. iatrogenic glucocorticoid excess
      4. sulfonyl-urea compounds, given without restriction of diet
   B. Agents that may affect thermogenesis and drugs
      1. phenothiazine tranquilizers
      2. cyproheptadine
      3. alcohol
      4. smoking, tobacco and type
      5. smoking marijuana
      6. other

(continued)

Table 24-1. A PROBLEM-ORIENTED APPROACH TO OBESITY: RECOMMENDED DATA
BASE OF FACTORS RELEVANT TO OBESITY IN MAN* *(continued)*

IV. Physical examination
    A. Distribution of excess adipose tissue
        1. android (upper trunk and abdomen)
        2. gynecoid (buttocks and hips)
        3. universal
        4. skin-fold measurements
                biceps: mm   triceps: mm
                subscapular: mm
                suprailiac: mm
    B. Indices of maturation†
        1. height
    crown to pubis: cm
    pubis to heel: cm
    ratio:
    2. height: cm
    span: cm
    ratio height to span:
    C. Evaluation of musculature
        Weak: Average: Well-developed:
    D. Hair distribution
        Android: Gynecoid: Excess:

V. Laboratory measurements‡
    A. Fasting plasma glucose: mg/dl
        Glucose 2 hours after test dose: mg/dl
            (specify dose)
        Contingency: 5-hour glucose tolerance
    B. With history of hypoglycemia during fasting:
        72-hour fast with plasma insulin and glucose determination
    C. Serum triglycerides and cholesterol (fasting)
        Contingency: Lipoprotein electrophoresis, serum uric acid determination
    D. Serum cortisol:
        Early AM: μg/dl; PM: μg/dl
        Contingency: Serum cortisol determination following 1 mg dexamethasone at 11 PM
        Urinary free cortisol with or without dexamethasone suppresion tests
        Skull roentgenogram for size of sella turcica
        Radioimmunoassay for plasma ACTH, if available
    E. Serum thyroxine (T_4): μg/dl Triiodothyronine (T_3) resin binding: %
        Contingency: serum total triiodothyronine (T_3):   ng/dl, serum thyroid-stimulating
            hormone (TSH):   mU/ml
    F. If other endocrine disorders, such as hypogonadism, are suspected on the basis of the
        case history and physical examination, then appropriate studies beyond the scope of
        this outline should be undertaken.

*Excerpted from Bray G (ed): Obesity in Perspective, Vol II, Part 1, 16. Bethesda, Maryland,
Fogarty International Center, National Institutes of Heatlh, 1973
†For investigative work or special cases, the Tanner classification of sexual maturation and
roentgenographic bone age may be indicated.
‡For investigative work, it is preferable to include measurements of the cell size and cell
number.

5. Current social relationships

Examples: A. What kind of support or sabotage might be anticipated during the period of weight loss?

B. Does the patient have interests in addition to those of his home or job?

6. Current level of physical activity

Examples: A. What routine physical activity does the patient engage in?

B. What opportunities for increasing physical activity are available to the patient?

7. Food supplies and storage

Examples: A. Which member of the family is responsible for shopping and for preparation of food?

B. What kinds and quantities of food are generally kept in the home?

8. Current food habits and attitudes

Examples: A. What is the patient's level of nutritional knowledge?

B. What are his preferred foods?

C. Does the patient feel guilty about eating high-caloric foods?

D. To what extent is food involved in the patient's social activities?

Following the appraisal of these factors, it is necessary to evaluate the patient's current eating behavior. This evaluation includes a description of the patient's eating patterns, their rates of occurrence, and the current determinants of these patterns. In order to obtain the information needed for this evaluation, patients should be taught to monitor their own eating behavior. The best way to accomplish this is to have the patient keep a daily record of his food intake. The record should indicate how frequently the patient eats, the foods and amounts he consumes, and his rate of ingestion. For each ingestion, the patient should record some of the important environmental determinants such as the time, place, and social situation in which eating occurs. In addition, it is very valuable to have the patient indicate his mood and degree of hunger prior to eating. The patient should record this information daily for at least a one-week period.

The information derived from the diagnostic inquiry and the analysis of the eating pattern yields a profile of the determinants that operate to produce both adaptive and maladaptive eating and activity patterns. The profile invariably reveals how the patient's eating and activity habits are intricately associated with his present style of life.

Prior to the assembly of all the information collected in this evaluation, no *a priori* decision can be made as to the relative importance of biological and psychological factors for an individual patient. For each patient, one must consider the interplay of biological and psychological factors in both the generation and maintenance of his obesity; in other words, one must assess the relative influence of these factors throughout the natural history of the disorder. There are four major stages in this natural history: becoming obese, remaining obese, reducing adipose stores, and maintaining a reduced body weight. As a patient progresses through each of these stages, a variety of biological and psychological phenomena are encountered.

CAUSATIVE FACTORS IN OBESITY

Biological and psychological factors of causative significance may help explain why the person had a disturbed energy balance in the first place and hence has stored excess fat.

The biological factors responsible for obesity have provided one of the more complex problems in medicine. No single biological factor has been identified that can account for all but a small portion of obese individuals; endocrine disorders are one such example. Another is the suggested genetic predisposition of children of obese parents to become obese themselves. The probability of obesity is as high as 80% if both parents are obese. Further investigation along the lines begun by Hirsch and Knittle (4) may provide insight into the relationship between fat-cell hyperplasia and genetics. Recently, a possible cause for the syndrome of binge eating, which has proved so resistant to current treatment methods, has been suggested by Greene and Rau (3). In their investigation of ten patients who exhibited compulsive eating disturbances, they found abnormal EEG patterns in all but one patient. Furthermore, in nine of the ten patients, episodes of compulsive eating were markedly reduced by the administration of anticonvulsant medication.

Like the biological factors, no single psychological factor has been identified that may be said to be the cause of most cases of obesity. Rather, there appears to be a network of contributing factors, some of which have been identified. Bruch (1) has described numerous cases in which intrapsychic and often intrafamilial psychopathology accounts for a patient's obesity. It would be a mistake, however, to assume that psychopathology is involved in all cases of obesity.

More important than possible psychopathological factors are the everyday experiences, especially those of early childhood, that influence the patient's eating and activity patterns. In every family, early learning experiences shape the patterns of behavior that tend to be stable throughout a person's life. Since each child has different genetic and environmental influences, each will develop different behaviors that enter into the regulation of his energy balance and body weight. Ullmann and Krasner (10) have outlined a number of ways in which a child may develop inappropriate eating-habit patterns. First, the child may be taught to rely on cues provided by a parent for terminating eating, and thus he will learn to depend on environmental cues rather than on those provided by his own physiological needs. Second, food may come to satisfy multiple emotional needs by being strongly and repeatedly associated with parental attention, comfort, and affection. Third, not only may parents actively teach inappropriate eating behaviors and uses for food, but, through initiation, the child may also acquire such patterns from his parents. Behavioral influences such as these are not limited in their influence to eating behavior alone, but they also have profound influences on the activity patterns of the growing child. Such activity patterns have been found to have causative importance in obesity. Mayer (6), in a study that compared thin and obese adolescent girls, found, for example, that the obese girls actually ate less than the thin girls, but they expended one-third less energy in physical activity.

MAINTENANCE OF OBESITY

A variety of consequences result from the state of being obese. These may not only explain the maintenance of the excess adipose stores, but they are important to consider in planning treatment.

Many biological phenomena have been found to be associated with obesity, but the causal relationships, if any, are not yet understood. Almost every organ system —and hence almost every medical specialty—is represented in the list of associated diseases. The most notable alterations are blood-pressure elevation, disorders of glucose metabolism including elevated blood glucose, elevated insulin levels, increased insulin resistance, and diabetes mellitus. Other illnesses associated with and often aggravated by obesity are cardiovascular disorders, pulmonary diseases, and diseases of the joints. It is also well known that obesity increases the risks in surgery, both from anesthesia and during the postoperative period.

An entire constellation of psychological effects results from the state of obesity. In this area, one must be careful to differentiate problems arising from intrapsychic conflicts from those problems arising from conflicts between the obese individual and a society that places a high value on thinness.

One of the major intrapsychic problems of the obese patient is a disturbance of body image. Bruch (1) and Stunkard and Mendelson (8) have commented on body-image disturbances in patients with obesity of juvenile onset. Glucksman and Hirsch (2) investigated this problem experimentally, and they found that obese patients with juvenile onset of the disorder have persistent feelings of obesity even after weight reduction. Stunkard and Mendelson (8) discussed two other factors that predispose an obese person to such a disturbance: the presence of other emotional disturbances and negative evaluations by his family and peers during the patient's formative years.

Many other psychological problems arise from the stigma that society places on obese persons. This negative regard for obesity is manifested by stigmatization in job promotion or college admission, for example, and in the general attitude that obese persons are mortally weak, sinful, lazy, and ugly. One result of this process of stigmatization is that the obese patient generally has a profound deficit in self-regard. This lack of self-esteem is most damaging during adolescence, when the value placed on personal appearance by peers is intensely regarded. Another result of stigmatization is that the obese person becomes very sensitized concerning the ingestion of food. Eating often becomes associated with guilt and shame, and, rather than providing a control over food intake, these feelings of guilt lead to eating in isolation and decreased satisfaction from normally pleasurable eating experiences. Furthermore, the obese person's overall life-style generally becomes more constricted. Social withdrawal sometimes occurs, but this is only one aspect of this change in life-style; all too often, both the medical effects of being obese and the constriction of the general life-style of the obese person lead to a considerable decrease in his physical activity, since fewer activities and resources may be available or utilized. In dealing with an obese person, then, the physician must assess the magnitude of the patient's disturbance of body image as well as his reaction to the pressures of his peer group and society. Ultimately, perhaps the stigma of being obese may be lessened in our society, and the problems resulting from societal pressure will decrease.

REDUCTION OF BODY WEIGHT

When an individual loses or attempts to lose weight, a number of unique medical and psychological effects may occur. These may help explain the difficulty that patients have in adhering to almost every treatment regiment.

The biological alterations observed during weight loss depend on the method used to create a negative energy balance. The effects of total starvation may be quite different from those of slow, gradual weight loss based on a moderately reduced caloric intake. Furthermore, weight reduction based on increased energy expenditure is associated with yet other alterations. If the weight loss is accomplished very rapidly, many of the phenomena that were observed by Keys and Brozek (5) in their study of normal weight men undergoing starvation may be seen in obese patients. Keys and Brozek noted the following effects among their 36 volunteers: 1) their pulse rate dropped, 2) their basal metabolic rate dropped, 3) general activity was slowed, 4) their libido was decreased, 5) their weight dropped (by six months, their weight had dropped an average of 24%), 6) tolerance to heat was increased, 7) tolerance to cold was decreased, and 8) vertigo and dizziness occurred. The first four observations reflect the physiological and metabolic alterations produced by the body's attempt to preserve its energy balance and maintain equilibrium. Since the subjects were unable to utilize responses that would normally lead to an increase in food intake, the last four changes reflect the organism's failure to maintain equilibrium. These alterations occur because the equilibrium of energy balance is disturbed, and when homeostasis is altered in any biological regulatory system, a series of control mechanisms operate to restore balance. These will operate even in an obese individual.

On the positive side, however, are the reversals during starvation of many of the biological alterations that occur as a result of being obese. Blood pressure may decrease, glucose metabolism may normalize, and many conditions aggravated by the obesity will be improved.

In addition to biological effects, the study by Keyes and Brozek (5) also found that significant psychological effects resulted from caloric restriction and weight loss. Among the most frequently encountered were irritability, depression, social withdrawal, loss of sexual desire, increased preoccupation with food, and marked changes in behaviors involved in the ingestive process. The same symptoms have been observed by Glucksman and Hirsch (2) and Stunkard (7) in obese individuals during caloric restriction. Glucksman and Hirsch (2) further reported that the magnitude of these changes is greater in patients who have been obese since childhood. They described four general categories of psychological change: 1) alteration in affect, manifested by increased anxiety, hostility, and depression; a dieting depression syndrome has been noted as an effect of many treatment regimens by Stunkard and Rush (9); 2) perceptual disturbances, especially those concerned with alterations of body size; the process of losing weight demands a continual readjustment of the obese person's perception of himself; 3) increased sexual fantasies and activities; as a person becomes thinner, increased self-esteem and increased sexual appeal require adjustment in his behavior and attitudes; and 4) increase in hunger sensations and preoccupation with food; feelings of deprivation are often experienced, and the person's interpretation of hunger and satiety often changes as the weight loss proceeds.

In addition, the ever-pervasive fear of failure may appear during any weight reduction attempt, the magnitude of which is determined by the patient's past experiences with weight loss. Frequently, a patient's sense of self-esteem is directly related to small, daily fluctuations in weight. On the other hand, unrealistic expectations about rapid weight loss can often produce frustration and erode motivation.

MAINTENANCE OF REDUCED BODY WEIGHT

Significant medical and psychological effects are encountered as a result of successful weight loss and the maintenance of lowered body weight. These effects may help explain why so many individuals are unable to maintain a reduced body weight.

The biological alterations that accompany successful weight reduction are the same as those mentioned in the preceding section. Most diseases, signs, and symptoms that are associated with or aggravated by obesity are improved and often may be reversed. Many of the metabolic abnormalities and the abnormal levels of circulating hormones and metabolites may be normalized following successful weight reduction.

Although marked improvement in these patients may be seen medically, many psychological problems persist or may develop as a result of successful weight reduction. It is apparent that patients who have returned to an ideal weight after a long period of obesity may experience profound psychological changes. Not only must they become accustomed to a radically different body size, but they must also adjust to being treated differently by other persons. Furthermore, the patient's family and close friends must readjust to his new appearance. Following the patient's weight reduction, the physician must be concerned with the possibility of disturbances in his interpersonal relationships. Each ongoing interpersonal relationship represents an equilibrium state, and individuals in the relationship tend to behave in ways that maintain this equilibrium. Thus, when an obese person alters his energy balance to produce weight loss, he also alters the equilibrium of his former interpersonal relationships. In reaction to this, his family members and friends may try to restore the former relationship. Often these attempts are perceived as sabotage by the patient and his therapist.

The formerly obese person has several additional problems that require resolution. During weight reduction, the patient derives considerable reinforcement from the weight loss *per se*. When an ideal weight is realized, this mode of reinforcement ceases and other means of reinforcement must be found. This is often a very difficult transition to make. The patient also encounters changed expectations from himself and his social environment. As a result, he must learn new and adaptive ways of behaving; this, too, is a most difficult period. The reducing patient may also expect his life problems to disappear when he reaches ideal weight. When this does not occur, the patient is often disenchanted. He will require assistance in evaluating the realistic merits of weight loss and in developing new skills to deal with these unresolved problems.

It becomes clear that the patient may require as much support and treatment for weight maintenance as he did during the weight reduction phase. Too often, intensive treatment is not continued into the weight maintenance phase, and the problems outlined remain unresolved. When the treatment is continued into the weight maintenance phase, however, the probability of long-term success is greatly increased.

From this discussion of the medical and psychological factors that are to be considered in the evaluation of the obese patient, it should be apparent that no single treatment modality can ever serve all the needs of all obese patients. As newer treatment modalities are developed, such as behavior modification, protein-sparing diets, or bowel bypass surgery, the physician will have a much greater range of treatment choice than in the past. This choice, however, must be made on the basis of all the information derived from a detailed, problem-oriented evaluation. Probably the most common mistake made in the treatment of obesity, regardless of the treatment techniques, is to try to treat all overweight persons in the same way.

We feel that if a physician can take the time to develop the skills necessary and to see his patients through the aforementioned evaluation, then there will be few obese patients that he or she cannot treat. If, however, sufficient time is not available, then the treatment of obesity will remain difficult and frustrating. Diets prescribed without regard to the patients' behaviors, attitudes, and food likes and dislikes almost universally fail.

If, after a detailed evaluation of the patient, the physician suspects that psychopathological problems are a primary cause of the obesity, then psychiatric evaluation and perhaps intervention are indicated. If one identifies a true "binge eater," as described by Green and Rau (3), then neurological evaluation should be considered. More common, however, than these rather exceptional cases are the large numbers of obese patients who come to the physician with unrealistic expectations of treatment.

Patients often expect 1) rapid weight loss, 2) the weight loss to be effortless, with the responsibility for control placed on the physician and not on themselves, and 3) a resolution of all their life problems when the weight loss occurs. Although there are other misconceptions and faulty expectations, these are the most often observed. Rapid weight loss seldom leads to permanent results, and it often reflects a loss of lean body mass as well as of fat. Patients must learn that their weight loss must occur gradually over long periods of time and, furthermore, that the change in their behavior and the control of weight is a lifelong process. The control must be within themselves and not provided by the physician. Any physician who feels that he can control his patients' eating behavior via diets, suggestions, or admonitions is bound to fail and be frustrated. Finally, they must learn that loss of weight will not solve all of life's problems, but it may actually create new problems. Some of these problems were mentioned previously in the context of the psychological problems associated with weight maintenance.

The single most important fact for the physician to remember, however, is that although our knowledge of obesity is far from complete, it is apparent at this time that a variety of factors can lead to the same result, namely, weight gain and the maintenance of excessive body weight. Treatment must reflect the uniqueness of each obese patient. The initial evaluation, the choice of treatment, and the therapy itself must always be considered within the context of the natural history of obesity. At different times throughout this natural history, and especially as treatment continues and hopefully is successful, the relative importance of biological, macrosocial, and experimental factors may change. It is therefore necessary to reevaluate the importance of each factor periodically throughout treatment.

REFERENCES

1. Bruch H: Eating Disorders: Obesity, Anorexia Nervosa, and the Person Within. New York, Basic Books, 1973

2. Glucksman ML, Hirsch J: The response of obese patients to weight reduction: a clinical evaluation of behavior. Psychosom Med 30: 1, 1968

3. Green RS, Rau JH: Treatment of compulsive eating disturbances with anticonvulsant medication. Am J Psychiatry 131 (4): 428, 1974

4. Hirsch J, Knittle JL: Cellularity of obese and non-obese human adipose tissue. Fed Proc 29: 1516, 1970

5. Keys A, Brozek J et al.: The Biology of Human Starvation, Vol 1,2. Minneapolis, University of Minnesota Press, 1950

6. Mayer J: Overweight: Causes, Cost, and Control. Englewood Cliffs, Prentice–Hall, 1968, pp 1–218

7. Stunkard AJ: The "dieting depression": incidence and clinical characteristics of untoward responses to weight reduction regimens. Am J Med 23: 77, 1957

8. Stunkard AJ, Mendelson S: Obesity and the body image. I. Characteristics of disturbance in the body image of some obese persons. Am J Psychiatry 123, 1967

9. Stunkard AJ, Rush J: Dieting and depression reexamined: a critical review of reports of untoward responses during weight reduction for obesity. Ann Intern Med 81: 526, 1974

10. Ullmann LP, Krasner L: Behavior Influence and Personality. New York, Holt, Rinehart & Winston, 1973

25 Gastrointestinal Disorders

DAN G. HERTZ, MILTON ROSENBAUM

The gastrointestinal tract is considered to be one of the sites where a wide range of emotional reactions may be manifested. According to most of the presently accepted psychological theories, personality development and personality traits are greatly affected by feeding habits and toilet training (8, 13). Symptoms involving the gastrointestinal tract are, however, often based on behavioral experiences imparted by the patient's environment in the form of the indoctrination into idiosyncrasies and negative learning.

In spite of continuous research into the possibility of there being a single cause in the pathogenesis of psychophysiological disturbances of the gastrointestinal tract, *no single, specific, causative agent has been detected.* The cause of these disorders must therefore still be considered as attributable to a combination of various factors, including constitutional, hereditary, hormonal, psychological, and environmental elements.

Our intention is to discuss two major clinical conditions affecting the gastrointestinal tract in which psychological factors often bear the major responsibility for their onset and exacerbations.

DUODENAL ULCER

In spite of the fact that in clinical practice the term "peptic ulcer" is used for both gastric and duodenal ulcer, a clear distinction should be made between these two entities. Our clinical concepts are basically oriented toward the duodenal ulcer. This condition is more frequent in younger men, it is characterized by high gastric secretion, and it is associated with a relatively low incidence of carcinoma. The gastric ulcer, on the other hand, occurs in both sexes with similar frequency, with normal or subnormal gastric secretion, and with a high incidence of gastric carcinoma.

At present, several different organic theories have been proposed to explain the development of peptic ulcer: the acid-pepsin theory, the theory of gastric mucosal damage, the relationship to blood group (O phenotype), the theory based on parietal cell mass, the vascular theory, and that involving mucosal-cell kinetics (1).

PSYCHOLOGICAL AND PSYCHOPHYSIOLOGICAL APPROACHES

Peptic ulcer was first clinically described by Cruveilhier in 1829 (2), and theories about its nature have continued to be put forth. It is impossible to give a detailed, historical overview of these various theories in this chapter, but readers are referred to the bibliography (8, 13).

The psychological factors involved in the development of duodenal ulcer have been increasingly emphasized since the observation of Wolf and Wolff (16) regarding the correlation of emotions and the activity of the gastric mucosa in their famous subject, "Tom."

Different personality patterns in a clinical population of male ulcer patients were described by one of the present authors and his associates (5). This classification categorized patients as pseudo-independent, passive-dependent, or acting-out. The results of this study seemed to point to an unconscious conflict in the patient between a deep, unconscious wish to be dependent and the denial of this wish in the form of strong, overt, independent behavior. It is as if these patients were saying, "I am strong and independent; I take care of others; I do not need or wish anyone to take care of me."

In recent years, Mirsky's studies (11) widened the scope of psychophysiological investigation of ulcer patients. His approach was based on the measurement of the excretion rate of pepsinogen in the urine and its concentration in the blood of ulcer patients, as compared to the data for ulcer-free subjects. His study indicated that in addition to the gastric hypersecretion, which is an essential determinant, other predisposing factors are equally present in the pathogenesis of the ulcer. His conclusion was that the physiological susceptibility to duodenal ulcer is reinforced by psychological conflicts that induce emotional tension and is enhanced by noxious environmental events. The presence of such a constellation leads, with great probability, to the development of duodenal ulcer (11). His findings were experimentally validated by Weiner *et al.* (15) in an elegantly designed study made on military recruits.

Stenback and his associates (14) reached a somewhat different conclusion in a comparative study of prisoners and factory workers that was performed to investigate the social, psychological, and physiological factors in ulcer formation. An analysis of the social factors and personality traits in duodenal ulcer patients revealed a high frequency of reactive depression in the prison group, whereas the factory personnel were characterized by an ambitious or perfectionistic makeup. This study emphasized that duodenal ulcer is to a certain extent an emotional stress disorder. There is no universally existing emotional process, however, that characterizes the ulcer patient. All factors that can produce a prolonged vagotonic state of sufficient intensity seem to be capable of producing a duodenal ulcer (14).

CLINICAL ASPECTS AND THERAPY

In different cultures, the emotional conflicts that precede or exist concomitantly with the development of ulcer may exhibit different patterns. The clinical investigation of the ulcer patient must therefore consider the multifactored pathogenesis of the disorder. Individual life situations show great variability, and the investigating physician must be satisfied with the realization that the central emotional conflict of his patient usually remains at least partly unconscious. No specific conflict has to be sought, and attempts need not be made to confront the patient with his conflict. Forced confrontation is often detrimental to the development of a proper doctor-patient relationship (4). In our experience, however, the most common precipitating factors are threatened or real object loss, separation, and situations in which strivings for success are blocked, with resulting frustration, anxiety, and mild depressive feelings.

In order to develop the proper therapeutic approach, the physician should make every attempt to determine the life events connected with the onset of the illness. It is important to determine whether or not precipitating emotional factors were involved in the onset or exacerbation of the illness. The physician should always explore this area by asking a few simple questions, such as, "Did any changes take place in your life around the time you became sick?" "How were things going at home or on the job?" "Did anything happen that might have upset you?" Sometimes the patient will answer by saying, "nothing particular happened," but, more often, he will respond by telling the physician of changes in his life, even though he may not connect these changes with the onset or exacerbation of his illness. The physician, by simply pointing out the temporal relationship between the distressing life event and the onset of the illness, may make the patient aware of this emotional component. This does not mean, however, that the physician should make an "interpretation." It is one thing to say, "perhaps you were more concerned about the added responsibility of another child during your wife's pregnancy," and quite another to say, "you were jealous of the baby, as you were of your sister when she was born."

The following vignettes illustrate the precipitating circumstances in the development of duodenal ulcer and emphasize the application of some theoretical considerations:

Case 1. The patient was 25 years old at the time of his admission to the hospital for a clinical examination because of suspected ulcer, nervousness, and difficulty in functioning. He was the second of three children and the only son. He had lost his father, "who adored him," when he was 15 years old. After his father's death, the patient became the center of attention in his family. His mother made extraordinary efforts to provide him with a maximum of care and love. The patient reciprocated her efforts with a continuous attempt to live up to her expectations. He was very successful in school and the leader of his class. The relationship between mother and son was a very close one; she shared with him all her concerns about the future.

His first symptoms appeared when he was inducted into army service at the age of 18.* He could have requested a deferment, but he insisted on proving his ability to cope with difficulties. After several weeks in the army, he began to suffer from gastrointestinal symptoms. In spite of this, he succeeded in becoming accepted for officer's training and completed this course at the top of his class. He was very much liked by his commanding officer, who became a "father substitute" to him. When his superior was killed in a car accident, however, he reacted again with localized pain in the epigastrium. After a short period of difficulty, he succeeded in becoming organized, and he was accepted at a university. At the same time, he also became involved with a young girl, a warm and understanding person.

The couple decided to marry while he was successfully continuing his university studies. He once more became active in community affairs. When his wife became pregnant, however, he again reacted with tension, nervousness, and complaints of physical pain. When the child (a boy) was born, the patient continued to react with nervousness and tension. Somehow, he felt that he had been rejected by his wife and that the baby had become the center of her attention. His condition deteriorated until hospitalization became necessary. The final conclusion of the medical workup was acute duodenal ulcer.

This case history illustrates a few of the characteristic points in the development of duodenal ulcer. Our patient held a central position in his family as the only son. The expectations of him arising from his environment were adequately met in his striving for success. Although he reacted with renewed effort to the threat of being abandoned after his father's death, his further success brought him the feeling of being praised and loved. In the protective environment of his home, he maintained an excellent level of functioning. The first difficulties arose when his army service caused temporary separation from his mother and a competitive situation with his peers. With his inner resources, he not only succeeded again, but he also gained recognition and support from his superior, a parent surrogate. The initial relation-

---

*Note the similarity in the findings of the study by Weiner *et al.* (15).

ship with his wife was similar to the one with his mother. The birth of his son, however, mobilized his basic conflict between the threat of the loss of love and the fear of competition. The external event, therefore, precipitated the psychological tension that was followed by the onset of symptoms of a duodenal ulcer.

This short case history defines the basic conflict of the patient: through the activation and mobilization of his emotional energy—his ego strength—he could repress his basic conflict—his need to be dependent, to be loved and taken care of for a long period of time. He became active and successful, and he was even able to take on the role of a leader, taking care of others instead of craving to be taken care of. After the birth of his child, the balance suddenly changed. He was confronted with a new situation: he had to assume further responsibility toward his son, whom he blamed for the loss of the security that he felt in relation to his wife.

It goes without saying that the patient could not be confronted with the jealousy and hostility that he was unconsciously harboring toward his son at the time of his psychophysiological crisis. Environmental changes could favorably decrease the psychological tension of the patient, and there was no need to add to the extent of the crisis by bringing in premature and haphazardous interpretations and confrontations.

This case also illustrates a principle in the management of certain patients with peptic ulcer. In spite of the fact that one could formulate the unconscious conflict quite simply, we recognized that it was reinforced by a life event to which he was vulnerable, the birth of the son. The environmental manipulation was therefore directed mainly toward the role of his wife, who could easily be persuaded to make certain changes in the family to prevent her husband turning into an egotistic and severely ill person in her eyes.

Case 2. The second patient was a 37-year-old man who was seen in the Psychosomatic Clinic—a clinic run by medical residents and supervised by internists and psychiatrists—because of chronic, recurrent, duodenal ulcer. He was seen for one hour each week for six weeks. The usual medical treatment was given, and the interviews were comprised of a discussion of problems in his job and with his wife. He became aware that the tensions associated with his problems seemed to cause exacerbation of his ulcer symptoms. An improvement in his symptoms was noted in three weeks, and, at the end of a six-week period, he was without symptoms and a gastrointestinal roentgenogram revealed that the ulcer had healed. He obtained a new job, and he stopped coming to the clinic because in his new job, he could not get time off to come there.

He was not seen until a year later, at which time he appeared in the emergency ward with a perforation of the duodenal ulcer. A history of the interval revealed that the day before the perforation occurred, he had been discharged from his job as a truck driver after a slight accident that he felt was not his fault. The next day, his wife left him following an argument, and a few hours later, while on his way to a house of prostitution, he was suddenly seized with the severe pain of the perforation.

In his case, we felt that if he had been able to continue his relationship with his physician and if we had originally involved the wife in the treatment plan, then the perforation might not have taken place.

ULCERATIVE COLITIS

No consensus exists about the nature of this serious inflammatory disease that affects mainly the mucosa and submucosa of the large intestine. If the inflammation is localized in the proximal colon, the manifestations of the illness are cramps, colic, pain, and occult blood; in the distal part, however, the disorder precipitates gross bleeding and diarrhea and may take the form of ulcerative proctitis.

The epidemiological and genetic features of the disease are also rather unclear. The illness seems to have a slight predilection for females. It is rarely reported in lower socioeconomic groups; it tends to be a disease of the middle class. The incidence in Jews is two to four times that of the general population, and a very low incidence is found among blacks and Spanish Americans.

The true origin of this illness is no more clear today than it was 25 years ago. Clinical investigations have studied allergic, infectious, genetic, neurogenic, nutritional, immunological, and psychosomatic aspects; however, no convincing evidence has yet been offered in support of any particular theory.

Clinical research in recent years has centered mainly around the autoimmune and infectious factors, and a series of aberrations have been described in patients suffering from ulcerative colitis. A cytotoxic action of lymphocytes, abnormal patterns of complement and immunoglobulins, and high titers of circulating antibodies have been reported in such cases by various investigators (17).

PSYCHOLOGICAL APPROACHES

Since Murray's pioneer study (12) in 1930, when psychogenic factors were first indicated in the causation of ulcerative colitis, other researchers have continued to support the importance of emotional components in the development and clinical course of inflammatory bowel diseases.

Engel's summary (3) of the findings of the earlier psychological studies reflects the symbiotic nature of the deep attachment that is shown by ulcerative colitis patients to a key figure, mainly to their mother. Even if the patients succeed in transferring this attachment to other key figures during further development, the attachment becomes distorted and turns into a matter of life or death in their need for extreme dependence. If external events (such as death, illness, or separation) or internal fantasy endanger the maintenance of this pathological relationship, the first clinical manifestation of the illness or the exacerbation of an earlier, existing condition may result (3).

The exaggerated, demanding attitude of ulcerative colitis patients supported the development of another theory, namely, that there is a genetic predisposition to the disease and that such patients develop certain psychological mannerisms and often bizarre ways of handling their emotions. The full-blown clinical picture, according to this view, develops only when the patients are exposed to an extreme type of stress. Under the influence of the stress situation, there then appears an unacceptable emotional reaction. The characteristic manifestations are egocentricity, overdependence, rigidity, and the expression of an excessive need for attention and love. The clinical course of ulcerative colitis often alternates between active colitis and other symptoms. Engel (3) observed that headache was a very common alternative symptom in colitis patients.

The importance of emotional maturation in avoiding the development of such reactions is demonstrated in the study of McMahon *et al.* (10) of the personality differences between patients with inflammatory bowel disease and their healthy siblings. They found that patients with ulcerative colitis exhibit fixation in a dependent relationship that makes them vulnerable to loss or separation. Their healthy siblings, however, went through normal identity crises and emerged as more independent and mature individuals.

A comparative study by McKegney *et al.* (9) of 123 patients with either ulcerative colitis or Crohn's disease indicated a similarly high incidence of emotional disturbance and life crises prior to onset of the illness in both cases. Examination of demographic, psychosocial personality, behavioral, psychiatric, and physical disease characteristics did not reveal any significant differences between patients with these diseases.

CLINICAL ASPECTS

One of the most extensive studies of ulcerative colitis in recent years was made by Karush and his associates (6, 7). Their systematic study of 30 patients with chronic ulcerative colitis is of particular value to the clinical practitioner because of its emphasis on the main clinical features, the pretreatment factors, and therapeutic approaches. Their finding of 14 schizophrenic and "borderline" cases indicates the serious psychopathology that often is found among ulcerative colitis patients. Even those who were not openly psychotic exhibited schizoid and paranoid features. Our clinical experience confirms their findings.

It must be pointed out that their egocentric and frequently bizarre behavior has proved to be one of the major obstacles in the management of hospitalized ulcerative colitis patients. The problem of how to deal with aggressive impulses against the outside world is handled by such patients by either of two means: they rarely act them out but instead they withdraw and either deny their emotions or project them. We found that this tendency is one of the frequent causes of conflict between hospitalized ulcerative colitis patients and the medical and paramedical staff.

Precipitating events similar to those reported in earlier studies were found in Karush's study: such events involved the loss of an object that usually symbolized dependency. Our own clinical observations are similar to theirs. Death (*e.g.,* of a parent), abortion, separation, or a change in environment (covering up the loss of physical closeness) were found to be the major causes for the precipitation of the clinical condition.

The prognosis of the physical condition parallels the seriousness of the emotional disturbance. The emotional immaturity of the patient indicates his inability to accept limitations and certain demands. The maintenance of symbiotic expectation on the patient's part usually works as an irritant on the physicians and nurses, and it causes rejection of the patient.

The following brief case histories show the characteristic features in the development of personality factors, environmental stimuli, family relationships, and interpersonal relations that lead to the manifestation of an acute state of ulcerative colitis.

Case 3. The patient was a slim, pleasant looking, 24-year-old single woman. She began to suffer from pain, abdominal cramps, and severe diarrhea two months before her admission to the hospital, which was her first hospitalization. She was an only daughter. Her mother lost her parents during World War II, and the patient was given her grandmother's first name. After her birth, her mother decided not to have any more children. This decision was made because of the father's cardiac condition, their financial difficulties, and her mother's feeling of inability to cope with an additional child. The mother felt that she had fulfilled her obligation toward her own mother by having given life to her daughter. The father accepted her decision without protest. He was a tired and silent person who did not make any demands on his family. He died when the patient was 11 years old, and she did not recall having reacted with great sorrow to his death.

The patient was a bright and intelligent child. By the time she had started nursery school, she had already learned the alphabet. She always felt the need to be close to her mother, however, and it took several weeks before she could stay in kindergarten. This took place only after she felt she had become the center of her teacher's attention.

After the father's death, the mother and daughter planned that she would become a doctor. Her uncle was a male hospital attendant, and she had heard stories about illnesses, operations, and doctors. She used to have nightmares about being operated upon.

The patient was a good student, but she became a loner among her peer group. She had the feeling that no one was interested in her but her mother. Both she and her mother blamed the teachers for not being nice to her. She never joined any youth movement or girl scout group. She never went out with boys; when neighborhood boys started to talk to her, she snubbed them. Both mother and daughter talked about the necessity for her to get a higher education; all the planning was on an abstract level. They apparently were both concerned with and afraid of the future. Her only pleasure and hobby was playing the flute. At the university, she passed her exams easily and was on the way to graduation as a high-school teacher. At about that time, her mother's friends brought a childhood friend of the mother's to their home. He was a pleasant, middle-aged man who had lost his wife a short while earlier. In the course of a few months, it became clear that he was seriously interested in marrying the mother. The patient became panicky and reacted with abdominal pains and diarrhea. Since then, she tried to avoid meeting the man. Within two months, the full-blown clinical picture of ulcerative colitis appeared, with eight to ten bowel movements daily. Her physical condition necessitated her admission to hospital.

She had great difficulty in getting along with the hospital environment. She refused to cooperate with the staff and complained that she was not used to "getting orders." She was critical about the physical facilities, and she felt that she did not have enough privacy. When her demands were not met immediately, she reacted with nagging complaints. The attitude that she reflected was that she was doing a favor to the medical staff by remaining in the hospital. Clashes and provocations with the nurses were daily features. Whenever any of her requests were refused, she either cried with an expression of having been insulted, or indicated that she was in pain and on the verge of bleeding. She played on her flute in the middle of the night and could not understand why the nurses interfered with her night concerts.

Her guilt-ridden mother felt absolutely helpless about her daughter's illness. She did not dare to think about continuing her relationship with her friend. Upon the patient's request, she once brought him to the hospital for a visit, and the patient's reaction was a combination of severe pain and diarrhea, followed by a long list of complaints about the cold and inconsiderate nurses.

Case 4. This patient was a 40-year-old single female, who was admitted to the hospital with the classic symptoms of ulcerative colitis. She was the only one in a family of five children who never married and continued to live with her mother. Her father died when she was in her teens. The relationship with her mother was a "symbiotic" one and, amazingly enough, she shared the same bed with her mother after the death of her father. The event that precipitated the onset of the ulcerative colitis took place as follows. A sister of her mother became widowed, and, shortly thereafter, she came to live with the patient and her mother. She also brought some of her furniture with her, which included a pair of twin beds. The mother then sold her large bed and substituted the twin beds so that she and her daughter (the patient) slept in separate beds. It was shortly after this that the illness started.

Once the emotional precipitating factor was uncovered in the weekly psychosomatic conference a mature and understanding social worker was assigned to the patient. Fortunately, the social worker was able to develop a close, warm, and supporting relationship with the patient, as well as to arrange for moving the patient's aunt to her own small apartment. This, together with excellent medical care, led to the patient's gradual recovery. After the patient was discharged from the hospital, she continued medical treatment with an understanding medical resident in the psychosomatic clinic and continued her relationship with the social worker, who became a "mother substitute."

THERAPEUTIC INTERVENTIONS

Considering the severe psychopathology of the majority of patients with ulcerative colitis, great reservation is recommended in the use of confrontation or interpretive therapy. The psychologically helpless patient often has no inner resources for coping with a confrontation with his unconscious motives. Episodes of profuse bleeding can be precipitated by careless remarks, even if these are intended to be constructive or necessary for the continuation of medical care.

Our view is in absolute agreement with that of Karush (7), namely, that patients with strong symbiotic tendencies can be helped through support, catharsis, ventilation, and suggestion.

A word of warning is in order regarding the use of insight therapy. In our opinion, it is preferable for ulcerative colitis patients to be kept under the comprehensive care of their family physician. As in other psychophysiological conditions, the maintenance of "continuous consultation" with a psychiatrist is recommended, instead of the abrupt and occasional "diagnostic consultation." Environmental manipulations can yield favorable treatment results when performed by the medical practitioner in close cooperation with the psychiatric consultant. The term *continuous consultation* implies that the psychiatrist also has a responsibility in the management of the family physician's patient, along principles similar to those involved in "mental-health consultation" and is available for continuous contact with his medical colleague.

REFERENCES

1. Bralow SP: Current concepts of peptic ulceration. Am J Dig Dis 14:655–677, 1969

2. Cruveilhier J: Anatomie pathologique du corps humain au description avec figures lithographiees et colorees des diverses alteration morbides dont le corps humain est susceptible, Vol I. Paris, Bailliere, 1829

3. Engel GL: Studies of ulcerative colitis: V. Psychological aspects and their implications for treatment. Am J Dig Dis 3:315–337, 1968

4. Hertz DG: Problems and challenges of consultation psychiatry. In Musaph H(ed): Mechanisms in Symptom Formation. Basel, S Karger, 1974, pp 67–76

5. Kapp FT, Rosenbaum M, Romano J: Psychological factors in men with peptic ulcers. Am J Psychiatry 103:700–704, 1947

6. Karush A, Daniels GE, O'Conner JF, Stern LO: The response to psychotherapy in chronic ulcerative colitis: I. Pretreatment factors. Psychosom Med 30:255–276, 1968

7. Karush A, Daniels GE, O'Conner JF, Stern LO: The response to psychotherapy in chronic ulcerative colitis. II. Factors arising from the therapeutic situation. Psychosom Med 31: 201–226, 1969

8. Lidz T, Rubinstein R: Psychology of gastrointestinal disorders. In Arieti S(ed): American Handbook of Psychiatry, Vol I. New York, Basic Books, 1959, pp 678–689

9. McKegney FP, Gordon RO, Levine SM: A psychosomatic comparison of patients with ulcerative colitis and Crohn's disease. Psychosom Med 32: 153–166, 1970

10. McMahon AW, Schmitt P, Patterson JF, Rothman E: Personality differences between inflammatory bowel disease patients and their healthy siblings. Psychosom Med 32:153–166, 1970

11. Mirsky IA: Physiologic, psychologic and social determinants in the etiology of duodenal ulcer. Am J Dig Dis 3:285, 1958

12. Murray CD: Psychogenic factors in the etiology of ulcerative colitis and bloody diarrhea. Am J Med Sci 180:239, 1930

13. Rosenbaum M: Peptic ulcer. In Freedman AM, Kaplan HI (eds): Comprehensive Textbook of Psychiatry. Baltimore, Williams & Wilkins, 1967, pp 1049–1054

14. Stenback A, Siurale M: Duodenal ulcer and functional dyspepsia in prisoners. J Psychosom Res 8:127, 1964

15. Weiner H, Thaler M, Reiser MF, Mirsky IA: Etiology of duodenal ulcer. I. Relation of specific psychological characteristic to rate of gastric secretion (serum pepsinogen). Psychosom Med 19:1, 1957

16. Wolf S, Wolff HG: Human Gastric Function. New York, Oxford University Press, 1943

17. Wright R: Progress in gastroenterology. Ulcerative colitis. Gastroenterology 58: 875–897, 1970

26 Neurological Disorders

HARRY A. TEITELBAUM

The clinical aspects of psychosomatic neurological diseases are much more complex than those of other systems, since they may embrace every system in the body, either individually or in various combinations. In addition, the psychopathology involves not only functions of the nervous system, but also the functions of other systems, such as respiration, digestion, and so forth. Because of this, any meaningful review of psychosomatic neurological disturbances requires attention to detailed and complex interrelationships.

PSYCHOSOMATIC NEUROLOGICAL PROCESSES

Psychosomatic neurological processes involve nerve impulse integration, which is neither additive nor cause-and-effect in nature. Healthy neurological function involves ongoing reintegration that is appropriate to the adaptation taking place. In pathological neurological conditions—whether organic or psychosomatic—nerve impulse integration is impaired, with associated disintegration and reintegration. Such reintegration can become compensatory in varying degrees and thus be adequately adaptive to the current situation, or it can be maladaptive, as I have discussed in detail elsewhere (61).

The nerve impulse may be viewed as the product of the metabolism of a variety of humoral agents and their enzyme systems (45). Therefore, the metabolism of such agents as norepinephrine, dopamine, and serotonin, along with the proper functioning of their essential enzyme systems, is basic to neurological integration. The impairment of these metabolic processes plays a significant role in psychosomatic neurological disturbances, as does dopamine deficiency in Parkinson's syndrome.

PSYCHOSOMATIC NEUROLOGICAL SYMPTOMS AND SYNDROMES

Psychosomatic neurological disturbances may occur either with or without the presence of organic neurological disease. Some psychosomatic neurological symptoms are clearly psychogenic in nature, such as midline-trunk hemianesthesia, concentric peripheral visual-field constriction, or polyopia; whereas others may mimic essentially organic disease, as in extrapyramidal syndromes, convulsive disorders, or aphasia (56, 57). In the latter category, whether a psychogenic element is present must be determined on the basis of the patient's history and the course of the illness.

Psychosomatic neurological symptoms may involve a limited anatomic area, part of a single system, several systems, or the entire body. Such symptoms may be constant or intermittent, or they may vary from time to time. The tendency to vary significantly suggests psychogenicity, but such variability and remitting tendency may also occur in multiple sclerosis. Syndromes can vary similarly. Groen *et al.* (26) referred to "syndrome shift" as occurring in organic as well as psychosomatic illness, even with both organic and psychogenic disturbances in the same patient. "Syndrome formation, suppression and shift, therefore," they maintained, "are phenomena of substitution, which develop under the influence of various factors of biological, somatic, psychological, and social nature, which are all integrated in the individual's total personality" (26).

Psychiatrists have long pondered the issue whether certain personality types are subject to specific psychosomatic symptoms or syndromes, or whether no such specificity exists. Kubie (32) advocated a concept of nonspecificity in psychosomatic cases, a view that is supported by my own experience.

CRANIAL NERVE FUNCTIONS

Psychosomatic disturbances involving the cranial nerves may occur as isolated symptoms, may exist concomitantly, or may be elements in various syndromes.

SMELL

Subjective smell experiences may be hallucinatory, as in the case of a schizophrenic woman who smelled the flesh of a decaying baby when she was pregnant. They also occur in uncinate fits in psychomotor epilepsy involving the temporal lobe of the brain.

The loss of the sense of smell may be psychogenic, or it may result from a variety of organic conditions. In a case that I reported elsewhere—"case 11" (61)—the psychogenic anosmia was unilateral and was associated with other homolateral disturbances such as those in taste and hearing.

VISION

Walsh (64) referred to various psychosomatic disturbances in vision, and I have reviewed this problem in detail (61). Psychogenic photophobia may be associated with eyelid spasm and concentric constriction of the visual fields. Such patients usually wear dark glasses, even indoors. Bartemeier (5) described psychogenic micropsia. Garvey (23) discussed hysterical homonymous hemianopia associated with midline body diminution of pain sensation and glove-and-stocking analgesia with rapid spontaneous recovery.

The differential diagnosis between psychogenic and organic blindness can be made by means of electroencephalography (EEG). I have previously described (60) a female patient with loss of vision and a multiplicity of other psychosomatic symptoms that changed from time to time throughout a number of years. Her EEG showed definite alpha blocking to light stimulation, although she was blind clinically. In organic blindness, alpha wave blocking does not occur. A patient whom I have described in another work—"case 10" (61)—had transitory unilateral blindness with marked constriction of the visual fields; this patient recovered promptly. Abrupt, remitting unilateral loss of vision is also seen in cases of multiple sclerosis, but it is associated with a central scotoma due to retrobulbar neuritis, which is readily identified opthalmoscopically. The psychodynamics of hysterical blindness have been formulated by Freud (22).

Subjective visual experiences occur in temporal lobe pathology. Jackson (27) described a classic picture of a patient with psychomotor epilepsy, who had a vision of a little black woman in the act of cooking. Visual hallucinations occur commonly in various psychoses as symbolic projections of the patients' inner conflicts.

EYE MOVEMENTS

Organic double vision results from dysfunction of the extraocular muscles, and it is evident only when both eyes are open. Psychogenic diplopia is monocular, since it persists with only one eye open. Monocular diplopia can occur, however, when there is a physical defect of the eye itself, as in a patient with corneal injury of his left eye. Polyopia—*i.e.,* seeing an object in triplicate or more—is psychogenic and may be either monocular or binocular. Nystagmus has a number of organic causes, but it, too, may be psychogenic.

FACIAL SENSATION

Psychogenic pain may present difficulties in differentiating it from trigeminal neuralgia. The syndrome of atypical facial neuralgia is a diagnostic problem. It is considered to be psychosomatic in nature by Engel (17). Psychogenic dental pain has been studied by Wolff (70).

Organic facial hemianesthesia has a clear midline demarcation for touch, pain, and temperature, but not for vibration, which is transmitted across the midline through the skull. If vibratory sensations also show a midline demarcation, the disturbance is psychogenic. Frequently, in cases of psychogenic facial hemianesthesia, homolateral disturbances also occur in other cranial nerve functions.

FACIAL MOVEMENTS

In unilateral facial paralysis due to a stroke, involving the lower two-thirds of the face, and sparing the forehead, the patient cannot contract the involved muscles voluntarily but he can smile on that side, so that the facial paralysis may be erroneously considered as psychogenic. After recovery from facial neuritis and Bell's Palsy, on one side, spasms, and contracture of the involved muscles may occur. This may give the impression that there was a shift of the impairment to the normal side, and it may be misinterpreted as psychogenic. Psychogenic fasciculations and spasms (tics) of the facial muscles are not infrequent and may be associated with spasms elsewhere in the body. Organic fasciculations occur in amyotrophic lateral sclerosis.

TASTE

Psychogenic loss of taste, if unilateral, is usually associated with the loss of other cranial nerve functions, such as smell, vision, or hearing, as in a case that I have described previously, "case 11" (61). Unilateral loss of taste also occurs in facial neuritis because the sensory roots of the facial nerve contain fibers conveying deep sensation from the face and taste fibers from the anterior two-thirds of the tongue. Subjective taste experiences, usually unpleasant, occur in uncinate fits involving temporal lobe lesions. Taste hallucinations occur in schizophrenia and other psychoses.

HEARING AND VESTIBULAR FUNCTIONS

Unilateral loss of hearing is fairly common in psychosomatic illness, and it is usually associated with homolateral impairment of other functions. Deafness is associated at times with vestibular symptoms such as vertigo or ataxia. Psychogenic sensitivity to loud noise and the tendency to hear ordinary noises as unusually intensified (hyperacusis) may occur, as does tinnitus.

Psychosomatic vestibular symptoms—particularly vertigo and, less often, nystagmus, ataxia, nausea, and vomiting—have been described by Moore and Atkinson (40). Nystagmus, vertigo, ataxia, and diplopia have been described in a schizophrenic patient by Grinker and Robbins (25). These symptoms are not unusual in multiple sclerosis.

SPEECH AND SWALLOWING

Psychosomatic speech disturbances involve aphonia, stuttering, hoarseness, or hypervocalization, and they are often associated with other symptoms. The psychodynamics of speech disturbances are discussed by Fenichel (19).

Dysphagia associated with the sensation of a tight feeling of the throat—or globus hystericus—is quite common. Considerable symbolic significance is related to dysphagia (19, 20).

TONGUE MOVEMENTS

In unilateral hypoglossal nerve disease, there may be homolateral atrophy, weakness, and deviation of the tongue to the weak side. In psychosomatic unilateral weakness of the tongue, however, the tongue deviates to the opposite side, so that the differential diagnosis is readily made. Hysterical spasms of the tongue and of the surrounding musculature do occur, and they may play a role in stuttering. Jackson's patient (27) with apraxia could not protrude his tongue or use it in speech, but he had no difficulty while eating or drinking. Phenothiazine treatment of long duration may result in a tardive dyskinesia with uncontrollable movements of the tongue and lips, which has been studied by Crane and Smeets (12) in geriatric patients. Tardive dyskinesia occurs less often in younger people.

SENSORY NEUROLOGICAL FUNCTION

Psychosomatic sensory changes are recognizable in many instances because the patterns of sensory impairment do not comply with established anatomic or physiological patterns of sensory innervation, as in well-defined glove-and-stocking anesthesia, midline trunk hemianesthesia, loss of vibratory sensation on one side of the midline and its retention on the other side, or in the psychogenic regional pain of Walters (65).

Noordenbos (42) discussed the difficulties in maping out sensory diminution or loss. Kelly (29) reviewed the natural variations in the distribution of the peripheral nerves; such variations might lead the observer to misinterpret the symptoms as psychosomatic. Nerve conduction studies may be very helpful in such problems.

Sensory disturbances are relatively common in cases of hysteria. With reference to the so-called hysterical personality, Ziegler, Imboden, and Meyer (71) found "hysterical characteristics" in less than half their patients, and they concluded that this type of personality structure is not essential for the development of conversion reactions. This complies with the concept of nonspecificity of psychosomatic disturbances with reference to personality. Seitz (51) showed, by means of hypnosis, that sensory psychosomatic symptoms could be converted to other sensory, motor, or visceral disturbances.

Walters (65) distinguished between "psychogenic regional pain" and hysterical pain; the former occurs in every type of psychiatric illness and results from maladaptation to various types of stress. The psychodynamics of regional pain are discussed in lucid detail in Walters' article.

Silverman (53) discussed the relationship of repressed hostility to psychosomatic pain, and Rosen (47) pointed out the hazard of excessive surgery in patients with hysterical pain. Such pain may involve various parts of the body and is often difficult to resolve. It is not unusual to see patients who have suffered injuries and who have pain that continues for years afterward, with no valid organic basis for the pain. Such problems are often complicated by issues of litigation and compensation. In addition, one has to be alert to the likelihood of erroneously diagnosing pain as psychogenic when it is not explainable on an organic basis early in an illness.

In a case previously reported—"case 27" (61)—the patient had had marital conflict, and she suffered anesthesia below the midlumbar region as well as paraplegia, but she demonstrated normal tendon reflexes as well as normal bowel and bladder function. She experienced complete, spontaneous recovery rather abruptly in several days. Such patients may later suffer a recurrence of the same symptoms or experience a shift to other psychosomatic disturbances.

MOTOR NEUROLOGICAL FUNCTION

Psychosomatic motor disturbances may resemble organic motor disease—such as parkinsonism, epilepsy, or chorea—or, sometimes, they can be recognized by their deviation from such well-defined organic disorders. The latter include astasia abasia, a bizarre form of instability in standing or walking, and camptocormia, a marked flexion contracture of the body at the waist (46). The feeling of tension in emotional disturbances is actually related to an increase in muscle tone, and it may be associated with tremors, clonic or tonic spasms, as well as pain. Shagass and Malmo (52) confirmed this with electromyographic studies. A muscle relaxant, *e.g.*, diazepam, may provide relief in such cases.

Torticollis or spastic rotation of the head to one side requires differential diagnosis from a number of organic clinical entities such as chorea, athetosis, and dystonia musculorum deformans. Torticollis may be a partial or early manifestation of one of these diseases, so that a diagnosis of hysterical torticollis might be made erroneously. Chorea, athetosis, and dystonia may also occur on a psychogenic basis, however, and they can then be treated by hypnosis or narcotherapy. Seitz (51) treated a patient with hysterical tremor by means of hypnosis, and the patient developed torticollis in the hypnotic state. Rosen (47) corrected the torticollis in a patient by means of hypnotic suggestion, but the patient became paranoid. The paranoid reaction cleared up when the torticollis was reestablished by means of hypnosis. Another of my previously reported cases—"case 26" (61)—showed a very stressful history, with torticollis and other psychosomatic symptoms, including epilepsy. The patient's electroencephalogram was normal, as it was in "case 11" (61).

Denervated muscle is subject to increased activity, as in the facial muscle spasm seen in Bell's palsy. This may lead to the erroneous conclusion that the disturbance is psychogenic. Bender (6) was able to demonstrate in monkeys that denervated muscle is hypersensitive to acetylcholine when the animal is under emotional stress. Bird and I (62) confirmed this by the observation that neostigmine augmented the fasciculations in progressive muscular atrophy by facilitating acetylcholine action.

I have previously referred to the various manifestations of psychogenic motor disturbances as fatigability, contractures, pain, tremor, and weakness that may range from partial to complete paralysis of various muscle groups (61). Psychosomatic disorders also occur along with well-defined organic diseases, and Brickner (9) stressed the importance of recognizing the degree of psychosomatic disturbance present.

PSYCHOSOMATIC NEUROLOGICAL SYNDROMES

BRAIN TUMORS

Premorbid personality plays a significant role in the emotional and personality changes in patients with brain tumors, so that the intellectual, neurotic, psychotic, and personality disturbances that are seen are often individual adaptations (10). Weinstein and Kahn (66) discussed the defensive significance of such adaptations. *e.g.,* in the tendency to deny illness.

The incidence of brain tumors in patients in psychiatric hospitals has been reviewed previously (61). Anderson (2) reported tumors in 3% of 5682 patients. Pincus and Tucker (45) emphasized that personality and thought disturbances, such as those occurring in schizophrenia and depression, may be significant early symptoms of organic brain disease, including tumors.

Hypochondriacal preoccupation with the brain tumor is similar to such preoccupation exhibited by patients with cancer or heart disease. Elsewhere, I have discussed the psychodynamics of the following case, originally "case 35" (61):

Case 1. The patient was a 36-year-old woman with dizzy spells and an obsessive preoccupation with the fear of having a brain tumor. The neurological examination was normal. She reacted with panic, heart palpitation, depression, weakness, and fear that her legs might give way. The patient's parents had fought with the patient and with one another. She felt inferior and terribly afraid of new people and crowds, and she believed that people did not like her and talked critically about her. She had repeated nightmares since childhood that involved rough oceans on which she was stranded at the mercy of giant waves. After her marriage, her dreams often involved being divorced. Her sexual adjustment was very turbulent. Her husband was an immature, irresponsible, dependent, aggressive person. At first she referred to him as being very wonderful, but later she was able to talk freely about their severe conflicts. In psychotherapy, the patient worked through many of her conflicts, became relieved of her hypochondriacal obsession with having a brain tumor, and made a much better adaptation to her ongoing life.

I have previously discussed tumor types and their localization as related to psychiatric symptoms (61). Although these relationships are variable, Brock and Wiesel (10) determined that frontal and temporal lobe tumors are more likely to be associated with characteristic psychiatric symptoms. Malamud (37) studied the pathology of tumors involving the limbic system of patients who had been misdiagnosed as having psychiatric disorders. Stevens *et al.* (55) demonstrated that psychological changes, like those that occur in focal temporal lobe lesions and psychomotor epilepsy, could be induced in patients by deep temporal-lobe stimulation.

HEAD INJURIES

Psychosomatic disturbances associated with head injuries are often complicated by litigation and compensation issues. Schilder (49) maintained that emotional disturbances related to head injuries may become evident years later. Goldstein (24) considered head injury symptoms as evidence of an individual's adaptability; such patients may do well in clearly defined, concrete situations, but not when dealing with abstractions.

Cerebral concussion has much psychosomatic significance. It involves a period of loss of consciousness, and there may be amnesia with regard to the events of the injury and afterward as well as sometimes regarding the period preceding the injury. In cases of concussion alone, there is usually no gross evidence of brain damage, although concussion may be associated with such damage. The symptoms may include headache, dizziness, nausea, vomiting, and many others. Denny-Brown (13) maintained that the electroencephalogram showed characteristic changes in cerebral concussion.

Head injury may involve intellectual, neurotic, psychotic, or personality disturbances; at times, all of them may result.

Case 2. A male patient felt confused following a head injury with loss of consciousness. He would awaken in a tremulous, fearful state, and he experienced numbness of both arms, a burning sensation in his chest, dizziness, and headaches. His memory and orientation were impaired, and he would get lost driving in a city that he knew well. He understood but would forget what people said. His speech became mixed up, and he was depressed and discouraged. He became paranoid and threatened to kill his physician and blow up his employer's plant because he thought that they were responsible for the accident and not interested in helping him. Following hospitalization, he became passive and did not express paranoid thoughts.

The neurological examination showed a positive Romberg test and diminished sensation on the right side, but the position sense was normal. Pin-prick elicited inappropriate laughter.

This patient's head injury and cerebral concussion resulted in memory loss and disorientation as well as in psychogenic diminution of sensation on the right side of his body and paranoid psychosis.

INFECTIONS OF THE NERVOUS SYSTEM

Infections can give rise to intellectual, neurotic, psychotic, or personality disorders. Weinstein, Linn, and Kahn (67) stressed the significance of the premorbid personalities of patients in their adaptation to encephalitis. Psychosomatic disturbances do not show any specific relationship to the type of nervous system infection.

I have reviewed (61) the psychosomatic aspects of brain abscess, meningitis, luetic encephalitis, measles, German measles, smallpox and vaccination, chicken pox, mumps, influenza, infectious mononucleosis, poliomyelitis, herpes zoster, and viral encephalitis, with particular attention to the extrapyramidal sequelae of the last mentioned. Differential diagnosis from essentially psychogenic illnesses in the early stages of such infections is often a problem. Recently, I saw a patient with meningitis who had been treated with apparent recovery six months earlier. He developed aberrant behavior, and was referred for psychiatric care. The neurological examination was normal at first, but he soon developed papilledema, and other somatic symptoms appeared later. A brain scan showed the classic halo of a frontal lobe abscess. Surgical evacuation of the abscess resulted in recovery.

Comparable to the case mentioned previously of hypochondriacal preoccupation with brain tumor was the case described elsewhere—"case 44" (61)—of a 14-year-old girl who became obsessively preoccupied with polio following a fainting spell when she received her polio inoculation.

Parkinson's syndrome, which may be postencephalitic, may also be psychogenic in nature. I have previously discussed this matter in detail and have discussed case histories to show the development of parkinsonian symptoms following bodily injury (61). Bird's patient (7) developed a parkinsonian syndrome following a very stressful experience in the Navy during World War II, although there was no bodily injury in this case.

Misra and Hay (39) reported three cases of encephalitis that were initially misdiagnosed as schizophrenia. These patients later developed elevated temperatures, Babinski's reflexes, slow EEG waves, and extrapyramidal symptoms. One patient recovered completely, another developed chronic schizophrenia, and a third developed postencephalitic parkinsonism. These patients resembled another of my previously reported cases, "case 45" (61).

CEREBRAL VASCULAR DISEASE

The vascular system, when under stress, is subject to a variety of abnormal clinical states, such as hypertension, transitory cerebral circulatory insufficiency, and arterial spasms, which may lead to significant psychomatic deviations. Engel (16) has related essential hypertension to unexpressed anger. The significance of the patient's personality in the development of the psychosomatic disturbances in cerebral vascular disease has been discussed by Wolff (70). Adler, MacRitchie, and Engel (1) reported that ischemic stroke usually developed during tense, emotional experiences involving the gratification of dependent needs or the need to appease the demands of others. These patients experienced marked frustration and shame when these goals were not gratified, and they developed an associated cerebral vascular thrombosis.

Several cases of psychosomatic cerebral vascular insufficiency, during which transitory somatic symptoms occurred, have been described (62). One patient, who had a long history of psychiatric illness, developed temporary paralysis and numbness of the right arm. Another patient suffered the symptoms of dizziness and temporary left hemiparesis associated with depression, which were related to the death of his son. Seidenberg and Ecker (50) demonstrated spasm of the intracranial portion of the internal carotid artery, as well as of other cerebral vessels, in patients with severe neurosis and rigid personalities, and they ascribed the vascular spasm to emotional stress.

Migraine is a classic psychosomatic cerebral vascular disturbance. Wolff (70) showed that the spotty vision and other somatic symptoms of this disorder result from cerebral vascular constriction, whereas the headache itself is due to the distension of relaxed cerebral vessels, particularly the branches of the external carotid artery, in patients with unstable personalities. Engel *et al.* (18) maintained that migraine attacks were related to unexpressed anger as well as to associated vasospasm of branches of the internal carotid artery. They reported focal EEG changes due to areas of acute cerebral ischemia. The latter may sometimes give rise to irreversible cerebral damage.

The following case—"case 49" (61) illustrates certain aspects of migraine:

Case 3. A 15-year-old female patient suffered episodes of bright spots and wavy lines before her eyes, numbness and weakness of the right side of her body, and difficulties with speech, followed by a throbbing headache on the left side. Although she knew what she wanted to say, her speech would be garbled and unintelligible, as in motor aphasia. She had had headaches since the age of 4 and "migraine headaches" since the age of 12.

The patient had "chorea" at the age of 5, and she feared new experiences. Her mother carried her around to protect her from any fatigue or stress, in order to avoid "rheumatic fever." The patient became "hysterical," according to the mother, if the parents tried to leave her with someone else. She cried, vomited, and threw herself out of bed. She had nightmares until she was 10 years old.

I have had a number of patients in psychotherapy with neuroses and migraine, but with these patients, little success has been achieved in relieving the migraine despite significant improvement in other respects. Drug treatment with ergotamine and other agents has not always been helpful. Migraine may improve considerably as patients get older; a 60-year-old man, for example, had had severe attacks since high-school days, but in more recent years, he has experienced occasional spotty vision but no headache.

Histamine headaches or cluster headaches are disturbing psychosomatic manifestations of emotional maladaptation. I have reported a patient—"case 50" (61)—who responded well to histamine desensitization without psychotherapy, despite severe neurosis. Desensitization, however, is not always successful.

EPILEPSY

Although the several types of epilepsy—such as petit mal, grand mal, jacksonian seizures, psychomotor epilepsy, and a number of variants—all have significant psychiatric aspects, the aberrant behavior in psychomotor seizures is of major interest. Dreifuss (15) ascribed complex partial seizures to a multiplicity of conditions, both organic and psychiatric and including neuroses and psychoses, with the temporal lobes and the limbic system playing a major role in giving rise to the symptoms involved. Barker (3) considered the epileptic spell as evidence of an organism-environment maladaptation that is equivalent to impaired ego integration. Penfield and Erickson (43) were able to reproduce seizures, including automatisms and psychotic states, by electrical stimulation of the temporal-lobe cortex in patients. Flor-Henry (21) confirmed that psychosis in temporal-lobe epilepsy is inversely related to the frequency of psychomotor seizures, and he maintained that the psychosis is related to the epileptic process.

Attempts have been made to differentiate essentially organic epilepsy from the psychogenic form by means of electroencephalography. Livingston (36) found the use of EEG to be helpful in this respect, but Wikler (68) did not. Barker (3) was able to correlate an abnormal EEG pattern with stressful experiences in the past in epileptic patients with emotional disturbances.

The personality of the epileptic patient has long been stigmatized as inadequate. This erroneous point of view was based on studies of institutionalized epileptics who also suffered character and mental disturbances. Diethelm and Jones (14) showed that there were normal and superior people among epileptics outside of institutions. Lennox and Markham (35) found, too, that the average intelligence of epileptics outside of institutions was normal or superior.

Pincus and Tucker (45) as well as this author (61) have reviewed the neurotic, psychotic, and character disorders that occur in epileptic patients. Such disturbances are more common in cases of psychomotor epilepsy. The significance of psychogenicity in epileptic seizures is strongly supported by a number of investigators, such as Barker, Burgwin, and Simmons (4) and others. Mulder (41) maintained that the psychiatric disturbances in epileptics are similar to those seen in other psychiatric patients. Psychotherapy has been effective in treating such patients.

I have previously described the case—"case 52" (61)—of a patient who suffered from a psychoneurosis and grand mal seizures but who had a normal EEG, and the following case—"case 53" (61)—is that of a patient with psychomotor epilepsy and a psychotic reaction:

Case 4. This patient was subject to monthly spells that lasted several minutes and consisted of disorganized motor activity, loss of consciousness, and amnesia. Following the attacks, she was confused; she had claimed that she and her "business" had been shown on television and that she had also seen her "baby in the sky" on television. When the patient was questioned about these hallucinations, she denied any knowledge about them. An EEG revealed mild, left temporal lobe disorganization that was compatible with the diagnosis of psychomotor epilepsy.

The treatment of epilepsy by means of a judicious use of anticonvulsant medication has been reviewed in detail by Pincus and Tucker (45). In addition to the use of such drugs, psychotherapy can be of inestimable value.

PRESENILE AND SENILE CEREBRAL DEGENERATION.

Patients in this category of illness show intellectual impairment, behavior disturbances, neuroses, or psychoses. Although cerebral arteriosclerosis is often the basis for senile psychosis, Schieve and Wilson (48) were able to differentiate a form of primary senile dementia that was not due to cerebral arteriosclerotic disease. The regressive aspects of the primary disorder are evident in memory loss for recent events but with retention of memory for events that occurred earlier in life, as well as in the deterioration of behavior with poor personal hygiene. Kahn *et al.* (28) found that the premorbid personality as well as the vocational and social background of the patient are significant in determining the mental changes, whereas age itself plays a less important role. Kiev *et al.* (31) observed that stress that resulted from the patients' difficulty in adapting to environmental demands because of their limitations, intellectual and otherwise, was significant in aggravating the mental disturbances of such patients. Williams *et al.* (69) reported that the stress of social isolation and insecurity was responsible to a significant degree for the disintegration of personality in people with dementia.

Pincus and Tucker (45) have discussed the pathology and clinical aspects of organic brain syndromes. That there is room for innovation in the area of treatment for the patient with chronic brain syndrome has been shown by the work of Ching-Piao Chien (11), who obtained significant improvement in geriatric patients, 70% of whom had chronic brain syndrome, by means of social beer-drinking sessions. Kern (30) reviewed the essential factors in caring for the aged from individual and social points of view, and Lehmann and Ban (34) have presented a broad discussion of drug treatment.

DEGENERATIVE NEUROLOGICAL DISEASES AND THOSE OF UNDETERMINED CAUSE

The psychosomatic aspects of the various entities in this group of diseases—which includes amyotrophic lateral sclerosis, progressive muscular atrophy, chorea, athetosis, hepatolenticular degeneration, dystonia musculorum deformans, multiple sclerosis, the hereditary ataxias, and the conglomerate of mental deficiences—have been reviewed by Bird *et al.* (8) and by myself and my colleagues (61, 63). Psychiatric disturbances occur infrequently in association with the muscular atrophies and dystrophies. The hereditary ataxias are sometimes associated with mental deficiency. The social behavior and the neurotic and psychotic aspects of the various types of mental deficiency have been reviewed elsewhere (61). Masland *et al.* (38) discussed the beneficial effects of psychiatric treatment and a supportive environment, which were also illustrated in cases—"case 63" and "case 64" (61)—that I have described previously.

Multiple sclerosis is associated with a wide range of psychosomatic disturbancs (33, 63). It has been pointed out that there is a difficulty in differentiating multiple sclerosis with psychiatric disturbances from essentially psychogenic illness with psychosomatic neurological symptoms. Slater (54) reported on patients who were diagnosed as having hysteria early in their illness, but were later found to have multiple sclerosis. According to Langworthy *et al.* (33) and Philippopoulos *et al.* (44), a patient's premorbid personality determines the psychiatric symptoms in cases of multiple sclerosis.

REFERENCES

1. Adler R, MacRitchie K, Engel GL: Psychologic processes and ischemic stroke (occlusive cerebrovascular disease). Psychosom Med 33:1–29, 1971

2. Anderson PG: Intracranial tumors in a psychiatric autopsy material. ACTA Psychiatr Scand 46:213–224, 1970

3. Barker W: Studies on epilepsy: the petit mal attack as a response within the central nervous system to distress in organism–environment integration. Psychosom Med 10:73–94, 1948

4. Barker W, Burgwin S, Simmons D: Studies in epilepsy. The significance of "spontaneous" abnormalities in brain wave patterns as observed during interview with epileptic patients. J Nerv Ment Dis 112:197–205, 1950

5. Bartemeier LH: Micropsia. Psychoanal Q 10:573–582, 1941

6. Bender MB: Contractions in denervated muscles induced by fright as evidence of secretion of a parasympathetic hormone. J Mt Sinai Hosp 5:418–441, 1938

7. Bird HW: Varying hypnotizability in a case of Parkinsonism. Bull Menninger Clin 12: 210–217, 1948

8. Bird HW, Teitelbaum HA, Dunn MB: Psychosomatic aspects of encephalomyelopathy with muscle atrophy. Psychosom Med 14:161–173, 1952

9. Brickner RM: Reluctance to move paretic muscles. Arch Neurol Psychiatry 69:129, 1953

10. Brock S, Wiesel B: Psychotic symptoms marking the onset in cases of brain tumor. Med Clin North Am 759–767, May, 1948

11. Chien Ching–Piao: Psychiatric treatment for geriatric patients: "pub" or drug? Am J Psychiatry 127:1070–1075, 1971

12. Crane GE, Smeets RA: Tardive dyskinesia and drug therapy in geriatric patients. Arch Gen Psychiatry 30:341–343, 1974

13. Denny–Brown D: The sequelae of war head injuries. N Engl J Med 227:771–780, 813–821, 1942

14. Diethelm O, Jones MR: Influence of anxiety on attention, learning, retention and thinking. Arch Neurol Psychiatry 58:325–326, 1947

15. Dreifuss PE: The differential diagnosis of partial seizures with complex symptomatology. In Penry JK, Daly DD (eds): Advances in Neurology, Vol 11. New York, Raven Press, 1975, pp 1–13

16. Engel GL: Fainting. Physiological and Psychological Considerations. Springfield Ill, C C Thomas, 1950

17. Engel GL: Primary atypical facial pain. Psychosom Med 13:375–396, 1951

18. Engel GL, Hamburger WW, Reiser M, Plunkett J: Electroencephalographic and psychologic studies of a case of migraine with severe preheadache phenomena: with comments on cerebral vasospasm and focal hypertensive encephalopathy. Psychosom Med 15:337–348, 1953

19. Fenichel O: The Psychoanalytic Theory of Neurosis. New York, WW Norton, 1945

20. Ferenczi S: Die "Materialisation" beim Globus Hystericus. Int Z Psychoanal 9:68, 1928

21. Flor–Henry P: Psychosis and temporal lobe epilepsy: a controlled investigation. Epilepsia 10:363–395, 1969

22. Freud S: Psychogenic Visual Disturbances According to Psychoanalytical Conceptions, Vol 2. Collected Papers. London, Hogarth, 1950, pp 105–112

23. Garvey JL: Hysteric homonymous hemianopsia. Am J Ophthalmol 5:721–722, 1922

24. Goldstein K: The Organism. A Holistic Approach to Biology Derived from Pathological Data in Man. New York, American Elsevier, 1939

25. Grinker RR, Robbins FP: Psychosomatic Case Book. New York, Blakiston, 1964

26. Groen J, Bastiaans J, van der Valk JM: Psychosomatic aspects of syndrome shift and syndrome suppression. In Booij J (ed): Psychosomatics. Nostrand, 1957, pp 33–59

27. Jackson JH: Case of a tumor of the right temperosphenoidal lobe, bearing on the localization of the sense of smell and the interpretation of a particular variety of epilepsy. In Taylor J(ed): Selected Writings of John Hughlings Jackson. London, Hodder & Stoughton, 1931, pp 408–411

28. Kahn RL, Pollack M, Goldfarb AL: Factors related to individual differences in mental status of institutionalized aged. In Hoch PH, Zubin J (eds): Psychopathology of Aging. New York, Grune & Stratton, 1961, pp 104–113

29. Kelly M: Spread of sensory and motor loss after nerve injury. Neurology (Minneap) 2:36–45, 1952

30. Kern RA: Emotional problems in relation to aging and old age. Geriatrics 26:82–93, 1971

31. Kiev A, Chapman LF, Guthrie TC, Wolff HG: The highest integrative functions and diffuse cerebral atrophy. Neurology (Minneap) 12:385–393, 1962

32. Kubie LS: The central representation of the symbolic process in psychosomatic disorders. Psychosom Med 15:1–7, 1953

33. Langworthy OR, Kolb L, Androp S: Disturbances of behavior in patients with disseminated sclerosis. Am J Psychiatry 98:243–249, 1941

34. Lehmann HE, Ban TA: Chemotherapy in aged psychiatric patients. Can Psychiatr Assoc J: 14:361–369, 1969

35. Lennox WG, Markham CH: The sociopsychological treatment of epilepsy. JAMA 152: 1690–1694, 1953

36. Livingston S: The Diagnosis and Treatment of Convulsive Disorders in Children. Springfield Ill, CC Thomas, 1956

37. Malamud N: Psychiatric disorder with intracranial tumors of limbic system. Arch Neurol 17:113–123, 1967

38. Masland RL, Sarason SB, Gladwin T: Mental Subnormality. Biological, Psychological and Social Factors. New York, Basic Books, 1959

39. Misra PC, Hay GG: Encephalitis presenting as acute schizophrenia. Br Med J 1:523–533, 1971

40. Moore HE, Atkinson M: Psychogenic vertigo. Arch Otolaryngol 67:347–353, 1958

41. Mulder DW: Paroxysmal psychiatric symptoms observed in epilepsy. Proc Staff Meet Mayo Clin 28:31–35, 1953

42. Noordenbos W: Pain. Problems Pertaining to the Transmission of Nerve Impulses Which Give Rise to Pain. Amsterdam, Elsevier, 1959

43. Penfield W, Erickson TC: Epilepsy and Cerebral Localization. Springfield Ill, CC Thomas, 1941

44. Philippopoulos GS, Wittkower ED, Couseneau A: The etiologic significance of emotional factors in onset and exacerbations of multiple sclerosis. Psychosom Med 20:458-474, 1958

45. Pincus JH, Tucker GJ: Behavioral Neurology. New York, Oxford University Press, 197<

46. Purves–Stewart J: The Diagnosis of Nervous Diseases. London, Edward Arnold, 193<

47. Rosen H: Hypnotherapy in Clinical Psychiatry. New York, Julian, 1953

48. Schieve JF, Wilson WP: The influence of age, anesthesia and cerebral arteriosclerosis on cerebral vascular activity to CO^2. Am J Med 15:171–174, 1953

49. Schilder P: Psychic disturbances after head injuries. Am J Psychiatry 91:155–188, 1934–1935

50. Seidenberg R, Ecker A: Psychodynamic and arteriographic studies of acute cerebral vascular disorders. Report of six patients under the age of fifty without gross pathogenic lesions. Psychosom Med 16:374–392, 1954

51. Seitz PFD: Experiments in the substitution of symptoms by hypnosis. II. Psychosom Med 15:405–424, 1953

52. Shagass C, Malmo RB: Psychodynamic themes and localized muscular tension during psychotherapy. Psychosom Med 16:295–313, 1954

53. Silverman S: The role of aggressive drives in the conversion process. In Deutsch F (ed): On the Mysterious Leap From the Mind to the Body. New York, International Universities Press, 1959, pp 111–130

54. Slater ET: A follow up of patients diagnosed as suffering from hysteria. Psychosom Res 9:9–13, 1965

55. Stevens JR, Mark VH, Erwin F, Pacheco P, Suematsu K: Deep temporal stimulation in man: long-latency, long lasting psychological changes. J Neurosurg 31:435–440, 1969

56. Teitelbaum HA: Psychogenic body image disturbances associated with psychogenic agnosia and aphasia. J Nerv Ment Dis 93:581–612, 1941

57. Teitelbaum HA: The principle of primary and associated disturbances of the higher cortical functions as applied to temporal lobe lesions. J Nerv Ment Dis 96:361–373, 1942

58. Teitelbaum HA: An analysis of the disturbances of the higher cortical functions, agnosia, apraxia, and aphasia. J Nerv Ment Dis 97:44–61, 1943

59. Teitelbaum HA: Psychosomatic aspects of cerebral vascular disease. J Sinai Hosp 9: 82–96, 1960

60. Teitelbaum HA: Psychosomatic aspects of nervous system disease. Psychosomatics 3:1–7, 1962

61. Teitelbaum HA: Psychosomatic Neurology. New York, Grune & Stratton, 1964

62. Teitelbaum HA, Bird WH: A study of fasciculations. J Nerv Ment Dis 108:455–469, 1948

63. Teitelbaum HA, Hall B, Phillips RE: Psychosomatic aspects of multiple sclerosis. Arch Neurol Psychiatry 67:535–544, 1952

64. Walsh FB: Clinical Neuro-Ophthalmology. Baltimore, Williams & Wilkins, 1947

65. Walters A: Psychogenic regional pain alias hysterial pain. Brain 84(1): 1–18, 1961

66. Weinstein EA, Kahn RL: Personality factors in denial of illness. Arch Neurol Psychiatry 69:355–367, 1953

67. Weinstein EA, Linn L, Kahn RL: Encephalitis with a clinical picture of schizophrenia. J Mt Sinai Hosp 21:341–354, 1954–1955

68. Wikler A: Clinical-electroencephalographic correlations, with special reference to epilepsy. JAMA 149:1365–1368, 1952

69. Williams HW, Quesnel E, Fish VW, Goodman L: Studies in senile and arteriosclerotic psychoses. I. Relative significance of extrinsic factors in their development. Am J Psychiatry 98:712–715, 1941–1942

70. Wolff HG: Headache and Other Head Pains. New York, Oxford University Press, 1950

71. Ziegler FJ, Imboden JB, Meyer E: Contemporary conversion reactions: a clinical study. Am J Psychiatry 116:901–910, 1960

27 Obstetrics and Gynecology

HANS MOLINSKI

The gynecologist deals primarily with situations that have an intrinsic emotional element, such as those involving pregnancy, infertility, or contraception. These physicians see a great many healthy women who are at turning points in their lives. The majority of women handle such situations well, and in dealing with them, gynecologists need only to use traditional gynecological expertise. Some women, however, suffer from neurotic distortions, and experience difficulties in facing life. These patients have a variety of misconceptions and unrealistic fears that complicate the gynecologist's task and make a rational approach to treatment difficult. In such cases, the patient's psychological problems must be dealt with if the doctor is to be able to use his gynecological expertise effectively. The gynecologist should, therefore, be thoughly familiar with the psychosomatic approach. This does not mean that the gynecologist should attempt to practice formal psychotherapy in addition to his more traditional role; rather, it implies that he should integrate psychotherapy into his own work by developing procedures adapted to the particular aspects of his own speciality. He must learn how to do his usual work in a psychosomatically oriented manner by developing new ways of communicating with and relating to his patients, he must learn to recognize and understand his patients' feelings and reactions, and he must also learn to recognize and understand his own reactions to various patients. Psychosomatic medicine exists only when an expert in somatic medicine applies both scientific knowledge and psychological skill simultaneously.

By integrating psychotherapy into gynecology, the gynecologist can achieve better treatment results and often can be of more benefit than the psychiatrist. With patients who are treated over a number of years, the psychotherapeutic process can, when employed by the gynecologist, reach a depth not always obtained by shorter psychiatric methods.

THE PSYCHIATRIST'S ROLE IN PSYCHOSOMATIC APPROACHES TO GYNECOLOGY

The psychiatrist's role in developing this integrated approach lies in instructing the gynecologist in the psychological aspects of medicine. He helps develop psychosomatic procedures adapted to the special situation of obstetrics and gynecology, conducts psychosomatic research, and takes over the more severe cases of psychogenic disorders.

A separate psychosomatic department within the obstetrical-gynecological service is better suited to these tasks than is liaison psychiatry. If the psychiatrist is a full-time member of the staff with his office in the obstetrical-gynecological service, then the resident gynecologist can learn from him during daily hospital routine, and both the gynecologist and the psychiatrist can work together on developing procedural methods that are especially adapted to gynecology.

271

It is also highly advantageous for the psychiatrist to be stationed directly at the gynecological hospital, since this allows him a special opportunity for psychiatric research. It provides him ample experience with gynecological patients, and it permits firsthand insights into the research problems presented by gynecology. It also helps the psychiatrist to become acquainted with and, to some degree, to identify with the special problems and attitudes of the gynecologist.

The psychosomatic approach to obstetrics and gynecology must not become a new and more or less independent branch of medicine, but it should remain as a viewpoint within gynecology. The size of the department determines whether psychiatric knowledge is added to gynecology or gynecological knowledge is merely employed in psychiatry.

PSYCHOSOMATIC ASPECTS OF PREGNANCY AND CONTRACEPTION

In actual practice, a gynecologist can profit from the psychosomatic approach in many areas. Since these areas cannot all be thoroughly discussed here, some of the psychological aspects of pregnancy and of oral contraception will be discussed, and a more cursory look will be given to the psychosomatic approach as it is used in other areas.

THE PREGNANCY CONFLICT

Insemination, the induction of ovulation, contraception, sterilization, and abortion have all become available as medical methods in many states and countries. Modern medicine allows control over conception and contraception to the extent that the only decisive factor seems to be the individual's choice. The conscious will and the unconscious, however, often do not coincide.

The decision to have a child by no means rules out the existence of subconscious fears and apprehensions. Both the desire for a child and the fear of a new child are almost invariably operative at the same time. The fears of having a child are partially based on various conflicts of interest that are rooted in reality. The child needs nourishment and costs money, and it thus competes with the mother for goods and the money that buys them. The child is perceived as an oral competitor, despite all the happiness it may bring. The child also demands time and energy, so it confines the mother's social life. Often, the fear of having a child stems from irrational and neurotic sources. Thus, both pregnancy and childlessness are invaribly accompanied by psychic conflicts.

The healthy woman will solve her pregnancy conflicts without great difficulty. This does not mean that she ignores or is unaware of her conflicts. It is precisely because she remains aware of her conflicts that the healthy woman is capable of achieving a compromise among her own needs and interests, the needs of the child, and the interest of third parties, *i.e.,* of her husband, her in-laws, and so on. Achieving this compromise may depend upon her willingness and ability to step aside where necessary.

The neurotic woman, however, often does not come to grips with her pregnancy conflicts but needs a doctor's help to do so. What, then, is the gynecologist's role in the solution of such a pregnancy conflict? Often, the gynecologist must help vacillating patients arrive at a decision. In doing so, he must avoid self-assured advice, because such personal opinion and direct advice are likely to have little effect as long as the patient's secret wishes, fears, and fantasies have not surfaced. What is most important is that the patient must be enabled to articulate her conflicts so that the doctor and patient together can discover an adequate solution. In order to enable the patient to articulate her conflicts, it is necessary for the doctor to listen carefully, even to what appear to be "absurdities." A family-therapy approach is often indicated, and the marital partner should also be consulted.

The gynecologist must be aware that the decision for or against having a child and the solution of inner conflicts are two different things. Measures such as insemination or abortion must not be overrated in regard to conflict situations; such measures do not eliminate or overcome these inner conflicts, they merely alter the outward conditions. Without such a psychic solution to inner conflicts, the alteration of outward conditions merely changes the content of the conflicts. The pregnancy conflict turns into a conflict about the medical measures. The gynecologist must realize that he cannot confine himself to altering the outward conditions through therapeutic measures; he must also face the task of coping with the psychic aspects of pregnancy conflicts.

A 33-year-old mother of two children complained sadly to her gynecologist of being pregnant again. She said that she had suffered many losses the previous year; her father had died, and her brother had been killed in an accident.

A colleague was asked for his advice. He thought that the doctor ought to decide whether the woman should have the child or not and then advise her accordingly. Before deciding, he should determine whether her income and lodging facilities were adequate to allow having another child, whether the patient was able to cope with the children she already had, whether she got along well with her husband, and whether she was, in fact, more depressed than she appeared to be.

The gynecologist himself, however, had a different idea of what constituted the best psychosomatic approach in this situation. During the usual antenatal check up, he responded in a very natural and sympathetic way by suggesting to her that this step could present a new start and should be regarded as a happy event. Before long, she was able to welcome her pregnancy.

THE CONTRACEPTIVE CLINIC

A description of the fantasies, fears, and conflicts that may arise in response to the use of oral contraceptives will help demonstrate the need for a psychosomatic approach in this area. These fears and anxieties are related to the psychological side effects of the pill. If there is no psychic solution to the pregnancy conflict, similar misconceptions and psychological reactions can occur with respect to all types of contraceptives, sterilization, insemination, induction of ovulation, and abortion.

FEMALE FEARS AND ANXIETIES REGARDING ORAL CONTRACEPTIVES

Fear of Loss of Self-Identity

Quite a few women refuse to take the pill and give as their reason, "I want to remain myself." Such a reaction is typical of women whose personality structure is characterized by a poor sense of self-identity and, in particular, by insecurity and conflict regarding their sex role. Such women fear that the intake of foreign hormones might alienate them from their own femininity. Conversely, some women with poor self-identity unconsciously yearn to be men, and it is precisely these women who strongly prefer oral contraceptives over other methods.

Fear of Self-Assertion and Power

The biological factors of menstruation, the ability to conceive, pregnancy, birth, and motherhood have far-reaching personal consequences. The female fate of conceiving and bearing children confronts a woman with the question, "Can I be a subject in my own right, or must I be a mere object?" Oral contraceptives, however, give the woman a large degree of independence from female physiology.

Whether or not a woman became pregnant used to depend largely upon her husband's volition and upon his contraceptive, or lack of contraceptive, measures. Now it depends upon the woman's decision and upon her action; she can create a situation where the man is practically powerless if she refuses to have the children that he may want. Oral contraceptives not only give women a greater independence from the female physiology, they also give women new power over men.

Although contraceptives are highly valued by many women, the power they represent can be a threat to other women. Those inhibited in asserting themselves tend to perceive oral contraceptives as something dangerous, and they are reluctant to take them. Oral contraceptives have been found to be practically 100% effective. This very asset can be perceived as a threat to two types of women: those who are preoccupied by the wish for more children and those who want to prove their genital health by becoming pregnant.

Fear of Remaining Childless

There are women who are characterized by a hypertrophied motherliness; pregnancy and motherhood are valued to the exclusion of other areas of experience. Such women find the 100% efficacy of oral contraceptives unbearable; it leaves no hope of gratifying their wish for a new child, not even as a result of a failure of the method, a failure in no way consciously wished for. Women who complain of becoming frigid through the use of the pill, (apart from the mood changes induced by oral contraceptives on a biochemical basis) often belong to this group. Other such women become irritated at their husbands, because the husband can obtain his gratification though he is unable to gratify the women's unconscious wish for a child.

Fear of Genital Damage

Some women would rather go through one abortion after another than to take oral contraceptives. Although they may be highly consciously motivated for contraception, the 100% efficacy of the pill appears to them as a threat. These women feel themselves to be genitally damaged, and they want to prove that they are genitally intact through their ability to become pregnant. Thus, they, too, need the hope of a contraceptive failure that is not consciously wished for.

Fear of Being "Eaten up from Within"

The fear of cancer, which is so common among the users of oral contraceptives, actually occurs in association with the use of all types of contraceptives. Quite frequently, though not invariably, this fear is voiced by women who are characterized by oral fears and inhibitions. The fear of cancer is an image of the fear of being "eaten up from within." The aforementioned fact that the child is indeed an oral competitor makes it understandable that pregnancy and the pill can be experienced by these women as being related to such fears.

Fears Associated with Tenderness and Surrender

Abandonment, in the sense of surrendering to one's feelings, and yielding, in the sense of offering oneself to another, are not to be confused with passivity. These are positive psychic acts. Women who are inhibited in these spheres tend to experience the use of oral contraceptives as a means to force them into the very activity and intimacy that they are most afraid of. They prefer to preserve their fear of conception in order to use it as a safeguard against overly frequent intercourse. Other women with fears in relation to tenderness and surrender tend to become, or to fear becoming, promiscuous while on the pill.

Neurotic Guilt Feelings and the Need for Punishment

Pregnancy may be unconsciously desired by some women as atonement for the sin of sexuality. In quite a few women, the use of condoms or coitus interruptus have led to so-called nervousness. Nowadays, women taking oral contraceptives may show similar signs of nervousness and irritability. These women feel nervous, not because of the type of contraceptives they are using, but because of their guilt feelings over using any contraceptives whatsoever.

MALE FEARS AND ANXIETIES REGARDING ORAL CONTRACEPTIVES

Fear of Lack of Potency

Some men fear being overtaxed by demands on their potency, or rather, they fear that they lack sufficient potency. They feel that women who take oral contraceptives feel much too free. An increase in female sexual responsiveness or sexual excitability is supposed, by these men, to threaten the harmony of society and to undermine the treasured values of "true womanhood" or "genuine femininity." Such apprehensions are widely voiced in certain magazines and newspapers. The doctor generally hears them from men, however, and hardly ever from the women involved.

Fear of Impairment of His Image of Femininity

Particularly important among the fears of the male is the fear that his image of femininity might be disturbed. The image of femininity is of particular importance to male psychology.

Fear of His Projected Arbitrary Attitude

In claiming that the pill is dangerous because it will make women go sexually astray, males are often projecting their own arbitrary attitude in sexual matters onto women.

The Wish to Punish Women and Keep Them Dependent

The more or less unconscious wish to punish the woman or to keep her dependent by further pregnancies can cause the man to feel aversion concerning the use of oral contraceptives.

Fear of Fading of Eros and Love

Still other men fear that love without risk may lose its attractions and become degraded to a purely biological function. Again, such fears are never expressed by women.

THE FERTILITY CLINIC

When the wish for a child is voiced emphatically the other side of the pregnancy conflict often remains unconscious. Problems frequently occur in the woman, in the man, or later in the child following insemination or the induction of ovulation.

Careful psychological evaluation of such cases is required when these methods are employed.

Heterologous insemination is a somewhat dubious procedure from an ethical, professional, and legal point of view. From the standpoint of the psychiatrist, however, homologous insemination is even more questionable, since this procedure is often requested by couples with overt or masked sexual disturbances. In such cases, the infertility that is circumvented by homologous insemination may represent the protective insurance against having children in a case where there should be no children.

ABORTION

It is our task as physicians to communicate with the patient so as to enable her to recognize within herself her own tendencies. When there is a question of abortion, it is necessary to allow the patient to talk freely, instead of inquiring after certain exact data. She ought to be able to express her whole motivational structure, life experiences, and attitudes, and she must be able to assess her ability to bear stress. Has her history shown that minor difficulties have produced serious consequences? Or, on the contrary, have serious events rarely, if ever, produced pathological consequences? Such handicaps as well as the positive means available to the patient should be discussed. The doctor should not adopt the role of an uncritical helper, yet he should be willing to allow the patient to find her own solutions. *Nil nocere* remains the prime law of his activities.

Not only is the pregnancy conflict often shifted onto the therapeutic measures when there is a question of abortion, but the pregnancy also is often handed over by the patient to the individual gynecologist and to the society at large.

PSYCHOSOMATIC APPROACHES TO MISCELLANEOUS GYNECOLOGICAL AND OBSTETRICAL PROBLEMS

ANTENATAL CARE

Oral symptoms—such as heartburn, hypersalivation, hyperemesis, excessive food intake, loss of weight, desires for or aversion toward certain food, and stealing—are frequently seen during pregnancy. Some of these women are orally inhibited and experience the fetus to an excessive degree as an oral competitor. This produces a level of anxiety that has to be lowered through expression of the symptom (2). An understanding of these relationships will enable the doctor to intervene psychologically without having to undertake uncovering psychotherapy during pregnancy.

Clyne (1) has written on the psychodynamic background of habitual abortion and has stated that uncovering and formal psychotherapy are not indicated in psychosomatic disorders during pregnancy, but that a therapeutic attitude of the doctor is required that is aimed directly at the particular conflicts.

PSYCHOLOGICAL CONDUCT OF DELIVERY

Obstetrics has, in the past, been mainly oriented toward the mechanics of delivery, but physicians are now beginning to recognize that the innervation and coordination of the structures that retain or expel the fetus are also dependent upon the affects and impulses that may be acting during delivery. There is normal and abnormal behavior during delivery. Disturbed behavior during delivery is not always directly correlated with anxiety, as might be assumed from the generally recognized concept of the anxiety-tension-pain syndrome. Other types of behavior during delivery—*e.g.*, retentive, annoyed, perfectionistic, aloof, puzzled, inactive, or aimless—are also of importance (3).

A knowledge of such affective situations makes it possible for the obstetrician to use adequate preventive approaches. Courses of prenatal psychoprophylaxis, for example, may prevent disordered behavior during delivery. They should not consist merely in learning techniques, but they should be designed to enable the woman to talk about her fears and anxieties. In these courses, it should be taken into account that in disturbed behavior during delivery, anxiety is not the only factor. Such courses are the best means of arriving at a solution of the pregnancy conflict once pregnancy has occurred.

PUERPERIUM

The multitudinous manifestations of perfectionism during puerperium, which are also the basis of many difficulties in breast-feeding, have been too little recognized. It is the gynecologist or the general practitioner engaged in obstetrics and gynecology, who is able to intervene favorably in such cases; he is frequently the only one who is able to help.

FUNCTIONAL SEXUAL DISORDERS

The training involved in the therapy of such disorders should, according to Masters and Johnson, be coupled with uncovering psychotherapy. It is possible to carry out such modifications in one-person gynecological practice, rather than with a team approach. This is the only situation in which gynecologists should practice procedures approaching formal psychotherapy.

SURGICAL GYNECOLOGY

Hysterectomy, mastectomy, and sterilization usually require that the psychological preoperative care and aftercare be carried out by the gynecologist himself.

Pelvic pains without organic findings, urinary incontinence, cosmetic operations of the breast, or sex changes by surgical means often indicate the need for cooperation between the gynecologist and a psychiatrist. The psychiatrist will be able to contribute toward the differential diagnosis and the determination of indications for operation. In some cases, he may recommend the use of formal psychotherapy instead of surgery.

ENDOCRINOLOGICAL CONSULTATION

Many psychosomatic symptoms represent the somatic correlates of inhibited impulses and affects. Pruritus vulvae and some types of vaginal discharge, for instance, are correlates of inhibited but active sexual excitation; other gynecological complaints may be correlates of inhibited anger.

No such direct relationships, however, have been recognized for psychosomatic symptoms in gynecological endocrinology. These symptoms are better understood from the point of view insofar as the energy needed for reproduction has also to be used for other vital functions. This difference in the pathogenesis of the symptom has practical consequences in the conduct of psychotherapy.

MENOPAUSE AND OLD AGE

The extent of the usefulness of estrogen administration is frequently overestimated. In many cases, psychic guidance and treatment with psychoactive drugs are indicated.

MASKED PSYCHIATRY

All general practitioners as well as specialists must deal with a large number of patients who have functional disorders or those who complain without presenting truly physical symptoms and signs. These are patients with overt or, more frequently, covert psychiatric and nervous disorders. Medical practice often does not facilitate the referral of such patients to a psychiatrist.

Here again, psychic guidance is of decisive importance, and the use of psychotropic drugs may also be indicated. Almost universally, organic gynecologists do not recognize that for many gynecological symptoms antidepressants are indicated, not tranquilizers or neuroleptics. This is particularly so in a subgroup of psychogenic pelvic pains, some types of urinary incontinence, some cases of frigidity, many cases during menopause and old age, and some cases of dysfunctional metrorrhagia. This statement must be emphasized, since such symptoms are frequently associated with masked depression. The antidepressant should be given in small doses only.

HANDLING OF THE ORGANIC PATIENT

This subject, which also includes the psychology of the gynecological examination, can only be alluded to here. Even in purely somatic disorders, the results of purely physical treatments, *e.g.,* of pharmacotherapy, will often depend decisively on whether the doctor is able to recognize and deal with the fantasies and expectations of the patient about his illness and the treatment.

REFERENCES

1. Abraham G, Pasini W: Introduction à la Sexologie Médicale. Paris, Payot, 1974, p 388
2. Bardwick JM: Psychology of Women. New York, Harper & Row, 1971, p 218
3. Clyne MB: Habitual abortion. Practitioner 83–90, 1967
4. Colette C: In Diederich N, Pundel JP (eds): Gynecologie Psychosomatique et Sexologie. European Press (in press)
5. Ey H, Bernard P, Brisset C: Manuel de Psychiatrie. Paris, Masson et Cie, 1974, p 1212
6. Fisher S: The Female Orgasm. New York, Basic Books, 1973
7. Goldman GD, Milman DS (eds): Modern Woman. Springfield Ill, CC Thomas, 1969, p 271
8. Howells JG (ed): Modern Perspectives in Psycho-Obstetrics. New York, Brunner/Mazel, 1972, p 469
9. Kaplan HS: The New Sex Therapy. New York, Brunner/Mazel, 1974, p 524
10. Miller JB (ed): Psychoanalysis and Women. New York, Brunner/Mazel, 1973, p 406
11. Molinski H: Die Unbewusste Angst vor dem Kind. Munchen, Kindler, 1972, p 203
12. Molinski H: Different behaviour of women in labor as a symptom of different psychic patterns. 4th Int Congr Psychosom Obstet & Gynecol. Basel, S Karger (in press)
13. Money J, Ehrhardt AA (eds): Man & Woman Boy & Girl. Baltimore, Johns Hopkins University Press, 1972, p 258
14. Nijs P: Psychosomatische Aspekte der Oralen Antikonzeption. Stuttgart, Ferdinand Enke Verlag, 1972, p 89
15. Pasini W: Désir D'Enfant et Contraception. Paris, Casterman, 1974, p 144
16. Pasini W: Sexualité et Gynécologie Psychosomatique. Paris, Masson et Cie, 1974, p 231
17. Rheingold JC: The Fear of Being a Woman. New York, Grune & Stratton, 1964, p 714
18. Sherfey MJ: The Nature & Evolution of Female Sexuality. New York, Random House, 1966, p 165

28 Psychiatric Aspects of Endocrine and Metabolic Disorders

CALVIN EZRIN

INTRODUCTION

The hypothalamus, the major interface between the nervous and endocrine systems, is a complicated connection of fiber tracts and nerve cells. It participates in the regulation of many autonomic functions and body rhythms and contributes to the control of body temperature, blood pressure, affect, energy, hunger, thirst, sex, and sleep. This region also contains cells that combine neural and secretory activity which collectively may be designated as the endocrine hypothalamus. The hormones it produces are delivered to the pituitary gland by neural and vascular pathways (Fig. 28–1).

The two catecholamines, dopamine and norepinephrine, and the indoleamine, serotonin, appear to exert important influences on the secretion of hypothalamic regulating factors. These neurotransmitters act in the hypophysiotropic area of the endocrine hypothalamus to stimulate or inhibit the activity of the transducer neurones that manufacture the peptide hormones destined for transport to the adenohypophysis. Pharmacological alteration of neurotransmitter function may occur in the treatment of psychiatric disorders with resultant endocrine manifestations. Prolonged phenothiazine treatment may lead to sufficient depletion of hypothalamic catecholamines to decrease the release of prolactin inhibitory factor into the hypophysial portal circulation, with resultant excessive secretion of prolactin, producing galactorrhea (10).

The hypothalamus also contains higher integrative centers that govern the activity of the sympathetic nervous system, via descending fiber tracts traveling in the intermediolateral columns of the spinal cord which emerge as the sympathetic outflow from the central nervous system between T1 and L2 to reach their respective paravertebral ganglia. The adrenal medulla is a collection of sympathetic ganglia in which the ganglion cells have lost their axons and have become specialized for endocrine secretion. Acetylcholine, released at the preganglionic nerve endings, stimulates the endocrine neurones of the adrenal medulla to secrete the catecholamine hormones, epinephrine and norepinephrine. In all other sympathetic neurones norepinephrine is the final product; the enzyme required to convert it to epinephrine is found in high concentration only in the adrenal medulla.

The catecholamines raise the blood glucose level by stimulating glycogenolytic enzymes and increase the circulating level of free fatty acids by activating adipose tissue hormone sensitive lipase. This increase in the supply of easily available energy is for survival during emergencies that induce fright, fight, or flight. This concept, which was first propounded by Cannon (4) in his "emergency theory of

Fig. 28–1. Anatomy and Physiology of the "endocrine hypothalamus" and its relationship to the neuro- and adenohypophysis. This figure illustrates the general organization of the region in which the nervous and endocrine systems meet most intimately.

At the *upper right*, the neuron, labeled HRF (for hypothalamic releasing factors) stands for the ill-defined groups of cells which secrete a series of releasing factors (hormones) into primary capillary network of portal circulation to govern activities of anterior pituitary cells. Various neurotransmitter substances affect the activity of these neurons. Norepinephrine (NE) and 5-hydroxytryptamine (5 HT) arise in neurons with cell bodies in the brain stem. Dopamine (DA) is made in cells that are found in the basal hypothalamus. Acetylcholine (Ach) is another important regulatory neurotransmitter active in this region. The amygdala and hippocampus are important higher connections of the "endocrine hypothalamus."

Two well-defined groups of hypothalamic cells, supraoptic (SO) and paraventricular (PV) nuclei, make vasopressin and oxytocin respectively, but these hormones are not released into the systemic circulation until they have reached the neurohypophysis. The shaded area surrounding SO cell body represents the "osmoreceptor" that is responsive to changes in osmolality of the fluid perfusing it. The thermostat symbol to the left of the osmoreceptor represents the variable "set-point" concept used to explain the regulation of many hormones.

The adenohypophysis contains a variety of cell types, possibly one for each of the hormones it produces. Six are shown here: somatotropic or growth hormone (GH); prolactin (PR); adrenocorticotropic (ACTH) and melanocyte-stimulating (MSH), which are made in the same cell in the human gland; thyroid-stimulating (TSH); follicle-stimulating (FSH); and luteinizing (LH) which are depicted in broken lines because their hormones also may arise in a combined FSH-LH gonadotroph (shown in unbroken outline). (From Ezrin C, Godden JO, Volpé R, Wilson R: Systematic Endocrinology. Hagerstown, Harper and Row, 1973)

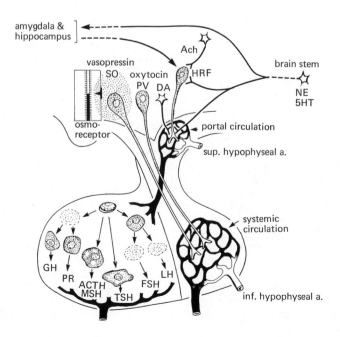

the emotions" and called the "alarm reaction," was expanded by Selye (23, 24) to include secondarily increased adrenal cortical activity in the "general adaptation syndrome" during prolonged "stress." The pathways underlying this sympathoadrenal interaction may spread from the cerebral cortex through the limbic system to the hypothalamus; increased secretion of corticotropin releasing factor then leads to pituitary corticotropic activation which in turn stimulates the adrenal cortex. Liberation of excessive quantities of catecholamines, chiefly epinephrine, may produce anxiety, hypertension, and irritability of the central nervous system in susceptible individuals.

ENDOCRINE ABNORMALITIES IN PSYCHIATRIC DISORDERS

ANXIETY STATE

Adrenal medullary and cortical secretion rates are often somewhat increased in states of sustained anxiety, (9) and prolonged emotional stress can reduce testosterone levels in men (13).

DEPRESSION

A frequent endocrine accompaniment of despondency is decreased sexual function, usually manifested as loss of libido. In many men, lithium carbonate may produce worrisome impotence, usually accompanied by decreased libido. Sexual hypofunction seems not to be the result of a reduction in testosterone secretion, although more studies are needed to settle this question. It is well known that in females emotional disorders can disrupt the sensitive central regulation of gonadotropin release producing amenorrhea or menstrual irregularities.

Lithium is also an antithyroid drug that may lead to myxedema, with sluggish mentation and apathy which may be erroneously attributed to depression. Although lithium-induced hypothyroidism is usually preceded by a goiter, thyroid enlargement may be slight enough to be overlooked. Since clinical hypothyroidism may by itself produce a severe depressive syndrome, care should be taken to avoid adding the burden of thyroid underactivity to the already depressed patient (27). Patients on long-term lithium treatment should have the serum thyroxine and serum thyrotropin (TSH) levels checked at least twice a year. If the serum TSH is higher than normal, even though the thyroxine remains within the normal range, a thyroid supplement should be given to bring the serum TSH to normal; usually L-thyroxine 0.1–0.2 mg daily will suffice (8).

Depression in women is often associated with salt and water retention which worsens the mental state. A large, rapid weight gain may follow a relatively small carbohydrate feeding, presumably by increasing insulin secretion which facilitates retention of salt and water by potentiating the effect of mineralocorticoid on the renal tubule. Premenstrual fluid retention seems to be related to the antialdosterone effect of progesterone. The adrenal reacts to this competitive antagonism and secretes excess aldosterone which along with other poorly understood mechanisms, favors transient sodium and water retention. When this phenomenon is prolonged and not related solely to the menstrual cycle, it is termed idiopathic edema, a disorder that is encountered chiefly in obese women in the late reproductive age group who tend to be easily depressed. There is often a history of large birth weight of babies, which is a prediabetic manifestation, and a strong family history of diabetes mellitus. The disorder may be related to a derangement of the regulation of insulin secretion as well as to other factors. Such patients do best on a program of calorie and carbohydrate restriction, even to the point of mild ketosis, which favors the renal loss of salt and water. Conventional diuretics should be used sparingly lest they lead to a worsening of secondary hyperaldosteronism and a further enervating hypokalemia.

SCHIZOPHRENIA

Since frank schizophrenia or a strong schizoid tendency is found in some patients with morbid obesity intractable to all conventional forms of treatment, the mental state must be carefully evaluated in all such patients being considered for the drastic procedure of intestinal bypass surgery. In the present state of uncertainty regarding the long-term consequences of such therapy, it is best to restrict its application to patients whose disturbed emotional state seems likely to improve with weight loss, which is not the case in schizophrenia.

HYSTERIA

The influence of emotions on reproductive function is well recognized. Psychogenic amenorrhea may follow a powerful emotional shock. In World War II a study of uterine biopsies from patients whose menses disappeared following air raids, showed that the arrest of endometrial development coincided with the day of the bombing raid (16).

Rakoff has studied the endocrine mechanisms in psychogenic amenorrhea (21). The rare subtype associated with an intense desire for pregnancy produces psuedocyesis or false pregnancy, which is associated with increased progesterone secretion.

Although emotional stress can reduce testosterone levels in men, in most patients with psychic impotence no hormonal abnormality can be implicated.

EFFECTS OF THERAPY

Galactorrhea due to phenothiazines is the result of a depletion of hypothalamic catecholamines which leads to increased prolactin secretion because of a reduction of prolactin inhibiting factor. As well as hypothyroidism already mentioned, lithium may produce a form of nephrogenic diabetes insipidus by interfering with the action of antidiuretic hormone (vasopressin) on the distal and collecting renal tubules.

PSYCHIATRIC MANIFESTATIONS OF ENDOCRINE DISORDERS

HYPOTHALAMIC–ANTERIOR PITUITARY DEFICIENCY DISEASE

Tumors or granulomas involving the hypothalamus may produce sleep disturbances, marked emotional lability, or inappropriate rage reactions. Alterations in appetite may rarely cause severe inanition or more frequently marked obesity, presumably because both of the paired medial satiety centers are more readily affected than are the more laterally placed feeding centers. A large lesion, such as a craniopharyngioma, may cause impairment of memory and intellect presumably from compression of the overlying basal portions of the frontal and temporal lobes. Surgical decompression or removal of the tumor may improve the mental state considerably.

Hypopituitarism, without accompanying hypothalamic involvement, usually presents as hypogonadism. Occasionally hypothyroidism dominates the clinical picture, and very rarely a selective deficiency of ACTH leads to hypoadrenalism manifested by easy nausea and vomiting, often with a marked hyponatremia. Since a relative adrenal insufficiency may be greatly aggravated by thyroid hormone replacement, patients with hypothyroidism with accompanying hypogonadism, however mild, should have appropriate pituitary studies conducted to establish that the ACTH reserve is adequate. If it is not, prednisone treatment, 2.5 mg twice a day, should be given before thyroxine is prescribed.

Sex hormone replacement therapy should not be overlooked in patients with pituitary disease even though it is not requested. It is usually gratefully received. Intramuscular injection of long-acting testosterone (400 mg testosterone cyclopentyl proprionate once a month) is safer than oral androgen. Methyltestosterone linquets, 10 mg three or four times a day, may produce a troublesome hepatocellular jaundice that occasionally proceeds to biliary cirrhosis. The intramuscular preparation, by avoiding transport of the androgen via the hepatic portal circulation to the liver, greatly reduces the risk of this complication.

In pituitary dwarfs, even those treated early enough with human growth hormone to achieve a substantial increase in height, there is always a disparity between the chronological age and the physical age. To look not fully grown constitutes a considerable emotional handicap to these patients, which is somewhat alleviated by the provision of sex hormones to achieve the appearance of adult sexual maturity. Since the response to human growth hormone seems to be greater in younger children, vigorous investigation of subjects with growth retardation should be pursued early in life to establish whether the cause is growth hormone deficiency (1).

Growth failure may be the result of emotional deprivation. Somatomedin (a polypeptide that is formed under the influence of growth hormone) levels are decreased in short patients with emotional deprivation, but this phenomenon may be related to their poor nutrition as well as to a lack of love (19, 20).

HYPERPITUITARY DISORDERS

Acromegaly and Gigantism

Growth hormone secreting tumors of the pituitary may produce considerable skeletal and soft tissue disfigurement. Gigantism in the child may produce psychological crippling. Early transsphenoidal removal of the offending adenoma preserving as much as possible of the surrounding gland seems to be the most rational therapy (11). A similar approach should be used in acromegalic women before irreversible bony changes have been produced. A considerable regression of soft tissue changes and some bony effects may be expected when the growth hormone levels are brought to normal.

Cushing's Syndrome

This disorder is usually considered an adrenal disease since it is expressed as effects of glucocorticoid excess. The most common cause of Cushing's syndrome now appears to be the ectopic production of ACTH by various malignancies, chiefly anaplastic lung cancers. In addition to stimulating the adrenal, ACTH may have important effects on cerebral function; however, more work remains to be done to define its precise role. Small pituitary ACTH secreting adenomas are sometimes found in patients with Cushing's syndrome. The transsphenoidal removal of a tiny adenoma may be followed by apparent cure of the disease. A hypothalamic contribution to some cases of this disorder is suggested by the recent report of control of the disease by an antiserotonin agent, cyproheptadine (14). Bilateral adrenalectomy will invariably cure the adrenal side of the disease. Usually replacement therapy with cortisone and a mineralocorticoid (9-alpha-fluorohydrocortisone) is no problem. However, some patients become deeply pigmented in association with an enlarging pituitary tumor following adrenalectomy

(Nelson's syndrome). (17). The increased pigmentation may be very trying emotionally. Pituitary irradiation preceding the bilateral adrenalectomy may not be sufficient to control the adrenal overactivity, but it seems to decrease the likelihood of postoperative increased pigmentation and tumor growth.

Galactorrhea–Amenorrhea Syndromes

With the establishment of prolactin as a separate human pituitary hormone, there was rapid recognition of the frequency of prolactin secreting tumors causing infertility. In addition, prolactinomas have been found in male patients with impotence. In both sexes galactorrhoea may not accompany the hyperprolactinemia. Prolactin has many undefined metabolic effects including an influence on cerebral function and mental state; it tends to favor water retention and thereby may aggravate depression.

DIABETES INSIPIDUS

This disorder is the result of insufficient antidiuretic hormone. It may arise from neurohypophysial or hypothalamic lesions, or may be due to a peripheral resistance to the effect of vasopressin. The most important differential diagnostic possibility is hysterical or psychogenic polydipsia. Usually these conditions are easy to separate from a consideration of the emotional background of the patient, and also the serum osmolalities in response to eight hours of fluid deprivation. Even a random serum osmolality is helpful because patients with psychogenic polydipsia usually have a somewhat dilute serum, whereas patients with diabetes insipidus (DI) are somewhat behind in their drinking and have a tendency to a more concentrated serum (the normal range is 275–295 mOs/kg). Patients with true DI cannot defend their serum osmolality which rises in response to continued polyuria during the fluid deprivation test; patients with primary polydipsia usually show very little change in serum osmolality and an increasing urine osmolality during the test. Sometimes prolonged drinking of water leads to a blunting of sensitivity to antidiuretic hormone and a response that is somewhat like that of a patient with nephrogenic DI.

Treatment with nasal vasopressin spray, long-acting vasopressin tannate in oil, or other agents such as chlorpropamide which increase the effectiveness of small amounts of endogenous vasopressin all may produce water intoxication with resultant mental changes. Aqueous vasopressin should be used with great caution postoperatively in patients with pituitary problems who seem to have diabetes insipidus. Water retention at that time can produce dangerous cerebral edema which may have fatal consequences. It is better to allow the patient to be somewhat dehydrated than to run the risk of water overload at this critical time. When chlorpropamide is used, the possibility of hypoglycemia producing mental changes should be remembered.

INAPPROPRIATE SECRETION OF ANTIDIURETIC HORMONE

This syndrome may present with mental changes caused by water intoxication. For a variety of causes excessive vasopressin may be secreted either from the neurohypophysis itself, or from malignant tissue in distant sites. Dilutional hyponatremia, hypoosmolality of the serum in association with a hypertonic urine, and increased renal sodium loss are the cardinal laboratory features. When the hyponatremia becomes severe (below 110 mEq/liter) clouding of consciousness and coma may result. Treatment consists of fluid restriction and possibly glucocorticoids which antagonise the effect of antidiuretic hormone and also to some extent interfere with its release (3). The use of lithium in the treatment of inappropriate antidiuretic hormone secretion has been suggested because of the peripheral antagonism of lithium to the action of vasopressin (26). However, lithium induces a renal loss of sodium that would further aggravate the excess renal excretion of sodium found in the syndrome of inappropriate ADH (2).

THYROID DISORDERS

Hyperthyroidism

Hyperthyroidism often produces emotional instability, with restlessness, irritability, and anxiety sometimes progressing to a state of severe agitation that may culminate in a toxic delirium. Some of the mental changes appear to result from associated increased sensitivity to epinephrine and norepinephrine that is characteristic of thyroid overactivity. The nervous manifestations of hyperthyroidism vary greatly, depending on the severity of the disease and the patient's underlying personality. Although the circulating level of thyroid hormone is important, there is a poorly understood mechanism that defends most patients against fulminating delirium in the presence of large excesses of thyroid hormone. This defence may be breached by infection, dehydration, or surgical thyroidectomy in poorly prepared patients, a rare event now that radioiodine therapy is so widely used. The earlier literature reports many devastating psychoses in the course of hyperthyroidism (7). Modern effective treatment for hyperthyroidism has greatly reduced the risk of serious mental complications in hyperthyroidism (15). However, when dangerous agitation does occur during therapy with radioiodine or antithyroid drugs, prompt treatment must be undertaken to prevent a fatal outcome.

Two drugs that have a prompt effect on the release of thyroid hormone should be stressed in the treatment of severe thyrotoxicosis; these are stable iodide and lithium carbonate, which has the added advantage of an antimanic effect in these restless patients. Propranolol in appropriate doses to control tachycardia, has been a great help with these patients. Diazepam and barbiturates can be used with good effect to relieve anxiety. Drugs that block the synthesis of thyroid hormone such as propylthiouracil or carbimazole should be used for several weeks to greatly reduce the circulating level of thyroid hormone; then a therapeutic dose of radioiodine can be administered. In unstable, unreliable, or paranoid patients, replacement thyroxine therapy of hypothyroidism that frequently follows radioiodine treatment may be unsatisfactory if the patient fails to take the drug regularly. Long-term antithyroid drug therapy for thyrotoxicosis has the same drawback. In most such cases the patient is more tractable if slightly hypothyroid, compared to the thyrotoxic state.

Hypothyroidism

Thyroid hormone is essential for normal development of brain function. Congenital absence of thyroid hormones leads to severe mental deficiency (cretinism), which may be permanent unless it is treated within the first few months of life. In adult myxedema a significant degree of intellectual impairment may be found, which is reversed by thyroid replacement. Lethargy and depression are common, but sometimes a paranoid psychosis dominates the clinical picture.

The administration of iodide in asthma medication may insidiously produce myxedema with weakness and hypoventilation that is wrongly attributed to the accompanying chest disease. Such patients usually show thyroid enlargement because of the goitrogenic effect of the iodide.

The nervous system is sometimes profoundly affected in myxedema. The term "myxedema madness" calls attention to a serious decline in cerebral function accompanying extreme hypothyroidism. There is impairment of psychic, sensory, and motor functions. The tendon reflexes are slowed, especially in their relaxation phase. Particularly striking is extreme somnolence culminating in myxedema coma.

In myxedema coma there is hypothermia, hypoventilation and respiratory acidosis, low serum sodium and high serum lactate, inappropriate secretion of antidiuretic hormone, sometimes hypoglycemia, severely disordered cerebral metabolism, hypotension, and imminent death. This terminal phase of long-standing myxedema, requires vigorous treatment including assisted ventilation and supportive steroids to prevent a fatal outcome. Because of its rapid onset of action, L-triiodothyronine is preferred to thyroxine treatment. It may be administered via a nasogastric tube in a dose of 0.01–0.25 mg every eight hours. L-thyroxine sodium is available for intravenous administration; a dose of 0.5 mg in a single injection is adequate to correct the estimated depletion of the extrathyroidal hormone pool (12).

PARATHYROID DISORDERS

Hyperparathyroidism

Parathyroid overactivity affects the nervous system via increased levels of circulating calcium which leads to decreased neuromuscular excitability and ultimately to profound muscle weakness. Mental confusion and even coma have been observed with very high levels of serum calcium (over 20 mg/100 ml). Agitation, paranoid personality disorders, and depression have been noted with hyperparathyroidism; these features disappear on removal of the offending adenoma and a restoration of normal serum calcium (6).

Hypoparathyroidism

With increased neuromuscular excitability due to accompanying hypocalcemia, hypoparathyroidism may present with convulsions and coma or as a chronic neurasthenic state. Since previous thyroid surgery may result in unrecognized hypoparathyroidism, such patients should be routinely checked for hypocalcemia. The stress of further surgery, such as the repair of a vocal cord palsy that resulted from recurrent laryngeal nerve damage at the time of a previous thyroidectomy, may bring out convulsions and a frightening laryngospasm in a patient with latent tetany from unrecognized hypoparathyroidism.

Babies born of hyperparathyroid mothers are at risk from neonatal tetany which may present as convulsions. This event sometimes leads to the diagnosis of the parathyroid overactivity in the mother, whose hypercalcemia has put the fetal parathyroids at rest.

Chronic hypoparathyroidism may produce papilledema and an increase in intracranial pressure. Calcification of the basal ganglia, the result of chronic hypocalcemia, may lead to the diagnosis of idiopathic hypoparathyroidism as a cause of convulsions. The treatment of hypoparathyroidism with vitamin D and supplemental calcium is hazardous and should not be undertaken lightly. Sometimes dangerous hypercalcemia with permanent renal damage, is produced resulting from associated nephrocalcinosis. For this reason the serum calcium should be checked at least twice a year in such patients and attempts made to keep the calcium level toward the lower limit of the normal range. This is usually sufficient to restore normal mental and neuromuscular stability.

ADRENAL CORTICAL DISORDERS

Hypercorticism

Cushing's Syndrome (Glucocorticoid Excess)

Profound mental changes accompany chronic hypercorticism. There is also some evidence that ACTH may have important effects on cerebral function. Steroid-induced Cushing's syndrome occurs with suppressed release of ACTH, whereas most cases of endogenous Cushing's syndrome except those caused by adrenal tumor, seem to have increased ACTH secretion.

When the disease is caused by endogenous overproduction of ACTH or related substances there is a high incidence of depression. Suicide is an important cause of death in this group of patients. In patients with Cushing's syndrome from exogenous glucocorticoid therapy, the most common psychological effect is euphoria, although depression is sometimes seen and may be severe. An acute toxic psychosis may appear in patients treated with moderate to large excesses of glucocorticoid hormones.

Following cure of the Cushing's syndrome by such procedures as total adrenalectomy or the complete removal of a corticotropin-producing adenoma of the pituitary, many patients undergo a difficult period of emotional vulnerability. The body seems to have become adapted to hypercorticism, and the return to normal steroid levels produces a withdrawal syndrome with tendency to depression and rheumatic discomforts. The postoperative period of adjutment, which may last six months, may be a difficult time for patient and doctor.

Aldosteronoma (Conn's Syndrome) Mineralocorticoid excess from an aldosterone secreting tumor usually presents with hypertension and hypokalemia. The low potassium level may cause profound weakness, and the associated alkalosis may contribute to attacks of tetany. Hypokalemic nephropathy may ensue with polyuria and secondary polydipsia. A functional emotional disorder may be suggested to explain the thirst and weakness in the absence of diabetes mellitus or insipidus.

Adrenal Virilism In women, severe masculinization can result from an adrenal cortical carcinoma overproducing androgens. Sometimes Cushing's syndrome due to bilateral adrenal cortical hyperplasia presents as virilization because of the dominant influence of adrenal androgen over glucocorticoid secretions.

Congenital enzyme defects in the biosynthetic pathway of cortisol may produce androgen excess *in utero* with resultant female pseudohermaphroditism. In the past girls with clitoral hypertrophy have been misdiagnosed at birth as male infants with undescended testes and hypospadias. Sex chromatin studies, including staining of buccal smears for nuclear heterochromatin characteristic of genetic females, has made the correct assignment of sex easy to achieve. From a study of a large group of such patients with female pseudohermaphroditism at Johns Hopkins Hospital, Money and co-workers derived the concept of psychogender being relatively fixed at about the age of 18 months. They advised that sex not be changed after this time if at all possible, since this would lead to a confused psychogender and a difficult sexual adjustment. The problems of gender ambiguity will be dealt with further under gonadal disorders, with special mention of both male and female transsexualism.

Feminising Adrenal Tumors Rarely in males an adrenal adenoma or carcinoma may overproduce estrogen, with resultant loss of libido and potency and gynecomastia.

Chronic Adrenal Insufficiency (Addison's Disease)

Major mental symptoms of this disorder include apathy, fatigue, depression, and anorexia usually leading to a substantial loss of weight. A paranoid psychosis is sometimes seen. There may be memory deficiency, confusion, and ultimately stupor. ECG tracings show high-amplitude slowing of activity, presumably due to glucocorticoid deficiency, since it is not affected by mineralocorticoid replacement but is reversed by giving glucocorticoids.

Treatment of adrenal insufficiency in females should include consideration of the effect of adrenal androgen on libido. A small supplement of testosterone in the form of methyltestosterone linquets, 5–10 mg daily, may restore sexual functioning of the patient with Addison's disease. The dose of life-maintaining glucocorticoid hormone, either cortisone or prednisone, should be increased under conditions of stress. Nausea is the first symptom of relative adrenal insufficiency, and insomnia, due to cerebral stimulation, is the most common manifestation of glucocorticoid excess. Therefore physicians are advised to steer a course for their patients between nausea and insomnia when dealing with an illness like viral influenza, that will require an increased amount of steroid for three or four days; usually a doubling of the maintenance dose of from 25–37.5 mg cortisone will be sufficient to keep them out of trouble. It is important not to allow the adrenal insufficiency to progress to vomiting which would then require parenteral administration of steroid.

ADRENAL MEDULLARY OVERACTIVITY (PHEOCHROMOCYTOMA)

Such catecholamine-producing tumors arise from chromaffin cells of the sympathoadrenal system. The most frequent symptoms during a severe attack are pounding headaches, sweating, palpitation, apprehension, tremulousness, pallor or flushing of the face. Psychoneurosis is sometimes diagnosed, particularly when the accompanying hypertension is intermittent as it is in about half the cases. Sometimes the menopause is blamed for symptoms produced by pheochromocytoma.

Reliable assay of catecholamines and their major metabolites in the urine is now the basis of the diagnosis of this usually curable condition. There are a number of drugs that can lead to false positive urinary catecholamine results, and others that contribute to the methylated urinary metabolites, measured as VMA. Extra care should be taken to discontinue these offending medications before testing lest nonspecific results lead to erroneous surgery (25).

PANCREATIC DISORDERS

Hyperinsulinism and Hypoglycemia

Because the brain is totally dependent on circulating glucose to supply its enormous demands for energy, hypoglycemia has profound effects on the central nervous system, similar to those of cerebral anoxia. Headache, confusion, restlessness, faintness, hunger, clouded consciousness, irritability, coma, and convulsions may be produced. Other symptoms are the result of increased secretion of epinephrine by the adrenals in response to the hypoglycemia; these include anxiety, tremulousness, perspiration, tachycardia, pallor, numbness, and tingling. Hypoglycemia is most commonly the result of excessive administration of insulin in the treatment of diabetes mellitus. However, it can occur from autonomous pancreatic islet cell tumors overproducing insulin or from other retroperitoneal tumors that either overutilize glucose or produce some hypoglycemic substance.

Reactive hypoglycemia is most commonly seen in postgastrectomy patients who have a very rapid rise in blood sugar which overstimulates the pancreatic beta cells to release excessive amounts of insulin. Multiple high protein, small volume feedings are usually all that is required to bring relief to these patients.

In early onset diabetes mellitus there also occurs a reactive hypoglycemia which appears to be related to disordered regulation of insulin release. At first insufficient insulin is secreted, and later in the course of a glucose tolerance test, at three to five hours, the blood sugar level drops to below normal because of an excessive discharge of insulin. A similar disordered insulin release is seen in some psychoneurotic patients who develop hypoglycemic and hyperepinephrinemic symptoms following concentrated carbohydrate ingestion. These patients are also prone to fluid retention that is aggravated by carbohydrate feeding. They also do better on a high protein diet which should be low in calories if they are obese.

In paramedical patients with puzzling episodes of hypoglycemia, special consideration should be given to the diagnosis of factitious hyperinsulinism, either from the surreptitious injection of insulin or the secret ingestion of an oral hypoglycemic drug. Insulin is sometimes used for suicidal or homicidal purposes by persons who have access to it.

Alcohol-induced hypoglycemia seems to be the result of a combination of previous undernutrition leading to a fatty liver and the additional interference of ethanol with hepatic gluconeogenesis. When hypoglycemia is suspected as a cause of convulsions or coma, the diagnosis can be rapidly verified by a blood specimen, and analyzed by a chemical or spot enzymatic test. While this is going on, glucose should be given intravenously; at least 25 g ought to be infused rapidly. Thereafter a continuous drip of 5% in glucose can provide about 12 g glucose per hour, which is sufficient to sustain the blood glucose even in the absence of any hepatic gluconeogenesis.

Diabetes Mellitus

Virtually complete absence of insulin causes progressive hyperglycemia, acidosis, coma, and death. Lesser degrees of insulin deficiency, particularly in elderly people who are fairly insensitive to thirst, may result in slowly developing hyperosmolar nonketotic coma which also may end fatally, if unrecognized. The timely administration of insulin and other supportive measures to correct dehydration and electrolyte imbalance should save all of these patients, providing the inciting event that led to the loss of glucose homeostasis is also controllable.

The acute and chronic complications of diabetes bring with them emotional burdens that should be recognized lest they overwhelm the patient. Acute neuropathy with muscle weakness or pain, and other sensory disturbances, usually responds quickly to proper control of the diabetes. Chronic neuropathy which may have a large autonomic component seems less related to the blood sugar level, but still general improvement may be expected with better diabetic control. Sexual impotence commonly accompanies autonomic neuropathy; libido is usually maintained, unlike hypogonadism from androgen deficiency. Hemochromatosis, which may affect both the pancreas and the testes as well as the gonadotrophs of the adenohypophysis, may produce hypogonadism in a diabetic patient. Reduced plasma testosterone will establish the diagnosis of testicular failure in these cases.

Diabetic retinopathy is now a major cause of blindness in young people. Repeated vitreous hemorrhage from proliferative neovascularization may give warning of impending visual failure. Hypophysectomy has given way to photocoagulation as the treatment of choice in progressive retinopathy, but the results are not entirely satisfactory. A strong permissive role of growth hormone in the pathogenesis of diabetic retinopathy is suggested by the improvement in some patients that followed selective decrease of this hormone by various means of pituitary destruction. Somatostatin (growth hormone release inhibiting hormone), one of the new hypothalamic regulating hormones, has been suggested as a possible means of controlling growth hormone secretion in long-term treatment of diabetic individuals. Clinical trials of this new agent in such a context are awaited with intense interest.

Diabetic nephropathy still defies anything but supportive measures for its control. Renal failure, hypertension, and its complications, including death from myocardial infarction, remain important causes of mortality in patients with diabetes mellitus, however treated. Decreased insulin requirements with uremia must be recognized to avoid hypoglycemia. Most physicians dealing with diabetes feel that once nephropathy is established, meticulous blood sugar control has little influence on the prognosis. At this stage of the disease the patient is most apt to become frightened and pursue good control in a vain attempt to help the kidney disease, with resultant dangerous hypoglycemia.

The management of progressive renal failure due to diabetic nephropathy has been broadened to include peritoneal- and hemodialysis as well as renal transplants. The family and personal resources available for sustaining the patient psychologically during these difficult therapeutic programs must be considered carefully before proceeding; if there is not a great deal of support these treatments may become intolerable.

GONADAL AND SEXUAL DISORDERS

The concept of sexuality involves two components: gender role and gender identity (psychogender). In addition there are five biological variables of sex: chromosomal, gonadal, hormonal, internal, and external genital sex.

Money and his colleagues were the first to recommend that the sex of a pseudohermaphroditic child should not be changed after the age of two, because by then psychogender is usually firmly established (18). However, when there is a confused gender identity, not consonant with the sex of assignment, change of sex even in adult life may produce considerable psychological benefits that would justify the maintenance hormone treatment and necessary surgery (5).

There is much evidence that sex hormones, particularly testosterone, control the differentiation of the central nervous system. During fetal and neonatal life these hormones act in an *inductive* way on an undifferentiated brain (as they do on the undifferentiated genital tract) to organize it into a male or female organ. During adult existence, the gonadal hormones act on the central nervous system in an *excitatory* or *inhibitory* way, thus regulating gonadotropin secretion.

The critical period for psychosexual differentiation in primates appears to be relatively early in gestation. More testosterone and less progesterone have been found in the plasma of male rhesus monkey fetuses as compared to female fetuses. It has been postulated that progesterone protects the female brain against the masculinizing effect of testosterone by interfering with androgen action on the central nervous system. The failure of this protective mechanism may account for some instances of masculine psychogender in the absence of androgen overproduction. Similarly, excessive progesterone interference with testosterone induction of masculine psychogender may be important in the pathogenesis of male transsexualism which, when studied later in life, seems to have no endocrine abnormality. Since the administration of progestational agents to prevent recurrent abortion has been associated with virilization of female fetusus, it appears that the time of administration and the metabolic handling of the exogenous steroid determines whether the administered steroid acts as an androgen or antiandrogen (22). Transsexuals are patients who are convinced that they really are persons of the opposite sex. In the light of new knowledge of fetal endocrinology and its effect on psychogender, it is easier to take seriously the repeatedly expressed protestation that "something must have gone wrong before I was born." In view of our current uncertainty, transsexualism should not be ascribed entirely to prenatal endocrine factors. However, due attention should be given to the endocrine abnormalities found in many of the biological females, at least one-third of whom have moderate androgen overproduction when they are first studied in early adult life. It is tempting to speculate that such oversecretion of androgen also occurred *in utero* imparting a masculine psychogender to the female brain. Transsexuals should be referred to special clinics that offer a coordinated program employing psychiatric, endocrinological, and various surgical consultants. Only in this setting can sex reassignment be handled with the proper safeguards for the patient and the involved professionals. Biological males accepted for sex reassignment receive estrogen treatment to develop breasts, and undergo surgical removal of external genitalia with construction of a vagina. Biological females receive testosterone treatment for virilization and somewhat later undergo removal of breasts with subsequent panhysterectomy, if there is troublesome menstrual bleeding.

Testicular feminization is an interesting extreme variant of male pseudohermaphroditism in which the tissues are completely insensitive to testosterone. Such patients present with primary amenorrhea, absent pubic and axillary hair (because of the androgen insensitivity), and excellent breast development. The testes are usually intraabdominal although occasionally they may present in inguinal canals. They should be removed because of the danger of malignant change. These patients have a normal male karyotype but are decidedly feminine in psychogender and body habitus. They long for marriage and make excellent adoptive mothers. Under no circumstances should they be told that they are really males. Such devastating information has led to suicide. They are very sensitive to female hormone so that after castration with removal of testicular estrogens, very small amounts of female hormone supplementation, *e.g.* 20 mg ethinyl estradiol will suffice to maintain normal feminine secondary sexual characteristics. These patients do not have fallopian tubes or uterus because the testis was capable of secreting mullerian inhibitory factor, a substance separate from testosterone, that prevents development of the internal genital tract along female lines.

The gonadal steroids are necessary for normal human sexual function. Prior to puberty in the male, there is a small amount of androgen secretion from the adrenal and the testis, but at the onset of puberty testicular secretion increases greatly. Plasma testosterone levels rise from 50 ng/dl to 500 within a two-year period in the midteens. Androgen causes an increase in sex drive as well as aggressive behavior. Similar psychological and behavioral effects are reported in older male patients treated for hypogonadism, who because of their belated start, rarely seem to achieve full psychosexual maturity and sex drive even though androgen levels are adequate.

Libido in the male is definitely dependent on androgen but psychic factors may strongly interfere with both desire and performance. Hormone regulation of psychosexual function in human females is more complex. It involves estrogen, progesterone, and androgen. In both sexes excessive prolactin from a pituitary adenoma may have profound effects. In males impotence usually results, due mainly to an interference by prolactin with the action of gonadotropin on the testes, but hypothalamic and pituitary effects are also likely involved. In females there is a tendency to fluid retention and depression, as well as galactorrhea and amenorrhea.

The syndrome of premenstrual tension with sodium and fluid retention seemingly contributing to depression and irritability, has been linked to a falling progesterone secretion that occurs in the postluteal phase of the menstrual cycle. Progesterone acts to block the sodium retaining effect of aldosterone at the distal renal tubule. Its sudden withdrawal allows an overshoot of this aldosterone effect. Treatment with spironolactone which also interferes with the action of aldosterone, helps some of these patients, particularly those with obvious fluid retention. Much more remains to be learned about the pathogenesis and optimal handling of this disorder.

The loss of ovarian function with the onset of the menopause usually has little effect on sex drive, but many estrogen-deficient women do report a loss of sexual interest. The regressive changes in the female genitalia that result from estrogen deficiency sometimes make coitus painful. For such patients small estrogen supplements should be provided.

In homosexuality the bulk of evidence indicates that gonadal function and hormone secretion are normal. Recent reports that some male homosexuals have lower than normal levels of testosterone have been challenged on the basis that this phenomenon might be secondary to the chronic anxiety that accompanies their somewhat troubled lives.

CONCLUSION

A review of the psychiatric aspects of endocrine and metabolic practice strongly supports the thesis that the brain is much more likely to be affected by endocrine and metabolic disorders than to cause them. Nevertheless the diagnosis and management of a wide variety of glandular disorders is greatly facilitated by an awareness of the frequent interplay between hormones, metabolites, and the nervous system.

REFERENCES

1. Aceto T Jr, Frasier SD, Hayles AB et al.: Collaborative study of the effects of human growth hormone in growth hormone deficiency. III. First eighteen months of therapy. an Raiti S (ed): Advances in Human Growth Hormone Research. Baltimore, DHEW Pub No. NIH) 74–612, 1973

2. Baer L, Glassman A, Karris S et al.: Negative sodium balance in lithium carbonate toxicity: evidence of mineralocorticoid blockade. Arch Gen Psychiatry 29:823–827, 1973

3. Bartter FC, Schwartz WB: The syndrome of inappropriate secretion of anti-diuretic hormone. Am J Med 42:790–806, 1967

4. Cannon WB: Bodily Changes in Pain, Hunger, Fear and Rage, 2nd ed. New York, Appleton, 1929 p 404

5. Cappon D, Ezrin C, Lynes P: Psychosexual identification (psychogender) in the intersexed. Can Psychiatry Assoc J 2:90–106, 1959

6. Dale AJD: Neurological problems in endocrine diseases. Med Clin North Am 56:1029, 1972

7. Dunlop HF, Moerch FP: Psychic manifestations associated with hyperthyroidism. Am J Psychiatry 91:1215, 1935

8. Emerson CH, Dyson WL, Utiger RD: Serum thyrotropin and thyroxine concentrations in patients receiving lithium carbonate. J Clin Endocrinol Metab 36:338, 1973

9. Froberg J, Karlsson CG, Levi L, Lidberg L: Physiological and biochemical stress reactions induced by psychosocial stimuli in society, stress and disease. In Levi L (ed): Vol 1. London, Oxford University Press, 1971, p 280

10. Frohman LA: Clinical neuropharmacology of hypothalamic releasing factors. N Engl J Med 286:1391, 1972

11. Hardy J: Transsphenoidal surgery of hypersecreting pituitary tumors. Diagnosis and treatment of pituitary tumors. In Kohler PO, Ross GT (eds): Amsterdam, Excerpta Medica, ICS 303:179–194, 1973

12. Holvey DN, Goodner CG, Nicoloff JT et al.: Treatment of myxoedema coma with intravenous thyroxine. Arch Intern Med 113:89, 1964

13. Kreuz LE, Rose RM, Jennings J: Depression of plasma testosterone levels and psychological stress: a longitudinal study of young men in officer candidate school. Arch Gen Psychiatry 26:479–482, 1972

14. Krieger DT, Amorosa L, Linick F: Cyproheptadine-induced remission of Cushing's disease. N Engl J Med 293:893–896, 1975

15. Lidz T, Whitehorn JC: Psychiatric problems in a thyroid clinic. JAMA 139:698, 1949

16. Loeser AA: Effect of emotional shock on hormone release and endometrial development. Lancet 1:518–527, 1943

17. Nelson DH, Meakin JW, Dealy JB Jr et al.: ACTH producing tumor of the pituitary gland. N Engl J Med 259:161–164, 1958

18. Money J, Ehrhardt A: Man and Woman, Boy and Girl. Baltimore Johns Hopkins University Press, 1972

19. Powell GF, Brasel JA, Blizzard RM: Emotional deprivation and growth retardation simulating idiopathic hypopituitarism. I. Clinical evaluation of syndrome. N Engl J Med 276:-1271–1283, 1967

20. Powell GF, Brasel JA, Raiti S et al.: Emotional deprivation and growth retardation simulating idiopathic hypopituitarism. II. Endocrinologic evaluation of syndrome. N Engl J Med 276:1279–1283, 1967

21. Rakoff AE: Endocrine mechanisms in psychogenic amenorrhoea. In Michael RP (ed): Endocrine Mechanisms and Human Behaviour. London, Oxford University Press, 1968, pp 139–160

22. Resko JA: The relationship between fetal hormones and the differentiation of the central nervous system in primates. In Montagna W, Salder WA (eds): Advances in Behavioural Biology, Vol II. Beaverton Oregon Regional Primate Research Center, 1974, pp 211–222

23. Selye H: The general adaptation syndrome and the diseases of adaptation. J Clin Endocrinol Metab 6:117, 1946

24. Selye H: What is stress? Metabolism 5:525, 1956

25. Sjoerdsma FAM, Engelman A, Waldmann K et al.: Pheochromocytoma: current concepts of diagnosis and treatment. Ann Intern Med 65:1302, 1966

26. White MG, Fetner CD: Treatment of the syndrome of inappropriate secretion of antidiuretic hormone with lithium carbonate. N Engl J Med 292:390–392, 1975

27. Whybrow PC, Prange AJ Jr, Treadway CR: Mental changes accompanying thyroid gland dysfunction. Arch Gen Psychiatry 20:48, 1969

29 Musculoskeletal Disorders*

W. DONALD ROSS

This chapter is concerned with understanding those patients who have special problems associated with disorders of the muscles, joints, or bones, with accompanying disability. Such understanding—which I have based on experience with patients on the psychosomatic ward and in psychiatric consultations on the medical and surgical wards of the Cincinnati General Hospital, on psychiatric consultations for occupational physicians, and on some pertinent points in the literature—provides the rationale for recommendations regarding the psychosomatic aspects of medical management of these patients by general physicians.

DISEASES OF THE MUSCLES

MYASTHENIA GRAVIS

A few years ago, we reviewed the combined medical and psychiatric findings for 13 patients with this disorder.* Nine of these had been seen in psychotherapy by psychiatric residents, and seven of them were observed in their interactions with other patients and staff on a small psychosomatic ward. In light of observations in the literature, we have been able to recognize the psychodynamic factors that contribute to the aggravation or amelioration of the symptoms of this disorder.

Even the earliest descriptions of this disease—which differentiated it from conversion hysteria, partially because of the sudden deaths that occurred with it—recognized that "emotional excitement" could precipitate crises (Maplet, 1659; Willis, 1672; and Wilks, 1870, as cited by Keynes [26], and Buzzard, 1905 [8]). Clinical psychiatric diagnoses of conditions concurrent with myasthenia gravis have been presented by Kennedy and Moersch (25), Collins (11), Levinson and Lim (29), and Oosterhuis and Wilde (41). Psychosomatic and psychodynamic aspects have been discussed by Hayman (21), Meyer (36, 37), Brolley and Hollender (7), "a doctor who has it" (1), Lennartz and Spiegelberg (27), Marcus (33), Claman and Johnston (9), Liskow (31), and Bernstein, Flegenheimer, and Roose (4).

The most frequent psychiatric diagnosis in our series was depression, which was seen in various degrees of severity. Other diagnoses included anxiety reaction, passive-aggressive personality, hysterical personality, and paranoid schizophrenia.

Several psychodynamic patterns were noted. Acute anxiety attacks with respiratory disturbances were the most threatening emotional storms. Feelings of rage related to shame over motor weakness or triggered by a separation or loss often led to an exacerbation of symptoms and to turning the rage against oneself in a

*Preparation of this chapter was supported in part by grant number T01 OH00129 from the National Institute for Occupational Safety and Health, DHEW.

*Appreciation is due to Louis Spitz, M.D., for assistance in the study of these patients.

depressive reaction. Conflicts over envious feelings seemed to be most marked in patients with the greatest fatigability in muscles innervated by the cranial nerves. Both hyperindependence and excessive dependence were noted to interfere with the optimal use of medications.

Remissions were noted when the patients were freed from depression or anxiety and when the patients were able to interact with others cooperatively without anger or withdrawal. Being able to anticipate the needs for muscular exertion by timing the doses of medication appeared to be of importance to these patients. Maneuvers that were accompanied by a reduction in symptoms and in the amount of the medication required included planning in an orderly fashion and manifesting a moderate degree of control over the environment.

On the basis of the experience with our patients, we do not recommend expressive psychotherapy except at those times when an exacerbation of symptoms has accompanied an unresolved grief reaction. We advise discussions of the circumstances contributing to an increase in symptoms, but the suppression of anger and the support of compulsive defenses are suggested. Doctors and nurses are advised to take the patient into partnership in deciding the dosage or frequency of medication. The nurse can particularly help the patient to learn the difference between symptoms of underdosage and overdosage and to plan the medication in relation to environmental demands for activity.

The drugs for which the participation of the patient is most needed are the cholinesterase inhibitors, pyridostigmine and neostigmine. In addition to these specific agents, the tricyclic antidepressants can also be used to alleviate a depressive component. We recommend, however, that the administration of antidepressants not be started until some therapeutic alliance has been established, so that the patient will not deny all emotional problems and be unable to discuss the factors that aggravate his disease.

Electroconvulsive therapy has been used for patients with severe depression, but caution must be observed in the use of any curarelike muscular relaxants in the technique for such treatment (14, 55).

Since at least two of the four known deaths in our series appeared to have been precipitated by emotional crises (such as feeling abandoned by a family member or a physician), the psychodynamic and psychotherapeutic considerations we have described may be lifesaving in severe cases as well as helpful in the rehabilitation of patients with less vital involvement of the disease process.

OTHER MUSCULAR DISORDERS

We have had sporadic experience in consultations with patients suffering from muscular dystrophies and myotonias. Our approach is to help the patient to recognize the physical basis for his complaints, including the frequently present hereditary factor, and to encourage him to talk about his individual life experiences, especially the personal circumstances that are accompanied by an increase in symptoms. The understanding of the patient as a person enables the physician to provide supportive psychotherapy along with the prescription of appropriate medication (27). Sometimes it is possible to reassure the patient that he is not as crippled as, say, some other member of the family who was a horrible example for him. It is usually considered wise to encourage the patient to continue walking and doing other light exercise as long as he can.

BACK PAIN

Interscapular muscular tension is a common cause of upper back pain in young women who are anxious and who are unconsciously making an effort to maintain a dignified posture. At the time of the initial physical examination, the physician should interview the patient to determine whether tensions are present in the life situations when the pain is experienced. The prescription of a minor tranquilizer (chlordiazepoxide or meprobamate) should be followed up by two or three office visits of 15–20 minutes each at one- or two-week intervals before the patient is discharged. The patient is then continued on the tranquilizer if required for tension or referred for more intensive psychotherapy.

Most experienced physicians are well aware that chronic low back pain or pain in the neck, which may persist in the absence of physical signs other than muscular spasm, is more difficult to treat. These patients also should be interviewed with understanding, especially regarding the life circumstances at the time of the injury or strain and subsequently.

When a protruded disc or other structural lesion has limited the activity of a previously athletic individual, it may not be possible to treat the "neurotic overlay" until the anatomic abnormality has been corrected surgically.

Many individuals, however, whose activity patterns have been altered by a back or neck incident, remain depressed and in a state of regression for many months if early attention is not given to the psychosocial factors that perpetuate the pain and muscle spasm (3, 15, 22).

Several papers in the last few years have reported abnormal scores on the Minnesota Multiphasic Personality Inventory (MMPI) for patients with chronic low back pain (3, 20, 52). The high scores have been on the hypochondriacal, hysterical, and depressive scales, and they have been correlated with chronicity of the physical disorder and pending litigation (52). For these persons, it is not only gold that glitters. They may be unconsciously seeking revenge because they feel that they have been mistreated at work. Whether this is the "secondary gain" factor or whether they are fighting for dependent "benefits," they are unhappy individuals, and their aggression may turn against themselves in depression. One survey in the state of Washington found that only one industrial claim per million was made by outright malingerers (19).

Few of these pain-afflicted patients are able to make use of insight psychotherapy. Marital counseling at an early stage may undo a reversal of roles that has taken place. Behavior modification has been successful in selected cases when it was carried out by a psychologist, psychiatrist, or other mental-health worker with special training in the technique. The use of tricyclic antidepressants can be helpful, not only to reduce the depressive aggravation of the pain and spasm, but also because of their direct analgesic effect, which reduces the need for "pain pills" (6). Sometimes, the goal of counseling must be to help the individual live with his or her pain and engage in gradually increasing, healthy, muscular exercise.

OCCUPATIONAL CRAMP

This is a functional motor disorder in which a specific, learned motor skill is impaired, such as writing, typewriting, telegraphy, musical performance, or comptometer or computer operation. Disabling muscular spasm, incoordination and discomfort, and sometimes tremor occur.

A tactful interview, after an examination of the involved muscles, will often elicit descriptions of conflicting, frustrating circumstances that face an obsessionally perfectionistic individual. If the patient or the physician is limited with regard to the therapeutic alliance that must be established for insight psychotherapy, success may still be achieved with a combination of supportive counseling, Jacobson's "progressive relaxation" exercises, and reeducation in the learned skill (39). Minor tranquilizers are sometimes used as adjuvants, although they do not seem to have direct muscle relaxant effects (54).

MUSCULAR-CONTRACTION HEADACHE

This type of headache is differentiated from the vascular (or migraine) and conversion headaches by the anatomic distribution of tension in the frontal or occipital muscles, which is symmetrical on both sides. Willingness to listen on the part of the doctor will elicit angry feelings "coming to a head," but the patient will often chastise himself for urges to "blow his top." Supportive counseling along with the administration of a minor tranquilizer may relieve the symptoms in a few weeks, but, bearing in mind that these patients are prone to addiction to analgesics, the physician should not procrastinate in referring the patient to a psychotherapist or in considering the possible need for antidepressant medication, especially if the patient's sleep is disrupted.

DISEASES OF THE JOINTS

RHEUMATOID ARTHRITIS

In recent years, much interest has centered on the immunological abnormalities in rheumatoid arthritis, and the burden of suspicion regarding its cause has shifted from streptococci to mycoplasmas and viruses (44). The clinical psychosomatic and psychiatric studies of patients with this disease, however, which have been done over many years, have left a heritage of practical principles applicable to the psychological aspects of the medical management of these sufferers (18, 50).

Several years ago, we published a report on the experience with 59 patients with rheumatoid arthritis, 14 of whom were treated in our psychosomatic unit of the Cincinnati General Hospital and 45 in the private practice of an internist in Indianapolis (49). In consonance with the previous and subsequent literature, we described some specific personality characteristics that accompany a predisposition to the development of the disease, and we reported the frequent occurrence of psychological stress immediately prior to onset or aggravation of the disease (18, 32, 51).

The difficulties in quantitation of psychological factors—especially in relation to pain, stiffness, and weakness, which do not have a direct relationship to the structural changes—have been dealt with before and after our study by a few investigators. Cobb and co-workers, in epidemiological studies employing psychological questionnaires and interviews, have established a number of statistical correlations between arthritis and certain psychosocial features, such as 1) severe arthritics more often perceive their mothers as being mean and the source of undeserved punishment, 2) they perceive their parents more often as being strict with discipline, and 3) women with arthritis are more likely to have come from high-status-stress families (10, 23). MMPI profiles for rheumatoid arthritis patients have been reported as being statistically higher than those of controls with regard to the scales for hypochondriasis, depression, and hysteria (42). It is not known whether these states are due to the crippling effects of the disease. Some less clear-cut psychological studies have indicated that these patients may fantasize a protective body boundary.

Moldofsky and Chester (40) have discriminated two pain-mood patterns in patients with rheumatoid arthritis; their experiments employed a dolorimeter and an adjective check list to determine mood. These patterns were described as a *synchronous state*, in which anxiety or hostility closely preceded or accompanied increases in joint tenderness, and a *paradoxical state*, in which there was an inverse relationship between the intensity of joint tenderness and the feeling of hopelessness. When they were observed again in one to two years, the patients in the paradoxical group were faring less well than the ones in the synchronous group. This study did not report any attempts to treat the depression in the "paradoxical" patients, although two of them were described as having showed improvement under gratifying life circumstances.

On the basis of our previously published experience (49), our experience with many patients seen in consultation since then, and the reports in the literature, we are able to outline several practical principles for the psychotherapeutic management of patients with this disease:

1. Doctors should be aware that usually these patients also have a diagnosable psychiatric condition, often a depressive neurosis, and that they sometimes have another medical illness in which emotional factors are playing a part, such as duodenal ulcer. Among these patients, personal conflicts have usually been long-standing, and the beginning or an exacerbation of the disease will be found to have occurred within a few weeks of some change in life circumstances.

2. These patients do not confide their emotional conflicts and personal history during the first interview. If the doctor expresses interest in their personal lives *after* he has pursued laboratory investigations and prescribed palliative medication, they will then reveal feelings of having been trapped by fate or frustrated by the behavior of others. Later, they may speak of deprivation or maltreatment and excessive discipline in childhood.

3. Such patients do not readily express anger, and yet they are sensitive to being slighted and concerned about rivalry with others for attention. The doctor should not suppress their expression of anger at him or other caretakers, nor should he discourage any initiative they may take on their own behalf.

4. Any consultation with a psychiatrist or clinical psychologist is best timed after the patient has voiced some awareness of his personal problems for which he might use further help.

5. Hospitalization can be used, not only when the rheumatoid process is progressing rapidly, but also as a haven from a stressful life situation, in order that the patient may recoup and regain his will to continue.

6. Medications should be used, not only for their antiinflammatory action, but also for their beneficial role in the patient-doctor relationship. One rheumatologist (13) has debated with a psychopharmacologist (5) in favor of the superiority of a phenothiazine-antidepressant combination (Triavil or Etrafon) over diazepam in treating the depression that aggravates the pain of this disease. We have found the tricyclic antidepressants to be the most helpful to depressed rheumatoid arthritics if the drug is prescribed after the patient has had the opportunity to talk with the doctor about his feelings of discouragement. At this point, the use of these drugs can facilitate the patient's verbal expression of aggression and aid him in constructive activity.

7. If antidepressant medications or steroids are given too soon—*i.e.,* before the therapeutic alliance has developed—they may then bolster a defense of denial and block the patient from solving his personal problems.

8. These patients are sensitive to separations and to the induction of shame or guilt. The doctor should take care not to make the intervals between visits too long, especially when the patient is subjected to stress or threats of separation. The patients should not be "weaned" from steroids at the same time that they are discharged from hospital, nor when the interval between their office visits is being increased.

9. This kind of supportive psychotherapy, along with appropriate medical management, is the best psychosomatic treatment for most of these patients (28). Some of them may be referred for insight psychotherapy for long-standing personality problems, but the general physician should remain available to treat exacerbations of the rheumatoid process.

ALLIED SYSTEMIC DISEASES

Several of the "rheumatic" and connective-tissue diseases—such as systemic lupus erythematosus (SLE), nonarticular rheumatism, psoriatic arthritis, ankylosing spondylitis, and others—may be precipitated or aggravated under depressing circumstances, *e.g.,* those of losses or of threats to self-esteem.

The previously described principles regarding the use of steroids or antidepressant drugs and its relation to the therapeutic alliance with the physician should be applied in treating these patients. When cardiac involvement may be present, the extent of this must be assessed by electrocardiography before proceeding with the administration of tricyclic antidepressants. One may have to prescribe diazepam, but this should not be done without providing repeated psychotherapeutic interviews to make sure that the patient is not becoming more depressed; such interviews will also facilitate working through the patient's feelings of loss or shame.

Patients with SLE may suffer from depression as well as schizophreniclike psychotic symptoms due to brain involvement, or they may have a psychotic reaction to steroids. The degree of impairment in immediate memory retention may be established to determine organic brain syndrome, or the electrolyte imbalance due to steroid administration may be measured by potassium levels or electrocardiography. The physician must then decide whether to decrease the steroids, to add antipsychotic medication, or to do both. Steroids can have an antidepressant action, but they can also increase paranoid or manic symptoms, even without producing hypokalemia. The preferred antipsychotic agents are thioridazine (which seems to have some antidepressant and antihypertensive effects) and haloperidol (plus an antiparkinsonian agent if necessary).

The prognosis is now better than what it has been in the past for some of these serious systemic diseases, provided that they are treated early with appropriate medication and supportive psychotherapy.

OSTEOARTHRITIS

One searches the literature in vain for reports on any psychological aspects of this more localized, degenerative form of joint disease. In our clinical experience, however, we have interviewed patients who presented the physical signs of this disorder and in whom the affected joints had not been subjected to trauma or unavoidable strenuous physical exertion. We discovered that some of these persons had a masochistic need to strain themselves during situations in which they were caring for persons toward whom they were ambivalent. Supportive counseling (or marital counseling if indicated) and a "progressive relaxation" regimen (as employed for patients with occupational cramp) would seem to provide the best psychosomatic approach to treating these individuals. If they are young enough and not in an irreversible life situation, they may be motivated for insight psychotherapy or psychoanalysis.

DISEASES OF THE BONES

FRACTURES

When Dunbar, a pioneer in psychosomatic investigation in America, decided to use fracture patients as controls in a study of the personality profiles of patients with cardiovascular and other diseases, she did not know that she was going to discover "by accident" that patients with fractures did not have randomly varying personalities, but rather that they tended to have "profiles" which they shared with other fracture patients (12). These patients were action-oriented, they resented strict control by authorities or by their own conscience, and frequently they had sustained their injury when their dependent needs were frustrated.

Probably only occupational physicians can use this information to prevent accidents, but other doctors can use it to understand their patients better who have healing fractures. The patient's conflicts and guilt may have been reduced by the punishing injury and by the care and attention obtained from others, but his aggressive urges may be frustrated if there is prolonged immobilization. Persisting pain and "uncooperativeness" may be manifestations of a depressive turning of aggression against the self. After listening to the patient's account of his own personal feelings before and after the accident, the physician can prescribe psychoactive medication to reduce the patient's increased tension. Tricyclic antidepressants are often more helpful in this respect than tranquilizers, which may threaten the patient with more enforced passivity. Depression may retard healing, especially if there is poor nutrition due to anorexia.

Complications resulting from psychological trauma will be considered below.

BONE DISEASES

Psychosomatic factors may play a part in osteoporosis, osteomalacia, osteitis fibrosa cystica generalisata, and osteosclerosis. Paget's disease and hyperostosis frontalis interna may be first diagnosed by roentgenographic examination during the investigation of a patient with psychiatric symptoms. Needless to say, the personal problems of the patient will also need attention, and the physician should not consider the symptoms as being entirely secondary to the bone disease.

Somatopsychic problems that need special attention in individuals with polyostotic fibrous dysplasia, osteogenesis imperfecta, and multiple myeloma or neoplasms of the bone that require mutilating surgery. For children whose problems of deformity, as a result of comparisons with their peers, warp their self-esteem, physicians—*e.g.,* pediatricians—should keep in mind the help that child psychiatry teams may give to these patients and their parents.

TRAUMA

Closely related to the problems of fracture patients are those of patients with other injuries such as multiple accidental injuries. The term "traumatic neurosis" is often used indiscriminately to refer to the specific sequelae of physical trauma (*e.g.,* damage to the brain or the loss of a limb of importance in the person's occupation) or to psychological trauma involving anxiety and ego restriction (24, 30, 38, 53). Either or both conditions may need attention during rehabilitation.

Psychological trauma occurs whenever the individual has had an overwhelming threat to his life or self-esteem, even if no physical damage actually occurred, as in near accidents or in survival after a community disaster. The sequelae of this kind of "trauma" can be recognized early if the doctor is alert to disturbed sleep patterns and repetitive dreams of the overwhelming situation, a phobia regarding the return to the activity in which the person was traumatized, or persisting guilt at being alive and physically intact when others have died or been crippled.

Early treatment is important to prevent the chronic disablement that is related to secondary gain and is often associated with psychologic compensation problems (47). The use of sedatives and minor tranquilizers, though perhaps helpful in relieving the symptoms, should not be allowed to preclude the opportunity for the patient to talk out his feelings of anxiety, loss, grief, and guilt. It may be advisable to refer the patient to a psychiatrist for intravenous-barbiturate analytic interviewing. This specialized technique is preferably employed within six months of the traumatic event (46).

The earlier that rehabilitation is achieved so that the individual may return to his customary activities or to the work situation in which he was injured (with changes in his work assignment if necessary), the less likely is the disablement to become chronic.

DISABLEMENT

Chronic disability has both somatopsychic and psychosomatic aspects (48).

The research on the somatopsychic aspects of the problem was thoroughly reviewed by Barker and Wright (2) over twenty years ago. These authors concluded that most of the preconceptions about disabled persons had not been validated, and that impaired persons must be treated individually, rather than as a group with special personality characteristics. The sociopsychological significance of the impairment was considered paramount. Problems were noted to exist in the communication between the patient and the doctor, since they have different views of the world. If the doctor can define the world of the disabled person and see how it differs from his own view, he can begin to understand how to help in rehabilitation.

Progress in the treatment of the psychosomatic aspects of chronic disablement in the two decades since Barker and Wright's review has been mainly along three lines: 1) there is now more understanding of the patient's regression to secondary gain in association with industrial or insurance compensation problems, 2) the use of operant conditioning has been initiated for patients with chronic pain or chronic illness behavior, and 3) antidepressant medication has been found useful for reducing pain and enhancing the patient's motivation to increased activity.

It has been recognized that the "secondary gain" component does not always take the form of a pursuit for dependent security, but it may also be manifested as an unconscious search for revenge by a depressed individual who has feelings of having been mistreated, as described previously in the discussion of back pain. Sometimes, it is necessary that any litigation be settled before the patient can be mobilized in a rehabilitation program, either in individual or group psychotherapy or in marital counseling (48). The attitudes of the physicians treating the patient are of great importance in dealing with the neurotic problems involved in disabilities following industrial injuries (34, 43). In order to understand such patients more objectively, the doctor must examine his own feelings to make sure that he is not being antagonistic to someone who may seem, in his view, to be trying to get away with obtaining a living without working for it (45). These problems would be easier to treat if there were liberal benefits granted to the patient for treatment in a work rehabilitation program, instead of an indefinitely continuing income for not working (48).

Operant conditioning techniques have been described in Chapter 14 on the behavior therapies. These techniques have been applied to patients with chronic pain or chronic illness behavior, and such applications have been described by teams of psychologists, physicians, and nurses in the Department of Physical Medicine and Rehabilitation at the University of Washington (16, 17) and in the Psychosomatic Unit of the Cincinnati General Hospital (56, 57). In studies of social contingencies, it has been found that these patients are inclined to reward others primarily for taking care of them. When the patients and their families are involved in planning treatment goals toward increasing the patient's independent activity, however, these patients can diminish their bids for care and attention, including their use of pain to get medication, and they can become better able to get along outside of the hospital and get back to the social and physical satisfactions of productive work. Even pain tolerance has been found to be increased when experimental subjects are given the opportunity to obtain the rewards of solving difficult problems on their own, as compared to when they are being given encouragement and attention by a solicitous experimenter in a white coat (58).

Although these experimental treatment programs were carried out in special units under the leadership of psychologists and psychiatrists with skill in behavior therapy, they still have relevance for the rehabilitation of chronically disabled persons by other doctors and nurses. Once they understand the patient's physical and psychological problems, the "caretakers" can enroll the patient and his family in a graded program of increasing activity, in which the patient is rewarded for progress instead of being given attention for complaining about his disablement.

Sometimes, chronically disabled patients are quite depressed, either as a result of exhausting effects of chronic pain, or as a result of bottled-up aggression due to enforced inactivity. As mentioned previously in the discussion of back pain, the use of a tricyclic antidepressant, such as imipramine or amitriptyline, may reduce the need for analgesics, improve the appetite, and give the patient increased hope that he can again obtain the satisfactions of greater mental or physical activity. If the patient's sleep has been disturbed by pain or restlessness, the prescription of a dose of 50 mg of one of these drugs at bedtime may be sufficient to give the patient a new lease on life.

These modern devices in treating the psychosomatic aspects of disablement are only aids, however, for the wise physician who seeks to understand his patients and help them to realize again their abilities. He is wise if he understands them in terms of William Cowper's poem:

Absence of occupation is not rest
A mind quite vacant is a mind distressed.

And, in the treatment of all these musculoskeletal disorders, the doctor should follow the aphorism of Hippocrates:

The physician must not only be prepared to do what is right himself, but also to make the patient, the attendants, and externals cooperate.

REFERENCES

1. A doctor who has it: myasthenia gravis. J Fla Med Assoc 42:815, 1956
2. Barker RG, Wright BA: Disablement: the somatopsychological problem. In Wittkower ED, Cleghorn RA (eds): Recent Developments in Psychosomatic Medicine. London, Pitman, 1954, pp 419-435
3. Beales RK, Hickman NW: Industrial injuries of the back and extremities. J Bone Joint Surg [AM] 54:1593, 1972
4. Bernstein AE, Flegenheimer W, Roose LJ: Transference and countertransference problems in a critically ill patient. Psychiatry Med 4:191, 1973
5. Blackwell B: Psychotropic drugs in use today. JAMA 225:1637, 1973
6. Blackwell B: Personal communication, 1974
7. Brolley M, Hollender MH: Psychological problems of patients with myasthenia gravis. J Nerv Ment Dis 122:178, 1955
8. Buzzard EF: The clinical history and post-mortem examination of five cases of myasthenia gravis. Brain 28:438, 1905
9. Claman L, Johnston RE: Effects of emotions on the use of medications in myasthenia gravis. Tex State J Med 61:49, 1965
10. Cobb S, Kasl SV: Epidemiologic contributions to the etiology of rheumatoid arthritis, with special attention to psychological and social factors. Proc Int Symp Pop Studies Rheumatic Diseases 3:75, 1966 (Excerpta Medica Int Congr Series No. 48)
11. Collins RT: Psychiatric syndromes in myasthenia gravis. Br Med J 1:975, 1939
12. Dunbar F: Mind and Body: Psychosomatic Medicine. New York, Random House, 1947
13. Dyer HR: Psychotropic drugs in rheumatology. JAMA 226:1572, 1973
14. Eaton LM: A warning concerning the use of curare in convulsive shock treatment of patients with psychiatric disorders who may have myasthenia gravis. Proc Mayo Clin 22:4, 1947
15. Farbman AA: Neck sprain: associated factors. JAMA 223:1010, 1973
16. Fordyce WE, Fowles RS, Lehmann JF, DeLateur BJ: Some implications of learning in problems of chronic pain. J Chronic Dis 21:179, 1968
17. Fowlers RS, Fordyce WE, Berni R: Operant conditioning in chronic illness. Am J Nurs 69:1226, 1969
18. Freedman AM, Kaplan HI, Sadock BJ (eds): Rheumatoid arthritis (psychophysiological musculoskeletal disorder). In Modern Synopsis of Comprehensive Textbook of Psychiatry. Baltimore, Williams & Wilkins, 1972, pp 471-473
19. Halliday WR: Prevention of psychosocial complications in workmen's comp. patients can cut cost (abstr). Clin Psychiatr News 1:10, 1973
20. Hanvik LJ: MMPI profiles in patients with low-back pain. J Consult Psychol 15:350, 1951
21. Hayman M: Myasthenia gravis and psychosis. A report of a case with observations on its psychosomatic implications. Psychosom Med 3:120, 1941
22. Jacobs S (ed): Backache: a multidisciplinary approach to its treatment (from Medicine Grand Rounds Touro Infirmary). Psychiatry Med 4:221, 1973
23. Kasl SV, Cobb S: Effects of parental status incongruence and discrepancy on physical and mental health of adult offspring. J Pers Soc Psychol 7 (2):1, 1967
24. Keiser L: The Traumatic Neurosis. Philadelphia, Lippincott, 1968
25. Kennedy FS, Moersch FP: Myasthenia gravis: clinical review of 87 cases observed between 1915 and 1932. Can Med Assoc J 37:216, 1937
26. Keynes G: The history of myasthenia gravis. Med Hist 5:313, 1961
27. Lennartz VH, Spiegelberg U: Psychopathologische Befunde bei Myopathien. Nervenarzt 27:98, 1956
28. Levinson JE: How arthritics can help themselves (abstr). Cincinnati Alumnus 41:22, 1967
29. Levinson A, Lim EL: Myasthenia gravis with mental retardation. J Pediatr 45:80, 1954
30. Lipinski E, Winslow WW, Powles WE, Ross WD: Occupational accidents: some psychosocial factors in the accident syndrome. Can Psychiatr Assoc J 10:299, 1965

31. Liskow A: Student essay: Emotional reactions of myasthenia gravis. University of Cincinnati, Dept of Psychiatry, 1965

32. Ludwig AO: Rheumatoid arthritis. In Wittkower ED, Cleghorn RA (eds): Recent Developments in Psychosomatic Medicine. London, Pitman, 1954, pp 232–244

33. Marcus J: The interrelations of myasthenia gravis and psychic stress. Isr Med J 21:178, 1962

34. Martin MJ: Psychiatric aspects of patients with compensation problems. Psychosomatics 11:81, 1970

35. Meyer E: Personality issues in myasthenia gravis. Presented at American Psychosomatic Society, 1950

36. Meyer E: Training in psychosomatic medicine: some observations on the hospital environment. In Advance Psychosomatic Medicine, Vol IV. Basel, S Karger, 1964, pp 47–57

37. Modlin HC: "Accidents" and traumatic neurosis. Cincinnati, 35th Annual AMA Congress on Occupational Health, 1975

38. Moldofsky H: Occupational cramp. J Psychosom Res 15:439, 1971

39. Moldofsky H, Chester WJ: Pain and mood patterns in patients with rheumatoid arthritis. Psychosom Med 32:309, 1970

40. Oosterhuis HJGH, Wilde GJS: Psychiatric aspects of myasthenia gravis. Psychiatr Neurol Neurochir 67:484, 1964

41. Polley HF, Swenson WM, Steinhilber RM: Personality characteristics of patients with rheumatoid arthritis. Psychosomatics 11:45, 1970

42. Raskin HA: Psychopathology following industrial injury—iatrogenic factors. Cincinnati, 35th Annual AMA Congress on Occupational Health, 1975

43. Rodman GP (ed): Rheumatoid arthritis. In Primer on the Rheumatic Diseases, 7th ed. JAMA 224:687–700, 1973

44. Ross WD: Accidents and their sequelae. In Practical Psychiatry for Industrial Physicians. Springfield Ill, CC Thomas, 1956, pp 151–167

45. Ross WD: Neuroses following trauma and their relation to compensation. In Arieti S(ed): American Handbook of Psychiatry, Vol 3. New York, Basic Books, 1966, 131–147

46. Ross WD: Differentiating compensation factors from traumatic factors. In Leedy JJ (ed): Compensation in Psychiatric Disability and Rehabilitation. Springfield Ill, CC Thomas, 1971

47. Ross WD: Prolongation of disability after a psychological traumatic reaction. Cincinnati, 35th Annual AMA Congress on Occupational Health, 1975

48. Ross WD, Browning JS, Kaplan SM: Emotional Aspects in the Medical Management of Rheumatoid Arthritis (#4 of Acta Psychosomatica Series). Great Britain, Geigy, 1961

49. Shafii M: Psychotherapeutic treatment for rheumatoid arthritis. Arch Gen Psychiatry 29:85, 1973

50. Shochet BR, Lisansky ET, Schubart AF, Fiocco V, Kurland S, Page M: A medical-psychiatric study of patients with rheumatoid arthritis. Psychosomatics 10:271, 1969

51. Sternbach RA, Wolf SR, Murphy RW, Akeson WH: Traits of pain patients: the low back "loser." Psychosomatics 14:226, 1973

52. Titchener JL, Ross WD: Acute or chronic stress as determinants of behavior, character and neurosis. In Arieti S (ed): American Handbook of Psychiatry, Vol 3. New York, Basic Books, 1974, pp 39–60

53. Wahl CH: Psychogenic muscular dystonia. In Arieti S(ed): American Handbook of Psychiatry, Vol 3. New York, Basic Books, 1966, pp 162–165

54. Williams RL, Silberman M: Electric shock therapy in a case of myasthenia gravis complicated by schizophrenic psychosis. Arch Neurol Psychiatry 66:783, 1951

55. Wooley SC, Blackwell B: A behavioral probe into social contingencies on a psychomatic ward. J Appl Behav Ann (in press)

56. Wooley SC, Blackwell B, Epps B, Harper R: A learning theory treatment model for illness behavior (abstr). Psychosom Med 37:78, 1975

57. Wooley SC, Epps B, Blackwell B: Pain tolerance in chronic illness behavior (abstr). Psychosom Med 37:98, 1975

30 Itching and Other Dermatoses

HERMAN MUSAPH

Itching is the sensation or perception that produces a compulsion to scratch or rub the surface of the skin where one feels or perceives the itching. Itching is associated with the corticothalamic pain system. There exist subliminal stimuli, which evoke itching outside consciousness, and liminal stimuli, in which the afferent pathways are sensorial.

The itching dermatoses are scabies, pediculosis, bites of insects, urticaria, atopic dermatitis, contact dermatitis, lichen ruber planus, Duhring's disease, and miliaria. The internal disorders that frequently can cause itching are diabetes mellitus, nephritis, diseases of the liver, gout, diseases of the thyroid gland, food allergies, Hodgkin's disease, leukemia, and cancer. Itching can also appear during pregnancy and senility.

We lack sufficient knowledge about how itching develops, how it is experienced, and why it finally ends. We do know that there are clear individual differences as to the perception threshold for itching. Some people experience low itching stimuli as unbearable, whereas others experience the same low itching stimuli as negligible.

The threshold of perception for itching stimuli depends on:

1. Organic disease. An organic disease may lower the threshold.
2. Personality structure. A rapid release of emotion leads to an increase in the threshold, whereas ego weakness lowers it.
3. Disposition, congenital or acquired. During the first days of life, a difference already exists in the degree of skin reaction in various babies (19). Some children clearly show a need for skin contact; others are less inclined to seek it. As we are not yet sufficiently aware of the factors that may explain these different patterns of behavior, we assume that constitutional factors play a role.
4. Stress situations, organic or psychological. A psychological stress situation exists when there is an unresolved and predominantly unconscious emotional conflict. The presence of skin disease itself may be psychologically stressful.

A decrease in the threshold value due to one or more of these enumerated factors can manifest itself clinically in fits of itching. It is likely that conditioned reflexes also play a role in threshold development.

During the first years of life, a human being is subjected to a series of frequently appearing tactile and itching stimuli. Skin contact with the mother and other key figures is of great importance. A normal mother-child relationship is essential for the development of an adequate itching and pain threshold. Disturbances in this relationship can facilitate conditioning that may lead to psychodermatoses in adolescence and maturity.

The kind of relationship that exists between the mother and child, or the father and child, can best be assessed by the way in which the child is held, particularly while it is still very small. In a good mother-child relationship, there is a maximum of contact between the hands of the mother and the skin of the child. The mother's hands are completely open, with the fingers slightly curved in a relaxed position. If the relationship between the mother and child is not as good, she will hold the child with clenched fists. In particular, the left hand of a right-handed person (or vice versa) will betray the fear of contact. In extreme cases, the mother may express her unconscious aversion and negative feelings toward the child on her lap by hitting, pinching, and boxing him with her left hand. More often than not, she is completely unaware of what she is doing. At the other end of the spectrum is the behavior of the mother who uses her left hand to stroke, fondle, and caress the child in the same way she strokes, fondles, and caresses her sexual partner. One can make similar observations in the father-child relationship.

We know that hugging or cuddling contact during the first months of life constitutes a sound basis for healthy emotional development. Such cuddling requires optimal tactile contact. This suggests that it may be desirable to advise mothers to present the naked upper part of their bodies to their nearly naked babies during nursing; this applies especially to bottle-fed babies (10).

PSYCHODERMATOLOGICAL SYNDROMES WITH SEVERE ITCHING STATES

PSYCHOGENIC PRURITUS

This disease is caused by emotional tension and is characterized by 1) the absence of an organic (internal or dermatological) explanation of the itching and 2) the coincidence of the perception of itching with the patient's attempt to ward off an emotion (1964). Fits of psychogenic pruritus can come into being through a decrease of the threshold level by psychogenic stress, *i.e.,* in an emotional conflict situation, or because of a disturbed personality structure, *i.e.,* one that is incapable of adequately resolving emotional conflict situations. In most cases, we are dealing with a combination of both factors.

The emotions that most often lead to an itching fit are repressed anger and repressed anxiety. These patients, as a result of their personality structures, have difficulty handling such emotions. Whenever they experience either anger or anxiety, they get a fit of itching and begin to scratch vehemently. Briefly, the personality structure of these patients is characterized by "semipermeability." The patient is hypersensitive to tensions that occur in others, especially in key persons. There is a real hunger for affection, but, at the same time, the patient is incapable of an adequate abreaction of his tensions and stresses. Typical of these patients is their taboo on the expression of aggressive impulses (1964). When these people encounter an attitude of hostility in a situation that they are powerless to alter, especially if such hostility is created by beloved persons, then their defenses may collapse. Each person has his own threshold level that cannot be crossed without symptom formation. Sometimes the aggressiveness of the beloved person is too strong; sometimes the counterforces of the patient are too weak. When the defense against these aggressive feelings collapses, an itching state may come about, and the attack is directed against the self.

ANOGENITAL PRURITUS

Many nonpsychogenic factors can give rise to itching in the anogenital region. The most well-known are worms, rhagades, hemorrhoids, eczema ani, scabies, and dermatomycoses. In males, the itching can appear on the penis and the scrotum as a result of eczema or infestation with *Phthirius pubis.* In females, pruritus valvae may appear as a result of vaginal discharge. This discharge may have many causes, the main ones being mycoses.

If all such organic causes can be excluded, then psychogenic causes should be considered. These may be primary—*i.e.,* there is no organic disease that preceded the beginning of the itching—or they may be secondary.

Case 1. A 49-year-old male homosexual consulted me because of unbearable itching of the scrotum. The dermatologist and the general physician could find no explanation for this pruritus. The patient had never had such a complaint before, nor was there any history of venereal disease or disorders of his genitals. He had been living together with a friend, who was also a homosexual, for more than 20 years. A few days before his pruritus started, his friend started a love affair with a young boy who had been a friend of the family. Nevertheless, there remained a sexual relationship between my patient and his friend. My patient suffered acutely from this emotional conflict situation and was unable to express his feelings of rage, resentment, and love. His friend pleaded for more sexual freedom and could not resist it. Two days later his pruritus started.

The term *secondary psychogenic pruritus anogenitalis* is used when the organic cause of the pruritus has disappeared, but the symptom of itching remains. This phenomenon can be seen in many neurotic symptoms, namely, those symptoms that originally had a certain function, but then started to live their own life.

Case 2. A girl of 21 came to the outpatient department because of severe itching over the whole body, which she had had for a few days. The diagnosis of scabies was easily made. A week before, she had bought a secondhand dress in one of the many artistic junk shops in Amsterdam. After treatment for scabies, the itching did not disappear. The results of several tests were negative: no *Sarcoptes* organisms were found. To be on the safe side, the antiscabies treatment was repeated, but the pruritus persisted. Therefore, the dermatologist sent her to me.

She was the only daughter of a strife-ridden family; she was eager to make herself independent and to move away from her family. Unfortunately, she was unable to support herself financially. During the preceding years, she had fallen in love several times, but all these affairs ended in disappointment. She blamed herself for choosing the wrong partners. Furthermore, she was struggling against the impulse to masturbate or to have sexual intercourse.

Her pruritus was exclusively localized in her labia majora. The itching sanctioned her desire to rub herself, and it simultaneously provided an outlet for her need to punish herself. The experienced itching states, which were originally caused by her scabies, obtained a new function as an alibi for her sexual and aggressive impulses. This new function had become instrumental in continuing the itching states.

In 1953 Wittkower and Russell (21) pointed out that pruritus vulvae not infrequently is a concealed form of masturbation and that, concurrent with elements of pleasure, it has a self-punitive and self-destructive psychological function. By rubbing the anal aperture, patients with pruritus ani unconsciously gratify an erotic need. Pleasure derived from performing this act is usually almost completely obliterated by an unconscious sense of guilt, which, in turn, changes the act of rubbing into one of scratching. Since it is obvious that the anus is more readily available as a site of expression of conflicts or of latent homosexual trends in men than it is in women, the preponderance of pruritus ani in men becomes understandable.

CHRONIC URTICARIA

As early as 1909, Kreibich and Sobotka (8) indicated that a psychological component must be included among the many possible causes of chronic urticaria. They described a 28-year-old house painter who, in an experiment, was provoked into developing urticaria in response to certain actions of a nurse in the hospital, which were irritating to him.

Several research workers in this field have recorded different character traits associated with this disorder. Saul (18) expressed the belief that urticaria is a substitute for suppressed crying. He suggested that the state of intense longing for love may increase allergic sensitivity. Graham and Wolf (5) described a specific attitude in urticaria patients. According to them, the skin eruptions develop in states where the patient feels powerless. Their conclusion was that the psychological disposition expressed by the complaint, "I was taking a beating," produces the same vascular changes as does a real beating. It is these vascular changes that give rise to urticaria. Several research workers in the field of psychodermatology were unable to corroborate this hypothesis, however (9, 16).

Among the patients in our Amsterdam study (9), we found a passive attitude evident in personal contacts. Heavy loads of partly conscious anxiety were found to coincide with a high degree of anxiety tolerance. Violent feelings of rage and resentment were strongly averted. In the majority of cases, it was demonstrated that the patients had been greatly annoyed shortly before the eruption of urticaria occurred; they had concealed their annoyance and were very distressed because of their pent-up anger.

Recent immunological investigations have revealed that the group of patients with chronic urticaria consists of several subgroups, in which different immune mechanisms can be detected. In our opinion, however, although immunological examination cannot be neglected, patients suffering from chronic urticaria need more help from psychiatrists than from allergists.

CONTACT DERMATITIS

In the pathogenesis of contact dermatitis, the most important features are external; *i.e.,* the dermatitis may be caused by toxic or allergic agents. Detergents, for instance, that change the physiological acidity of the skin by their strong alkalinity have a toxic effect on the skin. In response to toxic materials, the dermatitis usually occurs within 24 hours. The prodromal time is much longer—often months or even years—in cases of allergic contact dermatitis. In such cases, the skin of the patient is sensitized first; the effect of the allergen on the skin is the formation of specific antibodies, which may cause an allergic reaction if the skin is exposed again to the allergen. Such sensitizing compounds cause a reaction in very few people. Sometimes, toxic and allergic factors combine to cause the dermatitis: for example, detergents may have a toxic effect because of their strong alkalinity and an allergic effect because of the presence of sensitizing compounds such as nickel and chromate in very small concentrations.

The important question has not yet been answered as to why some people are sensitized by one of these compounds while others are not. During recent years, however, experimental immunological and biochemical investigations have given us more information about the composition of allergenic compounds and their antibodies. Psychiatric and psychological investigations have shown that the deprivation of love and affection is a powerful factor in the life histories of patients suffering from allergic contact dermatitis; their personality structure is abnormal. They have a passive, long-suffering attitude and an inordinate anxiety about losing contact with key persons. Life is hard for them; they are no fighters. They are afraid of their feelings of rage and are always apologizing. Because of their skin disorder, they are strongly preoccupied with their bodies, especially with the skin. They are aware of their inability to make contacts with other people and continually apologize for this. The long-suffering attitude, the passivity, and the deprivation factor are striking. It is of great value to understand the personality structure of these patients, because doing so makes it easier to enter into their problems.

It goes without saying that along with psychological help, the physician should also give the practical advice that the patient should avoid contact with any detergent.

ATOPIC DERMATITIS

The literature about this condition has become extensive since Greenhill and Finesinger (6) in 1942 pointed out that hostile feelings and depressive traits are found in patients suffering from atopic dermatitis. We now know that this disease is congenital. The occurrence of infantile eczema during the second part of the first year of life is almost pathognomonic.

Such children scratch their skin tremendously, which often leaves their faces grossly disfigured (7). Both mother and child may suffer because of these itching fits; the mother is apt to suffer from intense guilt feelings and may develop a reluctance to touch her baby. This behavior of the mother can have a pernicious effect on the child's emotional life. The mother and child develop a combination of repressed hostility and overt anxiety. This pattern can last a lifetime, and it is the basis of a neurotic distortion in both mother and child.

In some instances, the child with atopic dermatitis is immobilized in order to prevent him from tearing his itching skin. This immobilization is injurious to the mental health of the child. The restrictions imposed on the psychomotor functions of these children have repercussions on their character development. During an attack of itching, these children should be given an opportunity to express some of these motor functions in a different manner, such as by tearing up papers, kicking a ball, riding a rocking horse, or romping with the nurse or a mother figure. Dermatological treatment is obviously also of great value. Hence, the treatment of these patients should be entrusted, whenever possible, to both a dermatologist and a psychiatrist.

Atopic dermatitis is characterized by a frequent concurrence with other allergic manifestations. We speak of an "EAHT complex" (eczema-asthma-hayfever). It is not known why patients switch over from one part of this atopic complex to another. It is known, however, that disturbing life situations precipitate and aggravate atopic manifestations. Many attempts have been made to identify and to define the nature of precipitating and aggravating emotional conflicts, yet neither a specificity of emotional conflicts nor a specificity of personality structure has been established.

Three possible causative factors can be considered in the genesis of this disorder:

1. A congenital disposition to allergy, expressed in an overreactivity of the skin to stimuli during the latter half of the first year of life (19) and in an increased cathexis of the skin.
2. A disturbed mother-child relationship with insufficient skin contact.
3. Events of the critical phase during the first year of life, during which a disturbed ego development of the child can occur, resulting in a disturbed personality structure in adulthood.

In some patients, the presence of atopic dermatitis reduces neurotic tension and facilitates social adjustment. On examination of patients suffering from atopic dermatitis, one may justifiably ask oneself: which came first, the skin symptoms or the neurotic manifestations? It is often impossible to answer this question; frequently, a vicious circle exists that is very difficult to break.

FACTITIAL DERMATITIS

Factitial dermatitis is defined as self-induced eruptions of the skin. It occurs only in emotionally disturbed persons, and it is unconsciously produced by the patient, often during sleep (10). There are also many people who systematically damage their skin while they are concentrating on something else. This damage can be increased in various ways: they may clean the damaged skin by means that exacerbate the disturbance, *e.g.,* with turpentine, or they may corrode their skin with materials such as a 90% alcohol solution (17).

It is probable that sexualized aggressive feelings, originally aimed at key figures during the first year of life, play a role in the development of this disease. Such aggressive feelings directed against the patient's body-ego produce a regressive attitude. This is one reason why problems related to masturbation assume a central position for these patients. Furthermore, we have observed marked mechanisms of identification with respect to persons in the direct environment of the patient that were based on a pronounced ambivalent conflict situation. The exploration of such ambivalence and conflicts is an integral part of treatment and diagnosis. Self-mutilation cannot be evaluated apart from the context of the patient's personality structure.

TRICHOTILLOMANIA

Trichotillomania, or hair-pulling, is most often found in girls during puberty or early adolescence. Aggressive impulses play an extremely important part in the formation of the symptoms of trichotillomania as well as in factitial dermatitis.

There are also babies and infants who suffer from trichotillomania. When this occurs, it is apparent that we must determine whether something is wrong in the mother-child relationship. We can try to treat the baby *in absentia* by helping the mother overcome some of the difficulties in her relationship with the baby. It is also important to obtain complete information about the child's eating and bowel training.

ACNÉ EXCORIÉE DES JEUNES FILLES

This disorder was first described by Brocq as early as 1898. It was pointed out that the disorder is perpetuated by the patients because they systematically rub their faces. In this way, various defacing skin disorders may develop, which can very easily be diagnosed as self-induced. One observes a cheilitis on the lips, which is the result of the patient's compulsive tearing of skin from the upper and lower lip.

DELUSIONS OF PARASITOSIS

Patients suffering from this disorder typically complain of being troubled by small animals that creep into their skin, move around, and multiply. Every now and then these imagined parasites give rise to unbearable itching, and the effects of scratching can be seen on the skin. Other dermatological disorders are not demonstrable. These patients always use the same method to prove the existence of their parasitosis: they display matchboxes or cans in which very small amounts of scales or pieces of dirt can be found. They ask the doctor to investigate this material microscopically, expecting that parasites will be found.

The evident skin sensations in such cases are tactile sensory experiences, which are quite similar to those of chronic hallucinosis. Patients rationalize their delusions by pointing out that they are contaminated by certain forms of textiles, bedclothes, or carpeting. They think that everyone who enters their house can be contaminated, and therefore they try to have their homes fumigated. In certain families, a *"folie à deux or à trois"* occurs. This disorder occurs most often in patients of over 60 years of age, regardless of their sex. It is a monomorphic syndrome. Because the rest of the personality structure is often sound, I cannot agree with those psychiatrists who consider this disorder a form of schizophrenia.

The cause of this serious disorder is incompletely understood. One suggestion has been that it is the result of arteriosclerotic disorders that lead to vascular disturbances, especially in the region of the thalamus (4).

THERAPY OF ITCHING STATES

PSYCHOTHERAPY

Several psychotherapeutic techniques are at our disposal to help patients overcome the tensions that lead to itching. The choice of technique is dependent on the physician's training and experience and on the personality structure of the patient, his working alliance, his motivation toward treatment, the seriousness of his emotional disturbance, his specific illness behavior and the patient-doctor relationship. Some of these techniques will be discussed in greater detail in the section on therapy of self-induced skin disorders.

In cases where the itching dermatosis is not curable, *e.g.,* in atopic dermatitis, psychotherapeutic techniques may be used to help the patient to endure his pruritus.

PSYCHOPHARMACOTHERAPY

Unfortunately, a reliable antipruritic drug is still lacking. Nevertheless, drugs are of great help in combating repressed anger and repressed anxiety, which are the emotions most often responsible for triggering severe itching states, especially in psychogenic pruritus. The choice of drug depends largely on the strength of the repression and on the dangers of habituation and addiction.

Therapy for Patients with Repressed Anger

In some cases, we are able to help the patient by offering him the possibility of experiencing his anger. If the ego is strong enough, the patient is able to work through his conflicts; this requires a repetitive experience of the repressed emotion. A technique that is often used is narcoanalysis. We use either sodium pentothal (Thiopental), 250 mg intravenously, or sodium methohexital (Brietal Sodium), 50 mg intravenously. Sometimes it is preferable not to lift the repression, *i.e.,* not to make the anger conscious, for by doing so, we may seal off the emotions by strengthening the defense system.

Therapy for Patients with Repressed Anxiety

If the patient is able to tolerate a certain amount of anxiety, we can help him by means of narcoanalysis or other forms of abreaction. In most cases, we prescribe an anxiolytic drug, *e.g.,* one of the diazepam derivatives. Although they have no antipruritic effect, these agents may decrease tension, mitigate emotions, and disengage the patient's vehement feelings from their trigger mechanisms.

DERMATOLOGICAL TREATMENT

In nearly all cases, treatment involves a combined approach. If the dermatological treatment, whether local or systemic, is found to be insufficient, patients with itching dermatoses may be treated by a team consisting of a dermatologist and a psychiatrist. The general practitioner, who has the advantage of knowing the psychosocial background of his patient, could easily apply the results of psychodermatological investigations in the employment of such combined treatment.

THERAPY FOR SELF-INDUCED SKIN DISORDERS

It is not unusual for a doctor who diagnoses a self-inflicted skin disorder to assume an accusing, moralistic stance and insist that the delinquent patient "confess his crime." This reduces the patient's position to that of a defendant, which is hardly conducive to his mental recovery. Since we know that aggressive impulses play an extremely important part in the formation of the symptoms of factitial dermatitis and trichotillomania, it is easy to understand that a doctor's aggressive attitude toward the patient can reinforce the latter's aggressive impulses. Although it is sometimes difficult for doctors to accept their impotence in medical and pedagogical fields, they must be careful not to blame the patient for their own lack of success. The patient must be prevented from forming the impression that the doctor is a policeman or a judge (3). If the doctor has responded judgmentally, psychotherapy should then be performed by another physician, who must attempt to overcome the psychic damage created by this attitude as well as to treat the original problem.

In a psychotherapeutic situation, the desirable strategy entails 1) accepting the patient and his disagreeable habits, 2) trying to uncover the usually unconscious motivations of the undesirable habits, and 3) if the personality structure is sufficiently constructed and a good working alliance can be built up, trying to help the patient to overcome his emotional conflict situation that he is presently solving inadequately by means of his symptoms.

In practice we have a choice between two strategies: a psychotherapy or behavior therapy.

PSYCHOANALYSIS

We can suggest to the patient that we try to discover together the source of the compulsion to damage his skin. In doing this, we start from the working hypothesis that this compulsion fulfilled a function in an earlier period of life. This original function has disappeared, but the compulsive symptom has continued independently. Factitial dermatitis is seen as a neurotic symptom, *i.e.,* as the expression of an infantile, unconscious, and unresolved emotional conflict. The exploration of this conflict is essential in order to understand the hidden emotions, *e.g.,* guilt, anxiety, and anger.

The need for punishment is often a powerful motivating force. This need finds expression in tearing that part of the body which can be seen by everyone. The patient has a strong desire to reveal his guilt. This wish may be an unconscious expression of the wish to be punished, so that unbearable guilt feelings will decrease. In youngsters, an unresolved emotional relationship with their parents is usually apparent.

This dynamic working hypothesis has been applied in psychotherapy for many years. Unfortunately, it does not always result in a disappearance of the skin symptoms. Often, after months or even years of intensive therapeutic work, the patient is considerably less neurotic, but the neurotic skin symptom still persists. It is impossible to predict what the outcome of psychotherapy will be. It must be emphasized, however, that such therapy can only be carried out by highly qualified, psychoanalytically trained psychiatrists or psychologists.

BEHAVIOR THERAPY

During the past several years, a totally different approach has been developed. Here, the therapist does not start from the working hypothesis that the patient suffers from a neurotic symptom in the psychodynamic sense of the word, but instead he assumes that the compulsion to tear one's skin or to rub oneself is a bad habit. Then, on the basis of that assumption, an attempt is made to allow the patient to unlearn this habit, using techniques derived from modern learning theories (15). In so doing, the cause or range of causes of the symptom is not of primary interest. There are two possible forms of behavior therapy: aversion therapy or systematic desensitization (1; see also Ch. 14).

THERAPY FOR DELUSIONS OF PARASITOSIS

Therapy in this disorder consists of two strategies:

1. Psychotherapeutic approach to the patient's environment. Since we are dealing with a delusion, it is senseless to discuss the delusional nature of the disorder with the patient himself. For the general practitioner, it is important to convince public-health institutions not to accept any request of the patient to disinfect his home.
2. Psychopharmacological therapy. Clopenthixol, a thioxanthene with antipsychotic properties is useful. The patient can swallow these drugs without difficulty, and often it is possible to keep the patient in balance with their help. Social workers have the important task of offering guidance to persons in the patient's environment.

REFERENCES

1. Allen KE, Harris F: Elimination of a child's excessive scratching by training the mother in reinforcement procedures. Behav Res Ther 4:47–84, 1969

2. Bowlby J: Attachment and Loss, Vol 1. Attachment. London, Hogarth Press, 1969

3. Crisp AH: Therapeutic aspects of the doctor–patient relationship. Psychother Psychoso 18:12–33, 1970

4. Ganner H, Lorenzi E: Der Dermatozoenwahn. Psychiatr Clin (Basel) 8:31–44, 1975

5. Graham D, Wolf S: Pathogenesis of urticaria. JAMA 143:1396, 1950

6. Greenhill M, Finesinger J: Neurotic symptoms and emotional factors in atopic dermatitis. Arch Dermatol Syph 46:187, 1942

7. Jordan JM, Whitlock FA: Atopic dermatitis. Anxiety and conditioned scratch response. J Psychosom Res 18: 297–299, 1974

8. Kreibich C, Sobotka P: Experimenteller Beitrag zur Psychischen Urticaria. Arch Dermatol Syph 97:187, 1909

9. Musaph H: Itching and Scratching. Psychodynamics in Dermatology. Basel, S Karger, 1964

10. Musaph H: Aggression and symptom formation in dermatology. Psychosom Re 13: 257–264, 1969

11. Musaph H: Psychodermatology. Psychother Psychosom 24:79–85, 1974

12. Musaph H: The role of aggression in somatic symptom formation. In Lipowski ZJ (ed): Current Trends in Psychosomatic Medicine. Baywood, USA, 1975

13. Norton A, Hall–Smith P: A psychiatric view of skin disorders. In D O'Neill (ed): Modern Trends in Psychosomatic Medicine. London, Butterworth, 1955

14. Obermayer ME, Borelli S: Psychodermatologie. In Gottron HA, Schönfield W (eds): Dermatologie und Venerologie. Ergänzungsband. Stuttgart, Thieme, 1970

15. Ratliff RG, Stein NH: Treatment of neurodermatitis by behavior therapy: a case study. Behav Res Ther 6:397–399, 1968

16. Rees LW: The role of stress in the aetiology of psychosomatic disorders. Proc R Soc Med 42:274, 1959

17. Reiffers J: Les pathomimies. Schweiz Rundschau Med 29:887, 1974

18. Saul L: The emotional settings of some attacks of urticaria. In Alexander F, French TM (eds): Studies in Psychosomatic Medicine. New York, Ronald Press, 1948, pp 424–454

19. Spitz R: The First Year of Life. New York, University Press, 1965

20. Wittkower E: Psychiatry and the Skin. Proc Soc Med 43 (11):799–801, 1950

21. Wittkower E, Russell B: Emotional Factors in Skin Diseases. New York, Paul Hoeber, 1953

31 Psychosomatic Disorders in Children

RENATA DE BENEDETTI GADDINI

Certain psychosomatic disorders of early childhood are pertinent to everyday pediatric practice. The pediatrician's knowledge of psychosomatic medicine can be of enormous value for the child during this early period. His understanding of the dynamics of psychosomatic problems may give him the opportunity and the capacity for rational intervention or noninterference, which may entirely modify the course and future development of an illness. The rational approach to psychosomatic illnesses is based on prevention, for if a psychosomatic disorder is not understood and treated, it will enter the personality structure as a fixed and difficult-to-eliminate feature of adult life.

In the first months of the child's life, subtle mutual interactions take place between the mother and infant, which are characterized by the specificity of the cues involved. Unsatisfactory development of the child's self may occur at this early stage as a result of poor interaction and early environmental difficulties. If the mother-child interaction is pathogenic and if the environment of the first months of life is inadequate, early psychosomatic illness may occur, and, to a lesser extent, a specific vulnerability to all sorts of illness and physical injury may be found (6).

Psychosomatic illnesses can be classified on the basis of the theory of maturational processes: individuals can create only those symptoms that correspond to their level of development. Infants can create only physical symptoms, since their only means of expression is through the body. Early experiences of the body include those of the mouth, skin, and eyes, which is why we find illnesses of these organs early in life.

SPECIFIC PEDIATRIC PSYCHOSOMATIC DISORDERS

THREE-MONTHS COLIC

Colicky babies are those infants who, in their first months of life, have sudden spells of screaming with physical signs of pain and distress. Screaming and mounting tension may go on for hours, and there seems to be no way to console these infants.

From the point of view of mental development, the age of three months represents a crucial point for infant pathology. A minimum of mental and psychic activity already exists in a child of this age. Organization of the self is beginning to occur, and it is necessary for there to be at least one person who can enter into a relationship with the child. This does not have to be the child's biological mother, but, in order to feel whole, the child needs the contribution of a human being who can help integrate his innate self. For most infants at this age, the mother has not yet become a person but is still part of the infant's self. In a short while, however, it will no longer be possible to use her as a substitute, since the infant's personality structure will soon begin to organize itself, with its own ego.

Three-months colic occurs at a time when the relationship between mother and child is changing. By three months of age, the child's interest in his environment increases daily as his physical capacities increase. A seemingly infinite space separates him from his neonatal age, when he was more apt to feel the sensations derived from his various internal organs than the perceptions brought to him by his sense organs in relation to the external world. While this exciting development is going on, the "maternal preoccupation"—which we have come to know as an essential attribute of the "good enough mother"—begins to decrease. The mother begins to feel free of the emotional ties that previously provided a continuous link with the child. It is probable that the child perceives the noncontinuous availability of the mother, and this may be a cause of stress. The vaguely perceived threat of deprivation is the cause of those tensions that are translated into colics. This response is transitory and related to a part of the developmental process that is normally overcome very rapidly. I am convinced that the prolongation and complication of this syndrome may be due to various interventions, sometimes iatrogenic.

The possibility of using substitute mothering to treat a typically maturation-bound condition like three-months colic has suggested the utilization of foster grandparents. This tactic has been employed both at home and in the hospital, apparently with great success.

RUMINATION

In rumination, the infant fantasizes that he is the nursing mother; *i.e.,* he relives the experience that he once had in omnipotent fusion with his mother. This fantasy is inextricably connected with his previous bodily experiences and is expressed through his body. In the first months of life, nearly all ruminators initiate the syndrome by vomiting, an automatic organic response that can be self-destructive. In those cases where no vomiting has preceded rumination, we find without exception that there has been a sudden interruption of breast-feeding or a separation from the mother with a loss of comforting habits such as the use of a pacifier or thumb-sucking (5); the infant has experienced a sudden and severe bodily frustration.

As soon as it is biologically possible (*i.e.,* at three or four months), the child organizes a defense against frustration and disappointment by providing an entirely satisfactory bodily experience for himself through the act of rumination. The infant undergoes a number of bodily modifications in rumination that repeat previous experiences with the mother. Food or milk is repeatedly brought back into the mouth so that it is full; part of this flows into the corners of the mouth, part is again swallowed. Typically, it is the tongue that initiates the procedure of rumination, serving the function of the lost nipple, thumb, or pacifier. The fantasy that underlies rumination is a pathological one. In such autistic self-feeding, an infant regains omnipotent control. No evolution takes place in the process; it is an end in itself and the child does not mature. This psychosomatic syndrome indicates a pathology that can take place only at a particular level of development and is dependent on maternal and infant factors.

SELF-ROCKING

Self-rocking is another example of a pathological imitative fantasy of being the absent mother. The child imitates the rocking of the mother, but in so doing, he "becomes the rocking mother and loses his identity" (10). It is not certain whether the child is imitating his mother's rocking of him in her arms or the rocking that he experienced prenatally. Perhaps a sense of rhythm is inborn, and the relaxation the infant finds in rocking may be based on fantasies of return to the womb. When we consider the different modes of self-rocking, we tend to feel that a difference exists, in maturational terms, between head-banging and rocking of the whole body, the latter being a more primitive way of reliving early prenatal experiences.

Case 1. A premature child, who had been in an incubator for 40 days, spent most of her time after her return home in self-rocking. She reacted with visible anxiety when the mother tried to interfere with her rocking and rock her with a different rhythm. Her reactions on this occasion brought to mind the reactions of autistic children when one tries to enter their withdrawn world. This child's behavior can be explained on the hypothesis that the child, on emerging from the incubator, was maldeveloped and had a poor sense of self. Self-rocking gave her some sense of body reality through body sensations.

This interpretation applies equally well to self-rocking before going to sleep; it is reassuring at that moment when the threat of loss is most intense.

At present, we know only that an infant who is a self-rocker never develops a transitional object, and that the developmental process which leads to a sense of identity has been disturbed. We also know that for such infants, there was no object available in the outside world for libidinal cathexis at the right time, at least not one that was sufficient for the aggressive cathexes and requirements of an organism that did not yet have the potential to invest them mentally. The elements of imitative identity (*i.e.,* with the rocking mother) and of aggressive feelings turned toward the self seem to me to be significant for the elucidation of this syndrome.

ATOPIC DERMATITIS*

To illustrate some of the typical characterstics of children suffering from dermatosis, I shall describe in some detail the case of a five-year-old girl who, from the age of eight months, suffered from a most acute and distressing form of dermatitis. In this case, it is interesting to note that the child's mother used her infant and her relationship with her to reenact her own childhood. The mother also made the same omnipotent, dependent, idealized, but persecutory use of the medical institutions as her daughter made of her.

Case 2. Novella was born by cesarean section, presumably at full-term, and weighed 2.400 kg. The adults with whom she came into almost immediate contact were her parents and both grandmothers. The paternal grandmother practically raised the child. She was described by the mother as intrusive and overprotective: she "ruined" the child because she wanted her to be fed on demand with no discipline. "The doctor said it was a disaster and scolded me." For nearly three months, Novella was breast-fed on a rigid schedule. She was a poor sucker and often fell asleep at the breast, which caused a great deal of crying between meals. The paternal grandmother opposed this rigid scheme for the small baby, but the pediatrician felt that the baby's occasional regurgitation was caused by undisciplined feeding and imposed a sudden weaning to the bottle. At first, this immature infant refused the bottle but then seemed to capitulate, although she tended to refuse to eat altogether. Her bottles were prepared according to the pediatrician's instructions, which were based on "babies' needs," rather than the needs of this particular child. Novella's mother expected her to finish her voluminous feed to the

*See Chapter 30, pp. 306–307.

last drop. Forced feeding started, which was soon followed by vomiting and urticaria. Itching and scratching began almost simultaneously. At 7 months, diarrhea started. A diagnosis of celiac disease was made and a gluten-free diet was suggested. The child suffered from itching all night long and insisted on being massaged with talc or ointment by her mother, who was thus kept up all night. The interaction between mother and child proved Novella's extreme dependence on her mother.

We may suppose that in Novella's case, she failed to experience sufficient devotion from one person early in her development. Her mother longed to resume her work and may have been interrupted in a natural development toward independence. Novella's early somatic response was dermatosis. We may postulate that when she first had an allergic reaction to overfeeding (urticaria) and the itching began, the bond with her mother took place through the somatic symptom.

The mother, on the other hand, relived her own rather unhappy childhood, putting Novella in her own place, and fought with her mother-in-law as her own mother and aunt had fought about her. With this background, we can understand how this child's environment was pathogenic. Novella's atopic dermatosis, which required her mother's tranquilizing intervention with ointment and massage, is what I call a cry for help; it is a sign of hope as well as a denial of separation.

OBESITY*

It is possible that for a baby, the urges of hunger and for reunion with the mother are felt as one, rather than as two distinct urges. Perhaps what we traditionally think of as hunger is sometimes a stimulus hunger, a desire to be held and contained and to have skin-to-skin contact. Although hunger may seem to be a more physiological urge whereas being held and contained may seem to be more mental, both hunger and the need for contact acquire some mental meaning very early in infancy.

Bruch (1) finds that obese patients are unable to experience a sense of satisfaction. They are not particularly greedy, but they are compelled to eat almost compulsively to fulfill the self's goal of feeling solid and steady. For the obese person, this means being full, and their continuous eating has the unconscious meaning of protection from disintegration. The underlying fantasy is that the patient must sustain *himself*. The defense mechanisms that push the child toward obesity are imitative ones that hide omnipotence. Each obese child imitates (*i.e.,* wants to be) the feeding mother, who, in his fantasy, has disappointed him; he becomes the feeding mother. For the infant who will later become obese, separation from his mother at weaning has meant a loss of part of the self. From the child's point of view, this bond with his mother means nondisintegration, preservation of the self, and nonmutilation. Overeating is an attempt to recreate this bond. Since this imitative fantasy is not structuring for the ego but merely helps it to survive, then, if a sense of self-identity is achieved, it will be a disturbed one, because the ego is fragile. These patients need to find vicarious ego substitutes, which may sometimes include the mechanisms of artistic creation. If this particular substitute is employed, their creations always have an imitative quality that is retained from childhood.

CONCOMITANT (NONPARALYTIC) STRABISMUS IN EARLY CHILDHOOD

A special approach is necessary in order to reach young children with vision problems. A knowledge of the anatomy, physiology, and pathology of the eye is

*See Chapter 24, pp. 234–241.

of little use to the clinician who cannot communicate with his young patient. The high incidence of concomitant strabismus in early childhood is well known to the pediatrician, and all possible efforts should be made to insure that the child has binocular vision. An enormous amount of successful psychotherapy is being done all the time in the routine management of such cases.

Winnicott wrote, "The eye's complicated function works easily when the child uses it in the ordinary way, but what if the eye is used (unconsciously) instead of another organ of the body? What if the eye stands for an organ that contains erectile tissue and so is capable of changing when excited? In such a case the eye becomes not only the organ of sight, but also an excitable part of the body. Then symptoms may arise" (8). In my opinion, squint is a symptom that may arise in a state of excitement or fear. I have often observed that squinting at a threatening image is basic in the pathogenesis of concomitant strabismus. It takes place in the age period when "seeing" is a way of attempting to exert control over external reality. The unconscious reason underlying the strabismus may be to eliminate the clear-focused, threatening image. The case of a 3-year-old comes to mind, in whom spastic contraction of the ocular muscle did not allow her to focus on her newborn brother's genitals. She was a picture of tension and frozen denial when she approached him naked at bath time.

It is possible that a similar mechanism of denial takes place with respect to hearing, when an infant of 6 to 8 months of age cannot drown threatening noises with his screams and instead falls asleep. The gradual "becoming familiar" with things in the environment is an essential step toward the acceptance of reality.

THE PRACTICAL ASPECT OF THE PSYCHOSOMATIC APPROACH

Pediatricians must always keep both aspects of the mother-child relationship in mind and attempt to distinguish between the mother's hypochondriasis and that of the child. There is no sharp borderline between maternal hypochondriasis and natural concern, so the pediatrician must allow the mother to worry without exacerbating her feelings. Mothers need to be given the opportunity to mature, which they cannot do if they are threatened by all the possible dangers that may overwhelm their infant. The child's own hypochondriasis needs even more careful management. The simplest rule is that the child should hear the truth; true reassurance comes from statement of fact, not from reassuring words and tones that carry implications of danger. It is in its early development, when the mother-child integrations are inextricable, that the child may suffer most from his mother's unconscious fears about his health and integrity.

Empathetic listening is one of the ways of receiving the child's communication and is perhaps the most important way; only through this initial listening to the child and his parents can the doctor be aware of the former's needs in the particular situation. Listening must take place in conjunction with some knowledge of emotional development. I can understand the point of view of the pediatrician who, because he does not feel competent in psychology, prefers to ignore the symptom's meaning and tries only to cure it; however, because the whole field of prevention is pertinent to him, he may be brought to realize the strength of the psychosomatic approach to medicine.

THERAPEUTIC CONSIDERATIONS

The psychosomatic patient calls for our attention through the use of his symptom, and it is with that symptom that he tries to communicate with us (*e.g.*, as the environment or mother figures). Through his physical symptoms, the child tries to create a close bond with his mother that has not been achieved earlier on a more psychological level. When he is faced with the normal anxiety of growing, the psychic process of the fearful child turns inward and leads him to symptom formation. He has not been allowed to create, in early childhood, an intermediate area as a defense against anxiety. This potential space between inner and shared reality is founded on body experiences developed in the early relationship with a "good enough mother," and it provides the common ground between the infant and his mother in this state of ego-relatedness. If, at weaning time, the child has been allowed to create a transitional object to which he can turn for consolation, then his anxieties have that outlet and there is no need for him to turn to a psychosomatic symptom.

The patient's symptom deserves recognition and attention for itself. Nothing could be less competent on the part of a physician who is called in on the basis of a physical complaint than for him to talk to the patient only about his psyche and his feelings or emotions. In the case of a child, however, our acceptance of the bodily communication via his mother does not necessarily mean that we have to dissipate his symptom immediately. We may choose to accept it and give it full attention, definition, and containment. We can help the family to accept the child's regression to a bodily mode of communication. This requires, of course, that the physician must have a solid clinical experience in order to prevent mismanagement, as a result of either improper diagnosis of the illness or inadequate knowledge about it.

Hospitals, and institutions in general, do not have the same meaning for infant patients as they do for adults. If the child is over the age of four or five years, hospitalization, although often a last resort, can be a positive psychosocial experience. In the hospital, along with the vital physical interventions (each of which has a special meaning in the child's unconscious life), patients with illnesses such as anorexia nervosa or ulcerative colitis may find a detached yet empathetic atmosphere that contributes to the neutralization of the involved relationship between the mother and child. This may be fundamental for the possibility of later psychoanalytic treatment. In a few cases, such as three-months colic, when early pathology occurs in the mother-child relationship, some advantages may be found in the hospitalization of both mother and child. This gives their interaction the opportunity to pass through a corrective experience. In most cases, however, the home is the best place for the treatment of the ill child. Among other advantages, this approach respects family unity and gives brothers and sisters the opportunity to participate in the care of the sick child, thus neutralizing aggressive fantasies and guilt.

THE VALUE OF PREVENTION

We have already emphasized that in early occurring psychosomatic disorders, it is neither the child nor the mother who is ill, but rather the interaction between them. It is upon this interaction that we should focus our investigations. The child's doctor is the only person who can join a thorough knowledge of the child's development to the family context in which it has taken place. Over the last two years, I have had a girl, now 12, in analysis with a severe ulcerative colitis. While working with this patient, I discover again and again that all her problems have to do with the mother and the early care of the child. Because I am basically a pediatrician, I cannot help feeling regretful that I did not see this child in her first year, when my efforts to intervene in the mother-child interaction would have been made easier and could possibly have prevented the interactional pathology from becoming a somatic illness. As Winnicott wrote, "Mental ill-health arises imperceptibly out of the ordinary difficulties that are inherent in human nature and that give colour to the task of child care. . . . Prophylaxis against psychosis—and I would add, also against some kind of retardation and distortion—is therefore the responsibility of the pediatricians, did they but know it" (8).

Prevention in terms of mental illness, and particularly in terms of psychosomatic disorders, requires support without interference at the critical time of the child's early life when the mother must find her own feelings. The mother needs support while doing so. Many physicians are familiar with cases of infants brought into the hospital at night with severe attacks of asthma that gradually disappeared without the use of drugs or hospitalization while the mother was feeling relieved and supported. This provides a temporary relief, to be sure, but how can we tell whether, through a cumulation of such temporary reliefs, the child might not start growing without being frightened of disintegrating?

Interruption of the delicate natural processes that characterize a young child's relationship with his mother poses immense risks for his mental health. Minimizing unnecessary hospitalization and restrictions, trying to make diagnosis as non-threatening as possible, promoting the mother's self-confidence in handling health and illness of her child, and particularly the protection of the mother-infant in the first few months—these are the tasks that the physician can meet. The doctor must keep in mind that individual mental health, and particularly the achievement of psychosomatic integration, depends on this relationship of the first few months.

REFERENCES

1. Bruch H: The Importance of Overweight. New York, WW Norton, 1954

2. Gaddini E: On imitation. Int J Psychoanal 50: 475–484, 1969

3. Gaddini E: On father formation in child development—discussion in the dialogue on: "The role of family life in child development". Int J Psychoanal 57: (1): 1976

4. Gaddini R: Early psychosomatic symptom and the tendency towards integration. Psychother Psychosom 23: 26–34, 1974

5. Gaddini R, Gaddini E: Rumination in infancy. Dynamic Psychopathology in Childhood. New York, Grune & Stratton, 1959

6. Green M, Solnit AJ: Reactions to the threatened loss of a child: the vulnerable child syndrome. Pediatrics 34:58, 1964

7. Greenacre P, Freud A: Problems of infantile neurosis. Psychoanal Study Child IX: 18–31, 1954

8. Winnicott DW: Through Pediatrics to Psychoanalysis. London, Tavistock, 1958

9. Winnicott DW: Somatic illness in its positive and negative aspects. Int J Psychoanal 47: 510–516, 1966

10. Winnicott DW: Personal communication, 1968

32 Psychosomatic Problems in the Older Person

JOHN B. NOWLIN, EWALD W. BUSSE

The increasing number of older people and their more ready access to medical care renders the elderly an increasingly large proportion of the practitioner's patient population. Estimates in 1975 indicate that 10.3% of the United States population is 65 years of age or older; in that country alone, the elderly number over 21,000,000 (11). Moreover, the peculiar tensions that are engendered by a high-pressure, quickly changing society insure that a considerable fraction of the older patient's complaints will be stress-related or "psychosomatic" in origin. It is unlikely that the general practitioner will escape the probability of being at least a part-time geriatrician, and he will hence be often exposed to the older person.

A paramount consideration for the practitioner who sets out to deal with the psychosomatic illness manifested by the geriatric patient is that of attitudes about aging, both his and those of his older patient. Speculating about the nature of "old age" is seldom neutral. Popular terms such as "golden years" to describe the character of later life contrast sharply with the squalor and misery often associated with the lot of the older person. The invitation in Robert Browning's lines, "Come along grow old with me. . . . The best of life is yet to be," stands in direct opposition to the emptiness of the older Prufrock as he is protrayed by T. S. Eliot. This ambivalence about aging is universal, and it has contributed in no small degree to a widespread, often unrealistic mythology that surrounds aging and the older person. The medical practitioner, when he handles sickness in the older person, is himself vulnerable to the biases inherent to such a mythology. Successful outcomes in dealing with psychosomatic illness in patients of any age depend largely upon the establishment of a modicum of closeness in the practitioner-patient relationship. Incorporation of the practitioner's biases about aging into a working relationship with the older patient can provide sufficient distortion to disrupt an attempt at treatment. A necessary prerequisite, therefore, for the successful management of the geriatric patient whose complaints are "psychosomatic" in origin is a careful sorting-out of notions about aging on the part of both the practitioner and his patient.

THEORETICAL BACKGROUND

Pertinent to any discussion of psychosomatic problems among older patients is a brief summary of the physiological and psychological changes known to accompany the aging process. The precise definition of an "older person" is in itself elusive; the traditional criterion of 65 years as the time of onset of old age finds little backing in either physiological or psychological fact; rather, it has its origin in late nineteenth-century European politics, when that figure was designated as the age for initiation of old-age pensions. Currently, the aging process is no longer defined in terms of a specific age, but instead it is recognized as a continuum of the life cycle, as much a developmental phase of life as, for example, adolesence. Chronological age is only one of many markers employed to evaluate the broader concepts of the aging process. A large degree of person-to-person variability in response to the aging process is well documented; to base one's viewpoint and outlook toward an older person exclusively upon their chronological age is unwarranted and yet forms a considerable part of the "mythology of aging" mentioned earlier.

Despite the heterogeneous characteristics of older people, there are a number of physical and psychological concomitants that may be said to typify the aging process. With respect to physiological change, the best characterization is a concept that recognizes that there is a loss of reserve. The resting cardiac output, for example, is decreased by an average of 30%–40% between the ages of 25 and 65 (1). Kidney function also presents a decrement such that the glomerular filtration rate and the renal plasma flow fall an average of 46% and 56%, respectively, between the ages of 20 and 90 (6). Cerebral blood flow presents a similar decline (10). Despite a general picture of functional decrement with aging that is prevalent in almost every assessment of physiological function, these changes in themselves do not produce disease, but they merely represent the compromise of a vast physiological reserve. Only with the advent of an added stress on a particular physiological system of an older person does illness intervene.

Psychological changes are also noted to occur concurrently with the aging process. Tasks involving response speed, for example, show evidence of slowing. An often-cited decline in intellectual functioning (as measured by such test instruments as the Wechsler Adult Intelligent Scale) has been challenged by investigators like Eisdorfer (7), who have presented evidence that factors other than the aging process might well explain the apparent decrement. As for personality structure, Erikson (6), in his celebrated staging of the human life cycle, proposed that old age is an epoch of reassessment wherein a lifetime of experiences is summed up. This process of integration of the life experience presumably generates the wisdom traditionally attributed to the older person (8).

Old age, however, can be an era of attrition as well. There is often loss of family members, friends, and frequently, of physical vigor; the sense of stability and structure provided by work is disrupted by retirement. The extent to which the older individual can formulate a successful adjustment to these losses often portends his sense of psychic comfort or discomfort in later years. Presently accruing evidence strongly indicates that styles of coping with stress during the person's younger years are usually invoked again in later life. Appropriate or inappropriate adaptation to stress early in the life cycle proves often predictive of the response to stress in old age (3).

THE DILEMMA POSED BY THE SYMPTOMS OF THE OLDER PATIENT

The nature of the medical practitioner's decision-making demands that he sift through his patient's symptom report and clinical findings in order to determine a reasonable theraputic approach and the best method for reestablishing homeostasis. Guidelines for categorizing illnesses, which are usually explicit in dealing with the younger patient, are often less well-defined in assessing the symptoms of older individuals. The greater likelihood in old age of physiological and psychological vulnerability can muddle the practitioner's discernment. Two patient histories are provided that illustrate the dilemma confronting the physician when he deals with illness of the older person.

Case 1. A 73-year-old woman presented with a three-month history of back pain that was severe enough to limit her activity level. She was otherwise in good health, and she denied any unusual physical activity that might have produced her symptoms. The results of a general examination were normal, as were those of a careful neurological assessment of the lower extremities. Roentgenograms of the lumbar spine revealed extensive osteoarthritic change. Over the ensuing several months, the patient was offered a number of treatment regimens: enforced rest, muscle relaxants, physical therapy, and finally a back brace, but all produced minimal improvement. Throughout this time, the patient gave evidence of mild depression, which the practitioner considered related to the recent death of her husband and to the back discomfort itself.

Upon her return to the practitioner's office in a follow-up visit several months after her initial presentation with back pain, the patient reported marked improvement. Several weeks later, she was virtually free of symptoms and, coincidentally, much less depressed. Puzzled, the practitioner queried the patient about her own thoughts regarding the abrupt improvement in her symptoms. The patient herself offered no explanation, but she did relate the following set of circumstances that occurred during her period of back pain. Following the death of her husband, the patient's two sons were squabbling over possession of the family business. The patient was frequently called upon to arbitrate, often incurring anger from both her sons. Suddenly, one of her sons was offered an excellent position with another firm; he accepted the job, leaving the proprietorship of the family business to his brother. Enmity between the two sons ceased; it was at the time of the resolution of this problem that the patient first noted the beginning improvement in her back pain.

Such a patient report exemplifies the often-seen blurring of diagnostic criteria in the older patient. A not uncommon manifestation of depression among older people is that of back pain; osteoarthritic change in the lumbar spine, of course, can likewise be associated with back discomfort. It is most unlikely that even the most discerning practitioner would have stumbled across the association of the depression that stemmed from family discord and this particular patient's back pain.

A second report of a patient problem offers yet another example of the unclear diagnostic guidelines that are found not infrequently in dealing with the older person.

Case 2. A 68-year-old man complained of back pain, but he was also obviously depressed over the recent death of his son from multiple spinal injuries suffered in an auto accident. Normal physical findings were obtained on examination of his back; the radiologist reported that minimal osteoarthritic change was noted in roentgentograms of the lumbar spine. The prominent depression and the parallel between the patient's symptoms and the son's fatal injury were obvious both to the practitioner and to the patient. Time was spent counseling the patient in an attempt to work through a prominent grief reaction. After several weeks, the depression was much improved, although the back pain persisted. The medical practitioner then elected to give the patient a careful medical examination. On rectal examination, the patient was found to have a firm prostatic nodule; a second roentgenographic examination of the back revealed a single lytic lesion of the fifth lumbar vertebra. On hormonal therapy, the patient improved dramatically and was still free of symptoms several years later.

Although it is not unique to geriatric medicine, the diagnostic and therapeutic dilemma posed by such ambiguity in symptoms and findings occurs far more often in treating older patients. As documented by the two case reports just cited, the resolution of the dilemma will often require passage of time. In his dealings with the older patient, the practitioner has to be content with a temporary diagnosis and tentative therapeutic approaches far more often than in his management of the sick younger person.

DEPRESSION IN THE OLDER PATIENT

Psychosomatic symptoms among older patients are very commonly related to concurrent depression. Further, depressive reactions of varying severity are quite common in the geriatric population. The practitioner who is presented with a symptom complex that is probably psychosomatic in character should be suspicious of an underlying depression. Often triggered by events such as a specific loss, these depressive episodes may be quite shortlived and promptly resolved with appropriate intervention.

Case 3. A healthy 72-year-old woman fell on her out-stretched right hand while working in her garden and struck her wrist in falling. She was found to have a nondisplaced fracture of the distal radius, and a short forearm cast was applied. Within a week, she was complaining of severe headaches, abdominal distress with nausea, loss of appetite, and periumbilical cramping. Careful examination revealed no obvious physiological impairment. Upon questioning by her physician, she related stories about several neighbors, the gist of these stories being that "old people's bones do not mend well"; the implication to the patient was that of a permanent loss of function in her own right wrist. When reassured to the contrary by her physician, her symptoms promptly cleared. Within two months, she was again happily tending to her garden.

The more traditional theories concerning the dynamics of depression in the younger individual seem less applicable to the older person (4). Depression among younger people is proposed to arise from the real or fancied loss of a close interpersonal relationship wherein feelings were quite ambivalent. The anger that is characteristic of such an ambivalent relationship is interpreted by the patient as having produced the "loss," and this thus engenders feelings of guilt and self-blame. The associated affective state is, of course, that of depression. On the other hand, depression in the older person frequently arises not so much from loss in the context of an interpersonal relationship, but instead from a perceived loss of personal resources that werecharacteristic of that person when younger. As mentioned earlier, the potential for such a loss of personal resources is manifold in later years. The realization of resource decrement presumably creates feelings of hopelessness, and hence the depressive affect results; the role of guilt and self-blame in the older person's depression is often less obvious (2). This proposed age-related difference in the underlying dynamics of depression, however, need not be always precise or clear-cut. Particularly, the older person who experienced depression while younger often, when depressed in later life, expresses feelings of guilt. The more severe cases of geriatric depression often incorporate elements of both guilt and resource loss as their underlying causes. It is still likely, however, that the more common, less debilitating depression among older people is primarily a reflection of their preoccupation with the loss of personal resources.

One mode by which depressive affect masquerades in psychosomatic symptoms deserves emphasis: this is the so-called *depressive equivalent*. Not uncommon in the geriatric patient, the "depressive equivalent" is characteristically a single symptom or a set of symptoms that involves a single organ system. The musculoskeletal system is typically involved, with headache of muscular origin, neck pain and stiffness, or back pain being common symptoms. The depressive equivalent can be tenacious and recurrent; the patient may often use alcohol or proprietary pain medication in large quantity for relief. Despite the presentation of many signs of depression, sometimes even agitation, the patient disclaims the presence of such a feeling state. The patient attributes his discomfort exclusively to his symptoms; even if he will gingerly admit to having a depressive mood, the patient insists that it arises only because of the severity of his somatic symptom.

The use of antidepressant drugs is often quite effective in alleviating both the feeling state and the associated symptoms of geriatric depression. The use of these agents for treatment of the older person is described in a later section of this chapter.

More severe depression is not unusual among the geriatric population. In this instance, the somatic symptoms that are more characteristic of major depression are apparent, such as marked sleep disturbance, weight loss, withdrawal, or marked agitation. The treatment of this type of depression is usually outside the province of the general practitioner. Hospitalization, large dosages of antidepressants, or electroconvulsive treatment may often be required. Since severe depression is more responsive during its early course, the practitioner's primary responsibility is to promptly recognize such cases and provide speedy access to treatment.

Since depressive symptoms and their psychosomatic concomitants are so common among older persons who suffer injury or the onset of illness, the practitioner should take preventive steps when these situations occur. An early definition for the patient of the outcome to be anticipated with a particular illness or injury can prove important in mitigating the depression that may potentially arise.

HYPOCHONDRIASIS

An often troublesome patient is the individual whose symptoms can be categorized as hypochondriacal, and such patients are frequently found among the elderly. The problematic nature of this type of symptom presentation devolves upon both the patient and the medical practitioner. Hypochondriacal symptoms are unpleasant and cause no small discomfort to the patient; yet the symptoms are often persistent and difficult for the practitioner to manage.

Busse (5) has proposed that three mechanisms may underlie the presentation of hypochondriacal symptoms:

1. A withdrawal of psychic interest from other persons or objects and a centering of this interest upon one's self, one's own body, and its functioning.
2. A shift of anxiety from a specific psychic area to a less threatening concern with bodily disease.
3. The use of physical symptoms as a means of self-punishment and atonement for unacceptable, hostile, or vengeful feelings toward a person close to the individual.

His experience with this problem would seem to indicate a higher prevalence of hypochondriasis among older women.

The presentation of hypochondriacal symptoms highlights the practitioner's dilemma defined previously, *i.e.,* there is, in such cases, the possibility of coexistent structural illness that might jeopardize a patient. Moreover, the hypochondriacal patient often aggrandizes the dilemma. The physician's vigorous pursuit of a symptom with a host of investigative medical tests reinforces the patient's notion that he is experiencing a major illness; however, the failure to evaluate a complaint thoroughly may lead to the risk of overlooking important physiological dysfunction.

The resolution of this dilemma requires fuller knowledge of the patient. Fortunately, most complaints that reflect severe, life-threatening physiological derangement are associated with readily demonstrable signs that will become apparent even upon short acquaintance with the patient. The patient who complains of shortness of breath from rapidly progressive congestive heart failure, for example, will present sufficient physical findings to alert the practitioner to the likelihood of that circulatory disorder. In effect, the practitioner should perform a "mental" triage to determine the urgency of treatment required by the presentation of a particular symptom. Without the possible need to have to intervene in a "crisis situation," the practitioner can then afford the luxury of learning more details about his patient's illness. More subtle physiological derangements—*i.e.,* those that are not readily apparent—become manifest with the passage of time, yet usually soon enough that appropriate intervention can be undertaken.

A clue that is often of assistance in formulating an opinion about the patient's physical complaints is provided by his mode of symptom presentation. A parsimonious symptom presentation is well recognized to suggest an underlying physiological compromise; on the other hand, the embellished symptom more often tends to be less reflective of major physiologic malfunction. Since the exaggeration of symptoms is characteristic of hypochondriasis, this differentiation can often be even more easily apparent. Furthermore, hypochondriacal complaints often conform less to the established symptom patterns that have been associated with specific physiological derangements. Chest pain, for example, as a hypochondriacal symptom might be described as "stabbing" or momentary, in contrast to that of cardiac origin with its constricting type of discomfort and gradual onset and offset.

A number of common errors may occur in the practitioner's handling of a hypochondriacal patient. The natural instinct of the practitioner is to offer reassurance to a patient that no illness of consequence underlies his symptoms. With the hypochondriacal patient, however, an attempt at reassurance is usually counterproductive. Reassurance is interpreted by the patient as the practitioner's denial of the import of his symptoms, and it hence generates a loss of self-esteem. Often, the patient reacts either by breaking off his relationship with the practitioner or by presentation of a new cluster of symptoms.

Another approach that is usually unsuccessful is to provide the hypochondriacal patient with a specific disease diagnosis in the hope that he will improve over time. Such an approach at least indicates to the patient that he is being taken seriously. The specificity of "being diagnosed," however, also implies the possibility of "being cured." The patient's need to protect his symptom because of its symbolic meaning to him invariably causes this approach to fail.

The effective treatment of hypochondriasis is time-consuming, and it produces little dramatic, immediate impact. The practitioner's irritation at negligible initial improvement must be kept well disguised. A long-term maneuver that is helpful in diluting the practitioner's impatience at such slow improvement is to find, or even generate, an area of mutual interest that is not related to the illness and to make inquiries about this area at each visit. This connotes to the patient a flattering interest in him as a person, and it partially relieves the physician from hearing a constant visit-to-visit repetition of complaints.

At the beginning of any relationship with a hypochondriacal patient, the practitioner must be prepared to hear the individual out, long though the recital of symptoms may be. On the initial visit, it is mandatory to permit the patient to elaborate upon his symptoms; such attention communicates a willingness to take the patient's symptoms seriously. Likewise, a complete medical examination is quite important: first, to establish more clearly the physiological significance of the symptoms in the practitioner's mind and second, to satisfy the patient's expectations of the patient-practitioner relationship. Routine laboratory testing is in order, for the same reasons.

At the conclusion of the first visit, the practitioner should set the stage for his future dealings with the patient. First, there should be a noncommital attitude in defining the problem for the patient. Second, a follow-up visit should be scheduled, with the promise of even more visits in the future. Finally, the physician should prescribe a medication. The mention of a specific diagnosis, as mentioned previously, has no merit; a simple statement to the patient that there are indeed problems that bear watching is fully sufficient. The primary issue for the hypochondriacal patient is not the establishment of a diagnosis, but whether he is accepted by the practitioner. The promise of future visits indicates such an acceptance. The practitioner should be specific as to the dates of the return visits to emphasize his investment in the patient. Medication is prescribed to reflect again a serious consideration of the patient's symptoms. Since anxiety is often associated with hypochondriasis, a small dosage of a minor tranquilizer is useful (diazepam, chlordiazepoxide, or oxazepam).

Subsequent appointments should be reasonably close together, *e.g.,* every one to two weeks for a short visit of 10 to 15 minutes in length. The patient should be allowed to reiterate his symptoms, and possibly the "area of mutual interest" may be explored. The structure of subsequent visits should remain essentially unchanged. Once the patient recognizes his acceptance, the intervals between visits can be prolonged. Not infrequently, after the relationship with the patient is indeed well-established, visits every two to three months will suffice. The continuity of care in this fashion frequently generates trust to the extent that the patient will begin to offer personal issues in the place of a symptom recital. At this point, psychotherapy might be openly discussed with the patient and such treatment initiated. Even without psychotherapy, ready access to an accepting relationship provided by the practitioner is often more than enough to provide a great deal of comfort—both immediate and long-term—to the hypochondriacal individual.

USE OF PSYCHOTROPIC DRUGS AMONG GERIATRIC PATIENTS

As indicated previously in this chapter, the aging process is characterized by a gradual decrement in physiological reserve. This loss of physiological resilience has implications for any medication regimen proposed for the geriatric patient. The efficacy of a pharmacological agent depends, first, upon the rate and extent of absorption from the administration site, such as the injection area, or the gastrointestinal site in the instance of oral medication. Equally important determinants of the pharmacological effect involve the metabolism of the drug through hepatic enzymatic processes, secretion via the biliary tree, absorption by the intestinal mucosa, and excretion by the kidneys. Generally, the absorptive capabilities are less compromised with aging than are the mechanisms of elimination. Therefore, pharmacological effects are manifested more promptly in the older person, as compared to the younger individual, and they are less readily dissipated. Moreover, the muscle mass diminishes with aging so that there is a relative increase in the proportion of adipose tissue. Since many drugs, particularly the so-called psychotropic agents, are fat-soluble; the relative predominance of adipose tissue offers more storage sites and thereby induces a prolonged drug effect. As a general rule of thumb, the practitioner is well advised to initiate drug therapy at lower than usual dosage levels in his geriatric patient and to monitor the patient carefully as medication levels are increased.

Since depression and anxiety often underlie the psychosomatic complaints of the older individual, the physician should be familiar with the value and uses of the more commonly used psychotropic agents. For depression in which apathy and withdrawal seem typical of the patient's behavior and mode of interpersonal interaction, imipramine (Tofranil) is useful; therapy should initiated at a dosage of 10 mg three times a day, with incremental increases of the dosage levels every three days until the patient improves or until a level of 100 mg daily is reached. Most older patients do quite well at lower dosage levels, reporting relief from both depression and the accompanying somatic symptoms shortly after drug therapy is initiated. If the patient's apathy and somatic discomfort persist after daily imipramine levels of 100 mg are reached, psychiatric consultation is advisable.

For the more agitated depressed elderly patient, in particular for the individual who presents somatic symptoms suggestive of "depressive equivalent," amitriptyline (Elavil) is the drug of choice. This medication offers both antidepressant and tranquilizing properties, the latter being useful in managing agitation. Initial dosages of 10 mg three times a day are appropriate for this medication, with gradual increments as needed every three days until a maximum of 100 mg is reached. Older persons are often quite sensitive to the tranquilizing effects of this drug; to minimize daytime somnolence, the larger proportion of amitriptyline can be administered at night. A new, closely related drug, desipramine (Norpramin), is helpful for the agitated older individual with symptoms. It has a lesser tendency to produce sleepiness. The initial dosage of this drug is 25 mg two to three times daily, with three-day advancements of the dose level of 100 to 150 mg daily.

For anxiety, the benzodiazepine family of drugs is particularly useful for containing the symptoms. Barbiturates, the traditional anodynes for anxiety, often produce marked dulling of cerebral function in the elderly; this problem, coupled with the tendency toward habituation, makes this group of medications less attractive for use in the older patient. Similar problems exist with the substituted diols, such as meprobamate. Fortunately, the benzodiazepines are less of a problem in this regard, and they are quite effective in alleviating both anxiety and its often-seen somatic equivalents. Chlordiazepoxide (Librium) is useful in relieving anxiety among older patients, but it presents a slight tendency to habituation, similar to meprobamate. Diazepam has a minimal tendency to habituation, and it is equally efficacious in ameliorating anxiety. Low dosages (*e.g.,* 2 mg three times a day) are often sufficient, although amounts up to 20 mg daily can be employed. At higher dosages, the older patient might experience a slight ataxia, which subsides with a decrease in the medication level.

SLEEP DISTURBANCE IN THE ELDERLY

A frequent complaint among elderly people is that their sleep is impaired. In particular, a sense of sleep disturbance is a common endpoint in illnesses of psychosomatic origin. Electroencephalographic studies have confirmed that aging is accompanied by predictable changes in the nature of sleep. Rapid-eye-movement sleep—which is traditionally associated with the subjective experience of dreaming—decreases; so-called deep sleep or "stage 4" sleep, according to the electroencephalographic staging of sleep, decreases even more in its proportion of total sleep time, being almost absent in some older people. Further, an increased "sleep latency" (*i.e.,* the period of time required to fall asleep after "retiring") is found with aging, as well as a greater frequency of nocturnal awakenings (12). The question is, of course, moot whether or not these changes can be keyed to the older person's frequent notion that sleep is qualitatively "worse."

Barbiturates, though reliable in inducing sleep, are associated with some disruption of the electroencephalographic patterns of sleep (*e.g.,* a decrease in the rapid-eye-movement phase), and, in older individuals, they can produce a "hangover" the following day. Moreover, the tendency to habituation of this family of drugs, as already mentioned, renders barbituates a poor option for the older person, who might require prolonged use of sleeping medications. Chloral hydrate and paraldehyde, with their comparatively short-term effects, are useful, but there are sometimes problems with patient acceptance. The benzodiazepine family of tranquilizers may be useful for the induction of sleep; specifically, flurazepam has been extensively studied, and it has been found to produce minimal derangement of the electroencephalographic staging of sleep (9). Diazepam (Valium), which is closely related in structure to flurazepam, is equally efficacious.

REFERENCES

1. Brondfonbrenner M, Landowne M, Shock NW: Changes in cardiac output with age. Circulation 12:577, 1955

2. Busse EW et al.: Studies of processes of aging: VI. Factors that influence psyches of elderly persons. Am J Psychiatry 110:897, 1954

3. Busse EW et al.: Studies of processes of aging: X. The strengths and weaknesses of psychic functioning in the aged. Am J Psychiatry 111:896, 1955

4. Busse EW: Research on aging: some methods and findings. In Berezin MA, Cath SH (eds): Geriatric Psychiatry: Grief, Loss and Emotional Disorders in the Aging Process. New York, International Universities Press, 1965

5. Busse EW, Pfeiffer E: Functional psychiatric disorders in old age. In Busse EW, Pfeiffer E (eds): Behavior and Adaptation in Late Life. Boston, Little, Brown, and Co, 1969

6. Davies DF, Shock NW: Age changes in glomerular filtration rate, effective renal plasma flow and tubular excretory capacity in adult males. J Clin Invest 29:496, 1950

7. Eisdorfer C: The WAIS performance of the aged: a retest evaluation. J Gerontol 18:172, 1963

8. Erickson EH: Identity and the Life Cycle. Psychological Issues, Vol 1, No. 1. New York, International Universities Press, 1963

9. Kales A, Kales J: Effect of pharmacologic agents on sleep. In Usdin F (ed): Sleep Research and Clinical Practice. New York, Brenner/Mazel, 1973

10. Landowne M, Stanley J: Aging of the cardiovascular system. In Shock NW (ed): Aging, Some Social and Biological Aspects. Washington, Am Assoc Adv Sci, 1960

11. US Public Health Service: Working with older people. USPHS Pub No. 2459, Vol 1: 8, 1966

12. Williams R, Karacan I, Hursch C: EEG of Normal Sleep: Clinical Implications. New York, John Wiley & Sons, 1974

Index

Page numbers followed by the letter *t* indicate table content.